Also by G. WAYNE MILLER

BOOKS

NON-FICTION

The Work of Human Hands: *Hardy Hendren and Surgical Wonder*
at Children's Hospital, 1993.
Coming of Age: *The True Adventures of Two American Teens,* 1995.
Toy Wars: *The Epic Struggle Between G.I. Joe, Barbie and*
the Companies That Make Them, 1998.
King of Hearts: *The True Story of the Maverick*
Who Pioneered Open Heart Surgery, 2000.
Men and Speed: *A Wild Ride Through NASCAR's Breakout Season,* 2002.
The Xeno Chronicles: *Two Years on the Frontier of Medicine*
Inside Harvard's Transplant Research Lab, 2005.
An Uncommon Man: *The Life and Times of Senator Claiborne Pell,* 2011.
Top Brain, Bottom Brain: *Harnessing the Power of the Four Cognitive Modes* (with
neuroscientist Stephen M. Kosslyn, PhD), 2013.
Car Crazy: *The Battle for Supremacy Between Ford and Olds and*
the Dawn of the Automobile Age, 2015.

FICTION

Thunder Rise, 1989.
Since the Sky Blew Off: *The Essential G. Wayne Miller Fiction, Vol. 1,* 2012.
Summer Place, 2013.
Asylum, 2013.
Vapors: *The Essential G. Wayne Miller Fiction, Vol. 2,* 2013.
The Beach That Summer: *The Essential G. Wayne Miller Fiction, Vol. 3,* 2014.
Drowned: *A Different Kind of Zombie Tale,* 2015.

FILMS

On the Lake: *Life and Love in a Distant Place,* 2009.
Behind the Hedgerow: *Eileen Slocum and the Meaning of Newport Society,* 2010.
The Providence Journal's Coming Home, 2011.

KID NUMBER ONE

KID NUMBER ONE

Alan Hassenfeld and Hasbro

G. WAYNE MILLER

First Stillwater River Publications Edition 2019.

Library of Congress Control Number: 2019945275

ISBN-10: 1-950339-20-3
ISBN-13: 978-1-950339-20-4

1 2 3 4 5 6 7 8 9 10
Written by G. Wayne Miller. www.gwaynemiller.com
Design by Dawn M. Porter
Cover photo by G. Wayne Miller
Published by Stillwater River Publications, Pawtucket, RI, USA.

        Publisher's Cataloging-In-Publication Data
        (Prepared by The Donohue Group, Inc.)

    Names: Miller, G. Wayne, author.
    Title: Kid Number One : Alan Hassenfeld and Hasbro / G. Wayne Miller.
    Description: First Stillwater River Publications edition. | Pawtucket, RI, USA : Stillwa-
        ter River Publications, 2019. | Includes bibliographical references and index.
    Identifiers: ISBN 9781950339204 | ISBN 1950339203
    Subjects: LCSH: Hassenfeld, Alan Geoffrey, 1948- | Hasbro, Inc.--Biography. | Hasbro,
        Inc.--History. | Chief executive officers--United States--Biography. | Philanthro-
        pists--United States--Biography | Toy industry--United States--History. | LCGFT:
        Biographies.
    Classification: LCC HD9993.T692 M55 2019 | DDC 338.4/768872092--dc23

To my dearest, my wife and best friend, Yolanda.
With all my love, and my deepest gratitude for everything.

CAST OF CHARACTERS

MAIN

Alan G. Hassenfeld
Younger son of Merrill and Sylvia Hassenfeld, Hasbro CEO and chairman from 1989 to 2003; chairman until 2008; prominent philanthropist, human rights champion, political activist.

Henry and Hillel Hassenfeld
Sons of Osias and Chaya (Reich) Hassenfeld, immigrated to America in 1903 to escape religious persecution in their native Poland; founded Hassenfeld Bros. (Hasbro) in 1917.

Merrill L. Hassenfeld
Son of Henry and Marion (Frank) Hassenfeld, president of Hasbro Toys from 1943 until his death in 1979.

Stephen D. Hassenfeld
Older son of Merrill and Sylvia (Kay) Hassenfeld, Hasbro CEO and chairman from 1979 until his death from AIDS in 1989, propelled Hasbro from hit-or-miss to enduring Fortune 500.

Sylvia (Kay) Hassenfeld
Wife of Merrill Hassenfeld, long-time Hasbro board member, leading philanthropist and champion of Jewish and Israeli causes.

Vivien Maria Hassenfeld
Businesswoman, philanthropist, wife of Alan.

Ellen Hassenfeld Block
Daughter of Merrill and Sylvia Hassenfeld, noted philanthropist.

Alfred J. Verrecchia
Hasbro employee beginning in 1965, CEO and chairman from 2003 to 2008, chairman from 2008 to 2015, philanthropist.

Brian Goldner
Hasbro employee beginning in 2000, CEO from 2008 until present, chairman from 2015 to present; national corporate responsibility leader.

Mr. Potato Head
Iconic toy since 1952, husband of Mrs. Potato Head, father of son Spud and daughter Yam, alter ego of Kid Number One.

SUPPORTING

Steven Spielberg
Oscar-winning director.

George Lucas
Star Wars creator.

Bob Iger
Chairman and CEO of The Walt Disney Company.

Jill Barad
Former CEO of Mattel.

Margo Georgiadis
Former Google executive, short-lived Mattel CEO.

Ynon Kreiz
Current CEO of Mattel.

Li Ka-shing
Billionaire philanthropist, Alan Hassenfeld mentor.

Mechai Viravaidya
"Mr. Condom," credited with saving 7.7 million lives, Alan Hassenfeld friend.

Wayne Charness
Former Hasbro senior vice president of corporate communications.

John Frascotti
Hasbro president and COO.

Vincent A. "Buddy" Cianci Jr.
The 32nd and 34th mayor of Providence, serving more than 21 years; convicted felon, served 4½ years in federal prison for racketeering, running criminal enterprise from City Hall.

Bernard "Bernie" Loomis
Legendary toy man.

TOY STARS

G.I. Joe
Star Wars
Transformers
My Little Pony
The Game of Life
Monopoly
Nerf
Magic: The Gathering
Pokémon
Furby
Teletubbies
Flubber
Milton Bradley
Kenner
Parker Brothers
Tonka
Mickey Mouse
Power Rangers
Barbie
Ken

CONTENTS

Chapter Six: Dreaming

Chapter Seven: Natural Progressions

Chapter Eight: 'A Difference in the Lives of Those We Care About Most'

Chapter Nine: Responsibility

Chapter Ten: Fearless and Kind

Chapter Eleven: Reach for the Stars

FOREWORD

❧

TIKKUN OLAM

One summer afternoon, I joined Alan G. Hassenfeld for lunch at a seaside restaurant near his residence in Bristol, Rhode Island, his home state.

His wife, Vivien Maria Hassenfeld, joined us, together with two faculty members and five students from Brown University's Hassenfeld Child Health Innovation Institute, which had opened with a $12.5-million gift from Alan and his family. Utilizing research, education, and healthcare intervention, the Institute seeks solutions to childhood autism, asthma, obesity, and other pervasive problems. Alan had invited the Brown folks to lunch so he could learn about the early progress. The students, the first group of the institute's Child Heath Scholars, wanted to meet the man behind their mission.

Hassenfeld, former chairman and CEO of toy and entertainment giant Hasbro Inc., which reported record revenues of $5.21 billion in 2017 and $4.58 billion in 2018 after the collapse of toy retailer Toys 'R" Us, listened to the young women and men, asking questions and sprinkling the conversation with humor. The students may have expected a benefactor demanding a strict accounting of how his money was being spent, as some donors would have, but instead they found an amiable man with a mischievous laugh and a degree of humility that belied his stature. His youthful energy matched theirs. With his tousled hair, penny loafers, collarless shirt, and colorful wristbands, he looked like an unconventional sort of business executive.

He was, and he knew it. He enjoyed being Kid Number One, as he sometimes called himself—Pinocchio, he even said when feeling particularly impish. And he delighted in likening himself to Mr. Potato Head—"Pot Head," he affectionately called it—the whimsical toy that against odds became a national sensation the year it was introduced, 1952, when Hassenfeld was four and his only brother, Stephen, 10, was already dreaming of running Hasbro. On weekends and holidays, Stephen insisted on visiting the factories with the boys' father, Merrill, who was running the toy company in the post-war years. The younger brother only wanted to have fun.

Then, that is.

An hour or so into the lunch, Hassenfeld invited questions of himself.

"I want to hear a little bit more about your vision," one student said.

"I don't know if I can give you a real answer, but I won't give you a Trump answer, either," Hassenfeld joked.

The students laughed. They seemed no more enamored of the former reality-show host than was Hassenfeld, for whom the mere mention of the 45th president could prompt a denunciation of Donald Trump's demagogic intolerance.

Hassenfeld answered the students.

"The success of my family has always been through working in the toy industry and the entertainment industry, with children and families," he said. "I believe that if you're going to give back, your philanthropy should be related to things that are close to your heart."

Children, in other words.

Hassenfeld mentioned Rhode Island's Hasbro Children's Hospital, built with company and personal money during the 1990s while he headed Hasbro, and the newer Hassenfeld Children's Hospital of New York at NYU, founded with a $50-million family gift led by Alan's mother, the late Sylvia Grace Kay Hassenfeld. Alan could have gone on, although he did not, braggadocio not being among his traits. Kept internally, the unpublicized complete list of the diverse people and causes benefitting from Hassenfeld initiatives filled nine single-spaced pages. The Hasbro corporate philanthropy list also was lengthy, one of the reasons Corporate Responsibility Magazine rated the company number one on its 100 Best Corporate Citizens 2017 list, number five for 2018, and number 13 in 2019.

Hassenfeld discussed some of the new Brown institute's specialties: among other health issues, the rise in incidences of autism and asthma troubled him. Budget issues in "a school, a region, or a town" resulting in cutting child-nutrition programs did, too. And there were other matters that also bothered him that he did not mention but which he addressed philanthropically and with political activism.

The students were curious about Hassenfeld's motivation.

"All of these things I do because I have a debt to repay," he told them.

The promise to repay it, as they probably did not know, had been written in blood more than a century before, in a place far away.

Alan & Vivien Hassenfeld with Hassenfeld Child Health Innovation Institute faculty and students.(Miller photo)

At one point as we dined overlooking beautiful Narragansett Bay, where whitecaps danced beneath the August breeze, my thoughts drifted away from the students and their mentors, institute head Dr. Patrick M. Vivier and fellow scientist Annie Gjelsvik.

I imagined an excursion one might take.

If you travelled north on the bay, you would reach the city of Providence, founded in 1636 by Roger Williams after Massachusetts Puritans expelled him for his beliefs in religious freedom and separation of church and state, which the Founders would make bedrock principles of the American republic and which would make Rhode Island an attractive new home for other refugees. Continuing up the Seekonk River to the Blackstone River and into the city of Pawtucket, you would pass Slater Mill, a museum now but the birthplace of the American Industrial Revolution in the late 1700s when Samuel Slater, a British immigrant, opened a water-powered, cotton-spinning factory in partnership with Moses Brown, a wealthy industrialist and co-founder of the university where the Hassenfeld Child Health Innovation Institute is based.

Further up the Blackstone River, you would find old buildings in the city of Central Falls, where G.I. Joe toys once were manufactured—the factories that enchanted the young Stephen Hassenfeld in 1952. A ten-minute drive from there would bring you to 1027 Newport Avenue in Pawtucket, global headquarters today of Hasbro Inc., the company that made those toys—and still does, in China, India, Mexico,

Turkey, Ireland, and Massachusetts, though no longer in Rhode Island. Times have changed since "America's Movable Fighting Man" first hit the market, and today the line contributes but a fraction of the Fortune 513 company's annual revenues. Such other home-grown brands as Monopoly, Nerf, and Transformers, integrated into a blockbuster movie franchise—and licensed products including Star Wars, Disney, and Marvel now power Hasbro, second largest toy company on the planet, after Lego. Mattel, once the industry leader, had fallen on hard times.

The company's founders, brothers Hillel and Henry Hassenfeld, who immigrated to America in the summer of 1903, when they were penniless teenagers who spoke no English, could not have imagined such success. They left their native Poland to escape death at the hands of anti-Semites who slaughtered Jewish children and adults, not to build a global giant.

When they founded Hassenfeld Brothers, a Rhode Island textiles-remnants firm in 1917, Hasbro seemed destined for a modest place in global business history.

But the first Hassenfeld brothers expanded beyond textile remnants to pencil boxes, which they began to fill with writing instruments and rulers. On the eve of the Second World War, they used their boxes for play medical equipment, marketing them as junior doctor and nurse kits. The war brought Junior Air Raid Warden Kits. But until Mr. Potato Head, introduced in 1952, Hasbro still showed little indication of the corporation it would become. The toy and games industry then was ruled by heavyweights Marx, Ideal, Lionel, and Milton Bradley.

Pot Head, the first toy advertised on network TV and Hasbro's first monster hit, began a decade of unprecedented success for the company, which broadened its offerings and forged partnerships with Hollywood. Those ties would reap still greater rewards in decades to come. *Transformers* and *Star Wars* as well as Disney's *Frozen* and *Princess* today, for example.

And then came the fiasco of Flubber, which sold wildly when introduced in 1962 and crashed and burned the next year in a national scandal (the putty-like compound caused skin rashes, prompting lawsuits, scathing headlines, and a Food and Drug Administration investigation, a devastating development in those Camelot days). Merrill, who ran the Hasbro toy division while his only brother, Harold, ran the pencil-manufacturing side of the family firm, pulled Flubber from the market—and prayed for some new toy-business magic, which seemed the only way to survive the company's $5 million loss in 1963.

Merrill's prayers were answered with G.I. Joe, arguably the iconic boys' toy of all time.

Just as the character would in the heroic storylines surrounding his introduction the next year, G.I. Joe became an unprecedented best-seller. From record loss,

Hasbro earned a record profit of almost $6 million just two years later, a stunning turn-around in an industry beholden to the whims of kids and the pocketbooks of parents.

The company would continue to grow, albeit erratically with a succession of hits and misses characteristic of the toy and entertainment business—and another near-fatal blow in the late 1970s as the Vietnam War and the skyrocketing price of plastic forced G.I. Joe into the bunkers. Enter Stephen, who steered Hasbro to Fortune 500 glory in the 1980s by building internally and acquiring Milton Bradley Company with its Playskool brand and timeless classic games, including Candyland, Chutes and Ladders, and The Game of Life, first sold the year before the Russian Civil War began. Amazingly, and that really was the word, a toy company had become a Wall Street darling, sharing the same rarefied air as car manufacturers, petroleum producers, and venerable General Electric.

When Stephen died in 1989 at age 47 of AIDS, a disease he had kept secret from Wall Street and almost everyone else, even his mother, Alan succeeded him.

Some thought Kid Number One was ill-suited to run Hasbro.

Some thought he would kill it, and he almost did, though not for many years.

Alan was no Stephen, close as they were as siblings.

As a young man, Alan had wanted nothing to do with business, his family's or anyone else's. He wanted to be a writer or world-traveler—ideally, both, an adventure-seeking novelist roaming the globe and finding romance as he went. And then he volunteered for several months at an inner-city school named for Martin Luther King Jr., an immersion into a realm of poverty and racial discrimination that would profoundly influence his social-justice and human-rights beliefs, which his family had already begun to instill.

I'm making a difference, he thought.

He was nineteen years old.

Now there he was in 1989, forty years old and chairman and CEO of a mighty company—and an executive who gave some investors the shivers. Well, he *did* wear those penny loafers and colorful wristbands, one in memory of and promise to his first love, a teenaged girl left comatose in an accident who died as Alan, 18, stood vigil by her hospital bed. He *did* dance with Barney, the goofy purple plaything, at company meetings. He did try to see the good in everyone and he did take highly public stands against government corruption and for global human rights, regardless of how such crusades might affect the bottom line.

And he christened himself Kid Number One, which surely was no name that any of the straitlaced types who ran rival Mattel would have chosen.

But the last Hassenfeld brother made believers as the company continued to prosper and Alan acquired more crown jewels—Tonka Corporation, with its Kenner

Parker Toys division and its Star Wars licenses among them—and fended off a hostile takeover attempt by Mattel, whose corporate soul sometimes was compared to a killer shark, with good reason. Hasbro continued to climb the Fortune 500, reaching number 169 in 1994.

Kid Number One in the corner office, 1992. (Courtesy Providence Journal)

Alan's unlikely success as a CEO is told in my bestselling book *Toy Wars: The Epic Struggle Between G.I. Joe, Barbie and the Companies That Make Them,* published in 1998.

And there the story ended—my role as its teller, anyway.

In the years that followed, Hassenfeld and I have remained close.

I watched as Hasbro under Alan's later stewardship plateaued, then nosedived, resurrecting painful memories of Flubber. I knew Alan blamed some of his own decisions for the company's potentially fatal difficulties as the 20th century closed and how, putting pride and ego aside—not something you see every day in the corporate world—he decided to step down as CEO, leaving Hasbro in the hands of his long-time Number Two: Alfred J. Verrecchia, a financial wizard and another major character in *Toy Wars* and again now in *Kid Number One* with whom I also have remained close. Hassenfeld stayed on the board as chairman of the Executive Committee and he and his family continued as Hasbro's biggest stockholders, but he was done with day-to-day operations, although he continued to offer advice (sometimes annoyingly so, as he would admit) to Verrecchia and Verrecchia's successor, current chairman and CEO Brian Goldner.

Once again, the person who never intended to enter business morphed, this time from a part- to full-time philanthropist and social-justice and human-rights champion—a return, in essence, to the teenager who had made a difference. Only this time, he had not just conviction but deep pockets, including major holdings in a company whose stock at times in 2019 traded at more than $126 a share, a company and industry record. Retiring to a tropical island or buying a yacht or professional sports team was not for him, though his wealth would have allowed such indulgences. Like Bill Gates, Michael Bloomberg, George Soros, and others with great fortunes who believed in benefitting humanity, Hassenfeld would devote his remaining years to others.

So he closed his office at Hasbro headquarters, opened a headquarters for the Hassenfeld Family Foundation in the shadow of Brown University at the base of Providence's College Hill, and with his mother and sister got to work funding and supporting a multitude of causes, large and small. Goldner, the man he and Verrecchia had groomed to head the company, had proved his worth, and with Goldner and the Hasbro workforce lifting the company to new profitability, Hassenfeld enjoyed latitude not afforded everyone who dreams on a grand scale.

He was inspired by the legacy of his grandfather and great-uncle, the first Hassenfeld brothers, and his own father and his brother, Stephen, especially. Father Merrill died at work of a heart attack at age 61 in 1979, when Alan was just 30 but already entrusted with building Hasbro's international business, which Stephen would need during the ascent to the Fortune 500. A community leader and benefactor, like his father, Henry, Merrill left his estate—smaller than outsiders would have guessed—to his family only. He explained his rationale in a letter to his wife and children intended to be read after his passing.

Nearly four decades later, Alan could recall it nearly verbatim. It encapsulated Merrill's son's own philosophy.

"Dad said 'You'll be surprised to see that in my whole life I've been very philanthropic but I'm not leaving anything to charity,'" Alan said. "I leave it all to you because in my lifetime, I have believed in *living* charity. And to do things today while you're alive and able to see the fruits.'"

Alan's own heart attack years later gave the son further perspective.

Like Mark Zuckerberg, Larry Ellison, Marc Benioff, and other billionaires who have taken The Giving Pledge, "a commitment by the world's wealthiest individuals and families to dedicate the majority of their wealth to philanthropy," as The Pledge describes itself, Hassenfeld believed in the power of now, not the power of inheritance.

"The first day of the future is today," he said. "If you don't feed children today, if you don't educate people today, there won't be a future. So what are you saving your money for?"

More publicly, Hassenfeld also continued as an advocate for better healthcare, gun control, abortion rights, and political and ethics reform, among other issues—a man willing to commit not only his fortune but his voice to the common good, sometimes to the scorn of letter-writing and social media-trolling critics who mocked him as a bleeding heart, or worse.

Sometimes, cloaked in their cowardly anonymity, the trolls exhibited anti-Semitism that echoed that of which Henry and Hillel Hassenfeld witnessed more than a century before in Eastern Europe. This troll, for example, who reacted to the news that Hassenfeld would lead a coalition supporting gun-control candidates:

"They are a traitorous group to the American People… ALL a bunch of Jews BTW, all want our guns. History shows this jewish inlfuence will be the downfall of this country. They (jews) look upon all of us as Goyim, wake up folks."

This quote is verbatim, spelling and grammar as written.

But Hassenfeld was not deterred by such ugliness. His family never had been. Hassenfelds had survived worse.

And from that survival, they had embraced the Judaic tenet of Tikkun Olam, meaning "repairing the world." They believed in giving back, a commitment first made by the original Hasbro brothers—who, having found safety and prosperity in America, committed themselves to resettling European Jews and numerous philanthropic endeavors, religious and secular, domestically and abroad.

Every Hassenfeld—brothers, sisters, wives—had a debt to repay.

Alan was repaying it with generosity and humor—and some of the humor derived from the toy with which he most closely associated. Hassenfeld was often asked to name his favorite plaything, and he always responded that they were "all my children" and no good parent would ever single out one, but in truth, he placed Pot Head first among equals and not only because it was Hasbro's oldest toy still on the market and was roughly his age. Like Hassenfeld, Mr. Potato Head had continually transformed himself, becoming a succession of characters that suited his ambitions and reflected, if you will, what was beneath his skin.

Originally sold as plastic eyes, ears, mouths, and noses intended to be stuck into actual vegetables, Mr. Potato Head eventually was sold with a plastic body. Mrs. Potato Head appeared in 1953, a year after her husband, and the couple brought forth daughter Yam and son Spud, a playful sort of all-American family that mirrored the consumer aspirations and gender roles of the post-war nation with its blossoming Baby Boom. Later Potato Heads flew to the moon, joined the circus, time-travelled back to the Wild West, and took many more exotic (and mundane) journeys. Following the blockbuster movie *Toy Story*, released in 1995 while Hassenfeld was CEO, the toy has been reinvented in themes including Star Wars, Iron Man, Batman, The Simpsons, Indiana Jones, Three Stooges, and the Wizard of Oz. And *Transformers*, of course: among them, Bumble Spud and the Opti-Mash Prime Mr. Potato Head, a playfully punny mashup of two toy icons.

In one way or another, to greater or lesser degree, Hassenfeld has embraced the spirit of many of those things—though, he would have you know, "never Darth Vader!"

View Hassenfeld in a certain soft light and with a touch of imagination, and you can almost see a physical resemblance to his favorite toy. Visit Hassenfeld's office at Hassenfeld Family Initiatives, and you find it decorated with Mr. Potato Head sets, figures, and cartoons, alongside G.I. Joes, Monopoly games, and other Hasbro products and mementos. You could lose an hour exploring them all, and I have. Hassenfeld's office qualifies as a mini toy museum, albeit one heavily flavored by the company the first brothers founded.

Attractively framed, several of the Pot Head cartoons grace the brick walls.

One is by Garfield creator Jim Davis, who in 2001 produced a Mr. Potato Head cartoon. The three-panel strip shows Mr. Potato Head pounding hooks into a pegboard; Mr. Potato Head resting after the job was done; and Mr. Potato Head's arm and hammer hanging from the board, the rest of him nowhere to be seen.

"To: ALAN—Best Wishes!—Jim Davis" it is signed.

Another cartoon on Hassenfeld's wall, "The Mr. Potato Head Murder Trial," drawn by *Bizarro* creator Dan Piraro, depicts a prosecutor facing a judge in a courtroom. Tagged as evidence, several items commonly found in a kitchen cover a table next to the prosecutor.

"If it pleases the court," the prosecutor says, "the prosecution would like to enter the following items into evidence: a knife, a fork, sour cream, butter, chives, bacon bits…"

For birthday greetings, Hassenfeld might send a Mr. Potato Head card with a depiction of the toy standing at a bathroom urinal. "Oh great, I left it at home!" the toy is saying. "Getting older can make you a little forgetful," the card declares, and then, inside: "At least you don't have detachable parts. Happy birthday."

Yes, Pot Head's humor was Hassenfeld's. Or was it vice-versa?

It could be difficult to say. Hassenfeld sometimes spoke of Mr. Potato Head as a person, giving the toy a human voice and moral authority, as if it had a conscience matching Hassenfeld's. In an era of narcissism and self-serving men in power, a conscience counted.

***Toy Wars* was published in 1998,** when Alan Hassenfeld was still Hasbro chairman, president, and CEO, acing his corporate game. Much happened before the period documented in that book—events that have been barely mentioned publicly or completely untold, until now. Much has happened since that also has gone largely unchronicled, including disastrous decisions Hassenfeld made involving Pokémon that almost killed the company.

Thus, *Kid Number One* is really both prequel and sequel, a new contribution to the literature of an industry unlike any other, and the real people and fictional characters—a century-and-a-half's worth of toy, game and screen icons—that created and maintain it. Having become an elder statesman of that world, Hassenfeld is uncommonly qualified to serve as tour guide.

So this book is many interwoven stories—some entertaining, some educational, some historical, some inspirational to those who share Hassenfeld's belief in Tikkun Olam.

The first opens on that bloody Easter Sunday in 1903, when Christian mobs in Kishinev, now the city of Chișinău, Moldova, slaughtered Jewish children, women, and men until, as *The New York Times* reported, "at sunset, the streets were piled with corpses…"

G. Wayne Miller
August 3, 2019
Providence, Rhode Island

KID NUMBER ONE

CHAPTER ONE

❧

IN THAT DIRECTION LIES HOPE

PART ONE: BLOOD AND MURDER

When news of a terrible massacre in the spring of 1903 reached residents of the village of Ulanów, Galicia, which today is a part of Poland, the Hassenfeld family was among those deeply disturbed by what they learned. Osias Hassenfeld and his wife, Chaya Reich Hassenfeld, and their three sons—Herman, Henry and Hillel—knew nothing could ever be the same.

Many miles east, in the city of Kishinev, capital of a remote region of the Russian Empire near the Romanian border, anti-Semitic mobs during two days of madness had killed dozens of Jews, injured hundreds more, and burned and pillaged more than 1,000 houses and stores. In part thanks to a report smuggled out of Kishinev which reached *The New York Times* and other influential newspapers, the massacre, or pogrom, made international headlines, outraging the worldwide Jewish community and good-hearted people of many faiths.

The Jews of Kishinev, like those in much of Russia and Eastern Europe, already had been subject to persecution, and they could regularly read of the hatred expressed toward them in the popular newspaper *Бессарабец*, published by the ultra-nationalist racist Pavel Aleksandrovich Krushevan. Krushevan also was first publisher of *The Protocols of the Meetings of the Learned Elders of Zion*, a fake document that purported to be the minutes of a secret meeting of Jewish leaders who planned global domination by assuming control of world economies and the press. Henry Ford would later finance an American edition of *The Protocols*, and it remains in distribution more than a century later, a testament to the power of bigotry.

Krushevan's *Бессарабец* newspaper ran stories with provocative headlines including "Crusade against the Hated Race!" and "Death to the Jews!", and in 1903, such propaganda jumped from print to real life, undoubtedly orchestrated in part by Krushevan, in a succession of atrocities that began when a Christian boy was found murdered and a girl committed suicide by poison. The tragedies were unconnected and not of Jewish doing but *Бессарабец* suggested that Jews had killed both, in order to draw their blood for use in preparing matzo for the seven days of Passover. An outrageous allegation, but one that haters were eager to believe.

A proclamation that circulated in the tsarist city—today, such falsehoods are spread by social media and fake news sites, but the net effect, angry reaction, is the same—called on Christians to avenge the fictitious Passover obscenity.

"Our great festival of the Resurrection of Christ draws near," the proclamation began. "It is many years since, put to death by the Jews, Our Lord expiated by his blood our sins and those of all the world, pouring out in his mercy his holy blood for the salvation of all the nations of the earth, of us Christians as well as the adherents of other religions.

"But the vile Jews are not content with having shed the blood of our Savior, whom they crucified, and who suffered for them. Every year they shed the innocent blood of Christians. They shed it and use it in their religious rites. You have doubtless been told that at Dubossari they crucified a Christian youth, whose blood they offered in sacrifice. The story is quite correct. The authorities know it too, though they do not breathe a word in order not to excite our anger against these miserable, bloodthirsty men who should have been driven out of our country long ago. A similar case has just occurred at Kief, where they bled to death an innocent child and afterwards threw its body into the street.

"At the present moment, whilst we are preparing to celebrate the Passion of our Lord, they are drinking Christian blood among themselves… Brothers, in the name of our Savior who gave his blood for us, in the name of our very pious Little Father, the Tsar, who watches over the wants of his people, and alleviates their lot by generous manifestoes, let us join on Easter Day in the cry, 'Down with the Jews!' Let us massacre these sanguinary monsters who slake their thirst with Russian blood!

"Act in such a manner that they will remember the pogrom [i.e. massacre] of Odessa, where the troops themselves assisted the people. This time they will again aid us, inspired as they are, like ourselves, with the love of Christ. Brothers, lend us your aid. Let us massacre these vile Jews. We are already numerous."

The story is quite correct, the proclamation asserted.

Except it wasn't. It was a false assertion of authenticity, a favored tactic of the ignorant and the prejudicial—a tactic that Alan Hassenfeld would confront, many decades later. As would many other Americans, too.

The Kishinev pogrom began on Easter, April 19, and continued into that Monday, April 20 (April 6 and April 7 on the Julian calendar). Readers of *The New York Times,* published by Adolph Ochs, son of an Ohio Jewish family who had built the newspaper into one of America's most powerful, learned of the horrors in the April 28, 1903, edition.

> ST. PETERSBURG, April 25 – (Taken across the border for transmission in order to escape the censor.) – The anti-Jewish riots in Kishinev, Bessarabia, are worse than the censor will permit to publish. There was a well laid-out plan for the general massacre of Jews on the day following the Russian Easter. The mob was led by priests, and the general cry, "Kill the Jews," was taken up all over the city. The Jews were taken wholly unaware and were slaughtered like sheep. The dead number 120 and the wounded about 500.
>
> The scenes of horror attending this massacre are beyond description. Babes were literally torn to pieces by the frenzied and blood-thirsty mob. The local police made no attempt to check the reign of terror. At sunset, the streets were piled with corpses and wounded. Those who could make their escape fled in terror, and now the city is practically deserted of Jews. Just as in the riots of 1880-1881 there is a popular belief among the Russian peasants that the Czar decreed the slaughter of Jews. The immediate cause of the riot, however, is the ritual murder accusation against the Jews in Dubosary. Immediate relief is wanted.

Kishinev pogrom victims.

Further painful detail emerged in an account published by *The Times* of London, in which the author wrote that Monday had been the most horrendous day, when "besides the murders committed, the interiors of houses were utterly dismantled, pillows ripped up, Jewish Scriptures torn, floors destroyed and furniture thrown into the street... The local authorities took no effective steps to stop the riots, which continued unabated till 4 p.m., or later, the soldiers meanwhile being passive, if not sympathetic, spectators and the police contenting themselves with the arrest of minor criminals."

In "An American Eye-Witness," published in 1904 in *Russia at the Bar of the American People: A Memorial of Kishinef,* the respected politician and Civil War veteran Col. John B. Weber described the plight of Jews in Russia and East Europe during the century-long pogrom era—Kishinev being but the latest. The first is generally held to be that which occurred in 1821 in Odessa, founded by Russia's Catherine the Great. It was followed by pogroms again in that Black Sea city in 1859 and 1871; and a wave of anti-Jewish rioting and murder in Warsaw, Kiev, once more in Odessa, and elsewhere during the bloody years of 1881 to 1884. And the worst was yet to come: in 1905, pogroms in Ukraine, Odessa, Minsk, and other places claimed more than 1,000 innocent lives. Jews of any station lived under a shadow, for the hatred espoused by Pavel Krushevan and his kind was deep-rooted, and the rabble was willing to act.

Weber urged his fellow American citizens to welcome East European Jews to a land where they could be safe and enjoy prospects for prosperity. A two-term U.S. Representative and first Commissioner of Immigration at the port of New York City, Weber proved to be a leading human-rights activist of his era. From his perch at Ellis Island, he knew well the stories of those who arrived penniless but relieved to have reached the proverbial land of milk and honey.

"The Jew in Russia is an alien in the land of his birth, a subject who bears an undue share of the burdens of government without the privileges of its meanest citizen," Weber wrote in the Kishinev volume, which included a chapter, "The Authentic Account of the Kishinef Massacres," a truthful refutation of the "facts" as reported in the anti-Semitic press.

"Fettered in his movements, handicapped in his vocation, restricted in his educational opportunities, he is unable to protect himself and powerless to invoke successfully the protection of the authorities, a slave without the self-interest of a master to shield him from abuse, he stands helpless, friendless, and defenseless against brute force, egged on, not only by religious intolerance, but by contending forces that strive to strengthen the government on the one hand and to destroy it on the other...

"The Jew is therefore the sport of the rabble, the spoil of the official, the football of fanaticism, the buffer against which strikes the wrath of bigotry, intolerance and savagery.

"A poor uncultured Jew at Kovno who was about to sail for the United States, asked about the purposes of his weary voyage, textually replied: 'I am going to America, for in that direction lies hope. Here, I have only fears to confront me. The hope may be delusive, but the fears are a certainty. My great ambition is to breathe at least once the free air with which God has blessed the American people.'"

In America, that air was first felt in 1636, when Roger Williams founded Providence and Rhode Island.

In summation, Weber appealed to American idealism: "The persecution of the Jews of Russia, recently so hideously emphasized by the Kishinef massacre, should arouse all civilized nations but more especially the United States, for upon this country will fall the burden of furnishing an asylum of refuge for the surviving victims of racial hatred and religious bigotry."

The New York Times **wrote** that *immediate relief is wanted*—and it came, quickly and in abundance, especially from New York City, long the first step on U.S. soil for immigrants to America. By 1903, the Lower East Side of Manhattan had established itself as a favored destination for East European Jews, who brought with them many trades and talents. Grateful for their good fortune, those already there extended a hand to their brethren, joining Jewish residents of other parts of the city and places beyond. Non-Jews came aboard the cause.

A fund-raising vaudeville performance was scheduled for the Academy of Music and *The Times* described a "mass meeting of East Side Jews" during which "a committee of business men was appointed to solicit subscriptions for the relief of the victims in Kishinev." Contributions soon followed. By May 20, tens of thousands of dollars had been raised, with mining magnate and philanthropist Daniel Guggenheim, chair of a *Jewish Daily News* fund, announcing that his efforts alone had netted $20,000 (about $500,000 in today's dollars). The Central Committee reported similar success, with an official telling the newspaper that "among the letters enclosing checks or money were several from Christians." Committee treasurer Arnold Kohn said that "The Jews in this country realize that the American Government cannot effectively intervene. We do, however, believe that the press has served to arouse a sentiment of horror at the outrages of Russia which will reach all countries…"

Others believed the U.S. could intervene, and *The Times* reported that "the State Department was flooded with resolutions relative to Kishineff." One drafted by the East Side Physicians' Club was sent to President Theodore Roosevelt, "appealing to him in the name of humanity to protest to the Russian Government against the outrages at Kishineff and demand that all guilty be punished."

New York City politicians decried the massacre, with unanimous passage of a Board of Alderman resolution introduced by powerful Tammany Hall leader John T. McCall that called on "his Excellency, Theodore Roosevelt, President of the United States, in the name of humanity to protest to the Government of the Empire of Russia against these unspeakable outrages." In Jersey City, alderman passed similar resolutions sent to Roosevelt and Congress.

Perhaps no one at the time imagined that Kishinev would foreshadow something immeasurably worse: the Holocaust killing of six million Jews, nearly two thirds of all Jews in Europe.

The Hassenfelds of Ulanów, Galicia, likely read nothing that spring from the U.S. press, though they may have learned of the outpouring of American support. But Chaya and Osias (also known as Isaiah) needed no news from America to reach a decision. The news from Kishinev was sufficiently frightening to decide to send Hillel, 17, and Henry, 14, across the Atlantic. Herman, 21, would stay in Ulanów with his wife, Pesche Laufer Hassenfeld, also known as Pessel. The couple had a three-year-old daughter, Jean, and Pesche was several months pregnant.

Two objectives would be served with the departure of Hillel and Henry: the teenagers would find safety, and also receive the opportunity for a better life than would seem possible in Ulanów, a small trading center at the confluence of two rivers. Nearly half of its 3,500 or so residents were Jews, but shtetl life was hardscrabble and the economic future was, at best, dim.

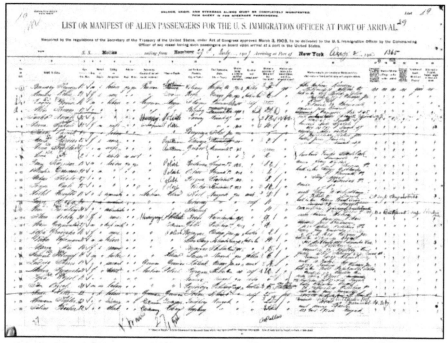

Manifest for S/S Moltke on arrival at New York, August 2, 1903. Hillel is line 15.

Aided by European relief societies, the brothers in the summer of 1903 made their way to Hamburg, Germany, where they boarded the Hamburg America steamer S/S

Moltke on July 22, 1903. After stops in Southampton and Cherbourg, the boys reached New York on August 2. For his immigration papers, Hillel listed his occupation as cigar maker, said he had four dollars in his pocket, and that his passage had been paid by an uncle who lived on the Lower East Side. The brothers first stayed with the uncle, in a tenement building two blocks from the East River, near where the Williamsburg Bridge to Brooklyn was nearing completion.

During the 19th century, the Lower East Side had been home to successive waves of immigrants, notably, in mid-century, Germans, who came in such numbers that an area had come to be called Little Germany. As the century ended, the immigrant mix was shifting to a growing presence of Eastern Europeans, including Jews from Poland, Russia, Ukraine, and other countries. Immigrants tended to cluster in neighborhoods defined by nationality, but the compressed presence of others in such a relatively small space and interaction with the greater city beyond, through which they could move without fear for their lives, provided for heterogeneity. A Polish Jew's views of America would be influenced by this multicultural environment—more so should he become involved in any manner of trade, as the young Hassenfeld brothers did soon after arriving.

In a remembrance of his Lower East Side childhood, an elderly man of Italian heritage wrote of his upbringing. "The tenants in our building were from Palermo, Naples, Minsk, Bucharest, and Warsaw, with a number of unidentifiables thrown in. How did we communicate? In Yiddish, partly… My father, [a] tailor, mastered conversational Yiddish in the needle trades; conversed in Italian with his compatriots; and spoke English at home. My [American-born] mother spoke enough Italian and Yiddish to show and communicate with in-laws and neighbors."

Hillel told the immigration authorities he made cigars, and he and his younger brother initially may have found employment with one of New York's cigar-manufacturing factories, or perhaps in one of its garment shops; at the turn of the century, the city offered abundant opportunity in both industries, albeit at low wages in inhospitable workspaces appropriately called sweatshops. Eventually, Henry and Hillel gravitated toward peddling, an occupation requiring skills in negotiation, persistence, and money-handling—and for the brothers, who spoke no English, an opportunity to learn a new language, a virtual necessity if their business were to greatly expand.

Hillel at first peddled gas mantles, Henry electrical supplies, but greater possibilities beckoned in cloth, which fueled the busy factories and showrooms of the city's mighty Garment District. The brothers began to peddle textile remnants—essentially, scraps—and their new business allowed them a living. At first, they bought from textile manufacturers, which made the cloth that became the apparel in New York, but eventually they began sourcing their remnants in Rhode Island, whose flourishing economy was owed to mills that traced their lineage to Samuel Slater and partner Moses Brown.

In factories on the Blackstone and other Rhode Island rivers—in Burrillville, Central Falls, Cumberland, North Smithfield, Pawtucket, Providence, South Kingstown, West Warwick, and Westerly, on the Connecticut border—workers transformed cotton from the south and wool from wherever into riches, at least for the families that owned the means of production.

PART TWO: THE SPIRIT OF ROGER WILLIAMS

The brothers would find something more in Rhode Island, reachable from Manhattan by steamship or J.P. Morgan's New York, New Haven, and Hartford Railroad. They would find the enduring legacy of Rhode Island's 17th-century founder, Roger Williams, a religious refugee, like them, who also had fled a place of intolerance: the Massachusetts Bay Colony, whose Puritan leaders tried and convicted him of heresy and sedition for his belief in separation of church and state, religious liberty, and freedom of conscience.

Banished from the colony, facing sadistic punishment or death should he return, Williams in 1636 established a settlement on the western shore of the Seekonk River, the tidal mouth of the Blackstone River as it meets Narragansett Bay. He was welcomed by the Native American inhabitants of the land, the Narragansett Indians, and he, in turn, befriended them. Like everyone regardless of race, Williams heretically believed, indigenous peoples were worthy before God.

Williams was still alive when Jews who landed in Newport, a distant corner of Rhode Island (in the 1600s), founded a congregation, Nephuse Israel— "Scattered of Israel"—as early as 1658. They were descendants of the "Marranos," people who had fled Portugal and Spain, where the Inquisition and state-forced conversion of Jews to Christianity led some to practice their Judaism in secret. Seeking asylum first in Barbados, these refugees had learned of this place, then officially known as the Colony of Rhode Island and Providence Plantations, where religious liberty was not only allowed but celebrated.

Dedicated in 1763, Newport's Touro Synagogue, today the oldest synagogue building in the U.S., was such a prominent symbol of freedom during the early republic that in 1790, in a letter to the "Hebrew congregation at Newport," President George Washington vowed that the new nation would give "to bigotry no sanction and to persecution no assistance." Some Jews capitalized on the seaport's thriving maritime-based economy, opening retail and wholesale trading companies that engaged in business with other colonies and beyond.

Newport's spirit of acceptance spread north, attracting new immigrants.

Jews began settling in Providence in 1838, when Dutch native Solomon Pereira and his wife arrived. Pereira ran clothing stores and became the first president of the Congregation of the Sons of Israel, or Temple Beth-El, when it was established in 1855. Providence's Jewish community was growing: from nine families listed in the 1850 city directory to about 250 in the 1885 directory and nearly 1,000 by 1895, an expansion attributable in part to an influx of immigrants from Eastern Europe. At the turn of the century, the Providence directory listed more than 1,600 names. The numbers firmly established the community in the capitol city, where the First Baptist Church, opened in 1775 and successor to Williams's original congregation, occupied a place of prominence on the East Side.

"As the community's size grew, so did its formal organizations and institutions," writes the Jewish Alliance of Greater Rhode Island. "By the turn of the 20th century, new congregations had appeared and were meeting in homes or rented halls. In the 55 years following the inception of the first temple in Providence, no fewer than 23 separate synagogues received charters... The emergence of so many congregations was a good indication of the growth and distribution of the Providence Jewish community. They originally were located near the center of the city, but as the population spread out, so did the synagogues — first to the more peripheral areas of the city and then to the suburbs.

"By the end of World War I, the tremendous growth of new organizations stopped. The institutional structure of the Jewish community of Providence was well-established, and few new organizations were chartered during the following decades. Thus began a period of consolidation and maturation, as the immigrants and their offspring built upon and molded the earlier structure to meet their changing needs."

Religion remained the foundation of the community when the Hassenfeld brothers discovered Rhode Island, but earthly needs were being addressed as well. Nothing perhaps exemplified that commitment more than Miriam Hospital—now a part of the Lifespan health system, which includes Rhode Island Hospital and Hasbro Children's Hospital—which began in 1902, a year before the Hassenfeld brothers arrived in New York, when a small number of women collected coins as they worked toward their goal of raising $1,000 for down payment for "a place to care for the indigent sick of the Jewish faith."

George Washington's Touro letter notwithstanding, bigotry, of course, had not been scoured from Rhode Island. The late Bruce Sundlun—Rhode Island's second Jewish governor (1991 to 1995) and the first Jew admitted to exclusive Bailey's Beach Club in Newport—often spoke of experiencing anti-Semitism while growing up in the 1920s and 1930s on Providence's East Side, home of Brown University and Moses Brown School, founded by Samuel Slater's business partner.

Sundlun remembered grammar school, when a Christian boy harassed him as he was walking home, calling him "you dirty Jew, you kike." (His father's advice was to punch the boy in the face and "run like hell," which is what Sundlun, who would join the French Resistance during World War II after being shot down over Nazi-occupied Belgium, did). "I'd go to dances and girls would tell me: 'I can't dance with you, I'd like to—but my parents told me I can't because you're Jewish.'"

Sundlun was a nine-year-old in third grade when he won a race at his school's annual field day. "The two guys who came in second threw me down on the ground and called me a dirty Jew," he recalled. "After the field day, they had a graduation ceremony and everybody got to wear white pants and dark blue jackets. You marched by classes and somebody carried the class banner. And I had been chosen to carry it. After this incident, the teacher called up my father and said, 'we're going to have to tell Bruce he can't carry the class banner.'"

The first Hassenfelds in Rhode Island also almost certainly were touched by bigotry, though no record survives to describe it.

What does survive is a record of the family's decades-long effort to help end it.

Henry Hassenfeld's travels through Rhode Island—a state whose motto was "hope" —brought him to West Warwick, where he met David Frank, a man who would change the course of his young life. By 1911, Frank had established a business buying and selling junk metal and scrap iron, and also lace and cotton remnants, which Henry and Hillel prized.

Frank was making a go of it, having the resources to buy a substantial ad in the 1911 West Warwick City Directory that boasted of a "telephone connection" for his junk yard and retail store on Main Street in the town's Phenix village, on the Pawtuxet River—which, like the Blackstone to the north, powered mighty textile mills.

Indeed, all of tiny West Warwick hummed with industry and commerce during the first part of the 20th century as fabric-making brought unprecedented prosperity to the town and Rhode Island, providing employment for increasing numbers of immigrants willing to work under trying conditions in exchange for modest wages and company housing and stores. Fruit of the Looms Mills, "The World's Most Famous Label"—makers of bedwear, book and print cloths, and clothing of all kinds—led the lineup of factories on the Pawtuxet, along which ran The Pawtuxet Valley Railroad Company, a short line connecting the town to the rest of the country. Suppliers of dyes, soaps, sizing, and softeners flourished, as did banks, insurers, contractors, grocers and more.

A visitor to West Warwick might dine or overnight at the Majestic, "largest and best hotel between Providence and New London,"a five-story building that served meals around the clock, offered "first class accommodations" with electric lights and steam heat, and invited "auto parties" to partake of its hospitality. A visitor might choose the Winsor Hotel and Cafe, "the best equipped and most centrally located hotel in the Pawtuxet Valley" and also a "headquarters for theatrical people and automobile parties," located on a trolley route and but "one minute from steam cars"—and all for $2 night, $1.50 for stays of three nights or more. Auto parties were welcome there, too: Henry Ford's Model T, introduced in 1908, was revolutionizing America.

And perhaps Henry Hassenfeld stayed at one of these establishments as he and his brother were building their still-Manhattan-based remnants business. Perhaps he conducted transactions with David Frank over a meal at the Majestic or Winsor, or called on him at his Main Street store.

The two had much in common beyond business.

Like Henry, Frank had immigrated to America from Europe as a teenager: leaving his native Austria and arriving in the U.S. in March 1889, three months shy of his 16th birthday. His first occupation, like Henry's, was peddling, his springboard also to growing enterprise. Both valued family (and the sons of each would follow them into the family business). Both were devout Jews, active in their synagogues and religious communities. Neither would return to live permanently in their homelands. Though they knew not then, of course, both would be buried at Lincoln Park Cemetery in Warwick, as would their wives, their children, and other relatives.

Sometime after meeting with Frank, Henry Hassenfeld met one of his and wife Minnie L. Frank's three daughters, Marion Lena Frank. Henry was smitten, and Marion likewise. On June 9, 1914, the 25-year-old groom married the 18-year-old bride, in Providence. City records state Henry's residence as New York City, his occupation as "travelling salesman." Philip Keller, a member of the Providence Hebrew Butchers Association, presided at the wedding. Marion went to live with her husband at his new apartment in a building on Honeywell Avenue that faced the Bronx Zoo.

Henry Hassenfeld and Marion Frank marriage license.

But Marion, Henry's "blond, vivacious wife," according to Henry's obituary decades later, "did not like New York but was pining for" her home state and by 1917, the couple had moved to an apartment on Somerset Street in South Providence—two blocks from where Hasbro Children's Hospital stands today. Jewish immigrants from Russia, Poland, and elsewhere in East Europe had settled in the district, creating a

... community of peddlers, butchers, grocers and jewelry-factory workers, and their families. Many worshipped at Robinson Street Shul, one of four Orthodox synagogues in South Providence, and just three blocks from the Hassenfelds' new home.

Contemporary religious writer Lester Bradner found virtue in these new Rhode Island residents, stating that "the development of Hebrew life in Providence is a comparatively recent feature, greatly accelerated in growth by the persecutions a few years past in Russia... They are by nature a self-contained and orderly people. Their family morals are above the average. They make good citizens, even if not agreeable."

Henry listed his occupation as broker in the 1917 Providence City Directory, but the city's tax records for 1917 confirm that he and Hillel, who apparently also had moved to Rhode Island from New York, remained partners in their textile-products business. That same year, as the Great War continued overseas, "Hassenfeld Brothers," eventually shortened to Hasbro, listed $900 in tangible assets and $700 in intangible assets.

Their business was growing, but for how long could it satisfy their ambition? *Why be only middlemen,* they surely wondered, *moving remnants from one party to another for modest gain when greater potential might be found in manufacture? Why not think on a grander scale?* They likely were encouraged and perhaps financially buttressed by Henry's father-in-law, who had opened the Phenix Lace and Remnant Store and was planning a dry goods retail business.

And so, the Hassenfeld brothers imagined new uses for their own remnants.

They could, for example, be made into wiping cloths. More imaginatively, they could be used to line wooden pencil boxes, making for a more appealing product with a potentially larger market. Real and artificial leather also could be fashioned into so-called novelties, and companies based in Rhode Island and elsewhere in New England made those materials in quantity and at competitive price, too.

Henry and Hillel took their success and reputations to investors. After they had secured $3,000 in financing, on April 14, 1919, Rhode Island Secretary of State J. Fred Parker certified the incorporation papers of their Leatherite Company, an expansion of Hassenfeld Brothers, whose stated purpose was "engaging in the business of manufacture of novelties and frames of all kinds and descriptions as well as buying and selling at wholesale and retail of said articles and the doing of all things incidental thereto; also the manufacture of cloth and leather merchandise."

The company that would make its mark under the brand "Hasbro" was now headed down a road that would bring them to toys. And while that was in the future, the brothers' expanded firm drew immediate attention at the time, with stories in the April 23, 1919, edition of trade journal *The Jewelers' Circular,* and the May 15, 1919, issue of *The Bookseller, Newsdealer and Stationer.*

Good fortune was theirs, but other developments, deeply alarming, tempered the brothers' enthusiasm. With the 1917 Bolshevik Revolution and the Russian Civil War that had followed, a new wave of pogroms was underway in Poland and other parts of East Europe, and reports of the latest atrocities were reaching America from the Associated Press and other sources. The Committee for the Defense of Jews in Poland, affiliated with the American Jewish Committee, was mobilizing support and rebutting Polish government officials who denied, despite uncontestable evidence to the contrary, that Hebrew blood was being spilled again on their soil.

After Polish officials in May 1919 dismissed the reports as "mere hearsay," Nathan Straus, a leader of the Committee for the Defense of Jews in Poland, produced AP reports for *The New York Times*, which, among other newspapers, had been publishing a succession of pogrom stories. The AP accounts described "Anti-Semitic riots… in western Galicia and Poland" and "slaughter of Jews" in the Ukrainian city of Lemberg, near the Polish border. They chronicled "wholesale massacre of Jews in Poland" and "slaying and plundering in Warsaw and Galicia" and "950 victims of Galicia pogroms buried so far" and more.

The Polish government's denial of these atrocities foreshadowed 21st-century propaganda and distortions of truth that would help elect a nativist to the American presidency. But the pogroms of 1919 and 1920 were not fake news. In a statement to *The Times*, Israel Cohen, a British human-rights and Jewish leader, spoke fact.

"Fortunately for the truth," Cohen wrote, "no barriers are high enough in modern times to conceal widespread movement, such as are the pogroms. From the testimony of men and women, eyewitnesses who escaped the inferno; from official representatives in Poland, Jews and Gentiles; from unbiased press correspondents who visited the scenes of pogroms; from reports of official investigation committees established in the places that were visited by mass barbarities; from reports of various social welfare organizations working in Poland; from an interpellation in the Polish Diet, we have gathered exact data as to the Polish pogroms. We have names, places, addresses. We can furnish all this to the Polish representatives here."

Through 1921, tens of thousands of Eastern European Jews would be killed, with many more left homeless. Henry and Hillel would help arrange to bring many of them—relatives and a much greater number of refugees they'd never met—to safety. Into Hitler's time and beyond, the Hassenfelds would prove savior to people facing misery and death.

The first relief mission occurred in the early spring of 1920, according to the passport application Hillel submitted and Henry countersigned in advance of the trip Hillel would take.

A naturalized U.S. citizen by then, like Henry, Hillel stated his business as "Hassenfeld Brothers, Jobbers and Converters, Cotton and Woolen Goods" and outlined his plans to visit France, Poland, and Czechoslovakia for the purpose of "buying merchandise" and to "see aged parents." Whether Hillel would have gone overseas to

...handise when it was plentiful in America was doubtful, so it is likely that the true mission was not just to see parents—in fact, there was just one parent left, for the mother had died—but to arrange passage to America for more Hassenfelds. Father Osias, 60, still lived in Ulanów in early 1920. So did older brother Herman and wife Pesche and their seven children: Jean, almost 20 now; Esther, about to turn 17; Jack, almost 16; Ruth, 14; Edith, 10; Joseph, eight; and David, five.

Thus began a tradition that Henry's son Merrill, daughter-in-law Sylvia, grandsons Stephen and Alan, and granddaughter Ellen Block would continue to the present day. Crises cried for relief, and they would answer the call.

"My grandfather died when I was 12," Alan said. "And I didn't necessarily go back in time and history to try and understand how many people—and how they did it—they brought from their village. Any number of people who worked at Hasbro had been brought over. The family brought them."

PART THREE: A TWO-STORY BRICK BUILDING

Arrangements were being made for the latest immigrant Hassenfelds—the father and third brother and his family—to leave for Rhode Island when, in June 1920, Henry and Hillel bought a small lot at the corner of Bowen and North Main Streets in Providence and hired Harry Marshak, one of the state's first prominent Jewish architects, to draw blueprints for a two-story brick building. Son of Russian immigrants, Marshak was known for his design of part of the Sons of Jacob Synagogue, where the Hassenfelds worshipped.

Ad for North Main Street headquarters of Hassenfeld Brothers.

Measuring 45 by 100 feet, the building would be a modest factory and office for the Leatherite and Hassenfeld Brothers Cotton Goods companies, names that the Hassenfelds used interchangeably at the time, but it was located in a prominent district in the capitol city.

That, too, spoke to the current success and future prospects of the business.

The Rhode Island State House was but a quarter of a mile distant; its predecessor, the Old State House, which dated to 1760, was two blocks away. City offices, wholesale and retail businesses, and the National Bank of Commerce were located along North Main, together with the Friends Meeting House and the Episcopal Cathedral of St. John. More sacred ground still was the congregation at 75 North Main: the First Baptist Church in America, established by Roger Williams in 1638 and now convening in a white steepled building completed in 1775. And just one block from Hassenfeld Brothers stood a house on the site of Roger Williams' home, which he had built in 1636, to be near what was then a freshwater spring.

The new building complete, Hassenfeld Brothers in 1921 listed $5,600 in tangible property, and their workplace was assessed at $40,880, more than a half million dollars today. The numbers in 1922 would all but confirm that Hasbro, as the enterprise eventually would be called, was here to stay.

That year, the value of the company's tangible property increased $2,000, to $7,600. The value of their factory was unchanged, but the revenues it produced were rising, and the workforce was growing in a workplace with sanitary conditions described by state inspectors as "very good," an early indication of Hasbro's kindly treatment of its workers. Hassenfeld Brothers in 1922 employed three men—Henry, Hillel, and Herman, the foreman—and twenty women, including Jean and Esther, both working as clerks. Henry and Marion continued to live on their apartment on Somerset Street, and Hillel lived in an apartment nearby. Herman and Pessel and their family shared a home on upscale Blackstone Boulevard, on the city's East Side, a five minutes' walk from where Sylvia and Merrill would raise the final Hassenfeld brothers.

And 1922 was the year that Henry and Hillel showed solid evidence that they were headed toward a mastery of marketing, which, like helping others, would be fused into the Hasbro corporate DNA. Exploiting the most powerful marketing tool of the era, print media, the brothers that year placed ads in *The Modern Stationer and Book-Seller: A Business Magazine for the Retail Stationer and Department Store Buyer* and *Geyer's Stationer: The Authoritative Weekly of the Stationery, Office Supply, Engraving, Greeting Card and Allied Trades*, among other publications. The ads, illustrated with drawings, showcased the brothers' No. 100 pencil set, a box encased in Leatherite material (available in different shades) containing four pencils, a rubber eraser, and a prism pencil sharpener; and, newly introduced in 1922, the more deluxe No. 299 set, "improved with a two-year calendar and multiplication chart" and five pencils.

"They make excellent premium items and may also be used by the mail order and syndicate trade," read one ad. "All these sets are sold at a saving to you, and no other concern can quote these prices on good of equal value." Read another, for the No. 100: "Very useful for the student as well as for home and library use. Made from genuine Leatherite Materials in assorted colors. We cheerfully send samples on memo on request." And another, for the No. 299: "We have perfected and completed this new and attractive pencil set to satisfy the demands of the large department store. It is faultless in workmanship and lowest in price."

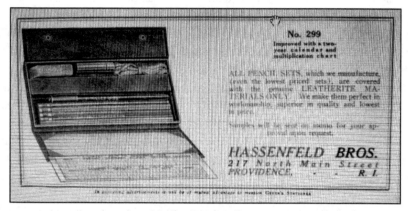

Leatherite pencil set.

Soon enough, the pencil sets were selling briskly nationwide through retail giants S.S. Kresge and F.W. Woolworth and other outlets. The demographics were favorable: the First World War over, America's population was rising, from 92 million people in the 1910 Census to 106 million in 1920, to 123 million in 1930, and to 132 million in 1940, on the eve of America's entry into the Second World War. Immigration helped fuel the rise, and also live births, with roughly 2.6 million children born every year from 1920 to 1940. Kids needed pencils and rulers for school, and parents saw added value in calendars and multiplication charts.

And as the Hassenfelds had concluded, pencils, erasers, sharpeners, calendars, and charts were not the only appealing items that could be added to their cloth-lined boxes.

A box could hold many things, practical and entertaining.

The brothers reached another milestone on January 7, 1926, when they met with lawyers Philip Joslin, Arthur Feiner, and Ira Marcus to sign papers creating Hassenfeld Bros. Inc., the entity they incorporated to give them legal right to own patents, trademarks, and copyrights, and to raise new capital for their burgeoning business, which the papers specified as the "manufacturing, selling and otherwise dealing in all kinds of leather novelties

[and] school supplies." Five hundred shares of preferred stock, each with a value of $100, netted $50,000 for expansion—$719,000 in today's dollars. Another 1,000 shares of common stock were authorized.

The year 1926 also found the Hassenfelds fully establishing themselves on the East Side.

Henry moved to a house on Elmgrove Avenue, near Herman and his family, and closer still to Brown Stadium and Temple Emanu-El. Hillel took up residence on Elmway Street, around the corner from Henry. The family's worship preferences were shifting, too, from The Sons of Jacob Synagogue, near the State House, to Temple Emanu-El. And Marion and Henry's family was growing: their first son, Harold, born in 1916, was now ten; their second, Merrill, born in 1918, was eight; and their last child, Muriel, was two. Hillel had married Esther Mollie Margolis, daughter of a Polish family, and the couple had two young daughters, Charlotte and Marion.

The influx in capital had the intended effect, and by 1929, the Hassenfelds had moved their headquarters to the corner of Dorrance and Pine Streets, in another leading banking and business neighborhood, four blocks from today's offices of the Hassenfeld Foundation. That year, Hillel was listed in the City Directory as president, with Henry holding the position of secretary-treasurer.

Their ambition unchecked, the brothers guided the company through the dark early days of the Great Depression, not merely surviving but flourishing, and in 1932, when (on July 8) the Dow Jones Industrial Average hit its lowest level, just 41.22, they moved all operations to a 65,000-square-foot facility on Broad Street that had been owned by a manufacturer of gold and silverware. According to the 1932 City Directory, Hassenfeld Bros. was capitalized at $300,000—$5.6 million in today's dollars. The depression may have dampened demand for silverware, but children and grownups still had to write.

And the Hassenfelds had new ideas on filling their boxes.

In 1940, Hassenfeld Bros. moved again, to a former textile mill with almost a half million square feet in Central Falls, another booming city on the Blackstone River, just north of Pawtucket. The company was employing more than 250 workers during the peak season. Annual sales passed $500,000—more than $9 million in 2019 dollars. The brothers had become captains of industry. Looming war was about to transform Hasbro once again, into a leading toy maker.

Busy though they were with their company, the Hassenfelds contributed their time and their money to Jewish causes—including, most urgently once again, helping to resettle hundreds of Jews from Eastern Europe and, with the rise of Hitler and the beginning of the Holocaust, Germany and other countries on the continent. These were mostly strangers to the Hassenfelds—people they did not know who faced suffering or death without a rescuing hand. This Hassenfeld family legacy of resettlement would be passed from Henry to Merrill, and from Merrill to Ellen, Stephen, and Alan. Merrill's wife Sylvia Hassenfeld, mother of the couple's three children, would herself embrace the mission, becoming, in 1988, the first female president of the American Jewish Joint Distribution Committee, founded in 1914 to provide refugee assistance and support services to Jews around the world facing persecution. And that would be but one of the many positions of leadership in helpful causes that she would assume.

Henry phrased the family commitment this way: "Making money, being successful—that's not enough. You have to believe in something. You have to have something to live and work for."

Domestically, as abroad, in religious and in secular endeavors, the first brothers put action behind their words. In Rhode Island, Henry and Hillel took leadership roles in two Providence temples, Emanu-El and Beth-Israel; the Shriners and the Masons; the Hebrew Free Loan Association; the Jewish Community Center; the Jewish Home for the Aged; and Miriam Hospital, among others. After Hillel died in 1943, Henry upheld the banner.

Hasbro Christmas party, 1947. Merrill with young son Stephen, center.

Henry would die of a heart attack in August 1960, less than two months after his wife, Marion, and just three months after one of their two daughters, Muriel E. Mann, passed. He was buried alongside his father, wife, sister, and two brothers in a

Jewish cemetery adjacent to the New York, New Haven, and Hartford Railroad tracks he likely travelled on his first visits to Rhode Island—the same cemetery where Merrill, Stephen, and Sylvia would be buried.

Alan Hassenfeld recalled the final two months of Henry's life, when his grandfather visited Marion's grave daily.

"The death certificate for my grandfather would show a heart attack," Hassenfeld said. "But it wasn't a heart attack. It was a broken heart. Every day, my grandfather would spend time at the cemetery. Every day, bar none."

In his obituary, Henry would be recalled as a "warm and friendly man," a description that would suit both his son Merrill and grandson Alan.

"When Mr. Hassenfeld was presented the 1959 B'nai B'rith Public Service Award," the obituary stated, "he was termed 'Mr. Community' by Rabbi Morris Schussheim of Temple Beth-Israel… Friends recalled today a poem he himself wrote and dedicated to his wife, which he read when he was presented with the B'nai B'rith award. Her death, they said, was a blow from which he did not seem to recover fully."

Henry had been a pillar of many communities, as his son and daughter-in-law also would be as well. But none of them would enter Rhode Island's political arena, where politics often—and correctly—is called blood sport. The younger of Henry's two grandsons would be the first Hassenfeld to go there, and he would be both praised and vilified for doing so.

1860	OSIAS HASSENFELD	ישעיה האזענפעלד	1933
1886	HILLEL HASSENFELD	הילל יוסף האזענפעלד	1943
1882	HERMAN HASSENFELD	צבי חיים האזענפעלד	1947
1882	PESSEL HASSENFELD	פעסל האזענפעלד	1968
1880	BENJAMIN OELBAUM	בנימין איילבוים	1951
1894	ESTHER OELBAUM	אסתר איילבוים	1947
1889	HENRY J HASSENFELD	יהושע העשל האזענפעלד	1960
1896	MARION L HASSENFELD	מרים לאה האזענפעלד	1960
1925	MURIEL L MANN	מידל ליבע מאן	1960

The Hassenfeld plot, Lincoln Park Cemetery, Warwick, R.I.(Miller photo)

Henry's younger son, Merrill, joined Hasbro in 1938, after graduating from the University of Pennsylvania, and with his father and uncle he was instrumental in broadening the pencil box concept to include sales of paints, modeling clay, and crayons, with which children played all year 'round. It was a marketing twist that helped fill slow periods—Christmas or Easter, for example—in the school supplies business. Further innovation came when Hasbro began selling its boxes with play pill bottles, stethoscopes, microscopes, needles, medical charts, and dental mirrors. The new line was actually two: Junior Doctor and Junior Nurse kits. This was, after all, a different era, when gender roles were more rigidly defined.

The Second World War brought warnings of air raids and preparations for defensive blackouts to the East Coast, and Rhode Island, long a seafaring state with its Newport Harbor and busy Narragansett Bay, seemed in the crosshairs. It had significant military value with its two Navy bases at Newport and Quonset Point, the latter of which also had an airfield. Another airfield, Naval Auxiliary Air Station Charlestown, on the southern coast, served as a satellite facility to Quonset. Among those training as a naval aviator there was future president George H. W. Bush.

Here again, the Hassenfelds saw opportunity.

The German blitz bombing of London that began on September 7, 1940, had affirmed the importance in England of air-raid wardens, volunteer civilians assigned to monitor compliance with blackouts and help assess damage after aerial attacks. With America's likely entrance into the war, the federal Office of Civilian Defense, established in May 1941, instituted a similar program in the U.S. It was designed for adults.

"The measures for safeguarding civilians against the effects of air attacks, which are described in the following pages have become a necessary part of the defensive organization of any country open to air attack," read *A Handbook for Air Raid Wardens,* from the Office of Civilian Defense. "Every State and municipality should take such legal or administrative action as may be necessary for the organization, direction and training of its Air Raid Warden Service." The office set clear protocol: "Each Air Raid Warden should be equipped with an arm band or similar uniform, steel helmet (when available), gas mask (when available), gas-protective clothing (as available), warden's whistle [and] heavy work gloves."

Merrill and Henry saw desire from youngsters, so they placed into Hasbro boxes kid-size arm bands, whistles, flashlights, and warden's caps, sold as junior air-raid warden kits. They offered the same appeal as a competitor, Kay Novelty Co., which advertised its junior kits as "an amazing opportunity for every full-blooded American boy to prepare himself and his buddies against enemy air attacks. Lots of fun! Exciting! Thrilling! Every one of your friends will want to play with you… you will become the most popular boy in the block."

Junior air-raid warden kits: a foreshadowing, if unknowingly, of G.I. Joe.

Henry confirmed his son's acumen by naming him president in 1943, a job he put on hold when he enlisted as a private in the Army in April 1945. But the war soon ended, and Merrill did not see combat. He continued to build Hasbro brands, bringing to market junior cosmetics kits, which had been inspired watching his young daughter, Ellie, sneak into Sylvia's vanity. ("Keeps mother's expensive cosmetics safe," one early ad assured.) Cosmetic kits beget sewing, embroidery, jewelry, mailman, and school kits.

A pencil box company was now something more.

But a quite different toy would define—and power—Hasbro as the country left war behind and transitioned into a stable era, one that beget the Baby Boomers. It would be the company's first monster hit—a whimsical character no one would have predicted would last more than 60 years, an unprecedented reign in the topsy-turvy toy business.

CHAPTER TWO

⚬

AN AMERICAN FAMILY

PART ONE: POT HEAD

Alan Geoffrey Hassenfeld was born at Providence's Women and Infants Hospital on November 16, 1948. As an adult, he would develop a fondness for this healthcare institution, as with others in Rhode Island and beyond, contributing to it financially while publicly supporting its mission as the state's leading hospital for newborns and women. And the hospital would work its way into a joke Hassenfeld would sometimes tell regarding his rejection while he was Hasbro CEO of a Mattel takeover bid that would have made him and his family fabulously wealthy—but essentially would have ended the company his grandfather and great-uncle founded, since Mattel likely would have consolidated operations in California.

When she learned of her son's decision to fight Mattel, not accept its buyout offer, Sylvia responded, Hassenfeld would joke: "Did I take the wrong baby home from the hospital?!"

This much was true: in personality and ambition, Sylvia's second-born son differed from her first. Alan would come reluctantly into the business—but Stephen, almost seven years his senior, seemed determined to work for Hasbro almost from his birth, on January 19, 1942.

"There was never a doubt in his mind that that's what he wanted to do," Sylvia would recall.

She remembered the adult who brought Hasbro into the Fortune 500 when he was a young schoolchild, pining for weekends so he could visit the factory where the pencil boxes and junior medical kits and play-cosmetics toys were made. "As soon as he was old enough," Sylvia said, "he loved the business. He could hardly wait for a Saturday to go in with Merrill."

The means of production captivated her first-born son less than the marketing and financial pieces, Sylvia said. "He just liked the creativity and the business end of it. He was not interested in the machinery and the technical sense of it."

The Hassenfelds were raised with strictness, the norm for the post-war era, a norm that Sylvia embraced. "You know, I hated spoiled children," she would say, "and I saw so many of my friends' children who took things for granted and we always thought that if we were fortunate, we were privileged, didn't mean that they had to be spoiled and assume that anything was theirs." That strictness was exemplified with groundings, the occasional wooden spoon or belt, and the washing-of-the-mouth-with-soap for use of profanity—disciplinary tools characteristic of the era. In grammar school, it was found in the use of the ruler on the back of the hand or the wearing of the dunce cap in the corner of the classroom, punishments the young Alan endured. And it was seen regularly at the Hassenfeld dinner table, where whatever food was served was to be eaten in its entirety, with not a morsel to be wasted, lest punishment result.

Hassenfeld possessed what he recalled as "very finicky tastes," and there were nights that he could not stomach what was served at dinner—liver, for example. "To this day, I can't eat it," he said. So he sat, sometimes with his also-wayward siblings.

And sat and sat, uneaten food on the plates.

"We'd sit down at six or six-fifteen," Hassenfeld said, "and there were some nights that I would stay at the dinner table or Ellie or Stevie would stay at the dinner table until nine-thirty or ten o'clock. And if we didn't get it down it would be waiting for us at breakfast the next morning."

Asked what message was being sent, Hassenfeld said: "You don't waste food, you eat what's put in front of you." Thinking further, he said, "I don't know what the message was. It was very bureaucratic."

None of this seemed to dampen the joie de vivre that, his mother said, characterized the younger Hassenfeld son from an early age. He shared that spirit with his father, whom Sylvia would recall as funny and warm, "a happy person, really an up person all the time, never had any moods." This in contrast to herself, and to a lesser extent, Stephen. Both could be tempestuous.

"Stephen was much more focused, much more disciplined," Sylvia said. "Alan was his own person, knew what he wanted to do—and he did what he pretty much wanted to do. Much more of a free spirit. Never as intense but probably one of the happiest people I ever knew."

The young Alan laughed easily and enjoyed making others do the same, and he was gifted with an imagination: the things that blossomed inside his head, inclining him toward writing and fantasies of travelling the globe to satisfy a craving for adventure. He collected stamps and baseball trading cards. He became a Cub Scout. He rode his bike from the Hassenfeld residence on Providence's East Side to the Blackstone

River, where he passed hours fishing. He attended sleepaway camp, like his siblings. Despite episodes of asthmatic hay fever, he enjoyed athletics, playing football and soccer as a young child and developing what would become a lifelong passion for tennis, at which he excelled. He became a Boston Red Sox fan, and with his father and brother, often went to Fenway Park, where hot dogs were the treat. The whole family played Scrabble, and Alan decades later would jokingly boast that he became the best player, dethroning Stephen, who at an early age had surpassed their parents.

Sylvia and Merrill Hassenfeld in 1961. (Courtesy Providence Journal)

And while the dinner table some evenings could be a sort of pillory, it also was a sort of academy in which local and world affairs were discussed and the importance of honoring the working person and giving back to the community were celebrated, particularly in Hassenfeld's formative years, before his parents' travel began to regularly take them away. Merrill became his younger son's North Star, and his beliefs would guide Alan after he left this earth.

"Dad was always there, always willing to listen, and always gave us a chance," Hassenfeld would recall. "He passed to us a humility and a compassion, especially about our Hasbro people, an appreciation for the people that got up at four or five o'clock in the morning to start the six o'clock shift in molding. He loved people. He loved giving back. He believed totally in *living charity*: giving while alive to things that can bring a smile."

Merrill and Sylvia limited television viewing, but Saturday-morning shows were allowed, and the young Alan took advantage. By 7:00 a.m., he was dressed in his cowboy boots and outfit and settled in front of the TV, tuned in to the screen staples of the era.

"I started with The Cisco Kid and Hopalong Cassidy and Roy Rogers: that was the bill of fare from about seven to nine o'clock," Hassenfeld recalled. "All I wanted to watch was cowboys." Westerns in the early 1950s still retained power in the culture, but it would diminish, John Wayne on horseback being replaced by soldiers who stormed the beaches of Normandy and intergalactic heroes who defeated evil aliens.

Hassenfeld's early toys in this pre-G.I. Joe era included Britain's Toy Soldiers, a line of metal figures representing many conflicts manufactured by an English firm, W. Britain Limited. And he was exposed to more toys, Hasbro's and others', on his annual trips with his brother and sister and their parents to Toy Fair. "One of the great experiences we had as kids was when Dad let us come to New York for Toy Fair," he said. "We'd take the train and then we'd go to the showroom. That was like Disney Land!"

But the Hassenfeld home did not overflow with playthings, despite what Daddy did and the boatloads of product he could have brought home.

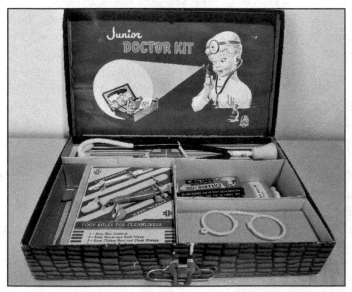

A Junior Doctor Kit that belonged to his dad is among Hassenfeld's prized possessions.

"I was not spoiled with toys by any stretch of the imagination," Hassenfeld said. "In those days, we didn't make great toys anyway."

One exception was the family firm's popular medical kits. "I remember the girl next door," Hassenfeld recalled. Her name was Marilyn. "She and I played doctor and nurse together. I was five, she was six. Her parents didn't understand, my parents didn't understand. I had the Hasbro doctor kit, she had the nurse kit. What did we know?"

Another exception, of course, was Mr. Potato Head.

Pot Head, as the grownup Alan Hassenfeld sometimes jokingly called the character, found Hasbro's Pawtucket headquarters the way many toys did and still do: a hopeful inventor walked through the door with a sample and a pitch. Then, as now, creative souls were welcome, for there was money to be made for everyone, if the inventor had found magic.

The man with the spud was George Lerner, from Brooklyn, New York. When he visited Merrill Hassenfeld one day in 1951, he was carrying a box with cartoon-like plastic eyes, ears, noses, eyeglasses, hats, moustaches, hair, and a pipe, much like the one the father played by Fred MacMurray a few years later in the TV show *My Three Sons*. Lerner also brought an actual potato or two, on which he demonstrated the play-pattern of his toy to the president of Hasbro. *Easy! Fun!* And many vegetables and fruits would work, although the spud seemed best-suited: the parts went in with minimal effort and stayed put, and most households kept potatoes in the larder.

Lerner had invented the toy in 1949 and he and his partner Julius Ellman, a fellow inventor, had tried to market it to several toy companies through their firm, The Lernell Company. All had passed: with memories of the Great Depression and World War II rationing still strong, the toy companies believed, consumers would reject the concept as an unconscionable waste of food. And there were other considerations that surely crossed the minds of those who sent Lerner and Ellman packing: *What a mess the thing would make! Imagine the smell when the darn thing gets lost under the couch and rots! See Mommy hunting for plastic parts everywhere! The dog will surely eat them!*

"George had done some work for Buddy L Toys during the war and even *they* turned it down," Ellman later said.

But he and Lerner had kept faith, and in 1951 a food firm purchased the rights for use as a cereal-box prize. "Not everyone could have had that idea," Ellman recalled. "But he not only thought of it, he believed in it and sold it, even though it was very controversial."

The cereal sale was for $5,000, a handsome sum for a toy inventor in that era, but a time-limited arrangement. Not the stuff of an inventor's dreams.

Royalties continuing for years and years were that stuff—and with giants A. C. Gilbert, maker of Erector Sets, and Louis Marx and Company, the world's largest toy manufacturer at the time, hardly beating down their door, Lerner and Ellman decided to try their luck with a small company in Pawtucket.

Merrill was sold.

He contacted the cereal company with an offer of $2,000 to cease production of their in-box prize plus $5,000 to cover their payment to Lerner. The offer was accepted. Merrill then offered Lerner a $500 advance against a five-percent royalty. Lerner accepted and Merrill ordered the toy into production.

Hasbro's 1952 catalog showed the toy as an apple, a banana, a cucumber, an orange, a pear, a pepper, and a potato. What the company actually sold in the box was an assortment of some 30 plastic pieces, including feet, hands, ears, two mouths, four noses, two sets of eyes, eyeglasses, three hats, a pipe, and pieces of felt meant to resemble hair and a moustache.

"The most novel toy in years," Hasbro proclaimed.

And all for 98 cents, with an order form inside the box offering the chance to buy more parts for even less: "Hey Kids! Get Loads of Extra Mr. Potato Head Parts—50 Different Pieces for Only 50¢" As a marketing tool, the bounce back was a brilliant stroke. Baby Boomer kids could use it as a gentle bludgeon against their parents.

Merrill launched Pot Head with newspaper and magazine advertising, which he had mastered selling his popular boxes and kits. But he also had been paying attention to a new medium, television. The year 1952 was another milestone for TV, with the surging national popularity of two shows introduced the year before: *I Love Lucy* and *The Roy Rogers Show*, which had spawned a burgeoning market for comics, playsets, and kids' western costumes and toy guns. *The Today Show* debuted in 1952, Canada got its first TV stations, and presidential candidates Adlai Stevenson and Dwight Eisenhower bought the first political ads. TV was here to stay.

Merrill arranged for a Mr. Potato Head commercial and bought airtime in a few local markets, making the toy the first to be advertised on network TV. The 1953 version of the ad featured the introduction of Potato Head's wife and the family's accessories. In the commercial, a cute girl and a handsome lad encounter the cartoon character "Hasbro." The boy speaks first.

Boy: "Hey, it's Hasbro! Hasbro makes toys. What's new Hasbro?"

Hasbro: "Mr. and Mrs. Potato Head with their own cars and trailers, that's what's new! See, Mr. Potato Head has a car and boat trailer. And there's a car and shopping trailer for his wife, Mrs. Potato Head."

The boy and girl play with the toys, placing a mop of hair on a potato, and then glasses on a nose.

Hasbro: "It's such fun to do! And so easy. Like this."

An ear is placed in a potato.

Hasbro: "Take any fruit or vegetable. Just stick in eyes, then ears, and then, the mouth! You can make the funniest looking people in the whole world."

The girl laughs.

A lineup of five Potato Heads appears on screen. A string manipulated by an off-screen hand pulls a Potato Head, with trailer, right to left (this was, after all, 1953 and low-budget).

Hasbro: "Potato Head people look different every time you make them."

The $2 box set appears.

Hasbro: "Mr. and Mrs. Potato head with cars and trailers come in one- and two-dollar sizes."

Boy: "What else is new, Hasbro?"

Hasbro: "A vanity case! With toy cosmetics and beautiful accessories. And real-looking doctor and nurse kits."

Boy: "Hasbro makes great toys. It's fun to play with Hasbro."

End commercial.

The new medium conveyed the magic of the toy as no static ad could. Expanding beyond local markets, Merrill bought national advertising on *The Jackie Gleason Show* as newspapers around the country wrote feature stories about the new sensation, a promotional crescendo that would foreshadow the digital buzz storms of a later era. Demand soared for Mr. Potato Head. The toy was so hot on the West Coast that distributors paid ordinarily unaffordable air freight to keep it on the shelves. In Rhode Island, Hasbro hired additional workers to increase production. The company had its first monster hit, and Merrill was determined to build on it.

Hassenfeld's office today features many iterations of Mr. Potato Head. (Miller photo)

Sixty-seven years later, the toy is still very much alive, with dozens of offerings, including Pirate Spud, Spudtater, Luke Frywalker, Darth Tater, Spider Man, Captain America, Transformers; and in the Mrs. Potato Head line, Mermaid, Unicorn, Fairy, Beach Spudette, Party Spudette, and Princess Spudette.

Hasbro already was gravitating toward Hollywood the year Mr. Potato Head debuted, with Mickey Mouse pencils, Roy Rogers pistol pencil cases, and Donald Duck doctor kits among its offerings. The company deepened its ties to film and TV during the remainder of the 1950s and into the presidential years of John F. Kennedy.

A tour through Hasbro's annual catalogs from the era captures both the firm's growth and the larger cultural developments in America that inspired the designers and marketers in Pawtucket from Mr. Potato Head's introduction through 1963, when Kennedy was assassinated. It confirms Merrill's wisdom in refashioning Mr. Potato Head every year, a sort of back-to-the-future strategy Hasbro would embrace into the present day.

The cover of the 1953 Hasbro catalog cover was devoted entirely to Mr. Potato Head, with drawings of hundreds of the characters standing on a map of the continental U.S. and a sizzling proclamation: "Nationally Advertised! Magazines, newspapers, trade papers. Television and radio spot announcements." Inside, buyers learned of new reasons to order, for the silly spud had married: "Mr. Potato Head the smash hit has a mate, Mrs. Potato Head," Hasbro announced. And like any all-American family, the couple had brought forth children, Yam and Spud.

All-American.

Hasbro in 1953 offered Walt Disney's Peter Pan Pencil Boxes, keyed to the February 5 release of the Disney animated film, which cost an estimated $4 million to produce—some $38 million in 2019 dollars—and would go on to become the fifth-biggest grossing movie of the year. The fact that Hasbro included the Disney pencil boxes in its lineup confirms that the company had negotiated with the studio before the movie's release—early evidence of what would become the time-honored formula of a movie opening at the same time as tie-ins including toys, merchandise, and fast food were available, a modus operandi that today is amplified by social media. The public could scarcely avoid such a blitz.

Hasbro's first relationship with Disney owed much to artist Al Konetzni, who with Pete Smith managed Disney's licensing operations.

An artist, designer, and self-proclaimed "idea man" and "Disney legend," Konetzni successfully pitched to Hasbro, Hallmark, Pez, and other companies during a lucrative career lasting decades. A graduate of the Pratt Institute, Konetzni designed the 1950s and '60s best-selling Disney lunchbox from Aladdin Industries, which sold in the millions and today is part of the Smithsonian's collection. Donald Duck pencil sharpeners sold by Hasbro and a Mary Poppins wristwatch are among the many other best-sellers he helped to develop and license.

Before he died at age 100 in early 2016, Konetzni's Florida hometown newspaper paid tribute to his role in expanding the Magic Kingdom. "From the outside of his door, where a stuffed Mickey dangles from a hook, to the inside of his one-bedroom apartment, no corner is spared a Disney relic," wrote a *Sarasota Herald-Tribune* reporter after a visit. "There are statues, awards, framed pictures gilded with Walt's autographs and a Mickey night light that Al designed for General Electric."

"I made them a lot of money!" Konetzni said.

Then his eyes misted over, the reporter wrote.

"We had the Mickey Mouse Club, 2000 Leagues Under the Sea, and Mary Poppins," he said. "It was the most exciting time to be at Disney and I feel like I was part of it and now it's in me forever."

That was Konetzni: a colorful, larger-than life figure from a golden era who never lost touch with the Hassenfelds.

"Hi, Alan!" he wrote in a letter in the summer of 2012 that followed a phone conversation. "Speaking with you was a real pleasure! Glad you are okay and mom, too! Even though I am 97 years old, I still feel and work like I was at Disney."

Konetzni wrote that he had forgotten to discuss obtaining a copy of catalogs featuring Hasbro's Donald Duck pencil sharpener and "an old photo or pkg. of Flubber, that we and your dad survived," which he hoped to include in a show he was planning. The word "survived" was an allusion to a toy that had almost ruined Hasbro.

Ever the showman, Konetzni closed his letter to Hassenfeld with a pitch.

"My Disney School bus lunch box is now on display in Washington's Smithsonian Institute! And it sold over 9,000,000. You'd be smart to add a school bag with that image on it—again, maybe millions would be sold! I'm still creating.

"Best to you!

"Al Konetzni,

"Disney Legend."

PART TWO: TAKE THEM TO THE MOVIES

The mid-1950s saw Hasbro strengthening its command of marketing, with an increasing emphasis on coast-to-coast ad campaigns. The 1954 cover boasted of ad placement with four high-circulation publishing stalwarts to spread word from Rhode Island to California and points between: Hasbro products, the text proclaimed, now were backed by "a hard-hitting national advertising program: *Parents, Saturday Evening Post, Good Housekeeping, Life.*" Also, "television, radio and magazines." It was impressive firepower, and it would be needed in the battles ahead, particularly with looming arch-rival, Mattel.

Disney was represented in the 1954 catalog with a line of pencil cases. The Potato Heads saw a pencil case to add to their line, which consumed two inside pages and featured the debut of The Spudettes, the "Potato Head pets," a line destined for longevity. There was a telltale new introduction, another testament to the soon-to-be-almighty tube: the TV Jolly Hobby Activity Kit, "designed to tie in with Television's pre-school play periods."

In 1955, an emerging symbol of parental frustration and amusement, the impish but lovable *Dennis the Menace,* who first appeared in the U.S. as a comic in 1951, became a Hasbro toy: Hank Ketcham's Dennis the Menace Mischief Kit, "loaded with harmless fun-provoking tricks and novelties." It received *Life* magazine exposure—and, like all Hasbro products that year, an implicit guarantee of quality. "Greater value because every manufacturing operation is performed in our own plants," Merrill assured his customers.

Disney made a bit of a Hasbro comeback this year, with the Walt Disney pencil-by-number set— "Drawn and pre-sold by the fabulous Walt Disney" —and the debut of Mickey Mouse Doctor Kits and Minnie Mouse Nurse Kits.

But the most significant development for Hasbro, as it would turn out, was not Mickey or Minnie.

In Pawtucket, attention was turning to games.

During the mid-1950s, the market was dominated by Selchow and Righter, Parker Brothers, and venerable Milton Bradley, which had achieved its first success in 1860, the year it was founded, with the introduction of The Checkered Game of Life, a timeless classic. Merrill foresaw possibility in games, and he stepped softly into the category, introducing (in 1954) Zig Zaggle, a knockoff of Selchow and Righter's Scrabble. Zig Zaggle returned in 1955, joined by the launch of Merry Milkman, the "exciting game and toy" that let players circle the board to deliver milk, cheese, and eggs in miniature plastic dairy trucks. Also introduced were Spot-a-Car Auto Bingo ("takes the 'drive' out of driving" but also suitable for "at home hours and hours of play") and Let's Face It!, whose parts, taken from the Potato Head assembly line, could be competitively arranged on a board.

But the frontrunning game in 1955 was the board version of *Two for the Money*, the Mark Goodson-Bill Todman CBS television show, which had been created as competition for Groucho Marx's top-rated NBC show *You Bet Your Life.* "TV's most exciting radio and television quiz game with thought-provoking questions," Hasbro declared. *Two for the Money* also received exposure with advertisements in *Life*, which by now was a Hasbro staple. Small wonder: with a weekly circulation in the millions, Henry Luce's magazine was seemingly in every home.

Attracting scant attention in 1955 was an item that coincided with the dawn of another technology that, like space science, would come to dominate the culture and its young (and old). With computer manufacturers including IBM beginning to flourish, Hasbro paid a sort of homage with introduction of its Adding Machine pencil case.

As the midpoint of the 1950s passed, Hasbro's fortunes were becoming ever-more entwined with the Magic Kingdom. Disney and Hasbro were both capitalizing on postwar affluence enjoyed by many, which had brought to the masses a motivation to purchase that was once largely the domain of the wealthy: buying on a whim. The overall pitch for products in Hasbro's 1956 catalog—in packaging, planograms, and appeal to buyers at Toy Fair—was summarized in 12 words, two of them so important they were repeated:

"Colorfully designed for impulse buying. Value and price to stimulate impulse buying."

Impulse buying worked, especially among parents who lacked impulse control or made the mistake of entering a toy store with nagging children in tow.

Reinforced by TV programs and print and TV advertising, impulse buying helped fuel demand for Hasbro's expanded Disney lines in 1956. Nine of the 40 pages in the company's catalog, nearly a quarter of the total space, featured Disney toys, crafts, and games.

Hasbro sold the Mickey Mouse Club Bead-o-Rama craft set, designed for ages four to 14, and an odd little toy that drew from the spirit of Mr. Potato Head: the Mickey Mouse Club Loony-Kins, "the funniest jitter-bugs in the world," the box declared. Hasbro also sold the Official Walt Disney Mickey Mouse Club oil paint-by-numbers ("drawn by Walt Disney, which will be the pride and joy of every Mouseketeer"); the Disneyland paint-by-number and pencil-craft painting sets; the Official Mickey Mouse Club nurse and doctor kits; and the Minnie Mouse nurse kit.

Hasbro reminded buyers of the reach of The Mickey Mouse Club television show. It aired, according to the Pawtucket firm, "every weekday 5 to 6 p.m. on over 100 stations reaching an estimated weekly audience of 125,000,000." Given that the total population of the U.S. was fewer than 170 million people in 1956 and many households still lacked television sets, the reach was probably hyperbole, but hyperbole could be friendly to the bottom line.

Merrill also trumpeted Hasbro's evergreens, notably Potato Head toys, medical kits, and pencil cases, freshened with introduction of the "Disneyland Space Ship Pencil Case." Declaring that it was "What Little Girls' Dreams Are Made of," Merrill introduced the Little Miss Seamstress Necchi Sewing Kit. It came with a doll, apparently the first doll Hasbro ever sold.

Merrill remained enchanted by games, and he was investing in new titles as he continued with Two for The Money, Merry Milkman and other favorites. Chonca, a variation of the centuries-old mancala, which enjoyed popularity in many parts of the world, was endorsed by the radio and newspaper gossip columnist Walter Winchell, who stated "Give a curtain call to the new game, CHONCA," which Hasbro described as a 2,000-year-old South Sea Game. Pooch, Mingo, Magic Miles, Playground, Let's Face It, Flip-a-Lid and Spot-a-Car Bingo rounded out Hasbro's games selection, largest to date.

By now, Disney was not the only force in the children's TV zeitgeist. Starring the avuncular Bob Keeshan, who had begun his career playing the clown Clarabell on *The Howdy Doody Show*, the *Captain Kangaroo* program had premiered in the fall of 1955. Hasbro negotiated immediately, concluding a deal that allowed the firm to introduce a Captain Kangaroo line within months. The 1956 catalog tantalized buyers with the promise that this "top-rated pre-school and primary age CBS TV sensation" would include—on air as a sort of supporting character—a Hasbro product, the Shoe Box Activity Kit. Merrill did not stop there. He gave the Captain the full Hasbro treatment, with Kangaroo Eras-O-Board Sets, Kangaroo Let's Play Conductor toys, and Kangaroo Play Clay. Potato Head had in on the action, with Captain Kangaroo's Pets, a group of three new Spudettes.

The 1956 line continued virtually intact into 1957, when the catalog copywriters decreed that Potato Head was "America's No. 1 toy for children ages 3 to 83." Another toy warranting Hasbro's title of "Outstanding Hit" was the Bub-L-Gun, apparently Hasbro's first entry into the toy-weapon category and a progenitor of Nerf. For one dollar, a child could have this "brand new idea in water pistols," which had a military look and a mission to be accomplished.

"With this realistic gun," the catalog stated, "one can blow a stream of target bubbles into the air, and then POP! Shoot them down by a squirt of the gun." And buyers surely paid attention to Bub-L's epic promise: "Never has there been a toy water pistol with so much play value." And what boy could pass Bub-L, with its "full color package for impulse buying," in the toy aisle without begging mom or dad to buy it.

Hasbro's advertising reach continued to grow. The back cover of the 1957 catalog listed details, noting new campaigns on ABC, CBS, and Dumont TV, a small network of three stations; national radio; *The New York Times*; and *Life, Good House-keeping, Look, Parent*, and *The Saturday Evening Post* magazines.

With its depiction of a happy family of four at the dinner table, the cover of the 1958 catalog could have been created by Norman Rockwell. Dad, wearing a tie, is seated, with Mom looking approvingly over his shoulder at their daughter and son, who are absorbed in Hasbro riches: Merry Milkman, a Teach-a-Toy map of the United States, Mr. and Mrs. Potato Head, a Disney numbered pencil set, a doll dressed in Cutie Clothes, and a Ponytail vanity case.

Disney was a reduced presence that year, but Hasbro did have a new Popeye license. The company also expanded its doll accessories, with the Cutie Clothes scissors-and-bows line and a toy tied in to trusted makers of baby products: the Jr. Miss Diaper and Feeding set ("just like mother's -- miniature nationally famous Davol polyethylene feeding bottles -- Johnson & Johnson baby powder and Q tips"). There was a new game in 1958, Police Patrol. Stitch-a-Story included Little Miss Muffet, Little Boy Blue, Hey Diddle Diddle, The Three Bears. The 'Tucket Toys line offered bowling, automatic bingo, bingo box, ring toss, table tennis, and games including Chinese checkers. With Americans increasingly taking to the road in their Detroit-made automobiles, Hasbro capitalized with its Gasoline Pump Pencil Cases bearing the logos of Texaco, Gulf, Mobil, Shell, Sunoco, and Esso, later Exxon.

The fast-food industry was in its infancy, but soon enough, Hasbro and other toymakers would find the value of ties to McDonald's, Burger King and others.

For all these businesses, population trends were in corporations' favor: The U.S. Census Bureau reported 150.6 million people in America in 1950, but ten years later, 179.9 million called the U.S. home. Many of the people in that nearly 30-million increase were children.

By 1959, when the U.S. and Soviet Union had launched satellites, Americans had their gaze fixed on space. Hasbro designers got busy, although they would not bring an extensive new line of space toys to market for another couple of years. Still, they managed to bundle space (somewhat oddly) into the company's newest license, *Leave it to Beaver*, with Hasbro's Leave it to Beaver—Rocket to the Moon game. "Thrills with Beaver on a race to the moon," the game cover teased. In 1959, Hasbro also offered the Space Scientist drafting set and a toy keyed to another American-Soviet rivalry, the competition beneath the seas, with the Atomic Submarine Torpedo Toy, "a realistic toy that will tax the skill and excite the imagination."

More light-hearted that year were three toys with lineage traceable to pop-culture icons: the Casper (the Friendly Ghost) Eras-o-Picture book, the Felix the Cat Eras-o-Card set, and the Maverick Eras-o-picture Book, tied to the hit TV show starring screen idol James Garner. An insider might have sensed the hand of Sylvia Hassenfeld and her daughter in the introduction of the Deb-U-Teen cosmetic sets, sold with toothpaste, perfume, and brush. Ellie had just entered her teenage years and debutantes were gracing the Society Pages of newspapers and magazines.

But the biggest introduction in the toy world in 1959 came from a competitor.

It was the Barbie doll, from Mattel, the California-based firm that already was an emerging titan, thanks to the success of its Uke-a-Doodle and Burp Gun, and its sponsorship, beginning in 1955, of Disney's *Mickey Mouse Club.*

Barbie debuted at Toy Fair in New York, where the industry's biggest meeting had been held annually since 1903, the year the Hassenfeld brothers reached America. Despite being modeled after Bild Lilli, a softly pornographic doll that was a popular souvenir at German bachelor parties, the mostly male buyers at the 1959 Toy Fair initially gave Barbie the thumbs-down, as had the mothers who'd participated in the market research behind transforming a German soft-porn icon into a tamer American version.

But Mattel's chiefs, Ruth and Elliot Handler, were not discouraged by finicky buyers or disapproving mothers; they had seen girls' enthusiastic reactions during their research, and they understood the power of nagging children. The Handlers commissioned advertisements that seemed to bring Barbie to life, tested the ads on girls, and began airing the ads in March.

By summer, Barbie was selling out everywhere, and the Handlers were planning increases in production—and recording record revenues.

Hasbro had no immediate answer. Nor, despite years of effort, would the man who would make Hasbro a Wall Street favorite: Stephen Hassenfeld, who enrolled at Johns Hopkins University in the fall of 1959.

His kid brother was soon to turn eleven, and his interests, unlike Stephen's, were anywhere but in the family company. Alan remained cerebral, a boy happy inside his head.

The first third of the Sixties saw America gaining ground in space race. With the 1958 establishment of NASA by President Eisenhower, a substantial government agency had been given the mission of beating the Soviet Union in what would come to be called the final frontier. Child (and adult) imaginations were fired, and toy people responded.

Barely a remnant of Disney was left in Hasbro's 1960 catalog, but space toys filled the void. Again capitalizing on a television personality, the firm sold Moon Rocks, an Art Linkletter Activity Toy. Another space toy was the Blast Away Rocket Launching Station, sold with the Targ-o-rama shooting gallery and Bubble-Jet plane under the Action Toys label; and the Lunar Launcher, "A triple-action skilled target game that launches three high-flying satellites."

Back on earth, Hasbro sold a new game, The Three Chipmunks, and something to please (and train) the budding gentleman: the Deluxe Jr. Shaver set, which came with Gleem toothpaste, Lifebuoy soap, "and a book on good grooming hints. Will be the delight of every young man 3 to 7." And there was the Huckleberry Hound pencil coloring set.

The next year saw Soviet cosmonaut Yuri Gagarin becoming the first person to fly into space, on April 12, 1961; less than a month later, Alan Shepard became the first American to achieve the milestone. The toy and entertainment industries cashed in. Hasbro introduced Space Doctor Survival Kits, "as imaginative and exciting as the space age in which we live. Kits designed to stimulate the young mind who knows we are on the brink of space travel." Closer to earth was the Pan American World Jet Flight Game, "devised by one of the world's leading airlines." Interested less in the air than the sea? Hasbro's Blinker Code Lights would allow a kid to "communicate and signal just as they do in the Navy and Coast Guard."

Computers continued to captivate the culture and Hasbro capitalized with the Electronic Brain Quiz Machine, which provided "the mystery, action, awe and fascination of a huge computer. Feed the data cards into the machine -- wheels turn -- lights flash -- and suddenly the answer is illuminated on the screen." Hasbro also announced its Mentor challenge game, "The wizard who thinks for himself... Maybe you can outsmart the Mentor but the odds are against it" and the IQ 190 toy auto, "the dream car with a brain... With the Data Drive brain board, you set the action." It is unclear, however, if IQ 190 made its past prototype into production.

More conventionally, Hasbro secured more screen tie-ins, including the Gunsmoke pencil craft and Gunsmoke coloring sets, the Bozo the Clown oil-by-number set, and the Dondi Potato Race game, based on the lead character in the cartoon that had become a staple of many newspapers. Hasbro in the early 1960s also found opportunity with new ties to leading consumer brands, including the Chiclets gum machine and a so-called "candy gun," which was sold "complete with M&M candy," holster, and badge. More sugar was available with the Hokey Pokey cotton candy machine. Also, with The Frosty Ice Cream Machine and Sno-Cone machine, which continued as strong staples.

Two other introductions in 1962 aimed for the mind. The Playing Grown-up line featured the Dolly Diaper and Feeding Set and the Junior Shaver toy. "Educators agree that toys that permit children to mimic their elders are worthwhile helps in a healthful development," Hasbro declared. An older child's development could be enhanced by the Great Inventions Model Kits—"authenticated by the Book of Knowledge, the children's encyclopedia"—with telephone, telegraph, printing press, and telescope sets. The affiliated Hasbro Book of Knowledge Science series allowed exploration of chemistry, hydroponics, magnetism, and more. With the G.I Bill allowing many Americans the chance to be the first in their families to attend college—and parents beginning to contemplate their children's future educational paths—the fact that learning and fun could go hand-in-hand resonated with Hasbro.

Merrill Hassenfeld. (Courtesy Providence Journal)

PART THREE: PARENT APPROVED? NOT REALLY

The message from Hasbro in 1962, according to the company's catalog cover, was "A Hasbro Toy is a Family Joy." And that sentiment carried over into 1963, when Hasbro went to Toy Fair with an excited sense that this would be the year Hasbro would break out of the pack.

The pack was thick.

American children had helped propel Arnold Clark Inc., makers of Silly Putty, to success. Azrak-Hamway was making its mark. Venerable Buddy L was thriving. Child Guidance, Corgi Toys, Creative Playthings, and Yo-Yo manufacturer Duncan prospered. Consumers could buy toys from diecast leader Ertl. There was Fisher-Price and A.C. Gilbert, which made American Flyer trains, chemistry sets, and Erector Sets.

There was Ideal, which had taken its View-Master toy to cultural icon, and James Industries, maker of Slinky toys. Kay Bee Toys and Toys 'R' Us were building retail empires, along with Sears, with its stores and catalog. Kenner and Lionel were household names, as was Marx. Mattel was flourishing. Milton Bradley, Ohio Art Company, and Parker Brothers stood proud and independent. Playskool, Remco, and Schaper products were forces. Tonka, Transogram, and Tyco muscled for market share. And there was Wham-o, the California company that sold Frisbee and Slip'n Slide, and had created a late 1950s craze with the Hula Hoop.

Still productive was the legendary inventor Marvin Glass, whose first big hit was Mr. Machine, introduced by Ideal in 1960. Glass also invented Mouse Trap, Operation, Hands Down, Rock'em Sock'em Robots, Lite Brite, Ants in the Pants and other favorites. Glass was an inventive genius—and a tormented human, paranoid and, despite success that had enabled him to build a mansion that rivaled his friend Hugh Hefner's, convinced he was a failure. Industry lore held that he shipped his latest inventions to Toy Fair in armored trucks and carried them in containers that he handcuffed to his wrist. His Chicago studio was locked and guarded.

Overseas, toy companies had their eye on the lucrative American market. Denmark's LEGO, founded in 1932, was rising, with innovations including lighted bricks, the "LEGO System of Play," and its signature stud-and-tube design. In Japan, Bandai, Takara, and Tomy were on the ascent, too. In England, Lesney, maker of Matchbox and Kiddicraft, hummed along, as did doll companies in Spain and Italy.

In Pawtucket, Hasbro was ready for all-out war. In 1963, Merrill believed, the company would win like never before.

The son of Henry Hassenfeld was so certain of success that he planned, for the first time ever in 1963, a second catalog, to be released in the spring.

New celebrities, brand names, and TV tie-ins—together with old standbys—were featured in the primary catalog, comprising many of Merrill's latest weapons. Some incorporated cutting-edge electronics that added sound effects, human voices, and even a crude form of voice-recognition: the Command Cannon, for example, the "spectacular new buccaneer gun that actually shoots when you say FIRE!"

And the Mickey Mouse Club Talking Telephone: "Hear the voices of Mickey Mouse, Minnie Mouse, Goofy, Donald Duck, Ludwig von drake and Jiminy Cricket."

And a new line of musical toys: Musical Chairs, Hurdy Gurdy and the Swiss Bell Ringers, which hinted of *The Sound of Music,* the Rodgers and Hammerstein musical, a Broadway phenomenon and soon to be a blockbuster movie.

And Hasbro games galore, with new titles including the Frankenstein, Wolfman, and Dracula mystery games; the Chiclets Gum Village Game; the Tootsie Roll Train Game; Archie's Fun Game; Ensign O'Toole's USS Appleby Game; The Mighty

Hercules Game; and the Deluxe Frankenstein Horror Target and Bull's Eye Target games.

Ben Casey and Dr. Kildare Luggage sets complimented Dr. Kildare and other medical kits, "Number 1" in America, Hasbro stated. The company sought to increase its share of the girls' category with its "exciting new concept" in Junior Miss Cosmetics, a new line that included Kathy Goes to the Prom, Liza has a Pajama Party, Babs Goes to the Soda Shop, Janie has a Bubble Bath, and Susie Goes to a Carnival. There was the New Little Miss Hasbro Quickie Cook Set, serving up a Chef Boyardee main course and a My-T-Fine dessert. Boys might want the Thinkatron ("the realism of a huge computer with wheels turning, lights flashing, and the answers illuminated on the screen") or the M-16 Combat Rifle, said to be "safe... as you fire, gun zings with a whining sound adding excitement and realism to youngster's play."

G.I. Joe had yet to storm the beaches, but a mighty force was about to be inleashed.

***Flubber,* it was called.**

Just like Mr. Potato Head 11 years before, Flubber was an exclusive product sizzling with excitement, and it had a Hollywood pedigree. Flubber was an essential character in 1961's fourth top-grossing movie *The Absent-Minded Professor*, Disney's most popular film that year, and nominated for three 1962 Oscars, including best cinematography and best special effects. And Disney had shot a sequel, *Son of Flubber,* which the studio released in January 1963. It went on to become the seventh top-grossing film of the year.

Flubber was a silly name—a portmanteau for "flying rubber"—but it was bewitching, and soon a nation had welcomed it into its vernacular. Invented by chemistry Professor Brainard (get it?), the lead character of *The Absent-Minded Professor* and *Son of Flubber*, the putty-like, "anti-gravity" compound accumulated energy when it contacted hard surfaces—bouncing higher and higher, to the delight of audiences and the consternation of the almost-but-not-quite-mad, absent-minded scientist. Add in the enduring popularity of Fred MacMurray, the *My Three Sons* TV star who played Professor Brainard in both films, and Hasbro surely had a category-killer.

"From Disney to Hasbro to you, the new kid craze," Merrill's 1963 catalog declared. "Flubber is a new parent-approved material that is non-toxic and will not stain... Flubber acts amazing. It bounces so high. It floats like a boat. It flows and moves." Moreover, "'63s hottest TV promotion" was supplemented by a comic book and Sunday newspaper comics, a full-front, seemingly foolproof marketing blitzkrieg.

Hasbro revved up production of the compound, made from pure rubber and Johnson & Johnson baby oil. An eager public responded, creating such demand that the company shipped millions of units, starting in September 1962.

Exciting product, Disney blockbuster tie-in—what could go wrong?

Pretty much everything.

Not long after Flubber reached the market, reports began to surface that Professor Brainard's invention was causing sore throats in some real-life children and prompting others to break out in rashes covering their whole bodies. Parent approval turned to parent anger and demands for compensation as the federal Food and Drug Administration began investigating.

Merrill at first pooh-poohed the reports.

"Ridiculous," he said in a March 15, 1963, statement. "Tests have been conducted by the laboratories of several leading medical schools and universities as well as by one of the outstanding private research laboratories in the country, and the results of every single test have indicated that the product is absolutely safe."

Well, no.

The next week, a Kansas woman filed a $104,000 lawsuit—almost $1 million in today's dollars—claiming Flubber-caused rashes were so severe on her and her three-year-old son that both had been hospitalized. The FDA, meanwhile, had tested Flubber on human subjects —who had no choice in the matter. The agency used prisoners at Alcatraz Federal Penitentiary, applying Flubber to their bald heads and observing the reaction.

Some prisoners were untouched. Others broke out.

"My understanding is that the rash was caused only in people that had improperly formed hair follicles," Alan Hassenfeld later said. "All people are different."

After more than 1,600 reports of bad reactions to Flubber (and similar toys from other firms), Hasbro in May recalled its compound and ceased production.

But tons of it remained in inventory.

"Dad got permission to take it to the dump in Providence," Hassenfeld said. Dumps burned trash in those days before the EPA, but Flubber would not easily combust.

"It created a black cloud over the city until we got this horrendous call, 'Get rid of it! Get it out of here!'" Hassenfeld said. "Dad then got permission to take it off to Newport and dump it in the sea. As the story was related to me, a day or two after dumping it my dad got a call. 'Merrill! What the hell are you doing? Newport Harbor has Flubber floating all over it!' Even though it had been weighted down, it rose back up."

Company legend held that the Flubber was skimmed off the Newport waters and trucked to Pawtucket, where it was buried near a company warehouse and sealed with pavement to make a parking lot—and that on hot summer days for years after it would bubble up from the earth, a ghostly reminder of the vicissitudes of the toy business.

"I don't think it's true," Alan Hassenfeld said, "because we checked and there's nothing there."

So where is it?

"My father never told me," Hassenfeld said.

CHAPTER THREE

✧

ASIA CALLING

PART ONE: ACTION FIGURE

One day during the year of the Flubber fiasco, Alan Hassenfeld's parents called him into the den of their new home on Providence's East Side. Hassenfeld was a freshman at Moses Brown School, which Stephen had attended. But Stephen and Ellie were both away at college now, and Sylvia and Merrill had decided Alan should be sent to boarding school. With the demands of Merrill's job and his numerous causes and Sylvia's involvement in causes of her own, many of them international, the Hassenfelds were just not around as much as before. Boarding school was their answer, and Alan did not have a choice in the matter. His only choice was which out-of-state school to attend as a sophomore: Andover, Exeter, Choate, Hotchkiss, or Deerfield.

He chose Deerfield and enrolled unhappily in the fall of 1963. He had to believe this was more his mother's decision than his father's.

"My mom was, I think, the stricter of the two and when I say I think stricter of the two, Dad was motivated more when mother was angry," he recalled decades later.

But there were new priorities in the Merrill and Sylvia Hassenfeld family household.

Three years after Henry's death, Merrill by 1963 had taken his place as heir to the family's philanthropic legacy. He had been instrumental in the 1948 founding of Brandeis University, named for Louis Brandeis, the first Jewish U.S. Supreme Court justice; in 1963, he was named a university fellow, as his father, another generous university benefactor, had been. Among other positions, Merrill had been or would be an honorary chairman and life trustee of the United Jewish Appeal; a member of the Board of Directors of the Council of

Jewish Federations; president of the Jewish Federation of Rhode Island, as his father also had been; a patron of the Jewish Theological Seminary of America; a board member of the Jewish Telegraphic Agency, the global news and analysis agency founded in 1917; an American Israel Public Affairs Committee executive board member; a Committee for the Economic Growth of Israel director; and a member of the Rhode Island Area Committee of the Anti-Defamation League of B'nai B'rith. He took leadership roles with the United Way of Southeastern New England, and the National Conference of Christians and Jews of Rhode Island. He was a co-founder of the Jewish Community Center and an original incorporator of the Hillel Foundation at Brown University. He served on the executive committee for the Jewish Home for the Aged and the boards of many corporations, including Narragansett Electric.

When he died, the Jewish Federation of Rhode Island president would praise him as a man "generous as a contributor to charitable causes," someone who "used his boundless energy in the support of an enormous number of humanitarian causes."

Here was someone Alan Hassenfeld might emulate as an adult.

Alan's mother was, as well.

Almost from meeting her husband, Sylvia had been instrumental in helping build the family company with her advice to Merrill, her eventual board membership, and, *The New York Times* would write, serving as a sort of household market researcher. Sylvia, the paper wrote after speaking with daughter Ellie, "was involved, as the mother of three children, in the early testmarketing of many Hasbro products."

In a 1995 interview, Sylvia told the author of *Toy Wars*: "Business is something from the time I was 20 years old I was involved in it. It was something that Merrill and I talked about. Merrill wasn't the kind of person who came home and closed it out. We discussed it all the time. So I sort of grew up with the business. I traveled with him all the time."

But her greater influence on her younger son, who initially balked at joining Hasbro, lay in the practice of good deeds—in Tikkun Olam.

By the time of Flubber, Sylvia had visited the young state of Israel and led a delegation to the concentration camp at Auschwitz, and the dinners that she and Merrill hosted for national and international philanthropists and dignitaries were not only much-heralded but occasions when much groundwork was laid for philanthropic causes. Much more lay ahead in her long life, which ended at 93 years of age in August 2014.

Like her father-in-law, husband, daughter, and two sons, she would contribute not just with substantial financial gifts, but also large gifts of her time.

Sylvia became president of the Hassenfeld Family Foundation. She was a trustee of the NYU Langone Medical Center, and a central force in establishing the Stephen D. Hassenfeld Children's Center for Cancer and Blood Disorders at Langone and Langone's Hassenfeld Children's Hospital, all in New York City, where she kept an apartment. She was National Chair of the Women's Division of the United Jewish Appeal, Vice-Chair of the Jerusalem Foundation, and a board member of the United Israel Appeal and the Jewish

Agency. She served as Vice Chair of the Brandeis board and was on the Advisory Committee of the Hopkins-Nanjing Center, a program administered by Nanjing University and Johns Hopkins University, which her son Stephen attended.

And she was perhaps proudest of becoming the first female president of the American Jewish Joint Distribution Committee. On her watch, she oversaw the rescue of Muslims and Jews from Sarajevo during the 1990s Bosnia War, and the airlift rescue, in less than two days, of some 14,000 Ethiopian Jews during Operation Solomon in 1991, a role that hearkened to the work of her father-in-law and his brother, who had escaped pogrom. She was on the first relief flight from Israel to Armenia after the Spitak earthquake in 1988 that killed tens of thousands; on the return flight, she accompanied victims requiring advanced treatment and care, including prosthetic limbs, a technology in which Israeli firms specialized.

The tradition, Alan later recalled, "had to have come from my grandfather: my grandfather to my father, and my mother absolutely worked into it perfectly."

Sylvia's insistence that Alan attend boarding school was met with his strong resistance. As a teen today might put it: *It's not fair.*

Alan had followed Stephen to Moses Brown School, and as he later put it, "I was just coming into my own. I loved it there. I had a beautiful girlfriend—not that I knew much, but we rode bikes together," a suitable enough early romance.

Resistance to his mother was futile. Longtime family friend Rabbi Leslie Y. Gutterman, who had met the Hassenfelds in the early 1970s when he arrived in Providence from seminary— and who would officiate at the funerals of Stephen and Sylvia—recalled not only Sylvia sending Alan to boarding school, but also, at an even younger age, off to sleepaway camp.

"There was not the kind of nurturing that I would have wished," Gutterman said. "I don't think that was Sylvia's strong suit. She was very austere and very strong. But that had nothing to do with a lack of loyalty; there was no son more devoted."

Gutterman found in that "a certain irony. She held him at a distance and held him very close, but she held a lot of people at a distance."

And he found it revealing that "she never talked about her childhood." Not that Gutterman suspected anything dark; rather, Sylvia seemed to lock her inner world to outsiders, and perhaps even to herself.

Still, boarding school might prove an adventure to Alan. He had read and adored *Rose of Tibet*, a recently published adventure novel by author Lionel Davidson that was set in Asia, and it had intensified his fascination with distant places—more specifically, China, the land of Marco Polo and Confucius. Davidson's novel echoed the mystical sensations of Shangri-La, the fictional paradise of James Hilton's 1933 book, *Lost Horizon*.

"Retraces the fantastic experiences of Charles Houston in the distant ranches of 'the lifeless land,' Tibet," is how *Kirkus Reviews* described Davidson's book. "Houston, whose brother had presumably been buried alive in an avalanche, goes there to secure a death certificate for an insurance claim... They reach the monastery of Yamdring... There, Houston is exposed not only to the practice but also the attraction of its she-devil abbess, and while shocked by her life of 'sacred prostitution,' falls in love with her... This is a stunning entertainment."

In September 1963, Alan shipped off to Deerfield. One of his earliest lasting memories would be sitting in study hall on November 22, when Kennedy was assassinated in Dallas.

With time, Hassenfeld came to like the boarding school. He smoked cigarettes and conspired with classmates to make a crude form of applejack from fermented cider and raisins. He lettered in tennis and joined the staff of the school newspaper and yearbook. He was aware of being one of the few Jews at a traditionally Protestant school, but did not experience any overt anti-Semitism, only, when he enrolled, what he later described as a degree of "aggravation."

Though physically distant now from his parents, he remained under their influence on certain issues, money in particular. Sylvia and Merrill did not want a pampered preppie who fancied he resided on Easy Street.

To wit: As the first semester of junior year neared its end, Hassenfeld began planning a visit to Nassau with classmates on Spring Break. He called home and asked his parents for a deposit on the airfare and hotel.

We thought you wanted to go to Nassau, now you want money? his parents replied. *Why don't you earn it?*

What do you mean? Hassenfeld said.

Well, you could work in the summer and earn some money.

The boy didn't get to Nassau. And his parents' lesson, he recalled, was "tough" but essential: *Look, you're 16 years old, if you're given everything on a silver platter at a young age, you'll never appreciate anything. You'll learn to appreciate things when you learn to pay for them yourself.* Hassenfeld embraced the philosophy and kept it for life.

The young Alan converted his adventure fantasies into reality the summer after junior year, when he traveled through Europe with two friends on a shoestring budget, and again the summer after he graduated, in 1966, when, in a life-changing experience, he lived with a family in a small town on the outskirts of the Australian Outback as part of The Experiment in International Living program, which counted among its first alumni Sargent Shriver, appointed by President Kennedy to realize his vision for the Peace Corps. Wanderlust had the young man in its grips, and it would never let go.

Having already decided that becoming head of the family company would never be for him (though destiny would hold otherwise), Hassenfeld also was spurning other occupations that might befit a well-educated son of community leaders.

"I don't think I ever wanted to become a doctor," Hassenfeld said. "I don't think I ever wanted to become a lawyer. I don't think I ever wanted to become an airline pilot. I loved the unknown and traveling. My idols were different than other people's; my idols were mostly the picaresque characters of literature." For example, Don Quixote, who fights against odds to destroy the wicked and protect the helpless, and Charles Houston, protagonist of *Rose of Tibet.*

"I never wanted to travel the path that other people had easily traveled," Hassenfeld said. "I didn't think that's what life was for: to basically live a humdrum existence."

During his summer on the Australian Outback (it was winter there) Hassenfeld worked with children living with intellectual and developmental disabilities, his first extended experience with them. But he did not consider himself a worthy advocate, he would remember, since his heart ruled his head, against advice.

"They explained to me in the beginning 'you can't become emotionally attached,'" Hassenfeld said. "Well, you do. I loved them."

Hassenfeld experienced his first crushing tragedy that summer of 1966, and from it emerged a principal he would thenceforth hold dear.

He met a 16-year-old girl in Australia and he fell in love—and then a car crash left her comatose. Hassenfeld sat at her bedside until she died.

And when she had, he promised to wear a rubber band on his wrist in her memory. More than that, he vowed to always wear one so that the girl "could live through me," he recalled decades later, when the promise remained kept, even as it puzzled some who already wondered about a man of such stature who preferred penny loafers and collarless shirts, and sometimes called himself Kid Number One and had this affinity for a toy with the body of a potato.

"The most important promises that you make are promises that you make to yourself," Hassenfeld said. "If you can't keep those, how can you keep a promise to anyone?"

Hassenfeld entered the University of Pennsylvania, his father's alma mater, the fall after his girlfriend was buried. He enrolled in a business course or two, in deference to his mother, and he declared English and creative writing as his concentrations.

But he was none too serious about those, either, at first. He was enjoying smoking marijuana for the first time and discovering a new sports passion: squash.

"I had the most incredible coach," he said, "and all of a sudden I developed into a pretty darn good squash player with a great deal of potential."

Enough to be nationally ranked—but it was at the expense of his studies. His partying and road trips with fraternity brothers in his Pontiac Firebird were not academically fruitful, either, and he finished freshman year with gentleman Cs.

None of this pleased his mother, who on a visit to Philadelphia scolded her son.

"Your dad and I have not worked so hard all of our lives to put a jock through school," she said. "You better make up your mind about what you want to do."

The younger brother wanted to journey to Asia, though not Vietnam, where an ugly war was getting uglier, so during the summer of 1967, Hassenfeld enlisted in the Air National Guard and left for basic training. Back at Pennsylvania in early 1968, he became sick with hepatitis and mononucleosis, and withdrew from college to convalesce at home in Providence.

During his convalescence, Hassenfeld experienced an epiphany, one that dovetailed with his time spent with children who lived with disabilities in Australia.

The epiphany occurred after Stephen travelled with him to the Dominican Republic for some recuperative time in a warm climate. Back in Rhode Island, Alan, having spent several weeks in bed and still unable to return to school, decided to volunteer at Martin Luther King. Jr. Elementary School. Located a short distance from the Hassenfeld residence, the school culturally and economically was a world away from the upper-class East Side of Providence. Children mostly from economically disadvantaged families attended, and many were African-American.

Hassenfeld bonded with these kids.

He played kickball with them and walked them home from school, past tenements he might otherwise have never seen. He became a friend and mentor to some, and he objected when he learned of a medical practice that disturbed him: prescribing medication to children whose only "fault" was what today would be called hyperactivity. Boundless energy seemed within reason for a healthy child, Hassenfeld believed. He had a touch of that energy himself.

"I felt I was doing something," Hassenfeld would recall. "I was an activist, trying to change, trying to make things happen."

He was 19 years old.

Hasbro, meanwhile, had literally bounced back from the Flubber disaster, thanks to a toy inspired by the real-life World War II soldier that had helped save the world from fascism. And like Mr. Potato Head, it originated outside, albeit along a different path.

It sprang from the imagination of Larry Reiner, a young games designer for Ideal Toy Co. who was daydreaming one day during a company meeting exploring how best to expand its Tammy doll line. Dolls, of course, were widely viewed as the exclusive domain of girls, *but why not a doll-size toy solider?* Reiner wondered. Something two or three times the size of the popular tin and plastic toy soldiers that had pleased boys for generations—a flexible, posable action figure, as it would later be known, that could hold toy weapons, drive toy army vehicles, and wear a U.S. Army, Navy, Marines or Air Force uniform.

Reiner's boss thought he was crazy: *Boys will never play with dolls,* he declared. But if Reiner wanted to take his nonsense elsewhere, well, *be my guest,* his boss said.

Licensing agent Stan Weston, an acquaintance of Reiner who was finding success with properties including Dr. Kildare and Universal's Frankenstein, was intrigued. During the February 1963 Toy Fair, just as Flubber seemed poised to ruin Hasbro, Weston met with Don Levine, Hasbro's marketing and research director who had developed monster games and Dr. Kildare doctor kits for Merrill's firm.

Back in Rhode Island, Levine and his small staff directed creation of wooden prototypes. The toy did not have a name when it was shown to Merrill after he and Sylvia had returned from a trip to Israel, where they had undertaken another of their philanthropic missions. And Merrill had many concerns, including how Levine proposed the toy be made: with molding of bodies, legs, and arms in Rhode Island, and the labor-intensive molding and painting of heads in Japan, where post-war labor was cheaper. Hasbro had never manufactured anything overseas.

Also troubling, Merrill thought, was the very sentiment that had drawn ridicule from Reiner's Ideal Toy Co. boss. *Boys? Dolls? Really?*

Still, Merrill saw potential, just as he had with a potato toy other companies had dismissed. And he found appeal in Levine's "razor/razor blade" principle, which would be applied to the toy: *sell a razor and you've also sold a continuing demand for razors...* in this case, G.I. Joe accessories. Mattel had perfected the concept with Barbie and her many must-have clothing, shoes, purses, jewelry, Dreamhouses, lunchboxes and more.

"Merrill, I have such a feeling about this," Levine said. "I think this can be it."

It was.

Merrill borrowed $15 million to begin mass production of G.I. Joe, America's Movable Fighting Man, the name Hasbro settled on, and the toy debuted at 1964 Toy Fair—but not, initially, to the smash reception Merrill and Levine desired.

Some buyers got it, but others were lukewarm. Orders trickled in and Joe could be found in only a few stores by summer, when Merrill decided to pull an old trick. He bought a daily TV ad on a station in New York, a critical and closely watched market—and within a week, the toy had sold out in the city. The frenzy was on, and Merrill fed it by purchasing national spots on the NBC network. Soon, Hasbro was selling The Next Big Thing, and the Christmas season beckoned.

More than $5 million of G.I. Joe toys were sold in 1964, contributing to a divisional profit of $895,000 for the year—a remarkable turnaround from the nearly $5 million in Flubber-related losses in 1963. Merrill rolled higher for 1965, investing another $2 million in advertising, which helped net $23 million in Joe sales, and a divisional profit of almost $6 million, a record.

Original G.I. Joe

G. I. Joe saved Hasbro, but 1964 witnessed another development that in the long term would prove more monumental: Merrill hired son Stephen, whose desire to work at Hasbro had prompted him to leave Johns Hopkins University before graduating, as his assistant.

The older last brother was just 22.

Finally where he'd wanted to be since childhood, Stephen moved aggressively, utilizing business and marketing instincts that seemed hard-wired into his brain. G.I. Joe's success had overwhelmed Hasbro's promotions and sales departments, but Stephen restored order. He restructured the national sales force, improved distribution, and immersed himself in marketing, promotion, advertising, product selection, and the packaging that could make or break a toy. Stephen kept his hand in everything. He was obsessed, and seemingly gifted with magic.

Stephen shepherded Joe to more record sales as the line was extended, so robustly that in 1965, the toy's second year, Hasbro devoted three separate catalogs to America's Movable Fighting Man: the G.I Joe, Backyard Patrol, and Backyard Patrol spring volumes, all of which extended the Joe storylines, much as new episodes of a TV show built an unfolding narrative. The company might have devoted more: Joe netted $23 million in revenues in 1965, a number that confirmed its status as the new iconic plaything for a generation of boys. Joe was a true mega-hit, and its fortunes, including the downturns, would influence Hasbro in ways young Stephen could not have predicted.

Stephen had wanted to join Hasbro since childhood, but the company attracted others with no deeper connection to the firm than a friend's recommendation or perusal of a help-wanted ad.

The 1965 *Hassenfeld Bros. Inc. Employee Manual* demonstrated the appeal of a job at Hasbro.

First published before G.I Joe's smash debut, the cover of the manual alone was inviting. It depicted a hand-drawn cornucopia spilling forth sketches of classic and newly popular Hasbro products that were staples in many homes: a pencil, a pencil case, a paint-by-number set, a Junior Nurses kit, a Dolly Darlings Doll, a Junior Vanity Case, a toy sewing machine, a Touch-a-Toy Plastic Puzzle Inlaid Map of the United States, and of course, a Mr. Potato Head, smoking a pipe and driving a car. "The fruits of our labor," read the caption beneath the toys.

Inside the manual, new and existing workers learned of incentives and benefits available to them, an array unusually progressive for a manufacturing firm in 1965. Hasbro offered performance and Christmas bonuses (up to three percent of gross earnings), supper money ($1.25) during overtime shifts, maternity leave, life insurance, seven paid holidays a year, an employee welfare fund ("set up to avoid taking up collections for weddings, deaths, hardship cases, etc."), full Blue Cross coverage, a scholarship fund, tuition reimbursement, a pension plan, the Hasbro Credit Union, and a Blood Bank, run with Memorial Hospital in Pawtucket. Few were the 1960s companies that offered such generosity, and fewer still in the toy industry.

"Merrill L. Hassenfeld, president," offered his personal greeting.

Reading this old manual, one sees evidence of what future Hasbro heads brothers Stephen and Alan Hassenfeld, Al Verrecchia and Brian Goldner would refer to as the company's DNA.

"All of us want you to feel at home here," Merrill wrote. "We want you to be satisfied and happy with your work. This manual will, I hope, help you over the rough spots as you start… At Hasbro, we are trying to create a real family feeling; a feeling of trust in one another as we work together. I hope you will soon share this feeling. I would like to suggest, too, that you let your family read this manual. They are naturally interested in your new job and your new Company. Good luck to you in your new job and my sincere wishes for a satisfying and successful career with Hassenfeld Bros. Inc."

The "family feeling," new employees learned, was rooted in actual family: In the Quarter Century Club of company employment, Merrill listed himself and Israel Hassenfeld, son of grandfather Osias; and Osias's second wife, Beile Meyerstein Hassenfeld, born in 1904. Other relatives with shorter service made the other longevity rosters, and the "Key Man List" included "Merrill Hassenfeld—President. Harold Hassenfeld—Vice President. Leon Mann—Vice President" and, untitled, "Stephen Hassenfeld," twenty-three years old.

Most on the lists, of course, were not related to Hassenfelds. But they were encouraged to share the Hassenfelds' values.

"Our Creed," the manual stated, was "to pay fair wages. To maintain reasonable hours of work. To provide healthful and safe working conditions. To encourage friendly and cooperative relations among all the groups within the Company. To provide opportunity for advancement. To give all applicants a fair and equal chance to qualify as employees. To exercise good business judgment and managerial skill in all our endeavors because we feel this policy is in the best interest of every individual involved. To be reasonable and considerate in all our mutual affairs."

As the second half of the sixties unfolded, Stephen shepherded a number of other hits (and some major duds, also a valuable learning experience). He broke new ground while also relying on tried-and-true formulas, expanding licensing and ties to movies and TV and nurturing the company's venerable icon, Mr. Potato Head. Ever-mindful of Mattel, he pushed more deeply into girls' dolls, the realm of Barbie, a category into which Stephen would invest millions of company dollars and untold personal psychic energy, all ultimately to naught.

But Stephen would master TV and movies and mine the rich vein of comic books.

From 1964 through 1969, Hasbro brought Hollywood into homes with toys, games, and crafts tied to *Superman, Superboy, Batman, Robin, Cinderella, Mary Poppins, The Munsters, Fess Parker's Daniel Boone, Flipper, Bozo, Popeye, Winnie the Pooh, Casper, Zorro, Snow White and the Seven Dwarfs, Disney's The Jungle Book, the Green Hornet, the Justice League of America, Tarzan, Dick Tracy* and more.

New Hasbro games included Cowboys and Indians, Challenge the Yankees ("the only official Yankees") game, The Dating Game, and The Newlywed Game. Bagatelle, a new line of pinball/gun games, some G.I. Joe themed, debuted. Nurse kits were hanging on, albeit fading. The Paint-by-Number line remained strong.

And there were dolls aplenty as the sixties advanced, though none even lightly mussed up Barbie.

During the period, Stephen and Merrill launched Flower Darlings dolls and the Dolly Darlings line, with its Sugar N Spice, School Days Cathy, Karen Slumber Party, Beth Supermarket, Nurse (the old medical theme, reworked once more), and other versions. They brought to market Flying Nun and Bobby Gentry dolls. And Storykins: the Rumpelstiltskin, Mother Hubbard, Goldilocks, Pinocchio, Prince Charming, Sleeping Beauty, and Snow White dolls that each came with a storytelling 33 1/3 LP record.

And Little Miss No Name, a forlorn, orphan-like character with turned-down lips and a large tear under her left eye. Pity or empathy seemed to be the intended emotional appeal, but the overall look of this 15-inch creation was off-putting, if not creepy, not what your ordinary young girl would hope to find under the tree the morning of December 25.

There was the uniquely strange Peteena, "The Pampered Poodle Doll" that was, yes, a fashion poodle, nine inches tall. Peteena wore a lime-colored bikini (which fit over her retractable tail) and also a raincoat, leotard, tights, ballet slippers, jumpsuit, ski goggles, sunglasses, hats, mittens, and jewelry that fit "Campus Capers," "Ooh La La," "Twinkle Toes" and other themes. Launched in 1966, as The Beatles, Donovan, and Herman's Hermits led the British Invasion, Peteena provided a sort of soft counterpoint to the only doll with which Hasbro had succeeded, G.I. Joe. The packaging declared:

"She's a pace setter! She's a swinger! She's where the action is, from skiing down the slopes to surfing in the sea! This Pampered Poodle Wheels right in with the new look—strong and outspoken! A bit on the wild side! Join the swing of things at groovy stores everywhere and pamper Peteena with chic-est wardrobe ever!"

The groove came and went in one year, 1966, although Peteena lives on today, with collectors and a robust online presence, including Facebook and Pinterest pages and a home at Vintage Doll Collector, which describes the doll's quirky appeal: "Peteena was the first animal fashion doll. But more than that, she embodies for us what collectors love about the swinging sixties - the wild and silly irreverence, the hip attitude and the fun, well-made fashions. She was heavily promoted, but perhaps she didn't live up to Hasbro's expectations, as she was made for only one year. Peteena is not hard to find, but her value has risen in recent years due to the interest of Japanese collectors."

Decades later, Alan Hassenfeld placed Peteena in his light-hearted Hall of Shame.

"Peteena was terrible," he said, joking, "it was Dad's idea!"

Try as they might, the Hasbro men just could not get a girls' doll right.

Stephen was intense, but he also was gifted with humor and charm, and he was loyal, which engendered loyalty to him, inside and outside of Hasbro, which in turn bolstered his management acumen. Merrill rewarded him with the executive vice-presidency in 1968, the year Hasbro finally went public after a soul-searching family discussion that ended with the conclusion that bigger growth would be more likely only with outside investment—with Wall Street. In 1974, when toy sales had reached $65 million, Stephen became president. Merrill assumed the board vice-chairmanship. His older son was the unchallenged captain now.

Meanwhile, a young University of Rhode Island student hired part-time in 1965 to audit invoices—at $1.75 an hour, less than $14 today—had been hired full-time and was ascending the corporate ladder.

Alfred J. Verrecchia proved so proficient with banking and the balance sheet that he was named treasurer less than a decade after his auditing gig, in 1974, when total toy sales hit $54 million. Flubber was forgotten, except for the fanciful story that on hot summer days, it bubbled up from beneath a company parking lot, an oily ghost of failure past.

Alan Hassenfeld had also joined the company by 1974, though by a much different route than Verrecchia. He wanted the opportunity to travel to Asia, land of his childhood fantasy.

His brother enticed him, early in 1969, when Alan, healthy again, had returned to college.

You know, I could use an extra hand in Asia this summer, Stephen said. Hasbro was now using factories in Japan and Hong Kong to manufacture G.I. Joe and a growing number of other toys, including Amaze-A-Matic cars, which Hasbro would introduce at the 1970 Toy Fair.

"Who would say no to a summer job in the Far East?" Alan later recalled thinking.

So he took it.

It was a time Hassenfeld always would remember fondly for the Japanese citizens he met, the hotels where he lived while in Tokyo and Shizuoka, the time he walked into a communal bathroom and found a woman urinating: "I went screaming out thinking I had created an international incident! But she took it in stride." During the last three weeks of summer, Hassenfeld travelled to Hong Kong, where he immersed himself in the details of manufacturing and shipping G.I. Joes. And where, years later, he would meet his wife.

"I was hooked," he would remember of that late summer of the counter-cultural year of 1969, when Flower Children still went to San Francisco.

With Stephen's gentle persuasion, Alan for the first time contemplated working for Hasbro.

Gentle was all it took, for truth was, despite their different temperaments and ambitions, Alan and Stephen enjoyed an unusual bond that dated to childhood.

"Steve was the brother that you were in awe of," Alan recalled later. "He always was there, and he always loved his kid brother. If I was having problems, or I didn't understand the reaction of mother or dad, Steve was the one I really went to.

"Whatever I was doing, he was the greatest cheerleader. He always thought that I could do even better. When I came into the business, I remember mom sort of saying, 'Steve, you've got a younger brother, you've got to bring him out a little bit.' And Steve would say: 'Don't worry, mom. He's great, he knows more of it than I do.'"

PART TWO: INTERNATIONAL OPS

Alan Hassenfeld came into the business full-time in 1970, with the job of overseeing Asian vendor operations. "There was really no one at the company who could be totally dedicated to the Far East or the international side of the business," he said. "There was a niche for me," the chance to take his own path, not follow in another's footsteps, and the rare opportunity to live in a place that had long entranced him.

But strong reluctance had preceded his decision to finally accept employment at Hasbro.

"I didn't want to come into the business," he said. "I was adamant. I wanted to write. I wanted to teach. I wanted my own identity."

Hassenfeld had read how businesses can destroy families, and he hated that. "Businesses make brothers go apart," he said, "and fathers and sons don't get along and it creates stress. I loved my father and my brother too much. My family was—and is—more important than the business."

So he came aboard on his own terms, which he made clear to Merrill and Stephen:

My family is more important to me than the business. If ever at any time I'm asked to sacrifice the moral values you instilled in me growing up, I'll leave. Second, if ever I see the business bringing separation to our family, I'll walk away.

And third, I work with you, not for you.

Deal.

During those earliest days of American toy manufacture in Asia—it was the era of ping-pong diplomacy, when Richard Nixon became the first American president to visit The People's Republic of China since Chairman Mao Zedong's revolution—Hassenfeld was essentially a one-man operation, working remotely, literally and figuratively, in that pre-internet era. Clunky cable transmissions were the lifeblood of communication and to reach Pawtucket by telephone required 12-hours' advance reservation for a few minutes of costly connection. Container ships were mostly a thing of the future, and everything moved at a snail's pace compared to 2019.

The silver lining?

Hassenfeld could find time to read, to write, to explore, to date beautiful women.

He was in his glory.

Decades later, when he was one of the handful of toy people still around who had experienced the reopening of China to the West, Hassenfeld recalled those days—his business coming-of-age—with reverence and still a measure of boyish wonder. So much of what he and Hasbro had become could be traced to the years when the Middle Kingdom was stirring, and Asia in general was beginning to boom economically as the Vietnam War wound down.

❧

Over lunch one summer day some while ago at his Rhode Island summer home, Hassenfeld walked that memory lane, with its start in Japan and progression to Hong Kong and China, punctuated by stops in South Korea, Taiwan, Thailand, and the Philippines.

Asia would bring many lessons, quickly, and one would reinforce what Merrill Hassenfeld always asserted.

Son, there are many people you can work with, Merrill would say. *Always try to work with people that you're willing to break bread with. In business, there are always going to be problems or issues between people you're working with. If it's people that you respect enough to have a meal with, you'll solve the problem. If the problem is one where you really don't enjoy the people or like the people or respect the people, the only people that will make money will be the lawyers. So always try and work with people you are willing to break bread with.*

That was the Hasbro way, in contrast to Mattel.

"They would sue anything and anyone walking," Alan Hassenfeld said, "and we would always try and mediate or try and find a solution."

On arrival so many years ago in Asia, Hassenfeld recalled over that lunch, "I learned so much being thrown into the arena, especially with the Japanese. Understanding that when you were in a meeting, where you were seated had an effect on what the meeting outcome might be. When you're able to look into someone's eyes, when you're able to watch someone's body motions, when you shake hands with someone, those are all indicators of different things. Also, in Japan, how you bow."

In Japan, which he described as his "first port of call," Hassenfeld also learned the value of negotiating with the assistance of a translator, even if the Japanese businessman across the table could speak English.

"Why? When you go through a translator, if the translation is good—and that's not easy, either—you have that much more time to think about how you answer. We tend as Americans or as Europeans to sometimes speak before we think."

Impulsiveness, Hassenfeld discovered, sometimes the hard way, could lead to bad deals.

He also began to form the conviction that later would underpin his philanthropy, particularly overseas. "You cannot put American values on other cultures and societies," is how he would phrase it. Rather, he believed, it was imperative "to understand their language, their history, their culture, their religion. Too often we think only we Americans do things the right way. If you want to make change happen, change comes from within, not from without."

While in Asia, Hassenfeld became attuned to which cultural issues belonged in conversations—and which did not. He told the story of negotiating warehouse space one day with executives from Mitsubishi Corporation, largest trading company in the Land of the Rising Sun.

"I'm a kid in his twenties alone in Japan, sitting with these two older gentlemen," Hassenfeld said. "I don't know how we got into it but somehow I asked what they did during the war. One of them turned to me and said: 'I was learning to be a kamikaze pilot.' And I said: 'Oh.' End of discussion. I didn't think you *learned* how to be a kamikaze pilot—I thought they just put you in an airplane and sent you in a direction! I learned never to ask questions about the war again."

On that summertime walk down memory lane, Hassenfeld also spoke affectionately of his lifelong friendship with Li Ka-shing, one of the world's wealthiest people and most generous philanthropists today at the age of 91, but a less prominent manufacturer of plastics when Hassenfeld met him a half century ago on his first trip to Hong Kong.

For context, Hassenfeld referenced Michael Shuman's book *The Miracle: The Epic Story of Asia's Quest for Wealth*, an international bestseller.

"Li took Alan under his wing, inviting him out for afternoon boating trips on weekends with his two sons, Victor and Richard, teaching him how to use plastic-molding machines, and sharing lunchtime bowls of noodles while squatting in the corners of Li's factory," Shuman wrote. "Li, no matter how busy, insisted on welcoming Alan at Hong Kong's airport and escorting him on the ferries to Hong Kong Island every time he flew into town. Alan says that Li, or 'KS,' as he calls him, 'had a great effect on my life' and 'became like a father to me.'"

A Harvard Business School case study also describes the man Hassenfeld calls mentor. "From his humble beginnings in China as a teacher's son, a refugee, and later as a salesman, Li provides a lesson in integrity and adaptability," the study states. "Through hard work, and a reputation for remaining true to his internal moral compass, he was able to build a business empire that includes: banking, construction, real estate, plastics, cellular phones, satellite television, cement production, retail outlets (pharmacies and supermarkets), hotels, domestic transportation (sky train), airports, electric power, steel production, ports, and shipping."

The summary does not do Li full justice, for it neglects his beginnings as someone who left school as a young teen after his father died and he became a blue-collar worker. It does not mention the simple lifestyle he has maintained as the world's 28th wealthiest person in 2019 (worth: $29.6 billion) according to Forbes, nor his status as a philanthropist who has given away billions, nor his nickname in Hong Kong, "Superman."

"He's my godfather," Hassenfeld said. "I won't go to Hong Kong without getting his permission. It's relationship. I'm one of the few people in the world he'll take my phone call. Whenever I go to Hong Kong, if it's humanly possible we'll have lunch and dinner together. At his penthouse. Just the two of us talking."

Such intimacy was possible only after Hassenfeld embraced his father's admonition, and heeded the advice of a friend, Michael Garrett, former executive vice President of Nestlé S.A. for Asia Pacific, Africa, and the Middle East, and later a Hasbro board member. Garrett, a citizen of Australia who was born in India and studied in Switzerland, shared business wisdom with Hassenfeld: "The Americans believe in the law first, the deal second, and relationships third. The Europeans believe in the deal first, the law second, and relationships third. The Asians believe in the relationship first, the deal second, and the law third."

Li smoothed the way into southern China, which in the mid-1970s was reached by riding a train from Hong Kong to the border crossing at Lowu.

Hassenfeld held vivid memories of the British flag on the Hong Kong side of the border, the covered bridge across the Ng Tung River, the Chinese flag on the other side, the searches and passport checks by Red Guards, the small village in Guangdong Province that you entered.

"Chinese military music would be blaring away as you walked across this slow, muddy river called the 'River of Blood,' because so many people had tried to cross and didn't make it," Hassenfeld said. "You got to what was called Shum Chun, and maybe you'd see a couple of water buffalo or water oxen—rice paddies forever—and a couple of kilns in the distance from the train station. Shun Chum today is Shenzhen. When I think of 1974, when I first went, to today—here you had a sleepy, muddy, little-nothing peasant village. And today it's a city of 10 million."

From Shum Chun, Hassenfeld would ride to Guangzhou, sometimes called Canton in the West, a manufacturing center and seaport with a history dating back more than two millennia. Hassenfeld went to attend the Canton Fair, a trade gathering held twice annually, and to negotiate Hasbro's first contracts with Chinese plastics manufacturers.

Watched closely by Chinese authorities, Hassenfeld and other foreigners stayed at the Dong Fang hotel, a luxury establishment today but not so luxurious then.

"When you were staying at the Fang," Hassenfeld said, "you brought your own toilet paper, your own soap, your own peanut butter. You used to sleep in a mosquito net. You would always leave water in your bathtub—showers you didn't have in those days—because you weren't sure when you came back at night that there would be water."

Decent food was served in the dining room—the dill pickles were especially notable, Hassenfeld remembered—and with little to occupy them in the evening, foreigners gathered at the Top of the Fang lounge.

"We would drink Maotai, which was like kerosene. They had ice cream up there also. I was there the night that Saigon fell [April 30, 1975] and became Ho Chi Minh City, so there were fireworks going off and everything. We used to play ping pong. I wrote more letters and postcards from China than I ever wrote in my life. Honestly, there was nothing to do."

As China opened, foreigners were allowed deeper into the country. Stephen accompanied Alan on his first visit to Shanghai and Beijing, cities where the brothers were beheld as exotic curiosities.

"As we were picked up in Shanghai—in getting to the hotel—all of a sudden on this beautiful, sun-lit day you couldn't see out the windows," Hassenfeld said. "We were like animals, such oddities: The Chinese had surrounded the car wanting to look at a foreigner, you know, a 'wide-eye.' There were times I'd walk in the park and I'd feel like the Pied Piper. There would be 150, 200 people following me. People just curious."

Ingenuity was a necessity in global business, Hassenfeld discovered, and an early test of his capacity to creatively problem-solve came during the West Coast longshoreman's strike that lasted from July 1971 to February 1972. Except for a Taft-Hartley Act injunction in the fall of 1971, the port of Seattle, which Hasbro used, was closed, together with other ports in Oregon and California. Hassenfeld had product to get to the American market. In Pawtucket, his father and brother had bet big on the G.I. Joe Adventure Team, with new storylines and a separate Joe catalog that had excited wholesalers and retailers at the 1971 New York Toy Fair.

As the July 1, 1971, strike deadline had loomed and no agreement neared, manufacturers panicked, their anxiety heightened by the approach of the holiday shopping season, which could make or break the year.

The Oshima Maru, last ship moored off Hong Kong that could reach Seattle before strikers closed the port, was soon to sail.

"Everybody and their second cousin was trying to get their cargo on board this ship," Hassenfeld recalled. "This was when you took the barges—what were called 'lighters'—with the pallets and you hoisted them onto the ship."

Hassenfeld called on an employee of Li Ka-Shing, who had an interest in the Japanese company that sailed the Oshima Maru.

"We'll get Mr. Hassenfeld on board," Li's employee said.

But the rest would be up to him. Hassenfeld would have to personally plead his case to the captain to accept a Hasbro shipment.

A bribe might help.

In Japan, he had discovered the value of Black Label Scotch. It was a symbol of success —"gold," Hassenfeld called it—so treasured that some Japanese didn't open it but placed it on the fireplace mantle for guests to admire.

Li's men brought Hassenfeld to the Oshima Maru.

"By the way, the captain doesn't speak English, he only speaks Japanese," one of them said. "Mr. Hassenfeld, good luck."

It was about 8 p.m.

"I remember the first couple of drinks with the captain, who had a good face," Hassenfeld said. "He knew why I was there. We drank—and I'm not a liquor drinker."

Meaning: he became inebriated.

Memory faded.

"The ship sailed on the tide at midnight. I found myself in my bed the next morning—but all of our cargo made it on board. I don't know any more!"

The strike havoc continued from there as the factories churned and product piled up, with no ships after the last trip by Oshima Maru able to transport it. It seemed unlikely that not even Verrecchia's financial sleight-of-hand could save the day if parents found empty spaces on shelves come the Thanksgiving start of holiday shopping.

It was shaping up to be another Flubber.

"All hell broke loose," Hassenfeld said. "We had to fly everything by charter."

The cost was enormous, compared to ocean transport—tens of thousands of dollars for each flight, on dozens of aircraft chartered from World Airways and Universal Airways. But there was no other option.

"These planes were carrying aid blankets to Bangladesh, fully loaded, and then they'd come back to Hong Kong empty and they'd pick up our cargo," Hassenfeld said.

Given the cost, every square inch counted and Hassenfeld and his crew used every one, even filling in the bathrooms with toys. They worked late into the night most days and into the autumn, crisscrossing an ocean and a continent. A token of appreciation from Stephen returned on one flight: fresh lobsters, bagels, and cream cheese, routed on an otherwise empty plane back from America.

One night as he labored inside the hot belly of plane at Hong Kong's airport, Hassenfeld developed excruciating abdominal pain. Back at his hotel, he ran naked between his bed and the bathroom as he waited the arrival of a doctor. The physician finally came, with a nurse, and a diagnosis of kidney stones caused by dehydration was made.

But by then, Hassenfeld was delirious.

"I can't hear anything, I don't care if I die, I am in that much agony," he recalled over lunch that summer day in Bristol. "They gave me Demerol and for about one minute I had complete lucidity. And in front of me is the most gorgeous Finnish blond nurse and there I am in my birthday suit going back and forth!"

Hasbro made it through the strike, but the company was entering another tumultuous period—and this time, there would be no G.I. Joe to carry the day. Sales of the action figure had peaked at $26 million in 1973 then declined steadily as Vietnam tarnished the image of the noble American warrior, a new generation of boys discovered a new sensation called Star Wars, and an oil embargo raised the price of plastic.

By 1978, Hasbro was hemorrhaging money again. Compounding the situation was the growing feud between Merrill and his brother Harold. The pencil side of the business, based in Tennessee, was prospering, while up there in Pawtucket, a kid named Stephen was yet to find the true Midas touch and Merrill's health was causing concern.

The seventies had begun promisingly enough, with strong sales of Joe grounded in the 1969 launch of an all-new line of Adventure Teams providing revenue for Hasbro to expand into what seemed, given the continuing growth of the population, a sure-fire business: nursery schools and daycare centers.

Specifically, a chain of centers bearing the name of *Romper Room*, the popular TV show created in the early 1950s by Bert Claster and featuring his wife, "Miss Nancy."

By1970, locally produced *Romper Room* shows were being broadcast in many American cities and foreign countries including Japan, England, Australia, and Canada. In a deal reported at $1.7 million in 1969 (some $12 million today), Hasbro also acquired Claster Television and the rights to produce Romper Room toys, games, and other products. That summer, before Alan headed to Asia, Stephen dispatched him to Scandinavia and the Soviet Union for some field work on daycare centers in those areas, where Romper Room also might be exported.

Structured play was a promising new subgenre of the toy industry, and with Alan's input, Merrill and Stephen invested time and money in planning for their Romper Room Schools, a chain of nursery and daycare centers. Hasbro hired the esteemed firm of Arthur D. Little to conduct market research, and working with architects, the firm had advanced sufficiently in its plans that the Hassenfelds sent representatives in March 1970 to unveil their concept at the Conference on Industry and Day Care, hosted by the Urban Research Corporation in Chicago.

Hasbro's intention "was to create children's services in selected communities," daycare expert Stevanne Auerbach wrote in her 1979 book, *Confronting the Child Care Crisis.* "Plans included the conversion of the school space for community purposes when the schools were not in session, acknowledging the need to strengthen community relationships. All racial and ethnic groups of varying incomes were included in the planning of this first phase. The people were involved in site selection, construction and financing."

Given the scarcity of quality daycare in the early 1970s and the rising demand, Hasbro was poised for a profitable new business. The power of Romper Room TV promised success.

Until Hasbro opened its first Romper Room School on Pawtucket's Newport Avenue about a mile from Hasbro headquarters, that is.

The first day went smoothly at the school. When it ended, the children went home by bus—all but one child, who fell asleep on the ride and wasn't discovered until the driver had parked the vehicle and left it, which is about when frantic parents called the authorities.

"We lost a child," Alan Hassenfeld recalled. "We said, 'this can't continue.'"

Romper Room Schools didn't: after one day, they were history.

More miscalculation occurred on Alan's direct watch. And once again, the allure of the screen played a role.

The show was *The Galloping Gourmet,* a two-time Emmy winner in the early 1970s hosted by Graham Kerr, the English-born master chef whose popularity in the pre-Food Network era rivalled Julia Child's. Hasbro hoped to cash in with a line of wooden Galloping Gourmet cookware, sourced in Asia—Alan's turf. Most of the products were manufactured in Taiwan, but the salad bowls were sourced in Thailand.

One day after the bowls has been shipped to America, a warehouse employee called the younger brother.

"Alan, something strange is happening," he said. "Those crates that you brought in—the salad bowls—every morning that we come in, there's sawdust on the floor around them. We can't figure it out."

Said Hassenfeld: "I probably got something I didn't pay for: tree termites."

Termites they were. The product was ruined, and the misfortune helped spell the demise of the line, along with an auto accident in 1971 in which The Galloping Gourmet host was badly injured, forcing the cancellation of his show.

Another sort of calamity at the start of the decade involved Hasbro's Hypo-Squirt Giant Hypo Water Gun. Introduced in 1963, the toy offered harmless backyard fun ("shoots over 20 feet—accurately," Hasbro proclaimed). A sort of ancestor to Nerf Super Soaker squirt guns, the toy looked like an actual, if outsized, hypodermic needle, a fact that initially seemed to concern no one; even *The New York Times* in a Nov. 23, 1966, story "For the Youngsters on the Christmas List," called it "fun for boys." And just $1 at Reiss Bros., 54th and 9th, Manhattan.

The toy was still on the market in 1970, the year Nixon signed into law the Comprehensive Drug Abuse Prevention and Control Act with its Title II Controlled Substances Act. With reports of rising heroin use in America, journalists began to dub Hypo-Squirt a "junior junkie" toy. Was the ghost of Flubber hovering? Hasbro pulled the toy from the market.

The company took another public-relations hit when, just four days before Christmas 1970, the federal Food and Drug Administration banned sales of lawn darts—popularly known as Jarts, for javelin darts—which had been labeled as child or family toys. Many other manufacturers of the darts, which had caused injury, were also affected, and some relabeled them as "adult" toys and returned them to the market. Hasbro, however, pulled its Javelin Darts, long a summer staple—"An exciting outdoor game of skill for the whole family!" —and ceased manufacture altogether.

The FDA's action on javelin darts, first under the 1969 Child Protection and Toy Safety Act, also included bans on certain stuffed animals and dolls that could expose sharp parts if broken. Among them were the Newborn Baby, Baby Beth, Honey Baby, I Cry Mama, Jackie Twisting Waist, Kooky Eyes, Your Dream Bride, and Little Sophisticate dolls.

None, however, was made by Hasbro.

❧

Hasbro dolls were safe, but still only marginally successful, despite Merrill and now Stephen's repeated efforts to find a winner. But Hasbro refused to give up and 1971 saw the introduction of the World of Love, a fashion doll line featuring Love, Peace, Flower, Adam, and the African-American Soul.

"Love is what's happening," the copywriters declared, echoing hippie culture, whose flavor, if not ethos, had permeated the mainstream. "Not because we say so but because Love is what today's young girls want to be: vibrant and warm and in love with life. Love is all around you." Peace and flower power indeed—but not the marketing power to dethrone Barbie.

The line disappeared after just three years.

Stephen and Alan in happy times. (Courtesy Providence Journal)

Alan Hassenfeld, however, was at Hasbro for good.

In 1972, Merrill and Stephen rewarded his ingenuity and energy by promoting him to vice president of International Operations, with responsibility for all the world but America—a job that included foreign licensing, a major source of revenue at a time when Hasbro manufactured and bought from vendors only in the U.S. and Asia. The kid brother was just 23, and his domain now included Europe, Canada, Mexico, Australia, New Zealand, and other regions with robust toy markets. From 1972 through decade's end, when he took on additional duties as vice president of marketing and sales, Hassenfeld was a sort of roving ambassador for Hasbro products and Hassenfeld philanthropic values.

Current chairman and CEO Brian Goldner articulated how these 1970s influences shaped the person and businessman who had the helm before him and Verrecchia. He noted the additional travels Alan undertook at Stephen Hassenfeld's request following the 1984 acquisition of Milton Bradley, with its rich brand library and vast global reach.

"Clearly the younger brother Alan spent a tremendous amount of time outside the United States," Goldner said. That contrasted with Stephen, who spent most of his hours in Rhode Island and New York. Goldner envisioned Stephen telling his brother: *We're launching all these brands, Alan, you help us figure out this burgeoning world called global business.*

"So Alan had this opportunity thrust upon him to go out around the world, including the Far East, and see how people were living, certainly how they were consuming brands, and enjoying playthings," Goldner said.

Goldner cited the best-selling book *Three Cups of Tea* with its memorable quotation from a resident of the remote Balti region of Pakistan, "The first time you share tea with a Balti, you are a stranger. The second time you take tea, you are an honored guest. The third time you share a cup of tea, you become family."

Said Goldner: "If you want to move a business or move a culture or inculcate yourself into an environment, go have three cups of tea with the people who live there. In other words, you have to spend the time, immerse yourself in that culture. It's not a 'one-and-done.' You can't show up and plant a flag and declare success. There's this inculcation process—acculturation—that goes on and Alan was seeped in international culture by the time he was done. You get this sense of how people around the world are living."

And that, Goldner asserted, contributed to Hassenfeld's later philanthropy, with its blend of domestic and international efforts.

"Alan was one of the earliest people that could see issues that existed in multiple cultures and multiple countries around the world," Goldner said. "Because some 40 years ago, he was travelling extensively—way beyond most contemporaries."

During his 1970s travels, Hassenfeld met Bernard Loomis, one of the giants of the entertainment and toy industries. Loomis's business acumen would prove providential not only for Hassenfeld personally, but Hasbro as well.

It would also be a double-edged sword.

Son of a poor Russian immigrant who was raised in the Bronx, which gave him kinship with Henry and Hillel Hassenfeld, "Bernie," as he was known, was an independent toy salesman in the 1950s who in 1960 joined Mattel, where he worked in sales and marketing. Barbie and the Chatty Cathy doll were among his products, along with Hot Wheels—the toy that Mattel in 1969 controversially brought to ABC TV, with an animated series. Consumers and rival toy companies complained that the show was a commercial, and the FCC responded by asking stations to record a percentage of the show as advertising time. The Hot Wheels show went off the air in 1971, but Loomis had created a new TV model, and he refined it in 1980, when the FCC did not contest the airing of a Strawberry Shortcake special, based on a new toy from Kenner, where Loomis had moved after his stint at Mattel.

Kenner at that time was a division of General Mills, which had diversified well beyond its 19th-century roots as a flour miller.

The company's first foray into toys had come in 1965, when it purchased Rainbow Crafts, which made Play-Doh, destined to become a Hasbro brand. General Mills was not the only food company desiring toys. Quaker Oats had bought Fisher-Price, which Mattel eventually would own, in 1969. Consolidated Foods in 1970 had bought TYCO, best known for its trains and slot cars; before Mattel purchased TYCO in 1997, the division would acquire companies that sold View-Master, Magna Doodle, and Matchbox toys. But eventually, the volatility of the toy industry prompted the food firms to get out; their business model was based on steady, predictable growth, not boom-and-bust cycles.

Loomis had left Mattel for General Mills. (He was head of Kenner when he and Hassenfeld met.)

The Minneapolis-based company was deep into toys by then, having followed the Rainbow Crafts purchase with the acquisition of Kenner, in 1967, and, in 1968, Parker Bros., the Massachusetts company that sold Risk, Clue, Sorry! and Monopoly. General Mills' empire was thoroughly global, with toy subsidiaries in Spain, Italy, France, Mexico, Australia, and elsewhere. Promoted from Kenner to Group Vice President of General Mills' New York-headquartered Toy Group in 1978, Loomis was hugely successful.

And, some said, legendary.

Not lacking in modesty, Loomis himself held that view.

In an interview before his death, he said: "During my Kenner/General Mills years I had the best record in the history of the toy industry: Snoopy Tooth Brush, Baby Alive, [car toys] SSP and TTP, The Six Million Dollar Man, Play-Doh Barber Shop, The Tree House, The Bionic Woman, Star Wars, Strawberry Shortcake, and Care Bears. Sometime in the late seventies the General Mills Group fueled by Kenner toys passed Mattel in volume and profit and I had now been part of the world's largest toy company when it became the world's largest toy company for the second time…"

His 1992 induction into the Toy Hall of Fame independently affirmed his importance. "During a career spanning five decades," his citation declared, "Bernard Loomis served as president of Kenner, group vice president of General Mills, partner in a joint venture with Hasbro, consultant to Tyco and head of his own toy design company. He brought to market an incomparable portfolio of blockbusters, once selling empty boxes at Christmas with the promise of a hit toy to be delivered later. An extraordinary marketer, he proved that breaking rules was often the best rule of all."

Loomis achieved such stature that *The New York Times* published a lengthy obituary after he died, on June 2, 2006. It acknowledged the revolutionary role he had played in the play and entertainment industries—a role that inspired, among others, Stephen and Alan Hassenfeld.

"Mr. Loomis originated the idea of producing television specials and series that promoted toys as much as they entertained," *The Times* wrote. "This reversed the suddenly quaint notion that toyselling followed the movie, book or television program. Similarly, Mr. Loomis pioneered the notion of selling lines of toys, not individual products. That created the possibility of concocting entire imaginary environments with ever more products, as exemplified by the Barbie doll, whose career he shepherded for a time. 'Manufacturers create a fantasy world, and this has led to a very sophisticated relationship between them and the child,' Mr. Loomis said in an interview with *Time* in 1985. 'We are now in the business of multiple sales to the same children in the same fantasy.'"

The obituary concluded: "He coined the word 'toyetic' to describe concepts or characters that could easily be massproduced toys, and prided himself in judging this elusive quality. He did have the occasional flops—Duke the Wonder Dog, for instance. But usually his instincts proved improbably right, as when engineers showed up at a meeting with a wooden model of a doll that chewed its food, then eliminated it into a disposable diaper. The group joked dismissively about peristaltic action, then moved on.

"'It's very funny, and I think it will sell a million dolls,' Mr. Loomis interjected.

"Named Baby Alive, it became a best seller."

As the 1970s wound down and sales of G.I. Joe declined, Loomis would prove both friend and foe to Hasbro. Alan Hassenfeld would find new meaning in the biblical saying *The Lord giveth and the Lord taketh.*

PART THREE: DOCTOR NO

Stephen Hassenfeld's dream of greatness had seemed plausible at the start of 1974.

G.I Joe sales had hit a record $26 million in 1973, and Hasbro's first line of infant products—Your Baby, from inventor and educational psychologist Howard Wexler—had performed well. Although not an NFL license, the Super Sunday football projection game (for two) capitalized on the growing popularity of the professional sport, where "Broadway Joe" Namath was the glamorous hero. Captain Kangaroo remained in the line, along with Mr. Potato Head and doctor and nurse kits, the time-honored staples. Leggy, a ten-inch fashion doll that looked like the real-life model Twiggy blended into Barbie, shared shelves with World of Love, which was breathing its last. Champion boxer Muhammad Ali's cultural influence was reflected in the Knuckle

Busters game: "Punch 'em, crunch 'em—with these bruisin' brutes! A rough, tough, boxing game for fast action fun. Punch 'em in the nose and over they go."

Beneath the seeming success of 1973, however, a precarious financial predicament was unfolding. Although he had not neglected inventory, cash flow, and bank credit, Merrill had not kept the most careful eye on them: he was by now an old-schooler, a toy man who put his faith in exciting product and smash hits covering the losses and then some for the inevitable losers. Hadn't that been the happy story of Potato Head and Joe?

But business basics mattered, and except for the new success of G.I. Joe, 1973 had seen no breakaway hit—and short-term debt had reached $16 million, an alarming one-fifth of total toy sales. The new year began with little cash on hand to begin manufacture of the 1974 line—and barely any cash flow, for who buys toys in January and February, except for birthdays? To keep Hasbro going, Merrill and brother Harold, the Tennessee pencil man, had been forced to put up personal property as collateral for painfully high-interest loans. Harold's resentment rose.

Merrill sought salvation in Al Verrecchia, whom he promoted to treasurer, and Stephen, whom he named president. The two went to work, and with superior forecasting tools and better controls on production and distribution, the balance sheet steadily improved during the mid-1970s. With Verrecchia's firm hand on the numbers and Stephen's command of licensing and Hasbro's growing international presence, Stephen gained confidence—cockiness, some whispered, for since when had Wall Street ever cared about toys? What investor would buy stock that surely would be valued no better than Monopoly play money?

In his 1976 presidential letter, part of that year's annual report, Stephen outlined his bold ambition: revenue gains of 15 percent annually, with earnings increases of 11 to 13 percent.

"Is it to swim upstream to believe that a moderate-sized company like ours can build strong investor credibility and confidence?" he wrote. "We believe not."

The belief was profoundly shaken as the 1980s approached.

Blame Barbie, in part.

His fashion doll fanaticism unchecked, Stephen in 1977 debuted the Charlie's Angels line, based on the hit TV show. He featured show stars Farrah Fawcett, Kate Jackson and Jaclyn Smith on the cover of Hasbro's annual report, and he believed that the dolls' California-hip look —the Black Magic metallic jacket and dress, the Golden Goddess swimsuit, as but two examples —would lure girls away from the original California babe, Barbie.

He was wrong. After only two years on the market, the dolls disappeared, as did the series itself in 1981, though it would live on in revivals and syndication.

By 1978, Alan Hassenfeld's home base had shifted to Rhode Island, where he could see first-hand the monetary troubles Hasbro faced. He began to work more closely with Verrecchia, who was plugging holes to keep the financial ship from going under.

"I had to begin to work on putting budgets together," Hassenfeld recalled one afternoon as he sat in his family foundation offices with his longtime friend and colleague. "Al was basically 'Doctor No.' He would never pay a bill on time. It was always 'in the mail.'"

"I had no cash," Verrecchia said.

"Al would buy us two weeks, three weeks, whatever it was," Hassenfeld said. "In the late seventies, we weren't really bankable. We were paying lenders 23-plus percent interest. We couldn't rub two nickels together."

"I used to keep a running tab of our daily bank balance," Verrecchia said. "If we collected $10,000 that day, I could let a check go out for $10,000. It was hand-to-mouth. We did that for pretty much most of the '70s."

"Al and his team had to play magician."

"We had one foot in the grave and another on a banana peel," Verrecchia said.

Al Verrecchia and wife, Gerrie, at a long-ago Hasbro event. (Courtesy Al Verrecchia)

Against that backdrop, the $1.6-million deal Hassenfeld negotiated with Loomis and general Mills in 1978 for the foreign licensing rights to G.I. Joe was, as Hassenfeld said, "a lot of money"—in fact, "a lifeline" for the ailing company. And it would reap further rewards when Hassenfeld later bought back the rights to Action Man, the name by which Joe was marketed overseas. For this and other licensing deals, Hassenfeld, along with Stephen, was inducted in 2011 into the International Licensing Industry Merchandisers Association's Licensing Hall of Fame, joining Walt Disney, George Lucas, and Charles Schulz.

But truly, Loomis did giveth, and Loomis did taketh away.

The same year he wrote Hasbro that $1.6-million check was also the year Kenner first shipped Star Wars toys.

Star Wars was an immediate hit, with first-year sales of nearly $100 million, a record-breaking sum that dwarfed the success of G.I. Joe even in his mightiest days. Backed by the success of Lucas's film, which had grossed an astounding $194.8 million domestically in 1977, Star Wars toys sucked the last oxygen out of Joe.

In 1978, Stephen pulled America's Movable Fighting Man from the market. No bugler played taps, and there was no 21-gun salute, not even a funeral. Hasbro closed out its Super Joe Adventure Team, a smaller version of the once-mighty toy; and Super Joe Commander, GOR King of Terrons, Darkon, and the clear-plastic Luminos with its interior light and "Fight by Night with Light!" motto, were relegated to the diehards, to enjoy a second life as collectibles selling for hundreds of dollars in 2019.

Distant galaxies, not the beaches of Normandy, were firing children's imaginations as the 1980s approached, and the Hasbro toys division was reeling. Hasbro sold Marvel Comics' Spider-Man, Captain America and Hulk tabletop pinball games in the mid and late 1970s, along with Super Heroes checkers, bingo and board games based on DC Comics characters Batman, Superman and Wonder Woman—but they were not enough.

Superheroes could not recharge the toy division—nor could the 1978 introduction of Hungry Hungry Hippos, a Hasbro mainstay today that came to the firm from inventor and agent Fred Kroll, who also brought the board game Trouble to Pawtucket. Originally sold by the Japanese firm Agatsuma, Hungry Hungry Hippos charmed youngsters—and also Alan Hassenfeld, who on Kroll's death in 2003 would tell the *Palm Beach Post*: "All of us are saddened by the passing of Fred Kroll. Two of his greatest creations, Hungry Hungry Hippos and the Trouble game, will continue to entertain children for many years to come."

In 1978, Harold Hassenfeld's pencil division made $2 million—but the toy side of Hasbro lost $5.2 million. If Stephen was to realize his vision, some products would need to be sacrificed, regardless of tradition or nostalgia.

Numbers mattered.

So did freeing toys from pencils. Reliable old pencils made steady money, but really, how large could that market ever be?

Stephen and Alan knew the family needed to divide the company—not only for business reasons, but to stop the bickering between their father and their uncle. But as 1979 began, no one knew that the death of one of them would determine the corporate fate of all Hassenfelds.

❧

In the seventh decade of his life, Merrill Hassenfeld kept a secret: He was, as it were, a closet diner, satisfying his appetite for unhealthy foods in restaurants that he and a select circle of friends frequented, often on the way home from work, when a brief indulgence could be tucked into the flow of his busy day. His wife in particular needn't know.

Merrill long had struggled with his weight, which dieting and Sylvia's nagging seemed powerless to reduce. "Mom always had Dad on a diet," Alan recalled. "I used to feel so sorry for him." Merrill loved to eat, but he was conscientious of portion and selection at the family table. He seemed the very model of compliance with the latest weight-loss program.

Yet, obesity persisted. And he suffered from high blood pressure, despite having stopped smoking cigars (he did, however, continue to chew on them, leaving a trail of stubs as he moved about the factories and offices).

"Dad was not well," Hassenfeld said.

On March 20, 1979, Alan was working in his Pawtucket office, back in Rhode Island from one of his international trips, when Merrill walked in.

"Mom is going to be away tomorrow night, let's have dinner," the father said. "We haven't had a chance to talk one-on-one for a long time."

"Pops, that will be great," Alan said.

The next morning, Merrill collapsed at Hasbro headquarters and died shortly after at Miriam Hospital. Like his father, Henry, a heart attack had taken him. He was 61.

The dinner they never had, Alan said, would remain one of the regrets in his life. But he would draw lessons from it.

"So I sometimes say to people 'too often we put off what we should do today until tomorrow.' And also, 'too often, too late, we appreciate.'"

Merrill's passing prompted an outpouring of grief from many communities. Memories were shared and favorite stories told. Among those his younger son held dear, with an impish humor Merrill would have shared, was the answer to a mystery.

"I will never forget when Dad was on one of his diets. There we were sitting, my brother and my sister and me, Dad and Mom at dinner, and Dad would get these little portions and we'd obviously have big portions. And my dad never complained. After father died, any number of people came up to me and said, 'Oh, Alan, I'm going to miss your father so much. I used to meet him at the New York System wiener joint at 5:30 every night for a hot dog.' And, 'Oh, Alan, I'm going to miss your father so much, I used to meet him for a bagel at Abelson's on Hope Street.'" Abelson's and New York System franks were Rhode Island traditions.

Verrecchia kept similar memories. He spoke of riding with Merrill and Stephen to Red Sox games and stopping for hot dogs on the trip to Fenway Park.

"Don't say anything to Mrs. Hassenfeld!" Merrill would say.

Merrill left no fortune when he died, though Hasbro's later successes would create one for surviving family members; he left, instead, a legacy.

"It would shock the world to know that when Dad died, we had some wonderful material things as far as a house and some art, but Dad had very little to his name," Alan said. "Dad believed in everything being today— living charity and giving. And giving today."

CHAPTER FOUR

❧

KIDS NO MORE

ART ONE: FORTUNE, GOOD AND BAD

Merrill's death further dampened what already was the lackluster year of 1979, when Stephen's first priority was returning Hasbro's toy division to profitability after the $5.2-million loss in 1978. Empire-building would have to wait. With G.I. Joe and Charlie's Angels both gone and no strong candidate for an explosive hit, Hasbro relied on longstanding revenue-generators including Disney products and medical kits, with only a Ronald McDonald doll and a Warner Bros. Looney Tunes line possibly qualifying as marquee products. The 1979 catalog was lean: just 54 pages long, compared to 86 the year before.

Stephen had pruned and was still pruning.

He also was solidifying his management team in this, his first year in full command, with Alan becoming executive vice president; Al Verrecchia, senior vice president for finance; and marketing, sales, and research headed by what would be known as The Three Musketeers, Steve Schwartz, Larry Bernstein, and George Dunsay. It was an unusually talented group of executives, though anything but a seamless blend of personalities. By temperament, Alan was as different from Verrecchia as Verrecchia was from Bernstein and Schwartz and Schwartz was from Alan.

But Stephen was the unquestioned visionary and leader, and his strong loyalty to his men was returned with theirs to him.

The center could hold, as long as he led.

That would turn out to be exactly ten years.

Hasbro toys did return to the black in 1979, albeit with a whimper, not a bang, but a whimper beat another drubbing, and Stephen had renewed confidence heading into 1980.

And that proved to be the year when momentum indeed began to build.

It also was the year of the corporate divorce, which had been a long time coming.

"There was always tension between my father and my uncle," Alan Hassenfeld recalled.

After negotiations involving Harold, Stephen, and Alan, on September 28, 1980, Hassenfeld Brothers was split in two.

Harold's half, Empire Pencil, would stay in Tennessee.

The last brothers' half would stay Rhode Island-based and retain the Hasbro name.

"It was the best thing for both families that we could have done," Alan said. "And both families did well by it."

After the split, Stephen remained top Hasbro executive and he gave himself a new title, too: chairman of a newly constituted board. He had a new residence as well. Stephen had continued to live at his parents' home until 1978, when he and Alan, who was in Rhode Island only sporadically, shared an apartment near Brown University. But now, with Merrill gone and Sylvia preferring her midtown-Manhattan apartment, where she could be close to fellow philanthropists and supporters of Israeli and Jewish causes, the brothers in 1979 purchased the bayside Bristol residence that eventually would be Alan's summer home alone.

The brothers had reason to raise a toast overlooking the water from their new home when 1980 ended, for Hasbro had turned a $5 million profit, best since the banner year of 1964. Verrecchia had liquidated all short-term debt and was chipping away at the long-term, and when 1981 dawned, Hasbro had a record $16 million cash on hand.

With Verrecchia's strong hand, Stephen was mastering the financial learning curve.

"It didn't take him very long to figure out that the banks were making more money off of Hasbro than Hasbro was making," Verrecchia recalled. "That incensed Stephen and from that moment on, he became one of the most financially astute CEOs that you can imagine. He wasn't a financier, but he knew how to make money and he knew he wasn't going to work his ass off all day long just to give interest checks to the banks."

When Hasbro had gone public in 1968, Verrecchia said, 75 percent of the stock was owned by the Hassenfeld family, with just a quarter owned by regular shareholders.

"I don't mean this in a negative way toward Merrill," Verrecchia said, "but Merrill didn't care much about the public shareholders. It was 'his' company; he owned

75 percent. When he passed on and Stephen took over, the public shareholders held a little greater percentage ownership and Stephen wanted to—and had to—pay more attention to them."

Stephen in 1981 focused on core brands, with only licensed Disney products and a new line based on Peanuts, the Charles M. Schulz cartoon, getting much marketing muscle.

Which, for those non-core brands, was substantial.

Having acquired Aviva, which had rights to Snoopy products, Hasbro in 1981 brought to market a Snoopy bowling set, a Snoopy ice cream machine, Push 'N' Fly Snoopy, the Snoopy copter pull toy, the Snoopy Jack in the box, and the Snoopy Playmate Electronic Activity Center.

Marketing genius had not been required for Hasbro to court Schulz. Peanuts had been a hit virtually from its start in 1950, reaching, at its peak, readers at more than 2,500 newspapers in 75 countries and 21 languages daily. In its obituary of Schulz, *The New York Times* wrote that "his saga of Charlie Brown, Snoopy, Lucy and Linus 'is arguably the longest story ever told by one human being,' Robert Thompson, a professor of popular culture at Syracuse University, observed on the PBS 'NewsHour' with Jim Lehrer, longer than any epic poem, any Tolstoy novel, any Wagner opera. In all Mr. Schulz drew more than 18,250 strips in nearly 50 years."

And he negotiated licenses for hundreds, if not thousands, of products, many still on the market today.

Hasbro's Peanuts licensing deal had been sealed over a game of tennis, Alan Hassenfeld recalled. When playing against Schulz, who went by the nickname Sparky, Alan said, Stephen had whispered jokingly to his brother: "Remember, this is customer tennis. Lose!"

But win or lose, the deal would have been theirs, Alan said.

"Charles was a wonderful guy," he remembered.

Still, despite the power of a Peanuts license, some pundits at the 1981 New York Toy Fair ridiculed Hasbro as "Has-been" for its decision not to enter the explosive new field of video games, which was bringing riches to companies including Coleco and Sega, the Japanese firm.

With its Intellivision platform, Mattel—eight times larger than Hasbro and nearing $1 billion in sales—was riding the craze. Stephen was unfazed. He saw too much risk in video, and his caution would prove wise, as Mattel would discover to its regret when aggressive competitors such as Atari flooded the market and the rise of the home computer added further pressure. Intellivision crashed in 1984, with Mattel suffering hundreds of millions of dollars in losses.

By then, the Hasbro coffers full, Stephen was stunning the toy world.

Stephen in Hasbro's New York showroom office. (Courtesy Providence Journal)

Inside Hasbro, consideration had been given in 1980 to a concept called Blastoff, an action-figure concept grounded in World War II that was little more than recycled G.I. Joe.

Stephen expressed no interest.

And thus it was with frustration when, early in the year of "Has-been," he listened to The Three Musketeers, who were eager to show him… G.I. Joe.

But this action figure was not the tall, tired warrior of days past.

For starters, the new Joes would be Star Wars-size: three and three-quarters-inch tall. And the storylines would be all new, too.

G.I. Joe: A Real American Hero was a concept built from the ground up, the new toy's only similarities to the old being the name and time-honored play pattern, conflict. *G.I. Joe: A Real American Hero* was a contemporary fighting force, locked in ongoing battle with an evil adversary, ready in an instant to confront an emerging threat, terrorism.

In the real world, this was the era of the PLO, SLA, and IRA, of skyjackings and Americans held hostage in Tehran. America was not storming the beaches of Normandy now, but it was defending against the horror of what frightening headlines implied could happen to anyone. Newly elected president Ronald Reagan had vowed strong policy in this new war against new adversaries.

"I believe it is high time that the civilized countries of the world made it plain that there is no room worldwide for terrorism; there will be no negotiation with terrorists of any kind," he said in the final debate with incumbent Jimmy Carter, who lost to the former California governor and movie star in the general election.

The proposed packaging for Hasbro's "The Legend of G.I. Joe" —the new legend—told the foundational story:

"The enemy army of COBRA Command (an international paramilitary terrorist force) wants to conquer the world! Only one group of heroic, dedicated, fighting soldiers can stop them. Code name 'G.I. Joe' this crack mobile strike force will go anywhere and do anything to fight COBRA. Each member of the squad is an expert in the use of ultra-modern small arms, vehicles and weapons systems. They are specialists, trained in the latest fighting techniques. Read their Combat Command File Cards and select the best team members for each perilous mission. 'Duty, Honor, Courage' is the motto of G.I. Joe. A Real American Hero!"

The heroic characters, each with his own back story, included Laser Rifle Trooper ("Code Name: Flash"), Commando ("Code Name: Snake Eyes"), Mortal Soldier ("Code Name: Short Fuze"), and Counter Intelligence ("Code Name: Scarlet"), the sole female member of the squad. Cobra Office and Cobra ("Code Name: Enemy" for each) were the villains. The figures were all 3 ¾-inch tall, Star Wars-scale and cheaper to manufacture than the larger original. Several accessories accompanied the figures, including the Rapid Fire Motorcycle, "RAM"; the Jet Pack, "JUMP"; and the Attack Cannon, "FLAK."

Well, Stephen?

Hassenfeld told the Three Musketeers he would think about it, but he was not encouraging.

Schwartz, Bernstein, and Dunsay were on a West Coast invention-hunting trip when he phoned with his answer.

"Years ago, I told the Wall Street community the reason we're stopping G.I. Joe is because we became dependent on this one line and that's what hurt us in the past," Stephen said. "And I can't think of a reason why we would be successful now."

Back in Pawtucket the next day, Schwartz told his boss: "You can't do this. You can't on one hand hammer us that we are not growing the business—and then when we show you what we think is the way, not let us do it."

Schwartz threatened to resign. He himself was a larger-than-life character, brilliant but fiery.

When he'd calmed, Schwartz said: "Give us one more meeting to show you the marketing."

Stephen issued a two-week deadline.

Joe Bacal, of Griffin Bacal Inc., Hasbro's New York advertising firm, took center stage in the presentation theater for the last-chance pitch. He noted the incredible success of Star Wars, and the timing of George Lucas's next film, Return of the Jedi. It was set for release in 1983, which gave New Joe a one-year window, 1982, when the line might not be overshadowed.

"We don't have a movie," Bacal said, "but we do have a book."

He presented Stephen with a mock cover of a *G.I. Joe: A Real American Hero* that Marvel had produced, and then showed storyboards of the animated television commercials that could be broadcast. They would advertise the comics, not the toys explicitly, but no one could miss the connection. This was an ingenious way to sidestep guidelines from the National Association of Broadcasters restricting toy commercials. But networks and stations were not bound by any regulations for comic book ads, for there were none.

As popular as Star Wars had become, comics remained untouchable in their penetration into households with boys. Many adult males read them, too, their passion having been formed in their own youth.

"We're going to reach more people than Star Wars reached with the movie," Bacal said. "We're going to put the fantasy of G.I. Joe into the kid culture."

Stephen had sat uncharacteristically silent during the presentation.

When the lights went up, he was standing at the back of the room, crying.

"I wish my father had been alive to see this," he said. "I'm going to tell my father."

He left for Lincoln Park Cemetery in Warwick.

The Real American Hero did not make it to market in 1981, but two Hasbro winners did: a Sesame Street line and My Pretty Pony, precursor to My Little Pony, which would become another of Hasbro's evergreen brands. Stephen teased of Joe in the 1981 annual report, placing the action figure line's new logo on the cover with a note inside of the launch planned for 1982.

Stephen was gaining confidence as a chief executive, and he was bringing that confidence to Wall Street as reborn G.I. Joe began to hit stores in 1982. On May 12 of that year, he convened Hasbro's annual meeting at the company's small showroom on 41 Madison Avenue in New York. This was the second consecutive year he'd held the meeting in Manhattan, not Providence.

In his address, Stephen reminded stockholders of the turnaround he had engineered since the death of his father and the corporate divorce. He predicted continued growth at historic levels.

"Since the first quarter, ended March 31, was the 13th consecutive quarter of record sales and earnings, and since bookings for all our toys are well ahead of 1981, we are confident of record operating results this year," Hassenfeld said.

That, he hinted, would empower Hasbro to become a major buyer of other companies, and not necessarily only companies in the toy industry.

In its coverage of the meeting, *The Providence Journal* signaled the new ambition.

"Hasbro Industries Inc. will be exploring potential acquisition of products or companies during the next 12 to 24 months, Stephen D. Hassenfeld, chairman and president, told stockholders at the company's annual meeting yesterday," the story began.

"The Pawtucket, R.I., toy and game manufacturer has been offered numerous potential purchases over the last year: 'It would not be out of line to say there were enough to choke a horse,' Hassenfeld said later. 'But the best transactions, so far, are the ones we haven't done, if you will,' he said.

"'Now, however, there are a number of situations that could be attractive,' he added. 'Hasbro isn't interested in acquiring products or businesses outside its own areas,' he said. 'We have worked hard to develop the experience we have gained over the years, and there are a lot of opportunities where we are; the grass is not greener in the other field,' he added.

"But a possible purchase isn't necessarily limited to toys and games, according to Hassenfeld."

Four months later, Hassenfeld marked the two-year anniversary of the splitting of Hasbro by declaring in an interview that "It's the best thing I ever did. Some things you may have second thoughts about, but there are no second thoughts here."

Nor about the relaunch of Joe.

"A profitable toy company in 1982 'must have a hot item' for Christmas, and Hasbro's G.I. Joe toy soldier is just that, says a Wall Street analyst who follows Hasbro closely," *The Providence Journal* reported. "Macy's in New York agrees, predicting strong sales for little Joe," 'little' being a reference to its three and three-quarter-inch size.

"Stockholders have already opened a few presents," the story continued. "Last year, Hasbro directors resumed payment of dividends on Hasbro common stock, 20 cents a share annually. Directors have since doubled the dividend to 40 cents and split the stock, three shares for two. The split-off of Empire Pencil obviously helped Hasbro's growth: No longer do the men in Tennessee have to compete with the men in Rhode Island over the whole gamut of corporate activities. Before the separation, there had been protracted negotiations over what should have been routine management decisions: long-term goals, operations and financing, advertising expenditures, allocation of resources, inventory management - even the selection of an appropriate fiscal year."

No more. Stephen now answered to no one but stockholders, and they were applauding, not feuding.

"Hasbro is about eighth in size among the toy companies in the United States - it's hard to be precise because some major toy companies are divisions of giant conglomerates," *The Providence Journal* wrote. "'But it is one of a very few toy makers to gain in both sales and earnings in recent years,' said Monroe Greenstein, senior analyst at the Bear Stearns & Co. securities firm. 'And Hasbro is continuing to increase its share of the market,' he said. Hasbro, he added, has 'transformed itself' from a company whose operations were both marginal and cyclical into a company with greatly improved growth and profitability."

Transformed, too, was Stephen.

The bookmarmish if brilliant young man who seemed most comfortable inside old factories was now middle-age and debonair, a master marketer and increasingly savvy chief executive who saw no limits to the riches a company that began, literally, with rags could bring home.

Hassenfeld told the newspaper that Hasbro continued to consider buying companies with annual sales of $5 million to $50 million, but that acquisition was not essential to the future.

"I think we have a tremendous ability to grow this business internally," Hassenfeld said. "We could develop everything from within."

Hassenfeld described to the reporter how his lifestyle and schedule had changed with Hasbro's new success.

"A few years ago, he says he was at his Pawtucket headquarters 80 to 85 percent of the time," *The Journal* wrote, "but now, 'probably no more than 20 percent of my time.' These days, another 20 percent of his time is spent in New York City, where Hasbro has an office for its Eastern sales force. In recent years it also has been where annual stockholders' meetings are held.

"Hassenfeld is also drawn to New York by the advertising agency that will help Hasbro spend an advertising budget of almost $19 million, by the annual two-week Toy Fair, which draws makers and buyers from around the world, by the city's importance as a financial center, and as home for major film and television studios that produce characters that Hasbro might want to adapt for its toys.

"In some cases, Hassenfeld feels he must travel because there are activities that require the presence of the Hasbro president; no lower level will do. In negotiating for a major license, Hassenfeld observes: 'If somebody from Hasbro at a different level were to get involved, that would signal that particular studio that this seemingly is less important to Hasbro than to, let's say, Mattel.'

"Hassenfeld is scheduled to be in California this week for this precise reason: 'I will spend half a day to a full day with Charles Schulz, who is, of course, responsible for Snoopy and Peanuts.' The Schulz creations have been a major item for Hasbro."

Accompanied by coast-to-coast advertising and an eight-page spread in Hasbro's 1982 catalog, measures that mattered to buyers, the relaunch of G.I. Joe was met with a feverish excitement rare even for the toy industry.

The reborn warrior was the unparalleled boys' toy Christmas sensation in 1982, and when the books closed for the year, Hasbro had recorded more than $51 million in sales. Stephen dropped medical play kits in 1982—their time had passed, emotional attachment no longer a reason to keep going—but the chairman was plowing fertile new ground with Big Bird, Cookie Monster, Weebles, and the second year of My Pretty Pony. Still undeterred on his quest for a fashion doll hit, Hassenfeld offered another Barbie-like line, Fashions by Me.

It was another dud.

But Stephen was not shooting blanks on the acquisition front. The year 1983 saw two major brands brought into Hasbro: Glenco, the infant-care company whose iconic item was the Tommee Tippee Sippy Cup, seemingly in every household that had a baby; and Knickerbocker Toy Co., a leading maker of plush products and Raggedy Ann and Raggedy Andy toys.

Meanwhile, Joe sales increased. My Little Pony, which as the years unfolded would beget a perennial toy, screen, and digital franchise, was introduced; it reached $21 million in sales, a number that would triple the next year, a girls' toy performance even Mattel could envy.

Overall in 1983, Hasbro posted revenues of $225 million with earnings of $15 million, each a company record. "Has-been" no more, Wall Street was responding.

"You want to talk about heady days," Larry Bernstein would remember. "That was a time when people were calling a broker at least hourly."

The next year, 1984, would prove another landmark for Hasbro, with two developments that would fundamentally remake the company, again.

One was the introduction of Transformers. Licensed from the Japanese firm Takara, the line put Hasbro in the new robot-toy genre in competition with Voltron, sold in the U.S. by Matchbox, and GoBots, sold by Tonka under license from Bandai. The new genre was so hot that *People* magazine devoted pages of coverage to the competition—primarily between Hasbro and Tonka—in a holiday-season edition.

"The kids may think the battle is between the hero robot Leader-1 and the sinister Cy-Kill, or between the noble Optimus Prime and the loathsome Megatron," the *People* piece began. "Parents may think the battle is between themselves and other parents scrambling around trying to find enough GoBot and Transformer robot toys in the stores to keep the kids from revolting at Christmas.

"But the real war is being fought not by moms and dads, or by some schizophrenic robots that can turn themselves into sports cars, jet fighters, dump trucks, tape recorders or jaguars. It is between three-piece-suited M.B.A. types in the corporate offices of Tonka Corp. in Spring Park, Minn. and the headquarters of Hasbro Industries in Pawtucket, R.I. And the weapons they are wielding are not laser rifles or heat-seeking missiles but multimillion-dollar advertising budgets and high-powered promotional campaigns."

People predicted that robot toy sales in 1984 could reach $300 million, easily besting the record $65 million that Cabbage Patch toys, the hot seller of the 1983 holiday season, had set.

"The robots have already turned that record into coleslaw, with both Tonka's GoBot series and Hasbro's Transformers approaching a $100 million turnover this year," the magazine wrote. "The GoBots and Transformers, both made of plastic and die-cast metal, are not alone either. Toy-store shelves are creaking and clanking with variations on the theme: Road-Bots, Zybots, ManTech robots, Robotix kits, Starriors and Robo Force figures, Diakrons and Robotroids, among others."

Noting that "the Hasbro-Tonka competition is an internationalization of a conflict that has been going on in Japan" between Bandai and Takara, *People* said that Hasbro had devoted $8 million in advertising for Transformers, an ad budget that had intimidated Tonka—which, with its GoBots, was recovering from its disastrous year of 1982, when it had laid off almost third of its 1,400 employees. "We quaked a little, but we didn't run" when Transformers hit the market, Tonka president Steve Shank told the magazine.

But *People* seemed to place its money on Hasbro. It was a wise bet: First-year sales of Transformers surpassed $100 million—almost a quarter of a billion 2019 dollars—a portent of the entertainment behemoth the toy would become, with five blockbuster movies netting in the billions. Transformers movies were destined to become the 11th-highest grossing screen series of all time, in the rarefied company of Harry Potter, Batman, Star Wars, and James Bond.

Transformers, *People* stated, were "more complicated, bigger and generally more expensive than GoBots. They also come with enough individualized idiosyncrasies to create a new subspecialty of psychology: robot therapy. For instance, among the evil Deceptions (the planet they and the good Autobots come from is Cybertron), Buzzsaw the spy is described on his package as having a 'large ego [and] will often sulk rather than proceed if his plans go astray.'"

One day, Tonka's plans would go astray, and Alan Hassenfeld would be the beneficiary when, as his brother's successor at the helm of Hasbro, he bought GoBots' maker.

Another man might have rested on Transformers laurels, but Stephen was no other man. On May 4, 1984, in a move that stunned even the new believers, he outmaneuvered multi-billionaire investor Ronald O. Perelman to acquire venerable Milton Bradley. The once-thriving Massachusetts-based company—$421 million in revenues as recently as 1980, quadruple Hasbro's that year—had answered the siren's call of videogaming by buying Vectrex, in 1982. The next year, the video game market collapsed, and Milton Bradley was eviscerated.

But with its rich library of brands, the venerable firm still had tremendous value, despite its newly precarious financial footing. Chutes and Ladders, Candy Land, The Game of Life, Yahtzee, Battleship, the industry's finest jigsaw puzzles—Milton Bradley sold these and many more. It owned Playskool, rivalled only by Fisher-Price in the baby and toddler sub-industry. Its international sales and marketing forces, as Alan could well appreciate, were to be envied. And now, it was Hasbro's.

"There can be little doubt that the acquisition of Milton Bradley has created the most profitable entrant in the toy industry—one that is running neck and neck for sales leadership," stock analyst David S. Leibowitz told *The Providence Journal*. "A key to the merger," the paper wrote, "is that the two complement each other. Milton Bradley's strength is in puzzles and board games, an area where Hasbro is relatively weak; Milton Bradley is a major player in Europe; foreign sales haven't been a major activity for Hasbro. This could mean even greater earnings for a company whose net income has already soared, in Liebowitz's view."

A stunning acquisition for Hasbro and Stephen Hassenfeld.

Paul Rothman, an analyst and vice president of research at Advest, a securities firm, told *The Journal* that he envisioned "a possibility for crossbreeding between the strongest lines of the two companies. 'You could take some of the hot things in the Hasbro line and turn them into games and puzzles' for Milton Bradley, Rothman said. 'For example, if Mr. Potato Head is so popular, why not a Mr. Potato Head game?'"

Exactly, and soon enough such games began to appear.

Hassenfeld had scored a coup, but behind the scenes, there was contention. Unknown to outsiders, a culture clash was unfolding after what Alan Hassenfeld would later describe as "the marriage with Milton Bradley."

A troubled marriage, at first. Most of Milton Bradley's executives and previous owners were no grandchildren of Polish immigrants, Verrecchia would note in recalling that period.

"These guys wore wing-tip shoes, as Waspy as you could get," Verrecchia said. "The idea that these two Jewish kids from Pawtucket, Rhode Island, owned the company? There was anti-Semitism up at Milton Bradley you couldn't believe."

George Ditomassi, Milton Bradley's vice president of marketing, did not hold that prejudice, and he proved instrumental in helping root it out. More decisive still were Alan and Stephen, who had never tolerated bigotry—in or out of business. Stephen moved and removed difficult characters, offering no apologies and leaving no question who now was boss.

"But in the beginning, it was a disaster," Alan Hassenfeld said. Rancor was rife.

Following the acquisition, Milton Bradley chairman James J. Shea Jr., the son of a former company chairman, had been given the title of president and CEO of Hasbro Bradley, the name Stephen decided fit during the post-acquisition transition period. But less than three weeks later, Shea announced his resignation and eventually moved to California. Stephen promoted Alan, who had been his executive vice president, to president and CEO.

Stephen discussed Shea's departure with a *Providence Journal* reporter during an interview in his office, a space, the reporter wrote, "that is unusually spare -- no pictures on the wall, no drapes at the windows, little furniture. Magazines sit in stacks by the dozen on the floor and a large conference table."

Hassenfeld spoke diplomatically, resisting the temptation to discuss anti-Semitism.

"I would have liked it to have worked out differently," he said. "It didn't, and it surprised probably no one; it didn't surprise anyone in the industry."

Hassenfeld described Shea as someone "whose style is quite a bit different from mine. I tend to run things on a much more participatory basis, but that doesn't mean that his style was wrong. Obviously, he is a very talented individual. But I can understand the problems somebody has in going from a chief executive officer of a big company like that to a number-two position.

"After all, if somebody came along and took away my opportunity to be the lead person in interfacing with Wall Street, to be the one responsible for mergers and acquisitions, to be the interface with the board of directors, well, that's taking away a big piece of everything that you've trained for. All that was defined up front. You can't have two people doing the same work. And as part of the acquisition, it was defined that I would do all those things. Nonetheless, it left him all of a sudden without things he was used to doing."

Stephen, like his brother, was a gentleman. But reading between the lines, one could infer his distaste for Shea.

As Christmas 1984 neared, reborn G.I. Joe and My Little Pony were flying high and the Transformers craze had reached dizzying levels. Newspapers and broadcast outlets across America wrote about the phenomenon and credited Stephen Hassenfeld and his Three Musketeers for the unprecedented success achieved by the toys and the company.

"On a recent Saturday, the line of impatient customers wound around Tons of Toys in Middletown," *The Providence Journal* wrote in a story headlined "Marketing makes magic of Hasbro," published on December 18. "When they finally reached the counter, the store was out of Transformers, the hugely popular robotic toys…the scene has been repeated around the country."

Deborah Smith, managing editor of industry publication *Toys, Hobbies and Crafts*, said that Hasbro had "tornadoed to the top. It's got a lot of marketing moxie, a lot of innovative toys, a lot of rapport with the trade and with the consumer."

And, yet again, a renewed appreciation for the power of the screen.

Debuting on September 17, 1984, just as Hasbro was beginning to ship toys for the holiday season, the half-hour animated TV show *The Transformers* brought captivating science fiction to children—and many parents. Coproduced by Marvel Productions and Sunbow Entertainment, the studio run by Griffin-Bacal, *The Transformers* ran four seasons, ending with an abbreviated season on November 11, 1987. But the program had laid the groundwork for bigger big-screen success in years to come.

"During the great Cybertronian War," *The Transformers* series summary on IMDb reads, "the Autobots and the Decepticons crash-landed on Earth. Millions of years later, geological activity revives the warring factions - the Decepticons want to strip Earth of its vast energy resources, and the Autobots seek to protect the inhabitants of Earth from that fate. And so an endless battle begins in a crucial race to find an energy source for their home world Cybertron."

The series featured the legendary Frank Welker, who voiced Megatron, leader of the evil Decepticons, and ten other characters. One of the most prolific actors in Hollywood history, prior to *The Transformers* Welker had voiced characters for *Pac-Man, Spider-Man, G.I. Joe: A Real American Hero, The Smurfs, The Fonz and the Happy Days Gang, The Flintstones, Scooby-Doo* and *Tom & Jerry*. When *Transformers* made it to the big screen, he would continue voicing characters for the blockbuster franchise. So, too, would Peter Cullen, who voiced Optimus Prime, honorable leader of the heroic Autobots, beginning in 1984.

Editor Smith cited other factors in the year that made Hasbro a force capable of challenging Mattel for industry supremacy. *The Secret World of the Very Young*, described by *The Providence Journal* as "a prize-winning CBS feature film for children" was one. A new licensing partnership with Disney was another—and a third, the newspaper wrote, was "*Mothers' Minutes*, 30- and 45-second daily informational segments on parenting topics delivered by ABC-TV's Joan Lunden, hostess of *Good Morning America* and followed by Lunden commercials for Hasbro preschool and Playskool toys."

Douglas Thomson, president of the Toy Manufacturers of America, gave proper credit to Hassenfeld's decision to forego entry into the video game market. "It was a very courageous decision," Thomson said. Tom Griffin, of ad agency Griffin Bacal, which Hassenfeld would pay some $75 million in the year ahead, agreed: "While the rest of industry was running to big-ticket bell-and-whistle electronic toys Hasbro focused on low-price concept toys based on fantasy play." And avoiding catastrophic loss when the video game market collapsed.

Hasbro's Schwartz explained the ultimately winning strategy in more detail, saying "We were in a less competitive marketplace for toys during the electronic boom because most people were chasing electronic toys and each other and they weren't doing action games or figures or dolls. It allowed us to establish ourselves in the marketplace."

As Alan Hassenfeld, Al Verrecchia, and Brian Goldner later would during their turns running Hasbro, Stephen confirmed branding as the bedrock of the company's marketing.

"With all Hasbro toys," *The Journal* reporter wrote, "the marketing strategy is based on the brand concept, which permits economies of scale in advertising and promotion. It encourages what Hassenfeld calls 'in-brand play' or collecting. Hasbro licenses are sold through a joint venture called Great Licensing and Design (GLAD), headed by Bernard Loomis, who as president of General Mills toy group orchestrated the licensing of *Star Wars* characters. The licenses, which produce about 50 percent of Hasbro's toy revenues, are released in a coordinated way to get the biggest bang for the buck in terms of trade, media, and consumer exposure."

Stephen described a sort of symphony behind every launch.

"Today, Hassenfeld insists," *The Journal* wrote, "the product comes first, but all the elements - product, packaging, price, delivery, and advertising - must work together to produce a successful toy. To come up with that winning combination, Hasbro Bradley works years in advance, buying ideas from toy creators, developing ideas and testing toys with parents and kids… Consumer testing rarely tells Hasbro to get into or abandon a toy concept, but it suggests nuances that should be stressed. For example, Hasbro planned to market a realistic My Little Pony with brown or palomino coloring until little girls gravitated to pastel ponies in the tests.

"Not even toy merchants always know what is going to sell. My Little Pony got ho-hum reviews from the big retailers. In 1982, when Gloworm, a glow-in-the-dark toy, was introduced to major accounts, it was panned. The one exception was Sears. Hasbro's solution was to sell Gloworm to Sears for one year on an exclusive basis. It became the best-selling toy in Sears catalog history, Hassenfeld says, and at the next Toy Fair and other toy retailers scrambled to buy it. He recalled:

"'All the people that hated it thought it was wonderful. You know the story about success having many fathers, failure having none.'"

Suuccess was the story of Hasbro when Hassenfeld in February 1985 announced the company's 1984 performance at Toy Fair in New York.

"Hasbro Bradley Inc. yesterday announced a dramatic net earnings," began *The Providence Journal* report. "The toymaker, which acquired Milton Bradley Sept. 10, said the record gains were fueled by internal growth as well as the acquisition." Dramatic and historic indeed: Net earnings for 1984 totaled $52.4 million, more than triple the $15.2 million the year before. Net revenues of $719 million were a 221 percent increase from 1983.

"Stephen Hassenfeld, chairman and chief executive officer, said the 1984 acquisition of Milton Bradley added about $205 million in revenue in the second half, and the new *Transformers* product line added about $105 million in revenue since its introduction in April," the paper wrote. "Even without the gains made in those two areas, growth from a 'broad range of continuing and new products' added to revenue increases by more than 80 percent."

The biggest news was yet to come. *The Journal* delivered it three days before Christmas.

"Santa Claus is going to be good to Hasbro," the paper wrote. "With revenues expected to reach $1.2 billion and net profits nearing $102 million for 1985, Hasbro becomes the largest toy company in the world, pushing aside Mattel, a California toymaker that long held the top spot. For Hasbro, the holidays mark the end of a year that makes the company as popular on Wall Street as at the North Pole."

Stephen had been unable to crack the fashion doll market, but he had dethroned the maker of Barbie.

Sales of Transformers, which *The Journal* described as "the year's hottest toy," were expected to reach at least $275 million in 1985, and three other Hasbro toys were expected to join Transformers on the Top Ten when the year ended, according to industry publication *Toy and Hobby World*: G.I. Joe, My Little Pony, and My Buddy, a boys' doll that had tested well despite initial skepticism.

For the first time ever, Hasbro in 1985 landed on the Fortune 500—number 373—in the company of industrial giants General Motors, IBM, Ford, and General Electric. Hasbro would remain on the list for the next decade and a half, into the tenures of Alan Hassenfeld and Al Verrecchia.

The National Association of Investors Corp., with a membership of more than 100,000 mostly smaller investors, selected Hasbro "Growth Company of the Year for 1985." And, *The Journal* wrote, "Hasbro led all 500 companies in its percentage gain in 1984 sales from sales of the previous year. It ranked second among the 500 in ten-year growth in earnings per share. It ranked third in total return (dividends plus stock appreciation) to investors for both 1984."

The final Hassenfeld brothers had hit their stride.

In 1985, Stephen and Alan dropped "Bradley" from the company name, and Hasbro was Hasbro again. They now oversaw an operation with a record number of employees, some 7,000 total, including at factories in seven countries and sales offices in nearly three times that many foreign nations.

"We are really beginning to span the globe," Alan said, adding that in 1986 and beyond, "one of the areas of extreme growth for the company will be in the European market."

Back home in Pawtucket, workers were in the last stage of converting Merrill's old factory at 1027 Newport Avenue into offices. Hasbro had expanded manufacturing at its plant near McCoy Stadium and was leasing warehouse space in West Warwick, where Stephen and Alan's great-grandfather, David Frank, had run a textile-remnants firm.

Schwartz, senior vice president of marketing—The Three Musketeers' first among equals—shared some of the secret behind the newfound success, stating that Hasbro in the rollicking '80s had not wavered from the marking strategy it had created during the depressing late '70s.

"That's the strategy that brought us here," Schwartz said.

It involved what he described first as an "offensive" marketing plan for a product, followed by a "defensive" strategy to fend off competitors once it reached consumers.

"That's really the impact of being as big as we are, that we find we have to protect our G. I. Joes and our My Little Ponies and our Transformers, as well as launch new products," Schwartz said. "When you have the lead that we have right now, the one thing we can't afford to do is sit on it because that's how you lose it. We have to continually push forward, even with existing brands like G.I. Joe and My Little Pony or Transformers."

That, he said, meant continual renewal of existing lines and launches of new ones.

"The reason why G. I. Joe stays great is that we continually invest in it every year in new tooling and new product," Schwartz said.

Layered over that, Alan Hassenfeld said, was his brother's managerial style and Hasbro's experienced management team.

"We've learned how to cover for each other, how to make that block, how to make that tackle, how to double team when we need to double team, how to move away," Alan said. "Steve considers his main job as that of chief personnel manager, in the sense that his job is to try and bring together the best people and make sure there is a forum for dialogue."

Also, for reflection.

"You've got ears; you're supposed to use them for listening," Alan said. "You don't always have to talk."

Standard & Poors' analyst Paul Valentine, a close follower of the toy industry, approved.

"I think the company has a bright future; one of their big opportunities is building up their presence overseas, in Western Europe," he said. "There's no doubt in my mind that Hasbro, through its broad base of staples and an ability to bring out successful promotional toys, is likely to remain the leading toy company in America."

If Valentine had a caveat, it was his assessment of shareholder value.

"We think the stock is fully valued at present and would avoid it," he said. "It's a wonderful stock but other stocks in the industry are cheaper on a valuation basis. I prefer Tonka and Coleco over Hasbro."

He could not predict, of course, Hasbro under Alan's leadership would buy Tonka, or that Coleco would crash and burn.

But Steven Eisenberg, an analyst for Bear Stearns & Co., declared no caveats regarding Hasbro.

"We continue to be impressed," he said. "They are just very good at what they do. They are the envy of the industry."

Focused as they were on business during Hasbro's explosive growth during the first half of the eighties, Stephen and Alan nonetheless found time to begin discussing what one day, a decade in the future, would be their first outsized contribution to bettering children's well-being: the construction of Hasbro Children's Hospital.

Through an insensitive product introduction, the brothers also experienced consciousness-raising. Health, they would never again forget, involved not just the body but the mind.

The product was Zartan, an adversary of G.I. Joe that Hasbro brought to market in 1984.

Zartan was, on first blush, a cunning enemy with a compelling back story, as the packaging stated. Zartan could "alter his skin color at will to blend in with his environment. He is also a master of make-up and disguise, a ventriloquist, a linguist (over 20 languages and dialects), an acrobatic-contortionist and a practitioner of several mystic martial arts. Very little is known of his background and origins, but most security agencies agree that he must have had European military academy training."

But the "Psychological Profile" stigmatized people living with mental illness.

"Extreme paranoid schizophrenic," the profile read. "Grows into various multiple personalities to such an extent that the original personality becomes buried and forgotten."

The associations now known as Mental Health America and the National Alliance on Mental Illness, or NAMI, were appalled. They already were engaged in a public campaigns to strip away obstacles to better treatment and care of the mentally ill, many of whom who had been warehoused under inhumane conditions in abusive intuitions and prisons. And now here was the worst sort of message on a wildly popular toy.

"For years, we have been trying to fight against the stigmatization and ostracization of the mentally ill," the president of the Canadian Mental Health Association told *The Globe and Mail,* of Toronto. "And now this company creates the notion that the mentally ill are alien and enemy creatures, rather than people who need our help and understanding."

The Hassenfeld brothers were listening.

"My brother turned this one over to me and said, 'Hey, you're the socialist! Please take care of it,'" Alan recalled years later.

So he met with NAMI officials.

Look, you're right, we're wrong, what can we do that's positive in trying to help you bring mental illness out of the closet? Alan said.

Hassenfeld promised to remove the offensive profile from the Zartan packaging (although Hasbro did not recall the almost one million $8.99 figures that had already been shipped). He agreed to partner with NAMI on an anti-stigma campaign and donate to mental-health causes. When he later became chairman of the trade group The Toy Association, he further raised awareness among manufacturers.

In a report published in *The New York Times* and other newspapers, the Associated Press reported on the controversy and Hasbro's reaction.

"A toy manufacturer, saying it used 'poor judgment'' in marketing a new doll as a schizophrenic adversary of its G.I. Joe soldier doll, will try to make amends by donating money to mental-health research," the story began.

Hasbro vice president and general counsel Donald M. Robbins apologized on behalf of his company. "This is just to show we're concerned about mental illness and we certainly did not mean any harm," Robbins said. The paranoid schizophrenic label, he maintained, "was just an error that was made—a poor judgment—and we're embarrassed by it. We hope to make amends to the mentally ill by donating money to help alleviate the illness."

Mental health advocates applauded, with the executive director of the Mental Health Association of Indiana, one of the local affiliates that had complained to Hasbro, calling the company's donations "a very positive reaction. I think this is a most tangible method of apologizing for an irresponsible act. I must say, I'm encouraged by their responsiveness to this issue, and I trust this will give a message to other manufacturers."

It did, and it reinforced for the Hassenfelds a lesson they had learned, albeit most painfully, during the Flubber fiasco.

"Problems are like ice cream cones," is how Alan put it many years later. "If you don't lick them, they quickly become very messy."

His message for CEOs, politicians, and others in positions of power?

"Tell people what the problem is. Tell people how you got there, what you're going to do to fix it, and then shut up."

Stephen's only other glaring missteps during the glory days involved—no surprise—a fashion doll. Hasbro's latest introduction and the lead item in the 1986 catalog was Jem, for which Stephen projected sales of $100 million. They were half that, and after two years, Jem was gone (Hasbro's revival film, the 2015 *Jem and the Holograms*, was a box-office flop, grossing just $2.2 million, less than half its budget).

Jem's failure did not dissuade Stephen from introducing, in 1988, the blond, blue-eyed Maxie with breathless wonder: "Whether she's hitting the books or hitting the beach, Maxie *is* what's happening with today's teens!" Despite an ad budget of almost $5 million, Maxie wasn't what was happening and soon followed Jem to collectors' shelves.

But the Hasbro workforce paid no price for Stephen's fashion doll missteps; like his father, he was solicitous of his employees. "We pay 8,400 people on a worldwide basis," he said in an interview. "That's a hell of a lot of responsibility, and a piece of my responsibility is that they have some security, something the toy industry generally hasn't given."

Hassenfeld did not ask his employees to embrace his own work ethic, which found him on the job 20 hours many days. Still, Stephen found time to connect personally with people. "He was always making notes to send a baby gift to new parents, or flowers to a patient or a call to someone in need," Rabbi Gutterman would remember.

He found time, as did his brother, to continue and deepen the philanthropic and public-service legacy of his parents and grandfather. Stephen founded the Hasbro Children's Foundation, which supported programs helping children and families. He was a director of the Jerusalem Foundation and a trustee of Johns Hopkins University. His efforts were rewarded with a humanitarian award from the Rhode Island Big Brothers Association, shared with Alan, and—also shared with his brother—the national humanitarian award of the National Jewish Hospital.

And he and Alan began to shape their dream of a free-standing children's hospital in their home state, which had none, only a cramped, antiquated pediatric wing at Rhode Island Hospital.

"Steve and I talked about it," Alan recalled. "We had great pediatric doctors in Rhode Island, but we really didn't have a pediatric place to go."

In this endeavor, as others, Stephen shared his brother's, sister's, and parents' conviction that Hasbro had a debt to repay.

"We grew up in a family that believed if we had the capability, we would give back to those who brought about our success and never forget them," Alan said. "And also remembering where we came from. Because too many people that are successful forget where they came from. And sometimes they even turn their back."

PART TWO: TATER SUPERHERO

Although numerous other hits had eclipsed him, Mr. Potato Head never left the Hasbro neighborhood. He and his kin remained the happy-go-lucky folks who lived in the tidy house on the corner, keeping the lawn cut and the hedges trimmed and never causing trouble. Nor ever stirring great excitement. Their glory days, it seemed, had passed with the '50s, though nostalgia and enduring quirkiness still provided them a modest living. And that seemed fine with the aging spud, born in an era when TV stations still signed off during the overnight hours.

So no one would have predicted that Pot Head in 1985 would not only make a comeback, but also create a sensation that the national media would cover, tongue planted firmly in cheek.

Rather, when 1985 began, it seemed the icon would be overshadowed again by the continuing sensations of G.I. Joe, Transformers, My Little Pony and Charmkins, and two newcomers: Wuzzles, "a unique co-adventure between Walt Disney Productions and Hasbro," and Roland Rat Superstar and Friends, billed as a TV "superstar." (The Wuzzles show lasted just one year, and Roland Rat, imported from Britain, soon disappeared as well.)

Indeed, Pot Head might have spent another year in relative obscurity if not for Idaho.

Idaho—as in home of the Idaho Potato Commission, established in 1937, which informs readers that it "is a state agency that is responsible for promoting and protecting the famous 'Grown in Idaho®' seal, a federally registered trademark that assures consumers they are purchasing genuine, top-quality Idaho® potatoes." Idaho—as in future home of the Idaho Potato Museum, in Blackfoot, which operated The Potato Lab and sponsored "Mr. Potato Head races and computer games designed by the Idaho Potato Commission." Darth Tater tee-shirts are sold in the museum gift shop, along with potato soup, the Idaho Cookie Cutter (in the shape of the state), Idaho Spud and Big Potato Country playing cards, and a postcard of Marilyn Monroe wearing a potato dress and standing in a potato field.

Yes, Idaho was—and is—big on taters.

So what better state for a Mr. Potato Head political candidacy?

On September 27, 1985, Pot Head filed papers as a candidate for mayor of Boise, the capital city. It was, of course, a stunt, and if national attention was the goal, it succeeded.

With appropriate whimsy and a generous serving of puns, *People* magazine recounted the story in an issue that November:

"City politicians are notorious for hurling epithets at their opponents in the heat of a close campaign. But these days one of the four men running for mayor of Boise, Idaho isn't going off half-baked when he calls his latest rival 'Mr. Potato Head.' He is merely using the proper form of address for the seven-foot spud who registered his candidacy at City Hall on September 27. In a combination prank (by some students at Boise State) and publicity stunt (by Hasbro toys), the 33-year-old children's plaything has been billed alternately as the first vegetable and the first toy to run for public office.

"The capital of the state known for its underground economy has taken to this unspoiled favorite in a big way. Why, just the other week the raw political recruit had a parade down Main Street as well as Idaho's highest honor, a 21-potato salute. In return, the talkative tuber, portrayed in public by actor Marc Grayson in a fiberglass costume, has been buttering up voters all over town. Presenting himself as 'a man of the soil,' Mr. Potato Head is full of 'down-to-earth promises' that include the weeding out of pessimism and the planting of optimism in Boise, which he affectionately calls 'the land of my roots.' In an emotional plea for votes, he also mentions making the world a better place for his newborn son, Chip.

"Mr. Potato Head's a-peeling personality seems to have forestalled the mud-slinging, backbiting and dirty dealing that have become staple fare in modern American politics. Outgoing Mayor Richard Eardley has endorsed the earthy candidate, and in a rare display of competitive largesse, rival Dick Kempthorne freely offered this advice to the idealistic newcomer: 'Go in with your eyes open, stay thick-skinned and try to stay out of hot water.' Obviously Kempthorne is unafraid of getting mashed in the polls next Tuesday, although at last report Mr. Potato was definitely a head." (Correctly quoted, "a head.")

Mr. Potato Head's purported early lead, however, did not hold. According to Guinness World Records, which has chronicled many Pot Head facts (including fastest assembly, 6.62 seconds, by a man in Turkey; and fastest marathon by someone dressed as him, three hours, 24 minutes and 19 seconds, by a British man), the toy received just four votes, all by mail.

As the Boise election brought laughs, Hasbro was producing a more substantial plat-form for Mr. Potato Head: an animated series based on the character. The series would prove half-baked, as the Potato Head punsters might have put it, but the lessons learned and the relationships made would be invaluable as Hasbro under Stephen Hassenfeld's leadership continued transforming from a company that primarily sold toys and games to one that marketed story and entertainment, in many media, for families and people of all ages.

The series was *Potato Head Kids* and it starred Mr. and Mrs. Potato Head and Big Chip, who was the leader of the kids: Spud, Puff, Lumpy, and girl Smarty Pants, among others. Conflict was created with Grease's Gang, the delinquents always in the Kids' faces.

But *Potato Head Kids* was hardly Emmy-worthy and the series folded in 1987 after just 23 episodes, passing into history with other kids' TV duds of the era including *Kissyfur, Foofur, Rubik the Amazing Cube*, and *Rude Dog and the Dweebs*.

Although ultimately failures, *Potato Head Kids* and another Hasbro show of the era, *My Little Pony 'n Friends*, which lasted only two seasons, opened new doors in Hollywood. Under Stephen and Alan Hassenfeld's supervision the shows were pro-duced by Sunbow Entertainment, the animation studio owned by Griffin-Bacal and Marvel Productions, and Claster Television, of *Romper Room* fame. Sunbow Entertain-ment would enjoy a degree of success in the screen world, but a woman at Marvel Productions would reach greater heights and her friendship with Hassenfelds would prove fruitful.

Marvel president and CEO Margaret Loesch in 1990 would become the founding president of the Fox Children's Network, and she would work with Israeli-American producer and businessman Haim Saban in creating the 1990s mega-hit *Mighty Morphin Power Rangers,* yet another brand that was destined to come into the Hasbro fold one day.

The Hassenfelds saw more than potential profit in Pot Head: they saw another chance to advance the common good. The toy had long been a staple of Hasbro's holiday-time donations to children, and it had been among the tens of thousands of Hasbro toys distributed to children traumatized by tragedy, including the fire that destroyed the downtown of the old industrial city of Lynn, Massachusetts, in 1981, and another fire, set by arsonists, that burned a Santa's Village in impoverished Bridgeport, Connecticut, in 1982. And Potato Head was among the $100,000 (in wholesale dollars) worth of toys the Hassenfelds sent to the 36,000 children younger than twelve following the October 1983 U.S. invasion of Grenada.

Alan Hassenfeld arranged that mission to Grenada, which brought children Raggedy Ann and Andy, Donald Duck, and Sesame Street toys—but, deliberately, no G.I. Joes, which would not have uplifted kids recently subjected to real-life war.

"We tried very hard to make sure what we selected would be appropriate," Hassenfeld told the media in December, as Rhode Island National Guard C-130 cargo planes carrying the toys were about to lift off from Rhode Island. No battery-operated toys or those with complicated instructions were to be distributed, either. The idea was immediate, continuing fun.

Hassenfeld said his company already had donated nearly 20,000 toys—and that he had calculated he would need about 12,000 more to give one to each child on Grenada.

The final tally was 36,000 toys, with a retail value of $210,000.

"It wasn't until two days ago that the State Department came back to me and said there were more than 30,000 kids on the island out of a population of 110,000," Hassenfeld said. "But fortunately we've done well this year and we're happy we could do it."

U.S. Representative Claudine Schneider, Republican of Rhode Island, flew on the relief mission, which reached Grenada after overnighting in Puerto Rico. The cargo included 2,496 Mr. Potato Heads, 1,104 Mrs. Potato Heads, 3,600 Raggedy Anns, 600 Raggedy Andys, and 1,800 Donald Ducks.

"I think it's important to note that this whole idea was the concept of Hasbro," Schneider told U.S. Ambassador Charles A. Gillespie when the C-130 landed on Grenada.

The ambassador spoke of the economic circumstances of the island, saying: "It is not a rich island… and its economy has not been well run by the people who tried to run it. They've got a lot of unemployment. A lot of people need work. And the country itself is not in good financial condition. The last government really did milk it pretty much dry. The banks are basically illiquid. They have very few funds."

The situation was similar to Puerto Rico after 2017's Hurricane Maria, when Hassenfeld would stage two relief missions from the U.S. to that devastated island.

Accompanied by reporters including longtime *Providence Journal* political writer and columnist M. Charles Bakst, Schneider and the National Guard crew on arrival on the island headed to Queen Elizabeth Home for Children, an orphanage in St. George's.

"I am happy to be here with you," Schneider told the boys and girls. "There is a very wonderfully generous company in our state that makes toys and they decided they wanted to share some of these toys with all of you. So with a great big hug and kiss from all of the Americans we want to deliver these toys."

"In truth, the children appeared to be startled and confused by the mass of media around them," a reporter covering the mission wrote in a story published on Christmas. "Some thanked the congresswoman, others were speechless. Some children seemed not to know, at least at first, what to make of Donald Duck or the Dial-a-Design kit. But they also warmed up to the gifts. Tony Byer, 10, who does not live at the orphanage, told me he really liked his Mr. Potato Head."

The Grenada relief flight set the pattern for future Hasbro and Hassenfeld missions to stricken areas, but with one difference: they would not include politicians, whose presence, however well-meaning, distracted from the job at hand.

Children needed to smile, not be presented with a political sideshow.

Four years later, the Hassenfelds sent Pot Head into the public-health arena—although, as Alan later liked to joke, the character in this case, as always, had called the shots.

"It was never *us* that told Potato Head what we wanted him to do," he would say. "Potato Head told us what *he* wanted to do."

By 1987, Stephen and Alan—who himself enjoyed an occasional cigarette—had decided that Mr. Potato Head's pipe, with him since he arrived 35 years before, delivered a bad message regarding tobacco. So they decided that the iconic character would abandon his pipe. For good. The pipe would no longer be included among the parts sold with the toy, which retailed for about $5.49. Perhaps more importantly in the public arena, Pot Head's new healthy lifestyle would be a cornerstone in 1987 of the American Cancer Society's 11th annual Great American Smokeout, credited with helping millions of Americans to quit smoking since the first event in California.

Twenty-three years after the landmark first Surgeon General's Report on Smoking and Health linked smoking to lung cancer, heart disease, and other illnesses, the annual Smokeout had steadily gained in popularity as many individuals and employers who were beginning to restrict smoking in the workplace embraced it. Smokeouts generated extensive media coverage, and C. Everett Koop, the 13th Surgeon General who regularly utilized the power of the press on public-health issues—and whose beard and admiral's uniform had helped make him a household figure—was the leading crusader against the habit.

So when Hasbro approached him with a proposal to have Pot Head drop his pipe in a public ceremony, he was game. He believed that adding a cultural icon to the arsenal would be advantageous, even if the icon was a toy. With cameras rolling, a life-size Mr. Potato Head surrendered his pipe to Koop on November 17, 1987, two days before the Smokeout, in a ceremony that was "beamed by television into living rooms across the country," United Press International wrote.

"We felt it was time for Mr. Potato Head to give up his pipe and join the American health craze," Alfred C. Carosi Jr., a Hasbro marketing executive, told *The Providence Journal.* "After all, we want Mr. Potato Head to be around another 35 years."

Big Tobacco pushed back.

"As long as it's his decision to do so, that's fine," said Carole Halicki, spokeswoman for The Tobacco Institute, a trade organization. "Smoking is an individual pleasure. It should be an individual choice."

Philip Morris U.S.A. distributed "Great American Smoker" kits with stickers that declared "I Smoke and I Vote" and "Don't Nag Me - I'm a Great American Smoker."

But Big Tobacco, which finally in a $206-billion settlement in 1998 would acknowledge its culpability, was on the losing end of the public-relations battle. And Pot Head was now a crusader for the forces of good, a tater superhero one might say. Christened as "spokespud," he left Koop's office and took the cause into the greater world, appearing on posters at anti-smoking rallies around the country and accepting an award at Harvard for abandoning his pipe. In Providence, Mayor Joseph A. Paolino Jr. presented him with the keys to the capitol city. In Warwick, Rhode Island's second-largest city then, he judged a contest at an elementary school.

Mr. Potato Head remained involved in the Great American Smokeout for several years, and having succeeded there, the toy broadened its public-health advocacy in 1992 when the President's Council on Physical Fitness and Sports enlisted it in a new campaign to improve family fitness through exercise. In a series of events culminating with a Presidential Sports Award bestowed May 1 at the White House during the third annual Great American Workout, Pot Head—the quintessential couch potato, one could say—vowed to get in shape, with weight training and fitness walking four decades after plastic-molding machines had given him birth.

"I couldn't think of a better way to spend my 40th birthday," the toy declared in a press release announcing his new role.

"He's been walking miles and miles every day," his wife, Mrs. Potato Head, said. "To qualify for the Presidential Sports Award, Mr. Potato Head needs to walk a minimum of 125 miles by his 40th birthday on May 1. That's no small potatoes."

Arnold Schwarzenegger, chairman of the President's Council, could not resist a pun, either.

"I am pleased that Mr. Potato Head has joined the campaign to help improve America's family fitness," said Schwarzenegger. "And believe me, this is no half-baked exercise plan...I will see to it that Mr. Potato Head continues his shape-up program."

"I'm beginning to feel better already," said an energized Mr. Potato Head after finishing up a brisk walk. "Instead of having a fit, I'll be fit when I turn 40... I'll be a new Spud come the first of May!"

President Bush did not mention Potato Head during the May 1 ceremony, but he did thank Schwarzenegger, singer Barbara Mandrell, comedian Milton Berle, actor Bob Saget, athletes Mary Lou Retton and Chris Evert, and others who joined him on the South Lawn.

In his remarks, Bush singled out the legendary comedian.

"A man with us, a special man, knows all about fitness," the president said. "He knows that an American that is physically and mentally fit is fit to take on the world. And at 83—sorry about that, Milton—Milton Berle still rides his stationary bike, he does a lot of walking, he punches a heavy bag, and he maintains a healthy diet. So no wonder he's just been named a special adviser to Arnold. I welcome his leadership, showing that nobody, put it this way, is too old to stay fit."

That same day, the toy "celebrated" its birthday "by spending a quiet evening in his Potato Head box with Mrs. Potato Head and their 12 children," a *Providence Journal* story declared.

"He wanted it that way," Wayne S. Charness, Hasbro senior vice president of corporate communications and close Hassenfeld friend, noted.

Asked if the spud had anything special planned, Charness quipped: "He might have some French fries."

PART THREE: TRAGEDY AND TRIUMPH

Hasbro's rocket-like trajectory continued after the Milton Bradley acquisition and the introduction of Transformers and My Little Pony.

A share of company stock traded at six cents in December 1978—and at $8.16 in September 1986, a jaw-dropping 13,500-percent increase in fewer than eight years. On the eve of the 1987 Toy Fair that February, distinguished guests and celebrities invited by Stephen arrived for a cocktail party at Hasbro's new offices and showroom half a block from the Toy Building, on Fifth and 28th, where lesser companies leased smaller rooms. An Andy Warhol screen print and a Richard Artschwager sculpture, "Exclamation Point," were among the fine-art pieces that graced the showroom, evidence of the hand of Robert Beckwith, Hasbro's corporate design director. The party and place elegantly illustrated Hasbro's entry into the Fortune 500.

But few, if any, of the celebrities or guests at that Toy Fair party knew that Beckwith and Stephen were involved in a committed relationship; or that Stephen's legendary energy had been sapped by two recent colds that kept him bed-ridden; or that Beckwith suspected Stephen had contracted AIDS, which a test later in 1987 confirmed. Stephen knew how Wall Street would react knowing this—how swiftly the stock price might fall, the empire perhaps crumbling—and so he confided in no one, not even his brother or mother.

He would soldier on, Beckwith his lone support, hoping for a cure.

It did not come, of course.

As his health continued to decline, Hassenfeld publicly attributed his lengthening absences from work to a case of endocarditis followed by a slow recovery. It was true, just not the full truth.

Stephen at 1989 meeting, one of last photos of him. (Courtesy Providence Journal)

Having led Hasbro to what would be $1.345 billion in sales in 1988, another record, Stephen presided over Hasbro's annual meeting on May 27, 1989, at his beloved showroom. His voice wavered and he seemed frail when, leaning on the podium for support, he told shareholders, analysts, and the press, some of whom had heard rumors that he was sick from some unnamed disorder or disease:

"I've been in this business 26 years and I hope, the good Lord willing, I'll be here another 26 years because I love it."

He was here less than a month.

On June 25, 1989, Stephen Hassenfeld died. He was 47.

On the morning he was buried, Stephen was transported from the Providence funeral home where his body had laid overnight to Bristol, for a final visit at the seaside home he shared with his brother, and then to Temple Emanu-El, where a stained-glass window and bronze tablets with names of Hassenfelds attested to the family's long allegiance to Jewish causes. The State Police-led procession from the temple to Lincoln Park Cemetery was three miles long, said to be the longest motorcade in Rhode Island history—longer even than for presidential visits.

Stephen now rested next to his father, and near his grandfather and great-uncle, who were born in a distant time and place.

During the days that followed, the mainstream and business media (still unaware of the true cause of death) bestowed praise on Stephen for his corporate successes and community contributions. His hometown newspaper, *The Providence Journal,* was best equipped to write his biography, and it did, in a lengthy Sunday story. A future president was mentioned.

"When toy industry giant Hasbro Inc. of Pawtucket formally unveiled a new board game at its New York showroom last February, it arranged for a visit by Donald J. Trump, the real estate tycoon for whom the game is named," the story began. The game was called Trump: The Game.

"With toys and games elaborately arranged beneath spotlights, the showroom resembled a theater, and Trump was center stage to publicize the product. He smiled and cameras clicked. He spoke and tape recorders rolled. Toy store buyers sought autographs. And executives of Hasbro's Milton Bradley games division joined him for commemorative snapshots.

"As the scene unfolded, Stephen D. Hassenfeld, Hasbro chairman and chief executive, stood unnoticed in the shadows above the lights on a catwalk that surrounds the showroom. Only when the event was over, and the crowd and camera crews had departed, did Hassenfeld come forward to greet Trump as Trump left the building. Then Hassenfeld returned to work.

"Asked later why he declined a more visible role, Hassenfeld said he thought it more appropriate that Milton Bradley executives get the attention. The new game was their product and their responsibility."

The Providence Journal story of Stephen's passing gave the cause of death at New York City's Columbia Presbyterian Medical Center as pneumonia and cardiac arrest, which technically was correct, if lacking in a critical detail. It described the steps Stephen had taken in his final months to ensure a smooth executive transition at the company.

"That's the true test of any manager," Thomas J. Kalinske, former president and chief executive officer at Mattel, told *The Journal*. "As much as he will be missed, he's left the company so strong and with such a superb management team that it won't miss a beat."

And it wouldn't. A week after Stephen was buried, the Hasbro board unanimously elected Alan to succeed his brother. Alan, for the moment, kept his brother's team intact.

The Journal recounted Stephen's ascension -- how an infatuation traced to childhood could not have fully prepared him for his responsibilities when Merrill died of his heart attack.

"Hassenfeld made his share of mistakes at first," the story declared.

Kalinske confirmed that fact.

"When he was first learning, he was easy to compete with and we beat him a lot," the former Mattel chief said. At Toy Fair, Kalinske said, "He'd come over to congratulate us and he'd learn from that. But he kept learning, and not too many years later, he'd be doing the beating and we'd be doing the congratulating."

The Journal quoted Paul Valentine, toy industry analyst at Standard & Poor's Corp., who acknowledged Hassenfeld's wisdom in diversifying—not going the route of "companies too reliant on one hot product, such as Coleco with Cabbage Patch Kids and Worlds of Wonder with the Teddy Ruxpin doll, which eventually wound up in Bankruptcy Court."

Hassenfeld, Valentine said, "saw that [toy] companies had to move from being single-product companies to broadly diversified companies. Stephen really stands out. He's the one who did it first." Kidder, Peabody & Co. analyst Gary M. Jacobson echoed Valentine: "Stephen was the guiding force behind the company as it grew tenfold in the past decade, and he has been instrumental in legitimizing the toy industry, making it a respectable industry."

And *The Journal's* biography provided fresh insight into Stephen's management style, which also would characterize Alan's tenure, although there would be differences.

Schwartz described to the newspaper Hassenfeld's insistence on seeking staff consensus in new products, during product reviews for each division held every month or month-and-a-half. "There'll be 30 or 40 people in a room and we'll go over product by product, detail by detail," the minutiae of packaging, pricing, and advertising, Schwartz said. The process could take hours, but in cases where, for example, 15 people opined unproductively, Hassenfeld had learned that one more opinion might have a breakthrough insight.

"Then the 16th person says something, and you'd say, 'Why didn't I think of that?' It makes it all worthwhile," Schwartz said.

Kalinske applauded the approach.

"He'd force everyone to participate and he'd really listen," he said. "It's not the typical CEO's approach. It takes a long time to get a consensus, to reach a decision. I don't know where he found the time." He found it in 20-hour days, until his health began to deteriorate.

Stephen, said Hasbro director Norma T. Pace, would "dig deeply into his knowledge of the industry and tell us about trends, about what competitors were doing and about strategy."

The late CEO, she said, "lived his company, lived his products."

In preparing for Stephen Hassenfeld's induction on February 16, 1991, into the Toy Industry Hall of Fame, the Toy Manufacturers of America asked 37 non-Hassenfelds to write letters of memory. They were incorporated into a book, *Remembering Stephen.*

"My memory goes back to Merrill hauling his huge suitcase up a flight of stairs to my office at 5th and Kay Street in Washington, D.C. The kid [Stephen] would sometimes come along," wrote Toys 'R' Us founder Charles Lazarus. "I've further memories of visiting Merrill and Steve in dingy downtown D.C. 'salesmen hotels.' After business, there would invariably be the family conversation over dinner. The importance of family to the Hassenfelds was wonderful, warm and infectious. Business, good or bad, was always secondary."

"He was a valued partner whose vision for the toy business built Hasbro into the industry leader while creating some of the most important products and programs of the past decade," wrote Frank Wells, president and COO of The Walt Disney Company. "Like Walt Disney himself, Stephen was much more than a talented businessman. He was a true creative genius who contributed fundamental values to his company and his industry. His innovation and creative flair made toys what they should always be: true gifts for our children's imagination."

"A special friend and a rare person," wrote Charles K. Gifford, president of the Bank of Boston.

Wrote Three Musketeer Bernstein: "I've started this letter too many times and I just can't do it. There are too many memories and too much pain. Stephen was a teacher, but he was my friend. I miss him and I loved him."

Addressing Sylvia, Ellie, and Alan, Verrecchia hand-wrote his tribute in his tidy script, recalling the nearly quarter-century they had worked together, often under difficult circumstances. "It's easy to share good times with someone but Stephen and I shared many 'not-so-good times,'" Verrecchia wrote. "The struggle in the early years made the good times that much sweeter. Our friendship was different than most. We did not socialize, except for an occasional Red Sox game or dinner. However, we knew that we were in it for the long haul. We never had to look over our shoulder to see if the other was there. We shared a deep loyalty. I will always remember Stephen and Merrill. Knowing them made me a better person."

In an essay he titled *Those Were the Days, My Friend,* Joe Bacal wrote: "What I remember most about Stephen is the joy he felt when he was doing the things he loved most. And when he could combine these things—racing along in the early morning during the America's Cup at full sail aboard an incredible vessel, huddling on deck later that day with close associates to come up with a breakthrough idea for the business and then at sunset, beginning a long and leisurely feast with good friends and good talk about everything from art, architecture and family to the future of Israel—these were the times he was truly exhilarated."

Elected by the Hasbro board to succeed his brother as chairman and CEO, Alan Hassenfeld propelled the company to yet-greater success after naming, in 1989, Verrecchia head of sales, marketing, manufacturing, and administration of toys; and Milton Bradley's George Ditomassi head of all games and international.

"Al and Ditto really became my survival," Hassenfeld later recalled. "I had never made a presentation before people. I didn't understand as well as I should a balance sheet. I understood about fighting for every nickel and dime in sourcing and licensing and whatever, but I didn't have any of the financial literacy that a CEO in theory would need."

Verrecchia and Ditomassi did and helped Hassenfeld achieve it.

But the new triumvirate angered others, particularly regarding Verrecchia, who had excelled with numbers and production more than with product. Dunsay had left the company by then, but the two remaining Musketeers received new titles, reporting to Verrecchia. Neither was pleased, and they both would follow Dunsay out the door, Bernstein later than Schwartz, who immediately quit on learning of his new role under Verrecchia.

"We don't like each other," he told Alan. "We haven't liked each other in 13 years, and I'm not going to put myself through what I know is going to happen working for him. So it's just better for everybody—the company and me and Al—if I resign."

"Talk to Al," Alan said.

"I don't want to talk to Al," Schwartz said. "I have nothing to say to him."

Verrecchia years later recalled the pressures on his new boss.

"The concerns that I had at the time or that anybody in the company had at the time was whether or not Alan was up to being the CEO of a public company," he said. "It wasn't a question of would he eventually be able to do the job. The question was: 'Do we have a long enough runway for him to get up to speed?'"

Stephen had made Hasbro a high-flier. Alan, as it were, was a rookie pilot.

"So now Stephen is dead," Verrecchia said. "Alan is suddenly thrown into this situation where he's got to run the company. He's got a bunch of tigers in the company that are all vying for positions and who's going to be in control of what. He's got the pressures of suddenly being the leader of the family. His own personal life—he's just gotten married, all of this coming down. The company's doing well, but he's not running a company where you can just come in in the morning and let it run itself. This is a company where 60, 70 percent of the product line has to change every year."

The new management structure settled, Hassenfeld looked to acquisition and internal growth, the proven strategy, to keep Hasbro on the trajectory his brother had set. Less than two years after Stephen died, in the spring of 1991, Hasbro acquired Tonka Corporation, with its Kenner Parker Toys. Having beaten Mattel to the purchase, Hasbro now owned not only such classics as Tonka trucks, Play-Doh, and Easy Bake Oven, but other revenue-rich icons including Risk, Trivial Pursuit, Strawberry Shortcake, Care Bears, and Risk!

And Monopoly. And Batman. And Star Wars. And Nerf.

It was an acquisition that would have made Stephen proud—and an affirmation that his kid brother had come with talent and leadership, not just legacy, to the corner office.

"It was important for a lot of different reasons in terms of the product lines it brought us, some of the talent, stronger connections to Hollywood, all that kind of stuff," Verrecchia said. "But it also was the event that made it Alan's company from Stephen's company. Every CEO needs something where people realize, 'OK he's in charge.'"

In integrating Tonka/Kenner into Hasbro and increasing revenues generally, Alan was guided by Stephen's playbook, which he had likened to Monopoly, even though it was not in the Hasbro fold before he died.

"When we talked about acquisition, we only wanted to buy properties that were on the Monopoly board—but in the toy industry," Alan recalled. "In other words, properties that could stand the test of time."

Personnel that could stand the test, too—and the Tonka/Kenner acquisition brought to Hasbro such a man, a man with rich Hollywood experience, Kenner head Bruce Stein.

The hip and charming Stein held an MBA and after rising through the ranks of Armour-Dial and Ogilvy & Mather, the Los Angeles advertising firm that held the Mattel account, he had become a marketing vice president at Barbie's maker. Lured by a headhunter to Kenner in 1987, he worked his California connections to win Kenner the lucrative toy rights to *Batman*, the 1989 hit starring Jack Nicholson and Michael Keaton. When Hasbro bought Tonka, he spearheaded the campaign to bring Hasbro the rights to a film that Steven Spielberg was developing for Universal Pictures after buying the rights to a book by best-selling author Michael Crichton.

The film was *Jurassic Park*.

At Toy Fair in February 1992, Hasbro reported its 1991 results: a 41 percent increase in revenues, to $2.14 billion. It was the first time any toy company had exceeded the $2-billion mark. The stock was trading at more than $12 a share.

In a stroke of understatement, Hassenfeld declared 1991 "a terrific year."

He was more ebullient a year later at the 1993 Toy Fair, when Hasbro reported 1992 sales of $2.54 billion, an increase of 19 percent. Hasbro's net income had more than doubled, to $179.2 million, or $2.01 a share. The performance exceeded analysts' expectations, and the price of a share of stock rose to more than $15 a share.

Hassenfeld offered celebratory Carrington cigars to visitors on the day the 1992 results were announced. He did not smoke them himself, but his father had and Merrill always handed them out at Toy Fair. After Merrill's death, Alan made a custom of bringing a box of them to Toy Fair in memory of his father, "so he could be there," the son said.

In announcing the 1992 numbers, Hassenfeld, smiling, said: "Nice. Our results were excellent."

A significant portion, 40 percent, came from the international division, the overseas business Hassenfeld had pioneered beginning as a young man still in college. Hasbro's chief financial officer, John T. O'Neill, said that overseas sales were growing faster than domestic.

"We see outstanding opportunities internationally," O'Neill said. Hasbro was now manufacturing in Asia, Canada, Mexico, New Zealand, Europe, and the U.S., and it had plans to use those facilities for two major launches the following year: Barney toys and toys from Spielberg's first *Jurassic Park* movie.

Jurassic Park grossed nearly $1 billion worldwide in 1993, and Hasbro's piece of the blockbuster—the most financially successful film to that time—together with Barney, Littlest Pet Shop, the Tonka Talk 'N' Play Fire Truck, and Milton Bradley games helped the company to yet another record year: net revenues of $2.75 billion and net earnings of $200 million for 1993. The crucial fourth quarter accounted for about a third of the year's success, with revenues increasing 12 percent, to $932 million, and earnings rising eight percent, to $70 million.

"It sounds repetitious, but again a very strong fourth quarter has brought us to the end of another year during which Hasbro remained in top form," Hassenfeld said at 1994 Toy Fair. He gave significant credit to international, saying "strong performances by our Canadian, Mexican, U.K., and German units helped to offset the negative effects of the strengthened U.S. dollar and the generally weak worldwide economic conditions."

What Hassenfeld did not mention, though perhaps it spoke for itself, was his mantra as CEO that "a company needs a heart and a soul." He later described this philosophy, which had roots with his grandfather and great-uncle, as "the triple threat" of direct monetary donations; in-kind donations, such as games and toys for needy children, and not just at holiday time; and employee volunteerism, in the form of paid time off for workers to engage in community service.

Verrecchia would later describe Hassenfeld's "triple-threat" successes as no mean feat, for he was able to weave it into corporate culture while still pleasing shareholders—some of whom applauded, and others who cared only about the return on their investment.

A bonanza of brands that Alan Hassenfeld brought to Hasbro.

"What Alan really did," Verrecchia said, "was to keep instilled in the company those attributes of a family company: caring about people, having concerns about the community, encouraging people to give back while still meeting fiduciary responsibility to shareholders."

In doing so, Hassenfeld rejected the philosophy of Nobel Prize-winning economist Milton Friedman, who is often quoted as having said "the business of business is business."

In its place, Hassenfeld embraced what he called "tangential philosophy" for a company.

"Corporate philanthropy should touch on your 'core,'" he said. "In the case of Hasbro, it's easy: it's family and children, and the communities you work in. That's what you should be going into. Where I disagree with Freidman is from my own reading of Voltaire, in *Candide,* where you're supposed to cultivate your garden. If you plant the seeds for the future by helping your community, they'll help you."

Hasbro reached number 169 on the Fortune 500 in 1994, an astonishing achievement for a toy firm, but a warning of trouble surfaced publicly mid-year when the company reported second-quarter results.

"Hasbro, which last year bet heavily on dinosaurs, says second-quarter earnings slowed to a prehistoric crawl, due largely to a 14 percent drop in sales," *The Providence Journal* wrote. *Jurassic Park* had left theaters and the Barney buzz was subsiding. Overseas sales remained strong and with "new products and relationships which we have under contract and development," Hassenfeld said, "we are enthusiastic about 1995 and beyond."

But enthusiasm was not a word anyone inside Hasbro would have used to describe company morale in 1994.

Hasbro had just lost a bidding war to Mattel for the overseas rights to Scrabble, a loss that was perhaps balanced when Hassenfeld beat Mattel in acquiring British game maker Waddington's, which gave Hasbro the foreign rights to Monopoly that Waddington's owned. But overriding all was the reality that the toy division was in the midst of a restructuring that before year's end led to hundreds of layoffs and reassignments and the closing of a plant in New Jersey, as the overseas cost of manufacture continued to be cheaper.

The company celebrated the 30th anniversary of G.I. Joe in 1994, but the celebration was muted, at least internally, by the reassignment of many of the core Joe marketers and designers to other duties as the management of the iconic action figure was transferred to the Kenner Division, still in Cincinnati, the group that had cut its teeth building Star Wars into a powerhouse. Among those affected was Kirk Bozigian, a passionate G.I. Joe collector as well as marketer. Bozigian was reassigned to Play-Doh.

When 1994 ended, Hasbro reported sales of $2.67 billion, a slight decline from 1993, and $175 million in earnings, or $1.96 a share, compared to $200 million, $2.22 a share, the year before. The fourth quarter, however, was a winner, with revenues of

$940 million, $8 million more than the prior year, and quarterly earnings of $75.8 million, a seven-percent increase.

In his remarks after the results were released, Hassenfeld emphasized the fourth quarter, saying he was pleased, "especially in a year of change—both within the marketplace and in our operations."

Hassenfeld all but promised improved corporate performance in 1995, which the restructuring would help make possible, declaring that "during the quarter, we completed the Hasbro Toy Group restructuring begun in August, took action to balance our domestic plant capacities with manufacturing needs, continued consolidation of certain international operations and, in early January, announced the formation of the Hasbro Games Group, which will manage our two game companies, Milton Bradley and Parker Brothers."

Hassenfeld delivered on that promise, with a record fourth quarter in 1995—sales hit $1.02 billion—and a record full year, $2.86 billion in sales. Sales among Hasbro's major units all increased, Hassenfeld told the press.

"The games group again led the way, up more than 15 percent from a year ago—that on top of an 11 percent growth in the fourth quarter of 1994," he said. "The toy group, after lagging 1994 during the second and third quarters of 1995, finished on a positive note, exceeding last year's fourth-quarter level." Robust lines included Batman and Star Wars action figures, Mr. Potato Head, classic games such as Scrabble and Monopoly, and new games, including Lucky Ducks and Chicken Limbo. An interactive CD-ROM version of Monopoly also was a hit, as the home computer revolution continued to transform the industry.

But away from the public eye, a threatening story was unfolding.

It began with a conversation a few weeks after the 1995 Toy Fair, when Hasbro and Warner Bros. threw a $650,000 *Batman Forever* gala that drew stars Nicole Kidman and Jim Carrey, director Joel Schumacher, Time Warner chair Gerald M. Levine, and studio bosses Terry Semel and Robert Daly. That April in Bermuda during a meeting of the Toy Manufacturers of America, Mattel chief John Amerman floated the idea of a merger past the head of Hasbro. Hassenfeld listened with interest and agreed to send some of his lieutenants to a series of meetings in New York and elsewhere.

But soon, Hassenfeld began to harbor doubts. How different the company's corporate cultures were. How insistent Amerman was. After a day of meetings in early summer, Hassenfeld thought: *I got into this as equals. This doesn't sound like equals to me.*

And there was another complication: concerned that Toys 'R' Us had pressured toymakers not to sell to warehouse clubs, the Federal Trade Commission was investigating the giant retail chain for possible anti-trust violations. In their investigation, the FTC had "requested boatloads of documents," Hassenfeld recalled, and hired expert consultants.

"Whenever the government hires an economist to look into something it goes to DEFCON 4. Really serious," Hassenfeld said. "We felt it would be better at that point in time if we were not talking. Let the government finish what they were doing vis-à-vis Toys 'R' Us and maybe at a later date reopen discussions."

The merger idea stayed back-burner for the remainder of 1995, and Hassenfeld and Vivien took their customary winter vacation to Thailand. Verrecchia's worry after formal talks broke off in early summer was forgotten.

He had said: "What if they were to decide to come after us at some point in time, fellas?"

That point occurred on January 16, 1996, when Hassenfeld's office phone rang. Amerman was calling, with a new merger offer that he faxed to Hassenfeld. It was a classic bear hug: agree to merge by the end of the next day or Mattel would release the letter to the press.

Seventeen days of anguish and stress followed, as Amerman, using a readily manipulated media as a weapon, increased the pressure. Hassenfeld rejected the offer, and, shock subsiding, he and Verrecchia and their executive team—with the strong support of Hasbro employees—mounted a counterattack. On February 2, employees at the Pawtucket headquarters staged Hasbro Pride Day. They wore Hasbro tee-shirts and "To Hell with Mattel" buttons and sang, to the tune of "Get Back," The Beatles tune, "Barbie was a doll who thought she was a goddess, wanted everything in sight. But she was just a plastic bimbo in a townhouse, and Joe, he was ready to fight." A model-shop worker brought a Playskool Magic Smoking Grille into the cafeteria, lashed a blindfolded Barbie to the motorized skewer, and sat G.I. Joe at the controls.

A Barbie-Q, the display was called.

That day, Amerman surrendered.

Hasbro went on to its best year ever, closing 1996 with a record 16-percent increase in fourth-quarter profits and record sales of $3 billion, up five percent from 1995.

"What a difference a year makes," Hassenfeld said. Yes, indeed.

The year ahead promised good tidings: The *Star Wars* Trilogy was being re-released, and *The Lost World,* sequel to *Jurassic Park*, and the latest Batman saga, *Batman and Robin*, were headed for the big screen.

But new trouble awaited as the decade neared its end.

This was, after all, the toy industry.

CHAPTER FIVE

⚘

GOOD HEALTH, BAD GOVERNMENT

PART ONE: TEARS OF JOY

Four months after Stephen Hassenfeld had been laid to rest, Alan Hassenfeld and his mother and sister joined Hasbro board member E. John Rosenwald Jr., vice chairman of the Bear Stearns Companies, in a ceremony with doctors and others at the New York University Medical Center in Manhattan. They were dedicating the Stephen D. Hassenfeld Children's Center for Cancer and Blood Disorders, on which construction had recently started. The Hasbro Children's Foundation had donated $1.1 million to help realize the project.

Today, the center at NYU Langone Medical Center, is a leader in the treatment and research of pediatric diseases including leukemia, brain tumors, soft-tissue and bone sarcomas, blood-clotting and platelet disorders, and vascular malformations. The center describes a four-fold mission: "To provide the most modern, effective therapy for children by a team of specialists who are leaders in their respective fields; to deliver personalized care in a healing environment that promotes the physical, emotional and spiritual well-being of children and their families; to use the tools of modern biology to identify the causes of childhood cancer and blood disorders; and to rapidly translate scientific discovery into better treatments for all children."

And that was the Hassenfeld family's vision on November 2, 1989, when Rosenwald remembered the man whose name the center bears.

Stephen "cared terribly about young people's lives," Rosenwald said on that dedication day. The new center would "celebrate his vision and compassion" and was "the best possible way that we could have honored one of the greatest guys who ever lived," Rosenwald asserted.

Overall Hassenfeld philanthropy was praised.

"This is a family that holds its arms open to a lot of strangers," Rosenwald said. Dr. Saul J. Farber, provost and dean at NYU Medical, paid tribute to Sylvia for raising "a generation of sons and a daughter" dedicated to improving children's lives. The family's generosity "is a model for us all to emulate," said Thomas S. Murphy, chairman of NYU Medical's trustees and chairman and CEO of Capital Cities/ABC Inc.

In its coverage of the ceremony, *The Providence Journal* elaborated: "Each family member is involved in a number of charitable and civic programs," the newspaper wrote. "Sylvia Hassenfeld heads a program that helps settle Soviet Jews in Israel. Alan Hassenfeld recently returned from a tour of the border between Thailand and Laos, where he helped coordinate a program to help refugees in camps there."

The details of Hassenfeld's recent "tour" were not reported—and indeed, even his family did not know the full story. But Hassenfeld told it many years later.

This part was publicly known: Before his brother died, Hassenfeld had taken a lead role in helping to reunite families and resettle southeast Asian refugees in Rhode Island, which had numerous Hmong, Miao, Cambodian, and Vietnamese expatriates. He chaired the Governor's Advisory Council of Refugee Resettlement for many years and worked closely with a Catholic nun and priest, Sister Angela Daniels and the Very Rev. Daniel M. Trainor, in arranging safe passage to America. The three in turn coordinated with Jonathan Moore, director of the U.S. Bureau of Refugee Programs and a man with long foreign service.

Still, Hassenfeld should not have agreed to lead a semi-secret mission to refugee camps in Thailand that September of 1989.

He had just become CEO at a time of family and corporate crisis, and a trip to a region still suffering from the genocidal atrocities of the Khmer Rouge was not without significant personal risk. This was a part of the world shocked by the barbarism depicted in the Academy Award-winning film *The Killing Fields.* But under the guise of "going to the Orient on business," as he had countless times before, Hassenfeld flew to Thailand—his true intent "unknown to my family because of the danger," he later said.

But salvation for strangers was not his only intent. He craved something for his soul.

"I needed my own pace," he recalled. "Even though I was doing something wrong because of the responsibility I had taken on at Hasbro, I needed my own shot of 'picaresque independence' and this was an adventure."

Rose of Tibet, the Asian adventure that had enchanted him when he was young, cast a spell still.

Hassenfeld visited several camps in Thailand along the Laotian border in search of people and families who might be brought to Rhode Island. He encountered three obstacles in screening candidates. First was polygamy, which some tribes practiced, but the U.S. government did not sanction. Second was opium addiction, which also precluded a candidate. Last was the potential obstruction or worse of "the resistance" —Hmong who had been abandoned by the U.S. after it withdrew from Vietnam in 1975 and who lived on either side of the border. Those who had not fled, been resettled, or slaughtered by Laos's Communist regime, that is.

"The resistance knew what I was doing, but if I wanted their help, I needed to meet with their leaders," Hassenfeld said. "That's not easy to arrange. You let certain people know what you're there for and you wait."

One night, a man knocked on Hassenfeld's door.

"Mr. Hassenfeld," he said, "we're willing to meet, but it's going to be a journey and you'll be blindfolded."

Hassenfeld was taken across the Mekong River into Laos, where he met with resistance leaders.

"I got nowhere," he said. "But I ended up back in my room four or five hours later safely." No one, not even his American companions, knew what had transpired.

Nonetheless, the overall mission was a success. Hassenfeld succeeded in bringing more refugees back to Rhode Island, where they were reunited with family members already there.

A year later, Hassenfeld, Sister Angela, Father Trainor, and others prominent in the refugee cause were honored at the State House in a ceremony marking the 10th anniversary of the Refugee Act. The first to be called forward to receive an Outstanding Contribution Award, Hassenfeld brushed aside media questions, saying only "a lot of people that they're honoring have done so much more than I have."

"Oh, he's so humble," said Lynn Kao August, director of the state Office of Refugee Resettlement when a reporter asked about him.

Seriously sick children from Rhode Island and southeastern Massachusetts in the 1980s had limited options for advanced treatment and care, unless they travelled to nationally renowned Boston Children's Hospital. Some community hospitals in the region operated pediatric floors or wings, but they typically were small, antiquated, and unlikely to attract and retain the finest clinicians and researchers. Even Rhode Island Hospital, the state's largest medical center and a leader in many medical and surgical fields, did not emphasize pediatric healthcare.

The regional status quo was captured in a newspaper story published in September 1991.

"Thursday's dawn is approaching, and Room 12 in Rhode Island Hospital's children's wing is a sleeping column of bodies big and small," the story began.

"In the bed nearest the window, a 2-year-old nestles against her mother. A 1-year-old is in the crib next to them, the child's father scrunched up in a nearby chair because there is no room for a cot. In the third bed, Gary Christopher rouses himself to check on 4-year-old Justin, who sleeps peacefully at his side. The bathroom is down the hall and must be shared by up to 25 children. At night, the warning sounds of one person's intravenous pump can wake everyone up.

"'This,' jokes Christopher, 'is the lousiest hotel I've ever stayed in.'"

It wasn't a joke for the 4,300 children hospitalized there annually.

The Potter building had opened on the eve of World War II, during an era when staffs at most hospitals discouraged parents from visiting their sick children except briefly; parents, the thinking went, got in the way. And they certainly did not belong there overnight. The original visiting hours at Potter were one hour, twice a week, which was eventually replaced with a 2 p.m.-to-4 p.m. daily schedule. Fathers were allowed from 7 p.m. to 8 p.m., provided they had secured special permission. The fact that the comfort of a mother or father (or both) can promote healing was slow to arrive.

But it did arrive, helped by such healers as Dr. Edwin N. Forman, associate chief of pediatrics at Rhode Island Hospital in 1991. "I remember when I was in the hospital, I could never stop crying," he said. "The old idea was that you [the parent] are totally incompetent from helping or protecting your child from illness."

Slowly, the old rules changed, and parents were allowed to sleep overnight—in quarters as tight as an overcrowded prison cell, as one newspaper story described it.

"Right now, parents sleep underneath beds or in chairs. One room has six beds," Forman said. "But parents make sure children eat better; they protect their children from falling out of bed and getting the wrong medications, and the parent feels competent."

Said the father of a boy who spent the night in a small bedside chair and sang his son back to sleep whenever he was wakened: "It makes a difference. The nurses are not going to stay and make sure he goes back to sleep."

In other words, parents were partners, integral members of the healthcare team, not to mention they were the people who knew their children best.

When Stephen and Alan Hassenfeld first envisioned a children's hospital in Rhode Island, Forman was one of the first medical professionals to join the discussion. He was a pioneering pediatric oncologist and hematologist known not only for his expertise but his kindly manner and first-hand knowledge of the inadequacies of pediatric care at the hospital where he worked. A native of Brooklyn, he had graduated from Brown University, completed medical school at the University of Pennsylvania, and then completed a residency in pediatrics at Johns Hopkins University.

Parents and children thought the world of Forman, even after he had delivered diagnoses of life-threatening illnesses. He listened. He was kind. He cared.

Those qualities were described in a newspaper story in 2005 marking the 20th anniversary of the Tomorrow Fund, a non-profit organization modeled after Boston's Jimmy Fund that provides emotional and financial assistance to families with children who have cancer. Forman was a co-founder. In the story, one boy's mother recalled the day Forman delivered the news that her son had leukemia:

"He was calm and comforting—grandfatherly—very reassuring. You're talking about your three-year-old, who could possibly die, and this man comes in and gives you the strength and the confidence in him to know that he's going to do everything he has in his power to make it better... He's just an amazing individual who really cares and really knows his job and mission—to help save children's lives."

Forman helped the three-year-old. Five years later, the boy was cancer-free.

In 1989, four years after the Tomorrow Fund debuted, Forman co-founded a Providence Ronald McDonald House, which offered low-cost housing for families whose children were hospitalized. And then he set his sights on a modern, free-standing hospital. His efforts received a major boost when he asked the Joint Commission for the Accreditation of Health Care Organizations to review the Potter unit and the commission concluded:

"Your children's area is an embarrassment."

The Hassenfelds agreed. The campaign for something better was on.

It advanced when another doctor of stature, William Oh, professor and chairman of the Brown University School of Medicine's Department of Pediatrics and a pediatrician at Women & Infants Hospital, signed on shortly after Stephen's death.

Oh was one of the 11 children of Chinese parents who emigrated to the Philippines, where they operated a small store that provided enough income to support their family and their children's education, which they prized.

"They made a living out of this little grocery store, but they put everything in our education. All of us went to colleges and were all successful, so we're very grateful to them," Oh told an interviewer with the American Academy of Pediatrics, which interviewed Oh at his home in Rhode Island in 2008 for its Oral History Project. One of Oh's siblings also became a medical doctor, two earned doctoral degrees in engineering and became executives with General Motors, two became teachers, and another became a successful businesswoman who owned a Philippines shipping company and an import/export firm.

Oh told of his childhood during World War II, when the Japanese occupied his native country. Shades of Henry and Hillel Hassenfeld, in their place of birth.

"My dad was a member of an anti-Japanese committee, so when the Japanese soldiers invaded the Philippines and took over this town, they were looking for my dad, because he was considered a spy," Oh recalled. "They really wanted to get him and, essentially, execute him. In fact, there were five members in that committee. Three of them were executed. My father was a lucky one. The whole family moved to a mountainside."

There, they planted rice and corn and kept a small chicken farm and were so poor that the children went barefoot, shoes being beyond financial reach. Oh joked—but it was true—that walking three years without shoes caused his feet to widen. As an adult, he wore triple- or quadruple-E shoes, the only size that fit.

Until the war ended, the Oh family lived in fear. Once a week, usually on a Monday or Tuesday, Oh recalled, Japanese soldiers patrolled the mountain area, searching for the two remaining men who had publicly opposed Japan.

"We had some sentinels out there, so when they saw the Japanese patrol coming by, they would run and warn everybody that the Japanese were coming," Oh recalled. "So we would pack up and hide in the river in the back of the mountainside town. The whole family would move into the riverside to hide from them, but they only patrolled on the highway. I still remember that every one of us had a responsibility. I remember my responsibility was to carry a bag of rice and a bag of clothing that I owned. Everyone was prepared. So whenever the sentinel came and said, 'The Japanese are coming,' we would each pack up our things and run until the sentinel come back and said, 'They're all gone.' Then we could come back and stay in the house.

"So it was a very interesting experience. The kind of experience that actually built your character, because you learned to be organized, you learned to be alert, and you learned to take care of each other. It really was a character-builder, those three years. I was very, in a way, fortunate to have that kind of experience."

Tikkun Olam.

After the war, Oh attended an American Jesuit-run high school and then a junior college run by the order. His mentor, a Jesuit from Wisconsin, so impressed him that he wanted to become a priest. Shocked and saddened, his Buddhist mother cried for three nights and days, Oh remembered. "You're not going to be a priest," she said. "I want a grandson from you."

"I was number six in the family, but I followed three girls," Oh said. "You know how Chinese are. They're very pro-male, so I was the first boy after the three girls. I was very close to her heart, I think. So anyway, I couldn't take it. I couldn't let my mom down. So I went back to Father Masterson, and I said, 'Father, I can't do this. I can't let my mom down like that.'

"And he was very understanding. He used to call me William, not Bill, and he said, 'Well, William, if you cannot save souls, you might as well save bodies.' He was encouraging me to go into medicine, and so I did."

Recruited by Dr. Leo Stern, head of pediatrics at Rhode Island Hospital and Women & Infants Hospital and professor at Brown University's new medical school, Oh arrived in the Ocean State in 1974. He had no intention of taking Stern's job.

But then, 15 years later, in 1989, Stern lost his life to suicide by jumping off the tenth-story roof of Rhode Island Hospital's main building.

"Every time I talk about it, I still get chest pain," Oh told the American Academy of Pediatrics. "The whole department was in tears. Everybody knew within 24 hours, around the country, that this bad news occurred."

Rhode Island Hospital president Louis A. Fazzano believed the suicide would make it difficult, if not impossible, to find an outsider to replace Stern. So he asked Oh, who said he would consider the offer over the weekend.

If I don't do it, this department probably will not survive, because the news is so bad, Oh thought. And the underlying news was terrible, too, he later recalled: "One of the reasons that Leo was in crisis was that the budget was something like $1 million in the red. In those days, the budget only involved $4 or 5 million. Apparently, they wanted him to fire his faculty members, and he refused to do it. He's very loyal. He was loyal to his faculty."

Fazzano's offer stood. When Monday came, Oh told him: "I'll do it."

"What do you need?" Fazzano said.

"You know, Lou, you know what I need?" Oh said. "We need a new hospital."

"You're asking me to write a $50 million check for you?" Fazzano said.

"You're damn right," Oh said. "But you will get it all back in due time. To build a new program, you need a facility. It's like to catch mice, you need to get a good mousetrap to attract all these people to come here."

"I will chair the fund-raising committee," Fazzano said.

The hospital president went to Hasbro CEO Alan Hassenfeld, who already was discussing possibilities with Forman, Verrecchia, Charness, and others.

"Everybody believed in the hospital," Hassenfeld later said.

His belief had solidified during a tour of Potter. Charness, who accompanied him on the tour, recalled seeing "a kid in a supply closet getting a chemotherapy drip." A supply closet was the only available space.

"Alan saw that and I swear he was crying," Charness recalled. "He said, 'we've got to do this.' That's when we went back and committed to five million dollars, of which we would give $2.5 million and we would help them raise another $2.5 million. Al and Alan were both very active [in raising the second $2.5 million] —Al especially, in going to all of our vendors around the world, Asia, the U.S., everywhere, to help raise this money. It was incredible."

Also, inspirational.

In years to come, Verrecchia would chair the board of directors of Lifespan, the parent system of Hasbro Children's Hospital, Rhode Island Hospital, and Bradley Hospital, the nation's first neuropsychiatric hospital for children and adolescents; he also would serve as president of the Rhode Island Public Expenditure Council, and on the boards of the Wheeler School and The Wolf School, among other positions. Charness would be vice-chair of the Hasbro Children's Hospital Advisory Council; become president of the Rhode Island Community Food Bank and Adoption Rhode Island; and serve on the boards of environmental group Save the Bay, adoption group Families First, and Give Kids The World Village, a nonprofit resort in Florida that provides free vacations to children with life-threatening illnesses and their families.

And Alan Hassenfeld's philanthropic commitments would broaden.

On September 19, 1991, Hassenfeld welcomed the community to a celebration that had been orchestrated by Charness in collaboration with Verrecchia and others. Under big-top tents made festive with balloons, guests enjoyed popcorn and soft drinks. Miss America 1991, Marjorie Vincent, daughter of Haitian immigrants, graced the crowd with her presence.

Officials were breaking ground for Hasbro Children's Hospital.

Scheduled to open in 1994, the $51.5-million hospital would have 87 private rooms, each with a bed for a patient and another for a parent, and a bathroom with shower. It would have a pediatric emergency department, four pediatric operating rooms, a four-bed bone-marrow transplantation unit, play and consultation areas, a gift shop, a chapel, an outdoor garden, and a library, a lobby, and a fountain. Every patient floor would have three circular nurses' stations, with eight rooms surrounding each. A child would always be able to see a nurse and a nurse would always be able to observe a child.

This would be no Potter Unit makeover. Bruce K. Komiske, the new hospital's vice president for planning, marketing, and business development, was clear about that.

"Kids are not little adults," he said, and they required their own facility. Parents would be welcomed when Hasbro Children's opened. They already were, having been involved in design decisions that had "a big impact on the layout of the room, the size of the rooms, how the bathrooms work and the types of furnishings," Komiske said.

"It will welcome children in a very specific way, trying to provide as much familiarity to them as possible so it will be less frightening," said Eleanor Elbaum, director of pediatric patient services.

Essential to "developing a world-class children's hospital," said president William Kreykes.

Hassenfeld explained to a reporter the reasoning behind his decision to name the hospital after his company, not his family. "This is for all the people who work in a business that is like a family," he said. "Too many times, we get the credit for what our people have done."

PART TWO: MISTER HASBRO

"The hospital that toys will build: Work begins on children's unit given by Hasbro," read the headline on the front-page *Providence Journal* story the day after the ground-breaking. Hasbro had donated its $2.5 million to the project, Verrecchia was securing the other $2.5 million from Hasbro vendors, and Hassenfeld had agreed to take a lead role in the community campaign to raise some $20 million more.

The campaign was quickly successful: Within a year, three-quarters of the $20-million goal had been achieved. A progress report in the fall of 1992, when construction of the building was about half-finished, revealed some of the major contributors solicited by Hassenfeld, Verrecchia, and hospital officials. Fleet Financial Group (a progenitor of Bank of America) gave $500,000 for the pediatric emergency room and another $500,000 to Brown University's medical school to endow a professorship dedicated to researching how social problems affect children's health. The Champlin Foundation contributed $1.5 million, The Providence Journal Co., $400,000, and Hospital Trust National Bank, $250,000. More than $1 million was donated by hospital employees.

Ironically, the old children's unit had become a powerful force for good.

"All you have to do is take a tour of Potter," said David R. Slone, vice president for public relations and development, and capital-campaign head. "Then it's a question not of whether, but how much they'll give."

Oh was delighted by the new Brown professorship, the "Fleet Scholar for the Study of Social Pediatrics."

"It will tie in very nicely with our research," the pediatrician said.

Seven months later, in May 1993, the capital campaign reached its $20-million goal—a year ahead of schedule. The total donated by hospital employees, trustees and volunteers had reached $7.5 million, and the Kresge Foundation had added an $800,000 challenge grant.

"The campaign is exceeding everybody's expectations," Kreykes said.

So the campaign leaders decided to go for more—$3 million more in donations, to be used for a pediatric out-patient clinic on the hospital's lower level. The original plans had envisioned that center being outfitted at some future date but completing it with the rest of the hospital was now feasible.

Hassenfeld continued to invest his time in raising money, succeeding with donations totaling another $1.5 million from domestic and overseas business associates; with his extensive connections to vendors and others in the Hasbro production chain, Verrecchia joined that effort.

"I basically committed to a gift—and committed to match that gift in raising funds—with a handshake," Hassenfeld told a woman who was writing a construction-progress report. "It was a bond of honor," one that his executives and employees shared.

Hassenfeld also was investing his time in design decisions that would set the atmosphere he and others wanted to be as comfortable as possible.

"What you wanted to do is make it nonthreatening," he told the woman writing the progress report. "You wanted to make it almost fun… It's a lot of the soft things and fuzzy things that we've really had an impact on. From the day that we agreed to be the foundation in the building of the hospital, if this hospital was going to carry our name, we just wanted to be involved."

Hassenfeld intentionally offered no opinion in medical-design decisions, but décor was an area in which he could legitimately make suggestions. No fan of the wall clocks that the designers had selected for the nurses' stations—Hassenfeld judged them too close to ones on school walls—so on his recommendation, *can't they be more fun?*, a cartoonist dressed them up.

Looking to the bigger picture, Hassenfeld disliked the original plans for the color palette, judging them unsuitable for a place where sick children needed cheer and parents wanted reassurance. He judged them "awful" —a description shared by Vivien, whose style sense was keen—and so he brought in Deborah Sussman, an award-winning designer whose touch had been put on the 1984 Summer Olympics, among many other projects.

"Surprising combinations" characterized the scheme Sussman created for the hospital, the writer of the progress report stated. "The lobby columns, instead of the bright cherry originally proposed, are muted salmon and aqua. Everywhere, the primary colors that children crave interact with the restful pastels that adults require."

Hassenfeld was self-effacing when describing his company's support.

"It's only in soft and fuzzy terms that Hassenfeld will speak of his contribution," the writer stated. "Asked what Hasbro gains from its donation, he says, 'Tears of joy.' Pressed for a businessman's response, he still doesn't say it's good advertising. He says the hospital will make Hasbro employees proud."

A community had come together. Perhaps the only naysay had been raised when Hassenfeld encountered Providence Mayor Vincent A. "Buddy" Cianci Jr. one day before the new hospital was completed while dining at the Capital Grille, a popular restaurant for politicians and power brokers near the State House.

Cianci held no admiration for the Hasbro CEO. In fact, it seemed, he despised him.

In 1990, in an episode that came to light years later with the publication of "The Prince of Providence: The Rise and Fall of America's Most Notorious Mayor," by *Providence Journal* investigative reporter Mike Stanton, a Pulitzer Prize winner, Cianci had mocked Hassenfeld during a breakfast meeting of lawyers, bankers, and business leaders.

Turning to him at the meeting, Cianci said: "Let's get one thing straight. You make fucking toys. I run a city. I have a police department, a fire department. You make fucking toys. And the only reason you do that is because your father left you the company, because you're a member of the Lucky Sperm Club."

Meaning, he had been born a Hassenfeld. That the family had benefitted humanity while the mayor first and foremost benefitted the mayor seemed lost on Cianci, whose final legacy would be of a criminal who served hard time.

On that day before the new children's hospital was completed and Hassenfeld encountered Cianci, the mayor said: "Alan? I got a problem."

"Whatcha got?" Hassenfeld said.

"You know there are air rights with the bridge between the two hospitals," Cianci said. The structure would connect Hasbro Children's to Rhode Island Hospital.

Hassenfeld wasn't sure what he meant, but a smart guess would have been that the mayor did not like being overshadowed by someone bigger than himself.

"You're going to have to pay for the air rights and that hasn't been negotiated," Cianci said.

Hassenfeld couldn't tell if he was kidding or not.

"Buddy," he said, "I'm raising money to build a children's hospital, what the hell do I know about air rights? That's for you to negotiate with others."

The mayor seemed unsatisfied with the answer.

"Buddy, I promise you one thing," Hassenfeld said. "I went to university at a time when we were fairly creative in protests and demonstrations sit-ins. I don't think your honor would like a sit-in outside City Hall—with children with IVs. Buddy, drop it."

The mayor did.

As the opening of Hasbro Children's Hospital approached, the capital campaign surpassed $23 million in contributions. They came in gifts of hundreds of thousands of dollars and gifts of dimes. Literally, dimes: from the "Dimes for Deeds" campaign conducted in public schools through Rhode Island, from sales of chocolate lollipops at shopping centers, from a month's worth of proceeds from a carousel at a mall. Nurses wrote and published a cookbook and raised money selling it. Providence College's nationally ranked men's basketball team donated $50 for each three-point basket during one stretch of a season.

The spirit of giving rippled through the community.

One fund-raising team sold Hasbro toys, working with the Rhode Island National Guard and visiting Rotary and Kiwanis Clubs, "any nook and cranny of the community where they could find interest," said vice president for public relations and development Slone. Artists donated hundreds of their works to the new building and painted murals on walls. A marina donated a 35-foot sailboat and a fire department gave, in memory of a boy who had died of cancer, an antique fire engine for the hospital's outside play yard.

In no better fashion, perhaps, was the spirit better exemplified than with the approximately 10,000 six-inch-square ceramic tiles that patients, parents, and students from all of Rhode Island's 39 cities and towns produced as part of the Circle of Clay project.

Overseen by stained-glass artist Peter Geisser, art director at the Rhode Island School for the Deaf and underwritten with more than $100,000 raised by Very Special Arts Rhode Island, devoted to involving people with disabilities in the arts, the Circle featured depictions of people, animals, dinosaurs, and even a pizza. Most told stories of joy, but a few spoke of death, the closing chapter for some seriously sick children. The choice was left to the tiles' creators.

One was made by a girl who was unlikely to survive.

"A hush fell over the intensive-care unit," said nurse Maureen Oberg. "Just incredible, as the mother did the little girl's handprint."

"You're looking at a house and tree," said Geisser, "then you encounter somebody saying goodbye to their dying child."

Major gifts had continued, with the charitable trust division of defense giant Textron, headquartered in Providence, giving a quarter of a million dollars, and The Rhode Island Hospital Surgery Foundation, the Haffenreffer Family Fund, and the Rhode Island Foundation each also giving $250,000. Providence Anesthesiologists and University Orthopedics each gave $350,000. Four-hundred-thousand dollars came from The Herald Group of Hong Kong, established by another friend of Hassenfeld and Verrecchia: the Austrian-born, British-educated George Bloch, who began building a toy and housewares manufacturing company after moving to Shanghai on the eve of World War II. Rhode Island Medical Imaging donated $1 million.

And this generosity blossomed during a time when the country was slowly recovering from a recession, which hit Rhode Island particularly hard.

"We've seldom had this experience of generosity, especially in such tough economic times," said Slone.

When the final coat of paint had dried, patients on the morning of February 12, 1994, were moved from Potter through Rhode Island Hospital's corridors and elevators to Hasbro Children's Hospital in an intricately choreographed transition, eight months in the planning. The opening followed a major snowstorm, but weather proved but a minor inconvenience to what was described as a procession of 60 patients in wheelchairs and on stretchers, assisted by hundreds of staff, parents, and volunteers. Reporters recorded the event. Musicians played and a nun distributed teddy bears to patients.

"It's very exciting," pediatric cardiologist Dr. Lloyd Feit said on that day. "It's finally happening. It's reality."

Lobby of Hasbro Children's Hospital when it opened. (Courtesy of Lifespan)

Minutes before 7:30 a.m., Barbara Crosby, a nurse on Potter since the early 1980s, began moving the crib where two-year-old Caitlyn Adler was awaiting surgery. Accompanied by her mother, Eileen Adler, the girl was wheeled from Potter to the passageway from Rhode Island Hospital to Hasbro Children's. A red ribbon and a crowd of officials and journalists awaited.

"Eileen Adler picks up her daughter and cuts the ribbon," *The Providence Journal* wrote. "Caitlyn sort of smiles. Her hand is taped to a board to keep the intravenous line in place. Caitlyn has a brain tumor that doctors hope to remove this week."

Caitlyn was settled into her new room, painted in pink, with a floor-to-ceiling window and a border of swimming fish.

"It's beautiful," Eileen Adler said. "It's cheery and bright. It feels nice and clean."

"It was like going from Kansas into Oz," a nurse recalled years later, on the 20th anniversary of the opening. "Like walking into Cinderella's castle," another staff member remembered.

Hassenfeld, Verrecchia, and Charness were in New York for Toy Fair during that second week of February 1994, but they visited the hospital following their return. Hassenfeld, in another event marking the opening of the hospital, struck a favorite theme.

"From the Wizard of Oz, Dorothy sings, 'Somewhere over the rainbow, skies are blue... and the dreams that you dare to dream really do come true,'" he said.

"Today, the dream that we dared to dream really does become reality. For almost 72 years, we have flourished in this community—from my grandfather to my father to my brother Stephen—three generations of Hassenfelds. They built Hasbro with a heart and always with a tradition of giving back. Today, I really represent the four generations of Hasbro employees, those who rise at 4 a.m. to work on the assembly lines, those in the community, and those across the seven seas. To so many of those who have dedicated their lives to Hasbro in Rhode Island, I can only say 'thank you.'

"So often, the landscape of our Rhode Island is painted as being negative and bleak," Hassenfeld continued, in reference to corrupt politics that he, as leader of an ethics-reform group, sought to defeat. "May this children's hospital be the beacon of light that shows the world we truly can be the best... From construction workers to nurses—from doctors to architects—from parents to the community as a whole—from Rhode Island artists to caring givers—we have shown that people can work hand in hand, without egos. What we have accomplished is truly monumental."

Hassenfeld paused in memory of a boy sick with cancer who had shared the spotlight three years before, when construction of the hospital had begun.

"Oh, how I wish I could wave a magical wand and bring Robert Eckert back," Hassenfeld said. "Robert held my hand as we walked to break ground in September '91. Robert died shortly after. It is not fair. How I wish there would be a way to alleviate all pain and sorrow. For the future, that must be another dream. For now, all we can do is ease the furrow on a brow—bring warmth, tenderness and a smile to a cloudy countenance."

Hassenfeld said the new hospital would be "a magical, non-threatening, enchanting home with the best doctors and nurses in the land," and then he quoted the lyrics from the Michael Jackson and Lionel Richie tune, "We are the World," recorded for the USA for Africa fundraiser: *There comes a time when we need a certain call, when the world must come together as one. There are children dying and it's time to lend a hand to life, the greatest gift of all.*

Turning emotional, Hassenfeld looked to another country he knew well.

"The Chinese believe that when one is married, it is best to have rain, for it is a sign of good luck. Confucius had not yet figured out snow, but let us say it is white rain, the purest and best of good fortune, as we unite tonight to bring our children a better tomorrow. I tremble and my eyes have tears of joy. A beacon of hope and a dream are becoming a reality because of all here, and so many others who are not, who have joined hands and heart to protect our greatest natural resource, our children."

Months later, on December 20, 1994, at the first of what became an annual tradition that they continued after both had left the Hasbro executive suite, Hassenfeld and Verrecchia, accompanied by Charness, visited the hospital. It was five days before Christmas.

Hassenfeld beamed, despite just learning that the Mexican peso had been devalued, bringing his Mexican business to near-devastation.

"This puts it all in perspective," he said as he followed gurneys loaded with toys into an elevator.

"Merry Christmas everyone!" he said at the first stop, the intensive-care unit.

"Is that Mister Hasbro?" whispered a nurse.

On Hassenfeld went, through a visit that lasted three hours.

"This is my favorite teddy bear," he told a boy with cancer. "He's going to keep you company."

But another child wanted no teddy bear, Transformer, Battleship game or other Hasbro toy on the gurneys—he wanted a Power Ranger.

"Mighty Morphin Power Ranger—this is hurting me!" Hassenfeld laughed.

But he promised to get him one.

"Aren't you nice," a mother said. "May I ask who you are?"

"We work at Hasbro," Hassenfeld said, letting it go at that.

In deciding to play Santa, he'd forbidden outside press coverage or internal announcement, except to the administrators who had to be informed.

This was not about him, nor even his company.

PART THREE: GOOD GOVERNMENT?

Three months after ground was broken on Hasbro Children's Hospital, at 10:30 a.m. on December 11, 1991, Hassenfeld had stepped to a podium in the Rhode Island State House. The sound of church bells ringing outside could be heard.

Within earshot, they rang in the belfries of the Gloria Dei Lutheran Church, the Armenian Church of Saints Sahag and Mesrob, the Cathedral of St. John, and the First Baptist Church in America, established in 1638 by Roger Williams, first person in America to espouse the principal of separation of church and state. Beyond Providence, they rang in churches around the state.

"Let the bells ring for a new dawn," Hassenfeld said in the House of Representatives lounge, where portraits of many of the state's most powerful politicians hung on the walls. "My business is toys, but we're here today—halfway between the first day of Hanukkah and Christmas—to give Rhode Islanders a different kind of gift. Today, we announce the formation of what we think is the broadest coalition in the history of Rhode Island."

Hassenfeld was correct. The state had never witnessed anything of the sort.

It was called RIght Now!, and it would take just such an extensive coalition of business, civic, education, faith, and other leaders to accomplish what Hassenfeld, founding RIght Now! chairman and fellow members, sought: change in a political system and statewide culture of corruption and crime that had deep historic roots.

At least as deep as 1904, when legendary muckraking reporter Lincoln Steffens documented in *McClure's Magazine* how a close-knit group of Republican politicians—among them the state's Nelson W. Aldrich, one of the notorious "Big Four" members of the GOP who controlled the U.S. Senate at the time—enriched themselves and their friends through their mastery of corruption.

Hassenfeld announces RIght Now! (Courtesy Providence Journal)

"The political condition of Rhode Island is notorious, acknowledged, and it is shameful," Steffens wrote. "Rhode Island is a state for sale, and cheap."

Yes, there was reason the state was nicknamed "Rogue's Island."

As the 20th century advanced, the roguishness intensified. Rhode Island became the Mob capital of New England under the crime boss Raymond L. S. Patriarca, whose murderous reign from the 1930s until his death in 1984 would be depicted in "Crimetown," the hit podcast series of 2016 and 2017 (his son, Raymond Patriarca Jr., succeeded him). Patriarca operated his Mafia empire from Providence's Federal Hill, with its view of the State House, a mile distant.

There was state Supreme Court Justice Joseph A. Bevilacqua, who resigned in 1986 after a *Providence Journal* investigation revealed that he associated with mobsters (the disgraced judge's son, John J. Bevilacqua, became state Senate Majority Leader in 1990).

And there was Cianci.

During his third term, in 1983, the mayor was indicted on charges of attempted extortion, conspiracy, kidnapping, assault, and assault with a dangerous weapon stemming from an incident in Cianci's home in which the mayor slapped and used a lit cigarette to burn the face of a man he believed was having an affair with his estranged wife. Cianci further threatened to smash his head with a fireplace log—all while his police bodyguard watched.

Cianci pleaded no contest before his trial started, and was given a five-year suspended sentence, which made him a convicted felon. Forced by the city charter to resign, Cianci became a radio talk show host. In 1990, he ran for mayor again—and in a three-way race, during which he vowed "honesty and governmental integrity," a slogan that begged ridicule, he was elected to a fourth term.

But even by these historical standards, 1991 had proved outrageous—and it was outrage that had moved Hassenfeld to take the podium and clergy to ring bells.

The year began with the gubernatorial inauguration of business tycoon Bruce Sundlun. During a ceremony on the front steps of the State House that featured cannons booming and aircraft flying over, Sundlun spoke of the $160-million budget deficit he had inherited—the worst fiscal crisis in Rhode Island in at least two decades—and of his "sense of deep and serious obligation" to root out corruption and insider politics.

"The voters not only wanted to change who governed them, but how they were governed," Sundlun, a Democrat, said of the election, in which he had defeated incumbent Republican Edward D. DiPrete, who in 1991 was fined $30,000 for ethics violations (and who in 1998 would plead guilty to extortion, bribery, and racketeering, a plea that brought a one-year sentence in the state prison).

"They wanted something different, something better," Sundlun said. "The people's trust has been abused over the years by endless disappointments. This year, they finally said, 'Enough'... Nothing can withstand the weight of public cynicism. Without the people's trust, our task will become an arduous, sullen struggle doomed to failure." Quoting President Grover Cleveland, Sundlun said "Public office is a public trust." And government, he said, should be "as honest and as hard-working as the taxpayers who pay for it."

In addressing what faced Rhode Island with its fiscal crisis, Sundlun, a decorated World War II bomber pilot, drew the analogy of navigating through a thunderstorm. "On the approach, the storm cloud is ominous and dark," he said. "Once inside, it's a rough, difficult, tumultuous ride. But once you get to the other side, there is sunlight once again."

Sundlun was describing, too, another monetary crisis—one that had just recently come to his attention. The private Rhode Island Share and Deposit Indemnity Corporation, or RISDIC, which insured more than $1 billion that belonged to depositors at the state's 45 credit unions, some 300,000 depositors in total, had collapsed. The collapse had been precipitated by the corporation's vice president, Joseph Mollicone Jr., who had embezzled millions of dollars from RISDIC. Unknown to the public, in

November, when he knew his malfeasance was about to be discovered, he fled to Utah and assumed a new identity.

When Sundlun's inauguration ended, the new governor went into the State House, where he signed an order that stiffened ethical standards for state employees. Then he held a press conference to announce the failure of RISDIC, and the closing of all 45 credit unions and the freezing of all deposits until the mess could be resolved, a decision that ignited the fury of many of those who had lost access to their money.

And it was only January 1. More corruption awaited as the year progressed.

The judicial system was tainted, again.

That July, Superior Court Judge Antonio S. Almeida was arrested for soliciting and accepting $45,100 in bribes from a lawyer, allegedly in return for favorable rulings (in 1992, after pleading guilty, he was sentenced to six years in prison, fined $50,000, disbarred and stripped of his judicial pension). Responding to Almeida's arrest, Superior Court Judge James C. Bulman called Almeida "a greedy, slimy son of a bitch" who deserved to be "boiled in oil" —after which Bulman was suspended several weeks for his comments, although many Rhode Islanders, including some lawyers, applauded.

The same week in July that Almeida was arrested, his alleged lawyer-partner-in-crime was suspended from practicing law for taking thousands of dollars from the estate of a comatose man (he later pleaded no contest to embezzlement). Former probate judge Marvin Brill was disbarred. Seventeen lawyers were censured for loans or arranging loans to former Family Court Judge John E. Fuyat Jr., who had resigned.

June brought headlines regarding Brian J. Sarault, mayor of Pawtucket. No friend of the media, Sarault two years before had responded to unflattering press reports by saying "We have a serious journalism problem in this city."

Furious, Sarault had added: "I am sick and tired of being treated as a criminal."

On June 12, 1991, he was charged as one.

An FBI special agent, member of a team that had been investigating him, walked into his office and arrested him for running a kickback operation in which he had collected about $1 million in extortion payments over four years. On November 14, 1991, after resigning as mayor, Sarault admitted in federal court to being the ringleader of a criminal enterprise, to violating the federal Racketeering Influenced and Corrupt Organization (RICO) Act.

"The administration of Brian J. Sarault was a group of individuals whose object was to derive money and property for personal benefit by corrupt and illegal means," Assistant U.S. Attorney Edwin J. Gale told Judge Ernest C. Torres. Eight other members of Sarault's administration were convicted of offenses including payment of bribes and receiving construction contracts on jobs at McCoy Stadium, located just over a mile from Hasbro headquarters. Sarault was sentenced to 5 1/2 years in prison.

Thus the year went, a barrage of painful publicity that some business leaders, Hassenfeld foremost among them, feared would damage the state's economy as it offended law-abiding citizens and taxpayers. Newspapers published negative reports about Rhode Island., as did magazines including *Time, Forbes*, and *U.S. News & World Report*.

And ABC's *PrimeTime Live* broadcast a segment on "Rogue's Island."

Correspondent Judd Rose began the report by saying "In a state where politics is often in the gutter, this year it fell into the sewer."

How bad was it, according to the network?

Rhode Island, Rose said, "might be the most corrupt state in the union."

It was against this backdrop that Hassenfeld had agreed to meet H. Philip West Jr., executive director of Common Cause, a nonpartisan citizens group, and a small group of reform-minded individuals. West would later write of what he saw in Hassenfeld's office: "Mr. Potato Head waved across the room while G.I. Joe figures scrambled along a windowsill. Bright blocks filled several bookshelves. A table held specialty versions of Monopoly."

And the CEO himself?

"With his unruly hair, an engaging grin, sleeves rolled up, and rubber bands around his wrists, Alan Hassenfeld shattered my stereotype of a corporate mogul," West wrote.

"I'm embarrassed to be from Rhode Island," Hassenfeld told West and the group. "When I'm in New York or Los Angeles or London, people ask why our little state has such terrible corruption. They can't believe we keep our company here."

Hassenfeld had implored politicians to clean house, but their reaction spoke volumes.

"When I talk to people from the legislature," Hassenfeld said to West and the group, "one senator actually told me that people will eventually see that they've done a pretty good job of running Rhode Island. I wanted to start screaming: 'If you've done a pretty good job, why is our state in such a god-awful mess? Are you really that blind?'"

As prominent as they had been in the community for much of the century, no Hassenfeld had ever plunged deeply into Rhode Island's turbulent political waters. Few business leaders of any kind ever had. But Hassenfeld during that first meeting with West not only agreed to join the ethics-reform coalition that would be named RIght Now!, he agreed chair it and take the fight into the proverbial belly of the beast.

Which is where he, West, and many others were gathered, inside the House lobby on that December 11, 1991, when church bells rang across Rhode Island.

"It's about time we finally did something," Hassenfeld said.

"It has to change," said West.

RIght Now! presented a 28-point platform of reforms which it hoped to accomplish through legislation and constitutional amendment. Hassenfeld asked that no one contribute to a state political candidacy in 1992 until reform had been achieved.

Strengthening anti-nepotism laws so that public officials could not use their office to financially benefit their relatives—whether spouse, child, sibling, grandparent, or grandchild—was one point on the platform. Among the other reforms RIght Now! demanded through legislation were a ban on corporate contributions to state campaigns; a prohibition on political parties contributing more than $10,000 to a candidate; a ban on cash contributions greater than $25; and a one-year waiting period before elected state officials and certain of their staff members could assume a permanent state job, including a seat on the bench. A proposed amendment to the state constitution requiring voter approval would lengthen terms for governor, lieutenant governor, and other general officers from two to four years and impose a two-term limit on consecutive terms; and establish a way for voters to recall a general officer accused or convicted of a crime.

In an interview the day before RIght Now! announced its platform, Hassenfeld referenced statements by Verrecchia in late October that had generated national coverage. Speaking at an economic conference, Verrecchia had outlined Rhode Island's high energy costs and taxes, and its burdensome workers' compensation insurance.

"If we were not in Rhode Island we would not come to Rhode Island, and certainly I do not recommend any expansion of our manufacturing operations in Rhode Island," Verrecchia had said. "We don't want to leave, but we have to remain competitive."

No other corporation or leading executive signed on to the RIght Now! campaign, but four chambers of commerce did and some of their leaders joined Hassenfeld at the State House on that morning two weeks before Christmas. The 21-member coalition represented a broad spectrum of interests including the Protestant Rhode Island State Council of Churches, led by executive minister Jim Miller; the Episcopal Diocese of Rhode Island, under the stewardship of Bishop George Nelson Hunt III; the Coalition Against Domestic Violence; the Environmental Council of Rhode Island; Rhode Island Lawyers for Reform; the Jewish Federation of Rhode Island; the Sierra Club; United Way of Southeastern New England; the Urban League of Rhode Island; the Women's Center of Rhode Island; Brown University President Vartan Gregorian; and the Rhode Island Public Expenditure Council, headed by Gary Sasse, who later would head Bryant University's Hassenfeld Institute for Public Leadership, established with a gift from the Hassenfeld Family Foundation.

Certain legislators feared the coalition, but RIght Now! had a friend in the speaker and many legislators and a strong ally in the governor. It helped that the rallies it organized drew thousands, and thousands more answered the call for telephone- and letter-writing blitzes to legislators and newspapers in that early Internet era.

❧

The first sign of victory came on April 28, 1992, when, after nearly two hours of debate, the House on a 94-to-5 vote passed a campaign finance reform bill. Supporters were ecstatic after the landmark vote was recorded.

"Today is truly an historic day," said Judiciary Committee Chairman Jeffrey J. Teitz, a Democrat, who co-authored the final bill with West.

"I'm so used to creeping in this area that when I get a chance to leap, I'm going to take it," said Republican representative David W. Dumas.

"It's great. It's spectacular," Hassenfeld said.

At 10:50 a.m. the next day, in a State House room graced by Gilbert Stuart's famous painting of George Washington, Sundlun signed the bill into law.

"Today marks an important milestone in the journey toward a more ethical government in Rhode Island," the governor said.

West and Hassenfeld watch as the votes come in. (Courtesy Providence Journal)

More milestones in RIght Now!'s campaign were marked in 1992, including one that fall when voters in what a newspaper report described as "a stunning turnaround" approved the constitutional amendment lengthening terms of the state's general officers to four years, enacting recall provisions, and limiting service to a maximum of two terms. Early polls had shown 70 percent or more of voters against the change, but RIght Now! had swayed the citizenry.

West was among those celebrating on election night.

"I think that within Rhode Island this vote tonight is really a victory over cynicism and suspicion," West told a reporter, adding that he had been disturbed by what he described as "toxic suspicion" of opponents of the constitutional changes as the election had neared. But RIght Now!'s own campaign, which relied on a quarter of a million dollars in donations, including from Hassenfeld, had prevailed.

Nine days later, RIght Now! suspended its major activities.

"Everything we had hoped to accomplish, we did," Hassenfeld said.

Hassenfeld noted the long slog to success, saying "it was the most draining thing I have ever been a part of." Perhaps naively, he had hoped for success more quickly. "I thought by the end of January I would be back to running a toy business."

And while RIght Now! had achieved its immediate objectives, Hassenfeld issued a warning to state officials. "If they don't work," he said, "then we'll have to come on back."

The next summer, they did. Once again, corruption had tainted Hassenfeld's home state—at the highest level.

Published on August 24, 1993, the latest installment of an ongoing *Providence Journal* investigation into corruption inside the state Supreme Court—the same court once led by disgraced chief justice Bevilacqua—had disclosed that then-Chief Justice Thomas F. Fay, Bevilacqua's successor, had used a crony network to steer court business to friends and associates, in violation of ethics laws. That evening, as a result of a concurrent criminal investigation by the state attorney general, Fay was charged.

He claimed innocence and remained on the bench. In an echo of Bevilacqua's own fall, calls for impeachment mounted.

The scandal was the second to hit the Rhode Island Supreme Court in 1993: state court administrator Matthew J. Smith, a friend and political ally of Fay and a former House Speaker, had resigned after *Providence Journal* and law-enforcement investigations revealed that he, too, was practiced in the art of cronyism.

On August 26, RIght Now! held a press conference in the State House rotunda, between the House and Senate chambers, and beneath the governor's office.

"We urge all Rhode Islanders to take personal responsibility for reforming the judiciary," West said.

"We're going to be even more tenacious this time around," Hassenfeld vowed.

"Until all state judges are chosen on the basis of merit rather than for their political connections, the citizens of Rhode Island will risk renewed embarrassment and outrage," West said.

Back in action, the coalition demanded creation of an independent commission to find and screen candidates for nomination to the Supreme Court and other Rhode Island courts. Bills to establish this merit-selection panel—which would replace a process controlled by the legislature—had failed in the 1992 and 1993 sessions of the General Assembly. Perhaps not surprisingly: in the summer of 1993, all five Supreme Court justices had served in the Assembly.

As the fall of 1993 progressed, events moved rapidly. With RIght Now! planning its latest campaign and the House accepting a resolution of impeachment against Fay, *The Providence Journal* on October 1 reported further malfeasance: the chief justice had attempted to use the power of his office to dispose of speeding tickets written to his brother-in-law and others.

One week later, Fay resigned.

As Thanksgiving and then Christmas approached, Fay was convicted of the ethics charges and sentenced to a year's probation and ordered to pay $3,000 in fines; was indicted on a charge of obstructing justice, a felony; was sued, along with Smith, by the state for more than $36,000 that allegedly was illegally spent; and was indicted, together with Smith, on another felony count that alleged they used state money for personal expenses.

On April 29, 1994, Fay, "looking gaunt and troubled," *The Journal* reported, pleaded guilty to all criminal charges he faced and was handed a five-year suspended prison sentence and placed on five years of probation. A convicted felon now, he surrendered his law license. Smith was later fined $1,000.

The Journal's investigative stories, capped by the masterful July 25, 1993 report "The Making of an Empire: Chief judge, top clerk reside over network of high-priced patronage," would earn the newspaper the 1994 Pulitzer Prize for Investigative Reporting. It was a year of intense competition for the prize, with *The New York Times'* Jane Fritsch and Dean Baquet, now the paper's executive editor, among the finalists.

On the eve of the 1994 legislative session, Hassenfeld returned to the State House rotunda on December to deliver another sharp rebuke—and issue another call to arms.

It was December 16, 1993.

In a speech that elicited deafening applause, Hassenfeld said state residents had again been "sold out by power, greed, and corruption." The words of Lincoln Steffens nine decades before could almost be heard in the background.

"Our agenda this time cuts to the very soul of our democracy," Hassenfeld said. "I am talking about the members of our judiciary and the flagrant abuse and embarrassment that we, as Rhode Islanders, have been subjected to."

Hassenfeld pledged his energy to the new battle: for a merit-based process to select all state judges. Governor Sundlun was behind the proposal.

"While no system is absolutely apolitical," Sundlun said, "other states that utilize merit-selection find that nominees to the bench are chosen on the basis of training, experience and temperament. Merit selection broadens the pool of qualified nominees and significantly diminishes the role of politics in the judicial selection process."

A year later, in December 1994, when Hassenfeld invited RIght Now! members to dinner at Hasbro headquarters, victory was celebrated. By a 211,394-to-92,294 margin, voters in the November general election had agreed to amend the constitution to establish judicial merit selection; the measure was approved by a majority of voters in every Rhode Island city and town. Less overwhelmingly but still encouragingly, voters had approved a second amendment reducing the size of the General Assembly (starting in 2003) and raising the part-time lawmakers' pay from $5 a day to $10,000 a year, another deterrent to graft, or so it was hoped.

"I'm thrilled you're all here," Hassenfeld said. "We've accomplished things together that are truly historic." Then he joked: "This is an astonishing assembly. I hope that you'll remember that there are only thirteen shopping days left until Christmas." During the holiday season, Hassenfeld never passed on the opportunity to make the old joke.

Rhode Island had been cleaned, if not quite purified. Hassenfeld's work was not done. New ethical transgressions and criminality would prompt him, with others, to resume the fight—a fight that would continue to the present day.

Even Hassenfeld's mother, ordinarily spare with praise, expressed admiration.

"He is thoroughly involved and he only gets involved in those things he cares very much about," she told this author in 1995. "He wants Rhode Island to have clean politics. He feels as if the state is killing itself because of what it's doing, driving out industry and doing all kinds of terrible things, very involved in philanthropy and the things he is involved in he cares very much about. Everything he does he cares very much about but he is very multifaceted."

Sylvia said: "The man is amazing. But I keep telling him he has to learn to say no. He must be more focused. He would take on the world if he could."

But Hassenfeld could not say no, though others besides his mother also urged him to. Speaking with this author in 1994, he stressed again the connection to those who went before him, and a commitment that went beyond making tax-deductible contributions to charity.

"My family has always been involved in the community and that's probably heredity or genes," he said. "If you go back to my grandfather's time or my dad's time, my brother, everybody was involved in trying to make the community better. It's almost as if 'why complain if you're not going to do anything about it and you always expect someone else to do it?' If you're not willing to get your hands dirty, you know, or be involved, why should anyone else?

"You can't always expect the other person to do something and if we [ever had] a total breakdown of society here, then no one is going to want to live here or work here. There is not going to be as decent an education system. There are not going to be decent support systems. Look -- we need good medical care. We need good education. We need a good fire department. We need a good police department."

Corporations, not just individuals, were morally obligated, too, Hassenfeld believed.

"To be a company going forward into the 21st century, you not only have to be well run and profitable and be a growth company, but you must be socially responsible," he said. "You must do things that are positive forces."

CHAPTER SIX

❧

DREAMING

PART ONE: STAR POWER, LITERALLY

On the day before the May 1997 release of *The Lost World: Jurassic Park,* Alan Hassenfeld sat in an auditorium with many of his Hasbro employees and watched a sneak preview of the film. His reaction could have been that of the millions of kids—child and grownup kids—who would flock to theaters to see *The Lost World,* which would gross $90 million in its opening weekend, largest opener of the year, on its way to a worldwide box office of $618 million. From theaters, the crowds would flock to restaurants and stores to indulge in food, Hasbro toys and tie-in products galore.

"Excellent! Spectacular!" Hassenfeld said when the credits rolled.

And those were the prospects as well for the many companies that had a piece of *The Lost World,* sequel to 1993's *Jurassic Park,* which with a global gross of $1 billion was history's all-time biggest commercial success until *Titanic,* which would do $2.1 billion worldwide.

Backed by Universal's $250-million marketing campaign, *The Lost World* had attracted JVC, Burger King and Mercedes Benz as tie-in partners. Tropicana and Timberland Co., which had never tied onto a film before, were on board. So were Hamburger Helper, Betty Crocker and General Mills, which put Jurassic Park Crunch cereal on grocers' shelves. Sega introduced *Lost World* pinball and arcade-video machines. Topps Comics published a four-part series. Kodak marketed stationery and photo albums, and Hershey sold dinosaur chocolate bars. Universal projected that the partners collectively could see profits exceeding $1 billion.

"If kids liked Jurassic 1, this is a better movie," Hassenfeld said as he was leaving the sneak preview. "More dinosaurs, more action. The toys will do very well."

Thirteen-year-old Jack Capobianco confirmed that they would.

"Awesome," he said after watching *The Lost World* on opening day, which played on three screens at the Rhode Island cineplex where he went.

"Way better than the first," said his friend Dean Perticig, also 13.

Ten-year-old Ricky Goff, whose parents had pulled him from school early so he could watch *The Lost World,* concurred.

"Cool," the boy said. "Better than the first."

"More scenes that make you jump," his father agreed.

The toys?

"I have a couple of dinosaurs," Ricky said.

"We're going to have to get more varieties of them now," his father said.

With the master toy license, Hasbro was prepared to oblige. The company was selling the Thrasher T Rex, The Giant Attack Dino assortment, the Dino Lab Playset with Allosaurus, the Electronic Bull T Rex, and the hand-held Raptor Run electronic game, which appeared in the film. And the Velociraptor FM radio. And Lost World puzzles and games. And more.

Spielberg was no stranger to Hasbro, nor to Rhode Island. Almost immediately after finishing post-production on *The Lost World,* he had travelled to the state for nearly a month of shooting for his next film, *Amistad,* about an 1839 slave-ship mutiny that starred Morgan Freeman, Anthony Hopkins and Matthew McConaughey. He filmed extensively in Newport, and also in Providence.

The arrival of the director and his cast and crew in March 1997 created a buzz in the state, which had seen its share of A-list talent film there over the years. Robert Redford, Arnold Schwarzenegger, Dustin Hoffman, Bruce Dern and Mia Farrow were among those who had all gone before the camera in the Ocean State—but Spielberg's presence overshadowed them, even though he held no press conferences, let no outsiders on the set, nor granted an interview until the eve of his departure, when he spoke exclusively with a *Providence Journal* staff writer.

Parents kept children out of school and brought them to Newport, where Spielberg shot exterior scenes in Queen Anne Square and interiors at historic Colony House, where Rhode Island legislators had first met in pre-Revolution days. Residents reported sightings to the local paper: the director's personal purchase of a spinach pie at a coffee shop, his dinner at a pub with wife Kate Capshaw and some of their children, the family's visit to a theater, where they saw *Jungle 2 Jungle.* Broadcast outlets and newspapers kept their reporters busy.

Busy, too, was *Amistad* author David Pesci, who granted interviews and appeared at bookstores. "Without him doing this movie," Pesci said, "I would not get the level of publicity I've been enjoying the last three weeks. I've been in about 10 papers and I've been contacted by *The New York Times*. Every book signing I've gone to I've either sold out or nearly sold out."

Spielberg's daytime shoots inside Colony House attracted spectators by the hundreds, even though they were kept outside.

"He's got the magic," said one of them, Joe Burke.

"I think it's awesome," said Hassenfeld. "There's no downside to Rhode Island. This is win-win."

Spielberg spent his final moments of the Rhode Island-based production of Amistad at the State House, where Hassenfeld had launched RIght Now! in 1991. Near the House lobby where Hassenfeld had declared war on unethical behavior, the State Room with its Gilbert Stuart rendering of Washington had been made over as President Martin Van Buren's office. Between takes, Spielberg—dressed in black pants, red shirt and hiking boots, and wearing a Capitol Police cap and dark glasses—granted his only interview.

The director, grandson of Jews who immigrated from Ukraine to America at roughly the same time as Henry and Hillel Hassenfeld arrived on these shores, turned reflective, speaking of the emotional toll of making *Schindler's List*, a story of the Holocaust that won seven Academy Awards, including Best Picture and Best Director, Spielberg's first. Spielberg had spent four months in Poland in 1993 shooting the movie.

"You can imagine how we felt," he said. "Only we felt it every day for four months."

Exhausted, Spielberg took time off after completing *Schindler's List.* Then, in 1994, he founded a studio, DreamWorks SKG, with entertainment moguls Jeffrey Katzenberg and David Geffen. Having not been filming for so long since childhood, he had to return.

"I missed it terribly," he said.

But after *Schindler's List,* he wanted lighter fare.

"I didn't want to throw myself back into another emotional film. *Lost World* was the perfect popcorn hiatus… an exercise in craft," he said.

He was into preproduction when he decided to film *Amistad.*

"I had kind of vaguely heard about Amistad," when producer Debbie Allen brought him the project, Spielberg said. After listening to the story and learning of Allen's research, he decided to make it. The issues it raised shared common ground with some in *Schindler's List.*

"It was a very interesting way of getting into the story of civil rights," Spielberg said. "It's a huge moral struggle."

He closed the interview with reflections on celebrity and children, whose sense of innocence and wonder suffuse many of his films.

Hubris seemed not in his character, despite his phenomenal success.

"I've witnessed so many celebrities be so cavalier to the people on whom they depend to be so successful," he said. "I don't understand the hypocrisy... I don't have to *think* about being a nice guy. I've just sort of been this way all my life."

And children, dear, also, to Hassenfeld?

"I love kids," Spielberg said. "I've directed kids all my life."

Spielberg's first ties to Hasbro dated to 1981, when the director and Universal Pictures negotiated with several companies regarding tie-ins for the 1982 movie *E.T. the Extra-Terrestrial,* which with an eventual box office of $792 million would surpass *Star Wars* as the top-grossing film in history until *Jurassic Park* dethroned it. Hasbro won only a sliver of the *E.T.* franchise—a small line that included Color-Vue Pencil by Number and The Extra-Terrestrial Talking Phone—but the relationship had started.

Seven years later, *Who Framed Roger Rabbit,* from Disney's Touchstone Pictures and Spielberg's Amblin Entertainment, became another hit, grossing $11.2 million on its opening weekend and eventually ringing up almost $330 million worldwide. But Hasbro again had only a sliver of the merchandising, with a line of 17-inch washable dolls dressed in overalls and polka-dot tie, like the film's cartoon protagonist. The pull-string talking version model, $22 retail, spoke lines including "I know it's raining cats and dogs. I just stepped on a poodle."

Not the big leagues.

At around this time, Stephen and Alan Hassenfeld traveled to California to pitch Spielberg a line of Hasbro toys tied to the movie *Hook*, which would be released in 1991 after years of development.

"We gave a great presentation," Alan recalled. "The last product was the skunk gun for *The Lost Boys.* It had a pellet that when you shot it smelled up everything. Steven was over the moon! He loved it."

He loved brother Stephen, too, Alan recalled, but affection did not decide the license; Brad Globe, who headed Spielberg's Amblin Entertainment consumer-product division, said no. The license went to Hasbro's chief competitor, and the brothers would be glad it did.

"Thank God Mattel got *Hook,"* Hassenfeld said, "because the movie was a disaster."

It was, in the view of critics, earning a 29-percent "rotten" certification on Rotten Tomatoes, the movie-review aggregator. The domestic box office was not quite rotten, but with a gross of $119.6 million against a production budget of $70 million, it was no winner, either.

The *Hook* experience did not portend a significant relationship with Spielberg—and then Hasbro bought Tonka/Kenner with marketing genius Bruce Stein coming into the fold. With Alan Hassenfeld, Verrecchia and other Hasbro executives, Stein persuaded Spielberg and Universal that the Pawtucket company was the best place for *Jurassic Park* toys and games. License in hand, Stein knew what to do: instruct the designers to create cool toys, and, as the movie's release approached, intensify the buzz that Spielberg's latest was creating.

A tease was always a useful marketing tool, and when the line was introduced at February 1993 Toy Fair, four months before the film hit screens, only buyers were allowed access to Hasbro's *Jurassic Park* lineup.

"Out front is a jungle of rhododendron and orchids," began a newspaper reporter's account of his visit to the Hasbro showroom. "Distant sounds of a waterfall and the roar of a dinosaur can be heard. 'You are now entering the lost world of the prehistoric past,' beckons a sign by the door. But we—meaning the press—aren't going anywhere. This is the showroom for Hasbro Inc.'s new toy line based on the forthcoming Steven Spielberg movie *Jurassic Park*, and a man in African safari garb has been instructed to let no one but industry buyers pass."

The tease worked. Industry buyers pushed *Jurassic Park* toys deep into the retail chain, and when the movie debuted, the buyers that mattered most, consumers, responded. In announcing second-quarter results that July, chief financial officer O'Neill said that strong sales of Jurassic products, together with excellent performances by Nerf, Littlest Pet Shop, and Barney, had helped boost earnings by 20 percent.

"We started shipping [*Jurassic Park*] in June and the initial reaction to both products, Barney in particular, has been very favorable," O'Neill said.

Spielberg's movie continued delivering during the third and fourth quarters, and the 1994 release of the home video would provide more boost. When the numbers were tallied, *Jurassic Park* toys proved a major factor in Hasbro's record 1993 year, when revenues reached $2.7 billion, an eight-percent increase, and earnings hit $200 million.

"Despite a challenging climate, Hasbro exhibited across-the-board strength powered mostly by the domestic market," said Salomon Brothers analyst Jill Krutick.

Michael Crichton's "The Lost World" was less than a month from hitting bookstores and another rapid ascent to the top of the best-seller lists when Spielberg, well-versed in the power of the sequel, decided to travel to Hasbro headquarters.

His planned trip had been kept secret from employees, but they knew something was up when they arrived at work on Tuesday, August 15, 1995. A giant tent had sprouted in one of the parking lots, and signs with a message from Hassenfeld had been posted on Main Street, the central corridor inside the main corporate building.

"As you know," Hassenfeld's message said, "Hasbro's senior management team has been hard at work shaping a cohesive global strategy that will allow us to succeed and grow in the 21st Century. On Wednesday, Aug. 16th, we will unveil important elements of this strategic vision to you."

Rumors immediately circulated: *Sega is buying us... No, it's Microsoft... Nope, I heard they finally got the licensing for the Star Wars second trilogy...*

Few suspected an announcement about DreamWorks SKG, which had been founded ten months before.

On the morning of August 16th, the tent opened. It had been made into an air-conditioned theater, with teleprompters, cameras, and a wall of television screens on which Hasbro commercials and crowd shots and were intercut as employees awaited... whatever it was that they were awaiting. A satellite link sent a live transmission to Hasbro outposts in England, Massachusetts and Cincinnati, where Kenner was still based.

Accompanied by family members, Hassenfeld, Verrecchia and Hasbro's other top executives walked in, to loud applause. Then they took the stage.

"We had originally planned on Big Bird and Barney," said Ditomassi. "So you'll have to accept Al and me. But you know what they say.'"

"Yeah," Verrecchia said. "Shit happens!"

The crowd roared. Most of Hasbro's employees had limited contact with Verrecchia and did not often see glimpses of his humor, but here it was.

After speaking about global branding, Verrecchia introduced Hassenfeld, calling him "the heart and soul of Hasbro."

Hassenfeld began his remarks by invoking the memory of his grandfather, this immigrant who had co-founded a company with 12,500 employees now—including some in Eastern Europe

"I really do sometimes wonder," Hassenfeld said, "if my grandfather, when he traveled from Poland, would have dared to dream of Hasbro as it is today. Or if my father would have dared to dream of a $3-billion company. Or my brother, Stephen, would recognize our fast-moving, ever-changing company."

Hassenfeld restruck the global theme, then said:

"Don't you believe in dreams? In the power, the magic, the pure joy of dreams? Don't you think dreams work?"

The sounds of "A Whole New World," the Academy Award-winning song from Disney's *Aladdin*, rocked the tent.

"Dreams *do* work," Hassenfeld said. "Dreamworks—a whole new world. I love it! I mean, I dare to dream that someday I'll be able to look to my right and look to my left and there, standing on either side of me, will be the DreamWorks dream team: Steven Spielberg and Jeffrey Katzenberg. And if it hadn't been for fog on Long Island, they'd be standing here right now!"

Weather had grounded the aircraft that was to have brought Spielberg and Katzenberg to Pawtucket from Spielberg's Hamptons summer home, but a phone connection to speakers in the tent had been made.

"I can't tell you how ecstatic and excited we are about being able to join your family and having you all be a part of our family," Hassenfeld said.

A monumental union it was. Hasbro and DreamWorks had reached agreement on an exclusive, long-term alliance in which the companies would jointly develop and market products from DreamWorks interactive entertainment, TV, and movies. In contrast to the traditional licensing arrangement, in which a toy company came on board after a studio's scripts had been written and production green-lit, Hasbro would have input starting at the idea stage. In the world of children's entertainment, only Mattel's relationship with Disney was similar.

Katzenberg, a former high-ranking Disney executive, spoke of Hasbro as "the center and foundation" of his new company's consumer products division.

Spielberg spoke of the level of intimacy the new relationship offered.

"We are going to be involved in Saturday-morning television, as well as Monday through Friday script series in animation and live action," he said. "We're going to be able to ensure that the products we come up together with will have a very long shelf life."

The announcement made mainstream and industry media headlines.

"The whole entertainment side of the toy industry has become more and more important. Half of all toys now are tied to some kind of license or another," said Frank Reysen Jr., editor of New York trade magazine *Playthings*. "Entertainment is a magic word in the toy industry. It's a major coup for Hasbro."

"This is a model for the rest of the industry to look at," said an analyst, as Hasbro stock climbed, ending the week up almost two dollars a share.

In interviews for an article published in *The Providence Journal,* the principals told the story of the Hasbro-DreamWorks courtship. Hasbro arch-rival Mattel had hoped for Spielberg's hand, but old friend Hassenfeld had won it. That the two shared a certain kindness, humility, and a child's sense of wonder, unlike some of the cutthroat executives at Mattel, was a factor.

So was Hassenfeld's persistence, coupled with Verrecchia's numbers touch.

"From the minute DreamWorks was announced, Alan was on the phone with us," Katzenberg said. "Alan lobbied early on and consistently pursued it."

Said Charness: "We were certainly aggressive from the get-go. But so were they… It was definitely a mutual attraction."

Katzenberg said a decisive factor was the "very creative" and "very entrepreneurial" culture that thrived at Hasbro.

Hassenfeld told a reporter that the DreamWorks agreement ranked with the Kenner/Tonka and Milton Bradley acquisitions as Hasbro's top three historic developments.

"This relationship, as far as I'm concerned, is a marriage made in heaven," Hassenfeld said.

Katzenberg returned to California, but Spielberg was determined to make it to Pawtucket. By Friday morning, the weather had cleared and Verrecchia met the director at the Providence airport and drove him to Hasbro headquarters, where security guards kept reporters at bay. Michael Jackson's surprise visit two years before had not created such excitement.

Verrecchia welcomes Spielberg to Hasbro. (Courtesy Al Verrecchia)

With Verrecchia and Hassenfeld leading the way, Spielberg toured headquarters, signing autographs and spending time in Fun Lab, the model shop, and design centers. Then he spoke to employees crowded into the cafeteria.

"My real interest is the generic toy line, the products that are what they are because they're created from your imaginations and our imaginations," Spielberg said. "They start from the ethers and they become standard operating childhood equipment in every home in the world. The original screenplay as a filmmaker interests me even more than the adapted novel—and the original toy, as a father of five, interests me more than the movie spinoffs. So I hope we'll be doing a lot of original toymaking together."

Hassenfeld listed the Hasbro Children's Hospital dedication and the Dream-Works deal as his two proudest moments ever, and said he now ranked Spielberg, Katzenberg, and third DreamWorks partner Geffen among Santa's elves—he, needless to say, being Santa. Then he gave Spielberg a 12-inch doll made with a likeness of the director's head on a fatigue-clad body of G.I. Joe.

"It's interesting because now I can see what I would have looked like had I served in the Vietnam War," Spielberg said. "And I looked pretty good! Thank you very much!"

After his tour, Spielberg and Hassenfeld emerged to speak with reporters.

"We're kindred spirits," Hassenfeld said.

"I finally met someone who's having more fun than I am at what he does," Spielberg said.

"What you need to make toys is to be young at heart and playful and creative," Hassenfeld said. "We're creating a road map of the future here. And that map is only as limited as our imagination."

Six months later, Spielberg joined Hassenfeld again, although not literally: putting aside the possibility that at some future date he might want to conduct business with the maker of Barbie, he publicly backed Hasbro during Mattel's hostile takeover attempt.

In a letter to Hassenfeld signed also by Katzenberg and Geffen and released to the press, Spielberg wrote that "you have our personal support in your bid to keep Hasbro independent... We believe it is in everyone's best interest that there should be two major independent toy companies competing on a worldwide basis. As a significant stakeholder in Hasbro, we also believe the greatest value to shareholders will be realized if Hasbro remains independent."

The year 1998 found Spielberg back in Rhode Island, for the graduation of stepdaughter Jessica Capshaw from Brown University. Six years later, another connection between the state and Spielberg was made when, on July 23, 2004, Hasbro announced that Spielberg would be executive producer of a movie it was developing with DreamWorks and Paramount Pictures.

The movie was *Transformers* -- the blockbuster that made Hasbro history, not the dud released in 1986, the company's first effort to bring the toy to the big screen.

An offshoot of *The Transformers* TV series that ran from 1984 to 1987, *The Transformers: The Movie*, an animated feature film, had been released in 1986. Despite an A-list voice cast that included Robert Stack, Leonard Nimoy, Scatman Crothers, Casey Kasem, and the legendary Orson Welles in one of his final roles—and Margaret Loesch as executive producer—*The Transformers: The Movie* became *The Transformers: The Bomb.* Made for $6 million, its box office was just $5.6 million.

In 1986, *Transformers*' big-screen future seemed dim.

Until Spielberg became fascinated with Decepticons and Autobots, that is.

A year after Hasbro announced it was trying again to bring its robotic characters to the cineplex, with a Hollywood production of a movie simply titled *Transformers*, the company revealed on July 23, 2004, that Spielberg had signed on as executive producer. Michael Bay, director of the hit movies *Armageddon* and *Pearl Harbor,* was already signed to helm the film, and Spielberg's involvement left Brian Goldner, Hasbro Toy president, effusive.

"We are truly fortunate to have the best talent in the entertainment industry on board for the Transformers movie and are excited at the opportunities this powerful collaboration will bring to the property," Goldner said. "The stars are truly aligned."

They were—for *Transformers* and the toy division chief alike.

Goldner was the relative new kid on the block—based in Pawtucket since early 2000, when Hassenfeld and Verrecchia had moved him from Tiger Electronics, an Illinois-based Hasbro subsidiary, where he had been executive vice president and chief operating officer. Goldner overflowed with energy and ideas, and by 2004, it seemed likely that one day he would succeed Verrecchia, CEO now that Hassenfeld, still chairman of the board, was moving toward full-time involvement as a philanthropist and social-justice advocate.

Goldner had been at Hasbro just two years when he began pitching Transformers to Hollywood studios, with his conviction that the characters could be the next *Spider-Man* movie franchise—the failure of 1986's *The Transformers: The Movie* notwithstanding. The studios weren't buying it, at first. Goldner later recalled encountering *Spider-Man* producer Avi Arad at lunch in Los Angeles. "He told me that I shouldn't embarrass myself because it was going to be impossible to execute," Goldner remembered.

Spielberg and Bay saw things differently.

The screenwriters got to work and the movie was cast, with Shia LaBeouf, Megan Fox, Jon Voight, Josh Duhamel, Grammy-nominated singer and songwriter Tyrese Gibson, and Rachael Taylor, a native of Tasmania, Australia, among others.

With all but the final editing tweaks on *Transformers* completed, Spielberg tele-visited Rhode Island on March 31, 2007, addressing a crowd of more than 1,200 at the Rhode Island Convention Center for a Hasbro Children's Hospital fundraiser.

"Rhode Island is lucky to have a world-class hospital like Hasbro Children's Hospital," Spielberg said, on a videoconference screen. After telling attendees that "being a dad is my most rewarding job," he rolled the *Transformers* trailer.

He drew applause, as did Rhode Island Hospital president Dr. Joseph Amaral, when he announced that the gala had raised almost $1 million for Hasbro Children's.

Hasbro continued to put *Transformers* to philanthropic purpose three months later, when Goldner, who had been promoted to chief operating officer in 2006, hosted a special Rhode Island premier a week in advance of the film's opening weekend. Proceeds from the $75-a-ticket evening—more than $50,000 total—benefitted Hasbro Children's Hospital, Adoption Rhode Island, The Rhode Island Community Food Bank and the Autism Project of Rhode Island.

"In the spirit of the *Transformers* brand, this exclusive premiere offers the opportunity to leverage the excitement around the film to help make a positive change in the lives of children in our home state," Goldner said. "We are delighted to be able to offer Rhode Islanders a sneak peek of the movie and a chance to help four wonderful organizations."

More than 600 guests attended the Rhode Island premier. In an interview, Goldner discussed Spielberg's early interest in the property, saying "Spielberg told us that he was a fan of the toy," Goldner said. Verrecchia said "it's a dream come true for fans. I hope the guests think that this event was what it was: cool, something special and global."

Cool, special—the presence of stars Taylor and Gibson had assured that.

Gibson, who had performed several times at the nearby Dunkin' Donuts Center, attended dressed in a summer suit and black loafers, and wearing diamond earrings. "Every time I come here, I find Providence to have good energy," he said.

Taylor, wearing a metallic sliver dress and white pumps, said the city reminded her of her hometown of Launceston, Tasmania, "a city with a small-town vibe," she said. "Providence is smart, comfortable, and hip. I liked going into the stores and meeting the designers and artists."

Gibson said when he heard the evening was not merely a premier but also a fundraiser, he decided immediately to come. "I'm here because I wanted to take this opportunity to give back,'" he said. "I'm hoping to talk to some of the kids here tonight and make a difference."

PART TWO: GET A LIFE, JERRY

One year after 1997's *The Lost World* opened, Hasbro had brought more star power to Pawtucket. With the acquisition of privately held Seattle-based Wizards of the Coast, for $325 million in cash, the company had secured the rights to electronic games, as well as plush toys and action figures based on Pokémon, the Japanese megahit that had rung up some $4 billion in sales. It was Hasbro's first major tie-in to Nintendo, the company that had emerged from the 1980s video game craze, in which many companies had perished, as a monolith. Nintendo meant Game Boy and The Legend of Zelda. It meant Super Mario Bros. The argument could be made that every American boy owned a Nintendo product, or wanted to.

Chairman and CEO Hassenfeld was ecstatic. Not only did the agreement promise to rank with the acquisition of Tonka/Kenner and the Jurassic franchise as one of the crowning achievements of his tenure, but Pokémon, the brainchild of Tokyo native Satoshi Tajiri, was a true child of Japan, the country where Hassenfeld became a Hasbro employee in 1969.

"Pokémon's phenomenal success in Japan demonstrates the power of this brand. We are incredibly excited to bring a wide range of Pokémon products to the rest of the world," Hassenfeld said in May 1998, when he revealed that Hasbro's Pokémon action figures, plush toys, electronic games, and other products would be on shelves in time for the holiday-shopping season. Hasbro's push would dovetail with Nintendo's autumn release of the first Pokémon Game Boy for the American market.

How could Hasbro lose?

The company could not—and did not—initially.

But if one were superstitious, one could find an omen of trouble ahead in the reactions of Japanese children watching a December 1997 episode of *Pocket Monsters*, a top-rated Pokémon cartoon TV show in Japan. Hundreds of children affected by what a medical school professor described as "photo stimulation" suffered seizures or convulsions, while others experienced confusion or headaches. All recovered—and the episode was never broadcast in America.

Still, one might wonder if the episode portended poorly.

Hassenfeld's "incredibly excited" enthusiasm for Pokémon continued through 1998 and he was similarly pleased with another addition to the Hasbro family: Teletubbies, the British preschool TV sensation that Hassenfeld had brought to America. The brand was managed by Playskool division head Meg Whitman, who also had responsibility for Mr. Potato Head. (Whitman would soon leave Hasbro for eBay, on a path that led her to Hewlett Packard after an unsuccessful campaign to become governor of California.)

One day during the week before Valentine's Day 1999, Hassenfeld hosted some 1,000 Hasbro employees attending Toy Fair for what was billed as the "World's Largest Tubby Toast" —an ode to Teletubbies characters Dipsy, Laa-Laa, Po, and Tinky Winky.

"There is much to celebrate," Hassenfeld told the showroom crowd, as they hoisted glasses of milk.

And not only the success Tinky Winky and friends had brought Hasbro. While other toy companies had seen frustrating results in the fourth quarter of 1998, Hasbro had witnessed a record 15 percent sales increase in that critical holiday-buying period, and a four-percent rise for the full year, to $3.3 billion sales. Earnings had declined somewhat in 1998—from $227.4 million to $206.4 million—but this was still a profitable performance, worthy of a toast.

And, milk glasses raised high, a chuckle or two—at the expense of Jerry Falwell, who was much on Hasbro employees' minds.

The conservative televangelist had made international headlines—and prompted widespread ridicule on both sides of the Atlantic—with the publication, during Toy Fair 1999, of an article in his *National Liberty Journal.*

"Parents Alert… Tinky Winky Comes Out of the Closet" warned mothers and fathers of the purportedly hidden dangers of the purple-colored Teletubbies character that carried a "magic bag." Where kids saw a funny friend, Falwell saw a sort of homosexual predator.

The article stated that Tinky Winky "has been the subject of debate since the series premiered in England in 1997. The character, whose voice is obviously that of a boy, has been found carrying a purse in many episodes and has become a favorite character among gay groups worldwide. Now further evidence that the creators of the series intend for Tinky Winky to be a gay role model have surfaced. He is purple—the gay pride color; and his antenna is shaped like a triangle—the gay pride symbol... These subtle depictions are no doubt intentional and parents are warned to be alert to these elements of the series."

Who knew?

"It's ridiculous," Michael Linnemann, coordinator of Baltimore's Gay and Lesbian Community Center, told the Associated Press. "It's news to the gay community. We didn't realize we had a doll. Is Barney gay too, because he's purple?" Falwell, Linnemann concluded, "is just looking for any excuse to get publicity for his cause."

Said Barry Lynn, executive director of Americans United for Separation of Church and State, "Who's Falwell going to out next, Winnie the Pooh? Or maybe, Barney; he's purple, you know... If Falwell and his fundamentalist friends had their way, there'd be nothing on the tube but TV preachers and the weather channel. I'd rather watch the 'Teletubbies' than televangelists."

Steve Rice, a spokesman for Itsy Bitsy Entertainment Co., which licensed Teletubbies in the U.S., also ridiculed Falwell. "The fact that he carries a magic bag doesn't make him gay," the spokesman said. "It's a children's show, folks. To think we would be putting sexual innuendo in a children's show is kind of outlandish."

Hasbro's O'Neill told reporters that Falwell's so-called alert had not affected Teletubbie toy sales. "Certainly, the product was well received before Jerry Falwell, and it's very well-received after Jerry Falwell," he said.

Hassenfeld's message to Falwell was short, if not sweet: "Get a life," he said.

Privately, when the minister had called him before the publicity exploded, he had told Falwell: "I wouldn't go there, I think you've crossed the line."

Falwell did not confine his absurd views to his publication. Appearing on NBC's *Today* show on February 11, he told Katie Couric that "Christians do not agree with" the notion that "little boys running around with purses and acting effeminate and leaving the idea that the masculine male, the feminine female is out, and gay is O.K."

Tinky Winky was not the only Hasbro toy ensnared in nonsense during Toy Fair 1999.

The company's 1998 acquisition of Tiger Electronics, for $335 million, had brought to Hasbro Furby, a robotic plush toy that used interactive electronics to respond to touch and speech.

Programmed to speak in its so-called native language, "Furbish," the toy with repetitive play could "learn" English; in other words, it could be trained. Modeling some of its capabilities after Tamagotchi, a hit Japanese toy sold by Bandai, Furby was the smash hit of the 1998 holiday season, rivaling the 1983 Cabbage Patch Kids and the 1996 Tickle Me Elmo crazes when demand outstripped supply, and desperate parents battled for the few toys left on shelves. Among the headline-making incidents were stampedes, arguments with fellow shoppers, and abuse of retail employees at Wal-Mart stories in Massachusetts, Illinois, Texas, and elsewhere.

But the National Security Agency saw something truly ominous in the toy.

Believing erroneously that Furby had internal recording capabilities, the NSA forbade its employees from bringing the toy onto its premises. CBS News was among the outlets that covered the story, with this report on January 13, 1999:

"In terms of sheer numbers, Furbies present a significant force. More than two million of the fuzzy owl-like creatures have infiltrated American homes with incessant chattering that delights children and aggravates adults.

"But you won't find a single Furby here at the National Security Agency, reports CBS News Correspondent Bob Orr. The U.S. satellite intelligence operation has banned Furby—in essence, accusing the toy of being a Chinese-manufactured spy, a secret-stealing bugging device capable of eavesdropping on sensitive conversations.

"The NSA, in this unclassified policy, reminded employees personal audio equipment is forbidden. 'This includes toys, such as Furbies, with built-in recorders that repeat the audio....' its policy reads.

"But there's a problem with the policy.

"'Furby has absolutely no ability to do any recording whatsoever,' says Roger Shiffman, who [heads] Tiger Electronics - the company that makes Furby.

"Shiffman says he gladly would have told the NSA that Furby has no built-in recorder if anyone from the spy agency had asked.

"'We know that Furby has artificial intelligence, we're just not sure what kind of intelligence the NSA is working with now,' Shiffman says...

"With Furby mania raging, there is no shortage of fans who believe the interactive electronic pets are nearly omnipotent.

"'I've been told that we're developing a Furby that can drive a car in the year 2000,' Shiffman says. 'We've also been told that the current Furby has the technology to launch the space shuttle. We have one woman who is absolutely insistent that her Furby sings Italian operas...'"

The London-based *Independent* newspaper also poked fun at the NSA. Columnist Andrew Marshall wrote on January 14:

"THE FURBY was one of the best-selling toys in America last Christmas. But now, the hirsute mechanical playmate has been branded a threat to national security, joining drug smugglers and arms traders as the latest target of US intelligence.

"The National Security Agency, America's equivalent of GCHQ, has banned Furbies from its premises.

"The toy mimics the speech of its owners, and gradually develops its own language. That could be a risk in a building where much of the talk is top- secret, the NSA has decided.

"In other words, having asked endearingly for a cookie, the Furby might then suggest bugging the Russian embassy and intercepting wireless traffic from the Iraqi military.

"Perhaps, in the long term, the playthings might make valuable additions to the staff of GCHQ. At least they would never go on strike."

Furby, Pokémon and Teletubbies had not carried Hasbro's banner year of 1998 alone. The acquisition of California toymaker Galoob, for $220 million, brought Hasbro deeper into the boys' and handheld-games markets and promised synergies with many of the company's existing lines. Galoob brought Micro Machines to Hasbro and was what Hassenfeld described as a "defensive acquisition." Galoob had rights to some *Star Wars* vehicles, and buying the company kept them from Mattel, which also had been bidding to buy the San Francisco-based firm.

"It's great. We're very excited. It's an exciting opportunity to make Hasbro the leading force in *Star Wars*," Charness said.

Indeed, *Star Wars* promised new riches as 1999 began. For the year, Hasbro was projecting sales of as much as $1 billion for product keyed to *Episode One: The Phantom Menace*, first of George Lucas's prequel trilogy. Hassenfeld had pushed hard for the prequel, even growing a beard and dressing as Obi-Wan Kenobi for the pitch to Lucas at his Skywalker Ranch. On a second presentation at Skywalker, he dressed as Bobba Fett.

Lesser lines packed a punch, too.

Hasbro had a piece of NASCAR with five new racing Micro Machines. Spice Girls fashion dolls sported a new look for 1999 and Pound Puppies had expanded beyond dogs to include sea creatures. Hasbro was selling Furbies, email games, interactive candy toys, and a new version of Scruples that asked adult players about ethical issues. There were Trivial Pursuit and Monopoly Millennium Editions, and anniversary editions of Candyland, Risk and Clue. And new Transformers, Barney, Batman, Tonka, Super-Soaker and Nerf toys.

Keyed to the November release of *Toy Story 2*, which featured again the voice of Don Rickles as Hasbro's iconic spud, Hasbro also was selling a Mr. Potato Head Says game and a Remote Talking Mr. Potato Head that walked and wisecracked, like the comedian.

"I think this is going to be a good year for Hasbro," Hassenfeld said.

But for the 150 workers at the company's last Rhode Island factory who had been laid off in 1998, it would not.

Announced by Hasbro on February 3, 1998, the once-mighty Central Falls plant—into which Henry and Hillel Hassenfeld had expanded their growing company in 1940—closed for good on October 2. Production of Play-Doh, its last product after

G.I. Joe manufacture had been phased out, was shifted to Milton Bradley facilities in East Longmeadow, Mass.

It was the end of Hasbro manufacturing in Rhode Island, part of a larger restructuring intended to save $350 million over five years that also saw the closing of a small Vermont factory that once made Scrabble's wooden tiles, and the shuttering of Hasbro factories in New Zealand, Mexico, and El Paso, Texas. Increasingly, China was the center of the company's production as Rhode Island, birthplace of the American Industrial Revolution, continued to shed thousands of industrial jobs across most sectors. State labor statistics told the grim story, one that would continue for years to come: At the close of 1997, there were 81,600 jobs in manufacturing in Rhode Island, a decrease of 800 in 12 months. The drop since 1987—34,700 manufacturing jobs lost—was staggering.

Rhode Island production, 1990s. (Courtesy Providence Journal)

Hassenfeld said he felt "awful" about Central Falls, telling a reporter in what was described as "an emotional interview" during which tears filled his eyes that economic forces beyond Hasbro's control had left him and Verrecchia no choice if the company were to survive.

"This is a toughie," Hassenfeld said. "We had to make a tough decision. Is it easy doing? Hell, no… [but] how long to do you continue to subsidize something?"

Said Verrecchia: "This is not the result of people who didn't do a great job. These are all very productive people who've worked long and hard for the company. It's just the competitive nature of the business and the world we live in."

In generous packages, the laid-off workers received job training, help in finding new positions and two weeks of benefits and severance pay for each year of employment, with the average worker receiving 36 weeks of severance. It was, Hassenfeld would recall, "a great severance package. We took care of our people. We helped a huge number of employees get their GED equivalency, and I believe within two years, more than 90 percent of our people had been re-employed."

Many of those laid off were immigrants, like the original Hassenfeld brothers.

"This is the only job many of them have had since they came here," said Stella Carrera, of social-service agency Project Hope/Proyecto Esperanza.

At a farewell picnic shortly before the plant closed, Tony Zarro, a Hasbro employee for more than a quarter of a century, called the gathering "the Last Supper."

"Will work for food," read a sign carried by a worker dressed as Mr. Potato Head.

PART THREE: SPUDNAPPERS

As the 1990s advanced, Hasbro's oldest icon receded from the limelight of an Idaho mayoral run, a national antismoking campaign, and a presidential fitness program starring Arnold. The 1980s TV show *Potato Head Kids* was all but forgotten. The spud seemed content once again to exist as a modest Hasbro staple enjoying modest popularity, the quiet neighbor living in the tidy little house, perhaps a grandfather now.

Enter John Lasseter, who had left Disney for Pixar Animation Studios, which had sprung from the genius of George Lucas and Apple's Steve Jobs.

Lasseter and his screenwriters wrote Mr. Potato Head into the script for *Toy Story*, about anthropomorphic toys including Woody and Buzz Lightyear, themselves destined to become cultural icons. With Jobs serving as executive producer and Randy Newman composing the music, Lasseter hired Tom Hanks, Tim Allen, John Ratzenberger, Annie Potts, and Nathan Lane, together with Rickles and others, to voice the characters.

The appearance of Hasbro's iconic character came as a surprise to Alan Hassenfeld. Disney had not informed Hasbro that Mr. Potato Head would have a starring role, he said.

More egregious still, the movie company wanted a royalty from the toy company for featuring the spud.

"We said, 'You know, guys…' " Hassenfeld recalled.

Disney received no royalty.

Toy Story—*Toy Story 1*, it would to be called after the first sequel—played on screens in dozens of countries including Poland, Japan, Estonia, Russia, Israel, and Uruguay and Kazakhstan and generated $373 million box office from its release on November 22, 1995.

That success awakened the toy, and not only at the checkout counter. Once more, the popular culture—and the political world—wanted Pot Head.

Toy Story remained on screens through September 1996, when the League of Women Voters named Mr. and Mrs. Potato Head as mascots for its Get Out the Vote drive that year. League president Becky Cain posed with the couple, urging voters to "head to the polls." A cute turn of phrase, befitting a cute toy, although what effect it had in the ballot booth was unknown. The League never again featured Pot Head, but a photo lives on at the lwv.org archives.

In Rhode Island, the toy returned to glory starting in March 1996 with a Mr. Potato Head display at Green State Airport in Warwick that was part of a marketing campaign featuring Hasbro, pen-maker A.T. Cross, defense firm Textron, and other Rhode Island-based companies. "Their hope: That business leaders and tourists will remember them after a visit to the Ocean State," wrote *The Providence Journal*. The displays coincided with completion of a new terminal, and the arrival of a new major carrier, Southwest Airlines, into the airport.

Two months later, a human-size Mr. Potato Head marched through the streets of Middletown and Newport with Ronald McDonald and bagpipers, floats, Clydesdale horses, and some 4,000 uniformed officers during the Aquidneck Island National Police Parade. Three months after that, the toy amused spectators watching "Roar on the River," a Formula-One powerboat race staged on the Seekonk River, tidal mouth of the Blackstone.

And in October, Pot Head marched again, in Providence's Columbus Day parade, led by Cianci, who was back in office. Potato Head already was a fixture of the Fourth of July parade in Bristol, where Hassenfeld kept his summer home.

A year passed, more or less quietly—and then Burger King, mindful of *Toy Story's* popularity and doubtless aware that Lasseter was deep into development of a sequel, bought the rights to use Mr. Potato Head in a French-fry war with rival McDonald's. The campaign generated coast-to-coast media attention.

"Burger King, which has taunted McDonald's for months with a successful Big Mac clone called Big King, is shifting the focus from burger wars to spud wars as it unveils ads for its new, crunchier fries, featuring the 45-year-old toy character Mr. Potato Head," *The Los Angeles Times* reported on December 10. "Burger King insiders said Tuesday Mr. Potato Head will start a 45-city tour Thursday." *The New York Times* provided further detail: "Among the television commercials Burger King will begin broadcasting next week is one intended to appeal to blacks," a spokesman said. "The spot shows the singer Isaac Hayes and Mr. Potato Head at a piano. Another commercial is aimed at Hispanic audiences, also featuring Mr. Potato Head and a play on the Spanish word for potato: papa."

But in Rhode Island, things turned troublesome when, three days before Christmas 1997, thieves stole a five-foot-tall Mr. Potato Head standee from a Burger King restaurant in Providence. The manager told police she saw a man loading the standee into a minivan and roaring off. The man—and an accomplice—were caught and charged with larceny.

In a state with a long history of criminal behaviors, this was a new twist.

Hassenfeld was nonplussed.

At Toy Fair in February 1998, he spoke of a new Pot Head TV program—*The Mr. Potato Head Show,* set to premiere that September—and of *Toy Story 2,* by then on course for release in late 1999. Showing off a new interactive Mr. Potato Head toy that told dozens of knock-knock jokes, Hassenfeld wise-cracked about his longtime fellow-traveler.

"Mr. Potato Head is giving me problems," he said. "I mean his ego—between being picked for Burger King, now going on television, and *Toy Story 2* coming out in December '99 and he'll have a role…"

The Mr. Potato Head Show lasted just 13 episodes, disappearing in early 1999 after posting low ratings, despite being broadcast on the Fox Kids network. The puppet format had proved a poor fit for the toy, although the supporting characters had playful (if bizarre) names, including Johnny Rotten Apple, Dr. Fruitcake, Queenie Sweet Potato, Miss Licorice Lips, Mr. Happy Whip, Ham Monster, Baloney, Mr. Giblets and Canny, a dog-food-can canine.

The show's demise took little sheen off the toy's post-*Toy Story* glory, however—certainly not in its home state, where, not long after the last episode aired, the governor presided over the unveiling of a $250,000 campaign promoting Rhode Island as a place for meeting planners to meet. Paid for by the Newport County Convention & Visitors Bureau and the Greater Providence Warwick Convention & Visitors Bureau, the *Rhode Island: Meet here for the fun of it* marketing blitz featured…

Mr. Potato Head as ambassador.

"We've all seen our children enjoy putting the pieces of Mr. Potato Head together. Now Mr. Potato Head is bringing two of our state's convention bureaus together to show the world all that Rhode Island has to offer," Governor Lincoln Almond said at the *Meet here for the fun of it* rollout, in the Hasbro headquarters' cafeteria, where a model in a Potato Head costume circulated, and potato puns were featured.

The campaign included industry advertising and a presence at trade shows. Hasbro donated licensing rights to Pot Head and other brands and distributed more than $100,000 in Potato Head and other products. Officials had built hype for the campaign by mailing a Potato Head body to some 2,000 meeting planners around the country, followed by the mailing of another part—tongues, eyes, arms—each week until the grand announcement. Recipients were asked to submit a photo featuring the toy. Many did, including a planner who cut the image of her husband out of their wedding picture, replacing it with Mr. Potato Head.

Pleased with the meeting-planner campaign, Rhode Island officials and Hassenfeld and his team decided Pot Head should serve as the centerpiece of larger efforts to promote Rhode Island as a "fun family" tourist destination.

Let the games begin.

They did, in early 2000, with Hasbro's announcement that it would offer people-size Potato Heads to worthy organizations around the state. The timing was right: *Toy Story*

2, which had opened on November 19, 1999, still played on screens on its climb to a global box office of almost a half-billion dollars. Spuds were back in the public consciousness.

The inspiration for this latest Potato Head twist was Chicago, where the "Cows on Parade" public art show set off what was described as "cow mania" —a phenomenon that helped draw an estimated additional million visitors to the city in the summer of 1999.

The brainchild of a Swiss man, Walter Knapp, who had debuted the concept in his native land the year before, Chicago's Cows on Parade included hundreds of forty-pound, lifelike cow models in various poses that businesses purchased for prices varying from $2,500 to more than $10,000—then dressed, painted or accessorized in fun themes and placed throughout the city. According to the Chicago Office of Tourism, the cow show helped generate as much as $200 million in new revenue during that summer of 1999. Plus, national and international media attention that motivated officials in other cities. Cows on Parade spread to other American cities including Denver, and to Spain, France, Australia and Argentina, among other countries.

Cows could be cute, but Pot Head had nearly a half century of proven charm.

Partnering with Rhode Island's tourism bureaus and the state Tourism Division, Hasbro in February 2000 invited business and others to participate in the "Rhode Island the Birthplace of Fun" campaign. For $3,500, a sponsor could buy a Mr. or Mrs. Potato Head statue and custom-decorate it within certain guidelines.

"It was basically carte blanche, within a measure of decorum because we didn't want to have the Foxy Lady Potato Head. Not happening," Charness said. The Foxy Lady was a strip club in Providence.

Charness announced the campaign in a February 3 press release, quoting state tourism director David DePetrillo, who said "our aim is to have millions of families become aware of Rhode Island as a fun place to visit as a direct result of the regional and national publicity generated by this imaginative approach to tourism marketing." Charness had his own fun, saying the campaign with its "bumper crop" of statues was "far from 'half-baked.' " Alerting the media to the upcoming official launch, he wrote: "Keep 'your eyes peeled' for 'what's cropping up in March: a special State House 'induction' ceremony when Governor Almond will officially recognize Mr. Potato Head as Rhode Island's Family Travel Ambassador."

Dozens of businesses, schools, civic groups and local governments purchased the undecorated the six-foot-tall Fiberglass Potato Heads (anchored by a 600-pound concrete base), and then, employing artists, created characters including "Couch Potato," displayed at the Providence Children's Museum; "Edgar Allen Poe-tato," Rhode Island Convention Center; "Fred the Friendly Fisherman," the South County Tourism Office; "The Independent Potato," a bronzed imitation of the Independent Man statue that tops the State House, in downtown Providence; "The Butterfly Queen," Hasbro

Children's Hospital; "Spud Light," Beacon Mutual Insurance; " 'Meet' & Potatoes," Newport Marriott; and the "Italian Potato Chef," outside Providence's Angelo's Restaurant, where signed photographs of celebrity diners hang on the walls. The Original Mr. Potato head was placed outside Hasbro headquarters in Pawtucket, where, lovingly maintained, it still stands today.

In the March 2000 "swearing-in" ceremony on the Rhode Island State House steps, Almond, Hassenfeld and others posed with some of the statues for photographs and stories that the wire services sent around the country. State Department of Economic Development spokesman John Martin's phone rang incessantly, as he granted interviews to TV and radio stations and newspapers coast-to-coast. "He is a native son," Martin said of Pot Head. "His success is in some part Rhode Island's... We see him as someone worthy of being a Rhode Island travel ambassador."

He did prove his worth. *Pittsburgh Post-Gazette* Staff Writer Marlene Parrish was among the out-of-towners who brought the ambassador's message home.

"A few weeks ago, I attended the annual conference of the International Association of Culinary Professionals" in Providence, Parrish wrote. "We food professionals are used to food themes greeting us in the host city, but we were unprepared for the sight of Mr. Potato Head clones all over town. The huge toy figures, a favorite of the nursery school set, greeted us in front of the hotel and at the door of the convention center, and stood guard on street corners. We were told they are all over the state, each dressed in artsy-themed designer outfits that would make Barbie jealous."

Hasbro employees, the memory of Mattel's hostile takeover attempt still fresh, could appreciate the jab.

"By the looks of it," Parrish continued, "they picked an easy row to hoe. Didn't we all have a Mr. Potato Head in the house either for ourselves or for our kids and grandkids to play with? If the idea of multiple barnyard figures in an urban setting sounds vaguely familiar, there's a good reason. It is the grandson of a related promotional inspiration, the famous cow sculptures of Switzerland and Chicago... Like the Chicago cows that milked every publicity ploy, Rhode Island's Mr. Potato Heads are going for the gold. They too are deeply indebted to puns and fun-by-association. The most obvious is the 'Couch Potato.' "

Parrish could not resist a few puns of her own.

"This is no half-baked idea," she wrote. "His a-peel has always been intergenerational... Sources say that should anyone try to vandalize the Mr. Potato Heads, there's a M*A*S*H unit ready to repair them."

Parrish even managed a swipe at 1992 vice-presidential candidate Dan Quayle, who had become the butt of a long-running joke when he misspelled "potato" during a sixth-grade spelling bee at a New Jersey school in the late spring of 1992.

"Dan Quayle was asked how he liked the potato promotion," Parrish wrote. "But as yet, he hasn't spelled out his position."

Hassenfeld was pleased to lend Potato Head as tourism ambassador—and source of a fresh round of potato cleverisms—but the campaign also served a cause. A portion of the proceeds from the $3,500 fee for each statue was dedicated to Kids Cafe, a national group whose local affiliate, the Rhode Island Community Food Bank program, provides free, healthy dinnertime meals to needy children who qualify for free or low-cost school lunches.

"A program like this is so wonderful," Charness told reporters. "It's a win for the state because it's really going to help bring people in. It's a win for Hasbro, taking something we love and making it that much more known, and it's a win for the kids of Rhode Island because the Kids Cafe is going to benefit."

Two decades later, *Rhode Island Monthly,* the Ocean State's magazine of record, recalled the campaign in its March 2019 issue with a page of photographs of some of the Potato Heads that remained—and the obligatory punning caption.

Copyright permission granted, Rhode Island Monthly Communications, Inc., 2019

No one benefitted from the vandals who struck just days after the Potato Head statues began appearing around Rhode Island in the spring of 2000.

It could have been predicted.

Vandals of the graffiti sort had long prospered in the state. Their defacing of public and private property was so pervasive that police departments had opened graffiti hotlines, and at least one, Providence, installed anti-graffiti cameras. The General Assembly passed a law prohibiting sales of spray paint to minors, with a $500 fine for each infraction.

It wasn't political crime, but graffiti *was* crime—and the state's most prominent political criminal, Providence Mayor Cianci, in 1993 had seized on it as another opportunity to satisfy his appetite for publicity, with a nod to the common good.

One day that October, Cianci summoned the press to a grocery parking lot, where a truck that was a frequent target had recently been spray-painted. Dressed in an orange jumpsuit that matched a "graffiti-buster" city van painted in the same bright color, Cianci, joined by citizens and two mounted police officers and their horses, announced a new campaign.

"We are rallying all of our forces to aggressively rid the city of graffiti," the mayor said. "Graffiti isn't art. It's vandalism… a crime… And we're going to make sure that the criminals are arrested. We're driving home the message and we're driving it home hard. There is nothing beautiful about graffiti."

The issue was gold for the man who had disparaged Hassenfeld as a member of the "lucky sperm club"—Hassenfeld, a man who had led a campaign against crime and who spent his money on worthy causes, not hawked a "Mayor's Own Marinara Sauce" intended to raise money that would be "Benefiting Providence School Children," but in fact contributed only three dollars to that cause from 2009 to 2012, according to an Associated Press investigation.

So, yes, an observer of Rhode Island culture might have predicted the fate of some of the Mr. Potato Head statues constructed for the "Birthplace of Fun" tourism campaign. No sooner had the Newport County Convention and Visitors Bureau erected their "Hospitality Spud," vandals struck: Pot Head's nose was ripped off and his body was spray-painted.

"We hope he gets well soon," bureau president Robert Rosenberg said.

He didn't: Two weeks later, police arrested a man for tearing off one of Hospitality Spud's arms. At about the same time, vandals ripped both arms off "Mr. Potato Head Bulb," a statue near Providence's nationally renowned Trinity Repertory Theater sponsored by an electric utility. A month later, in mid-May, "Wannabee Surfer," which welcomed visitors to the town of Narragansett's historic seaside center, lost his ear, eyebrow, nose and surfboard to vandals; and in Providence, Potato Head Chef, outside Angelo's Restaurant, a dining institution, lost his right arm.

In the most widely publicized vandalism, a secret group of Brown students who called themselves "Carmen Sandiego" managed to unbolt the unnamed Potato Head outside *The Providence Journal's* headquarters, two blocks from City Hall.

A *Journal* reporter could not resist a pun.

"The spudnappers are on the loose," her story began.

The copy desk could not resist, either.

"All eyes peeled for stolen spud sculpture," the *Journal* headline read. "Mr. Hot Potato."

The story related how, at about 3:25 a.m. on May 15, an observer spotted two unidentified young men unbolting Pot Head and loading him into a U-Haul truck. The person called police, and when Patrolman Amy Mello arrived the crime scene, she found a note:

"Don't worry, you'll get it back."

Detective work brought no results, only threats of prosecution, but the thieves were unintimidated. Less than 12 hours after the abduction, Brown security guards found the stolen spud on the college green. A student later reported seeing two masked men carrying the statue, covered by a white tarpaulin, and unveiling it in the early afternoon before fleeing.

Eventually, vandalism faded from "Birthplace of Fun" coverage, supplanted by headlines of national renown and significantly increased tourism in the Ocean State. In 2000, revenues from travel and tourism surpassed $3 billion for the first time, reaching $3.3 billion. The number of people who visited the state for leisure, conventions or business increased more than 16 percent, to an estimated 15.7 million travelers.

The overall success of the Potato Head campaign inspired Hasbro to seek legislative and gubernatorial approval for production of fund-raising Potato Head license plates. Half of the $40 fee from those buying one would be donated to the Rhode Island Community Food Bank, and Hasbro would cover the costs of design and manufacture.

The idea originated in Indiana, home of *Garfield* cartoonist Jim Davis; Indiana had sold Garfield license plates, with proceeds donated to a public-education fund. Hassenfeld enjoyed a relationship with Davis, having granted him and collaborator Brett Koth permission to draw a Mr. Potato Head comic strip that debuted in the summer of 2001, in the afterglow of *Toy Story 2*.

At Hasbro's request, Rhode Island Senate Majority leader William V. Irons introduced a Pot Head plate bill in early 2002, the 50th anniversary of the toy. Irons waxed nostalgic in supporting the legislation, saying "I remember when the toy first came out; I remember the novelty of it, and it was very popular." These many years later, he said, "I have grandchildren who love it, and I like playing Mr. Potato Head with them."

The General Assembly passed the bill and the Mr. Potato Head plate was unveiled at a State House ceremony on August 22. The design was intriguing: an original Mr. Potato Head holding a Food Bank sign on the left, with a "Help End Hunger" message on the bottom.

Irons presided over the ceremony, which, predictably, drew widespread coverage, and the gratitude of Food Bank executive director Bernie Beaudreau, one of Rhode Island's leading social-justice and volunteerism leaders. The plates, he said, "will remind many more people that ending hunger is not only a possibility, but a necessity. With all the phenomenal capability that we have as a country and a state, all the wealth that we have and all the enormous amounts of food we have that's just wasted, there's really no excuse for hunger."

Said Charness: "This is all about doing a good deed and trying to raise awareness and money for the Rhode Island Community Food Bank."

Not every citizen agreed.

In a letter to the editor, one curmudgeon wrote: "The soon-to-be-released Rhode Island license plate featuring Mr. Potato Head should reaffirm to every motorist in the country the mindset of Rhode Island politicians. Of all the slogans the politicos might have adopted ('Seacoast State, 'Golfing Wonderland,' 'Land of Roger Williams'), they pick a potato. And to top it all off, the lower third of the plate reads, 'Feed the Hungry.' Why not go the rest of the way and call it the 'Meat-and-Potato State.' Duh!! Anyone else share the embarrassment of this loony approach?"

Few did. Most agreed with the spirit expressed in letter to the editor from a woman responding to the grump: "I have ordered the Mr. Potato Head Rhode Island license plate, because part of the money will be donated to the Rhode Island Community Food Bank! I'm sorry some [letter] writers are embarrassed about giving food to the needy and putting a smile on my grandchildren's faces when they see the new plate."

Hassenfeld smiled with them and ordered a Potato Head plate for his "HH 11" registration, which he had inherited from his grandfather, Henry Hassenfeld. Charness jumped in, with his "Wayno" plate. When the campaign ended, more than 2,000 plates had been sold, raising $45,000 for the Food Bank.

If further evidence were needed of the unbreakable bond between Hassenfeld and Pot Head, it came on May 22, 1993, during commencement exercises at Roger Williams University.

In addressing the graduates, Brown University President Vartan Gregorian spoke of philanthropy, declaring that "service to the neighborhood and the nation is not solely the product of altruism but the duty of free men and women."

And then honorary degrees were conferred, on Gregorian, Rhode Island Supreme Court Justice Donald F. Shea, *Providence Journal* publisher Stephen Hamblett and Hassenfeld, who, the paper reported, "got a loud cheer from the graduates when he was described as the maker of Monopoly, Nerf balls, and Mr. Potato Head."

This was not Hassenfeld's first honorary degree, nor would it be his last. The first had been in 1985, when Bryant University conferred a Doctor of Humanities degree. In 1994, he would receive an honorary Doctorate of Business from Johnson & Wales University. More honorary degrees would follow: from Ireland's Waterford Institute of Technology in 2004; from Rhode Island College, also in 2004; from Salve Regina University, in 2008, when he was the principal speaker at graduation; the University of Hartford, in 2009; the Fashion Institute of Technology, in 2010; and the University of Rhode Island, in 2011.

In his address to the Salve Regina University Class of 2008, Hassenfeld urged graduates to be generous, live creatively, accept responsibility for one's own behaviors, and do all they could to "help make a better world for children."

And always, give back.

"We can never truly enrich ourselves unless we enrich others," Hassenfeld said. "Dare to dream with me of a world of caring and sharing."

Hassenfeld's first major recognition for his philanthropy had come in 1982, when he was named an Outstanding Young American by the United States Junior Chamber of Commerce, or Jaycees (he repeated the next year). In 1984, he and his brother received national humanitarian awards by the Rhode Island Friends of the National Jewish Hospital/National Asthma Center. Two years after that, he and Stephen shared the Rhode Island Big Brothers "Cy" Killian Humanitarian Award, and in 1988, Alan received the Jewish Federation of Rhode Island's Never Again Award, a Holocaust remembrance-themed honor given to an individual who has labored against anti-Semitism and prejudice and racism of all kinds.

More recognition followed, starting with another that Stephen shared with him posthumously: the Southeastern New England Chapter of the National Conference of Christians and Jews' 38th Annual Brotherhood Award, in 1990. The year 1990 also marked the tenth anniversary of the Refugee Act of 1980, a measure amending a previous version in order to "revise the procedures for the admission of refugees [and] to establish a more uniform basis for the provision of assistance to refugees..." Hassenfeld was among those honored on that tenth anniversary for his work in helping persecuted and homeless foreigners to America with his acceptance of the Rhode Island Award for Outstanding Contribution in Refugee Resettlement.

Thus the roster grew, with more awards for citizenship, humanitarianism, community service and more, and induction into the Rhode Island Heritage Hall of Fame—and, in 2001, yet another refugee-related honor his grandfather and great-uncle would have appreciated, the Ellis Island Medal of Honor, from the National Ethnic Coalition of Organizations. Rosa Parks, Coretta Scott King, Muhammad Ali, Elie Wiesel, and Joe Biden are among the other recipients of the medal, awarded to "individuals who have made it their mission to share their wealth of knowledge, indomitable

courage, boundless compassion, unique talents and selfless generosity with those less fortunate," according to the coalition.

By 2008, when he turned the Hasbro chairmanship over to Verrecchia, Hassenfeld had been or still was chairman, trustee, member or leader of a diverse group of
boards, organizations, campaigns and causes, many of which he had also aided with
financial support. Operation Smile, which mobilizes surgeons volunteering their services for needy children around the world, was one. Save the Bay, the environmental
group, was another. And the International Tennis Hall of Fame, which celebrates his
favorite sport; Miriam and Hasbro Children's Hospitals; Harvard's Kennedy School;
the Warren Alpert Medical School at Brown University; Bryant University and two
alma maters: the University of Pennsylvania and Deerfield Academy. And Brandeis
University, where a conference center, a residential hall, and an innovation center devoted to research and entrepreneurship bore the Hassenfeld name.

Despite such busyness, Hassenfeld remained a force in politics. The RIghtNow!
movement had receded, but not all of the ethical issues it addressed had—notably, the
undue influence of campaign contributions on the democratic process. More than a decade before the landmark 2010 Citizens United Supreme Court decision gave the
wealthy unprecedented power to influence elections, Hassenfeld, who had spent significant amounts of his own money on local and national political campaigns, cried foul.

Back into the public arena he stepped.

The backdrop was a national controversy embroiling President Clinton at the
start of his second term. During Clinton's 1996 campaign for reelection, the Democratic
National Committee had accepted millions of dollars in illegal contributions from for-
eign sources, including individuals with "extensive ties to the People's Republic of
China," according to the House Committee on Government Reform and the Senate
Governmental Affairs Committee.

The Clinton Administration stonewalled both investigations, creating tension
between the Democratic White House and the Republican-controlled Congress in a
foreshadowing of Washington paralysis in years to come.

The campaign-contribution controversy was still young when, in April 1997,
Hassenfeld declared a personal moratorium on giving to candidacies until legitimate
reform had been enacted. He urged other individuals to join him.

"It's just gone crazy," he said of the large sums of money contributed to campaigns. "I've gone back to people, and I've said because of the times we are in right
now, until I see something happening in campaign finance, I don't think it's advisable
that I give."

Hassenfeld said he allied himself with the Campaign Reform Project, which
had been started by a retired investment banker and a former congressman Mike Synar.

He was also in sync with the Hollywood Women's Political Committee, led by stars Barbara Streisand and Tom Hanks, which had contributed millions to progressive candidates but could no longer participate in a system that "promotes the buying and selling of office."

And Hassenfeld had consulted with Philip West, his partner in RightNow!, which had initiated a similar moratorium that gathered some 2,000 signature during the organization's most active period. West had been cautious, noting that not all like-minded people, those in business especially, would be willing to speak as publicly as Hassenfeld. He favored instead support for a related effort: the petition drive that sought to gather 1,776,000 signatures by July 4th endorsing campaign finance reform. West's group, Common Cause, was hoping to contribute 30,000 Rhode Island signatures to the Independence Day drive.

"One of the problems with a moratorium is that you are really striking such a direct blow at people in high places," West said. "People are afraid that if they come out on this, until they are confident that there is going to be a big group with them, that it's very frightening, because you can really get punished."

True, but Hassenfeld was willing to take the risk. He also was transparent, disclosing that he had contributed about $150,000 of his own money to both Democrats and Republicans during the previous decade.

In the end, few joined Hassenfeld, and no reform measures were passed in Washington, as he had predicted. "If you talked to each and every individual congressperson and senator, I think they would tell you individually there should be reform," he said. "But put them together, and I just don't think anything is going to happen."

Still, Hassenfeld won praise for trying.

"Though campaign finance abuses have been mounting steadily year by year, it has by no means seemed certain that anyone would finally say, Enough.' But now, someone has: Rhode Island businessman Alan Hassenfeld," a *Providence Journal* editorial, "Hooray for Hassenfeld," began.

"Given the absence of any real progress on this issue, attacking it from the donors' side is worth a shot," the editorial ended. "Congress and the President have persistently lacked the will to pass even the most watered-down reform, so addicted have both parties become to the large sums of money that pay for campaigns. If the spigot were turned off, our national politicians might find it easier to enact new rules.

"Hasbro, the world's second largest toymaker and a Fortune 500 company, could lose some clout, or worse, if Mr. Hassenfeld holds to his principled stand, and others do not follow suit. But somebody had to act. Mr. Hassenfeld deserves credit for recognizing this, and for taking the risk."

CHAPTER SEVEN

NATURAL PROGRESSIONS

PART ONE: POCKET MONSTER

One Friday in April 1998, Hassenfeld was driving with Vivien to Deerfield Academy for a trustees' meeting when he felt uncharacteristically tired. He read little into it; he did, after all, have many preoccupations.

At dinner that evening, Hassenfeld lacked his usual appetite. He felt fatigued when he awoke on Saturday, and after the trustees had met, he forewent what ordinarily would have been an afternoon of tennis for a nap. That evening, Vivien was so concerned that she shared her fears with headmaster Eric Widmer. They arranged for Hassenfeld to be transported to a hospital.

"You've just had a heart attack," a doctor said when tests had been completed. He was sent east by ambulance to Boston's Massachusetts General Hospital, a Harvard Medical School affiliate with one of the nation's top cardiology departments. There, he underwent surgery to implant a stent to restore proper flow through a clogged artery.

Alan was 49. A heart attack had killed Merrill at age 61. Alan was not overweight like his father but he was a smoker.

The heart attack did not scare him, Hassenfeld later said, though it did motivate him to cut back on cigarettes. And his relatively young age gave him pause.

How could this happen to me? he thought. *I'm not 50 yet.*

That November, he did turn 50. Hasbro continued to hum. The year ahead would prove to be another record-breaking one, but within that success, seeds of disaster had been planted.

❧

The year 1999 was nearing its midpoint when Wall Street, once so skeptical of Hassenfeld's management abilities, praised him and Hasbro for the performance that had raised the price of company stock 135 percent during the preceding three years to more than $34 a share in mid-May.

Hasbro, said analyst Jill Krutick of Salomon Smith Barney, was "riding the top of the wave with a whole slew of hot products and a potential mega-blockbuster about to launch." That was Lucas's *Star Wars: Episode I - Phantom Menace,* which was soon to open.

But in Rhode Island, former Governor Bruce Sundlun viewed Hassenfeld in a less flattering manner, declining to forgive his former RIghtNow! ally for closing Hasbro's last manufacturing plant in Rhode Island. Speaking to a *Providence Journal* reporter whose May 16, 1999, story "Alan Hassenfeld: Cheers on Wall Street, mixed reviews in Rhode Island," Sundlun also took aim at Hassenfeld's and Hasbro's philanthropy.

"I do not think they're a significant company in Rhode Island at the present time in communal activities," Sundlun said. "I regret that Alan, representing the Hassenfeld family, and the company itself has greatly lessened its activities in, interest in, employment and community position in Rhode Island."

Hassenfeld was blindsided.

"Questioned about Sundlun's comments," *The Journal* wrote, "a visibly disturbed Hassenfeld in New York last week responded that he and Sundlun have had a falling out. He said he felt a 'sense of betrayal' when Sundlun broke a promise not to seek a third term as governor in 1994. 'He broke a pledge,' Hassenfeld said.

"Hassenfeld said he remains deeply involved in a variety of social and charitable causes in Rhode Island and worldwide. He is on the board at Bryant College, a trustee emeritus at Brown University, and chairman of the World Scholar Athlete Games. He also works with the food bank in the state, and is on the board of Refugees International..."

Hassenfeld elaborated: "As far as being a leader in Rhode Island, if being a leader means having to be in politics, I'm not a leader. As far as being a leader in the community, I would say I'm one of the first people to be socially responsible. Am I not as active? I'm active quietly. I spend a lot of time with World Scholar Athletes, the Food Bank. I'm trying to make a difference for people who have less. I'm trying to make a difference in the world."

Several prominent Rhode Islanders came to Hassenfeld's defense.

Bryant University president Ron Machtley, a former Republican Congressman, noted that "like every other company in" America, Hasbro "had to make sure they're providing good shareholder value and they're competitive in the manufacturing of their product. They're global sourcing, but they have not moved their corporate headquarters." As for Hasbro's chief executive, Machtley said "I would strenuously argue that Alan has continued to be a strong leader who has roots in Rhode Island and continues to put energies beyond most people to ensure we have a bright future."

Good-ethics ally Phil West joined in, saying "Last year, when we were engaged in the effort to get national campaign finance reform, he proposed one of the same tactics that helped in Rhode Island: a moratorium on campaign contributions until campaign reform would pass. That was a sign he still cares, and is still out there."

And in a letter to the editor following publication of the story, Lifespan chairman Bruce M. Selya, a U.S. District Court judge, took the *Journal* writer to task.

"Strikingly, your article omitted any mention of the most visible (and in many ways the most salient) of Alan's civic accomplishments: the Hasbro Children's Hospital," the judge wrote.

"This world-class institution is a model for modern pediatric care and a critical part of this state's health-care complement. I can assure you that, without the efforts of Alan Hassenfeld and the corporation that he heads, that project could not have been brought to fruition in so successful a fashion. I can also assure you that both Alan and his company continue to support the hospital in a wide variety of ways. Their sense of commitment is exceeded only by their generosity - and the children of this state are the direct beneficiaries."

Mr. Potato Head graced the cover of Hasbro's 1999 annual report, published in early 2000. The toy "continues to appeal to all generations," the copy read, no pun apparently intended. But Pot Head was not the star of the year just ended. He had been upstaged by Star Wars, Furby and Pokémon's Pikachu character, which filled most of the report's second page.

"POKéMON'S popular PIKACHU is beloved around the world," the report stated, and the character's popularity was one reason Pokémon's overall 1999 had helped push Hasbro to historic numbers.

"Hasbro had its best year ever in 1999," the report declared. "Overall, we delivered record financial results and we met or exceeded our most ambitious business objectives. Today's Hasbro is stronger than ever. The heart of our business is making great games, toys, lifestyle, and entertainment products that are enjoyed by people of all ages. Hasbro enters the 21st Century with a balanced and deep portfolio — from our popular classic board games to products with the latest technologies and everything in between. Hasbro has what it takes to succeed.

"In fact, more than half of the 66 most notable toys and games of the last century, which were identified by a leading trade publication, are ours. We believe this unmatched content, combined with our emphasis on technology, toys, and game play, will contribute to delivering the outstanding results you expect from Hasbro. Simply put, we intend to be the number-one company in the toy and game industry, the leading provider of play and fun the world over."

It was an ambition that would continue to today, with Goldner at the helm.

The report gave no hint of the troubles that awaited in the first year of the new millennium, when the Pokémon craze began to cool.

"Net revenues climbed to record levels in every quarter of 1999, and increased 28% for the year to a record $4.2 billion," the report stated. "This reflected balanced growth in core brands and key licenses in the U.S. and internationally, led by STAR WARS, FURBY, hand-held electronic games, plus a wide range of new POKéMON toys and games. We are especially pleased with the outstanding performance of our international businesses during 1999, where revenues increased 24% in local currencies and 19% in U.S. dollars.

"STAR WARS: EPISODE I: THE PHANTOM MENACE is the second highest-grossing motion picture of all time. Retail sales of Hasbro's STAR WARS toys and games were approximately $500 million (in wholesale dollars), the largest annual sales of any Hasbro product line in our history. STAR WARS is a powerful global brand with proven long-term appeal, and we are working hard with our partners to ensure its continued success for years to come. The continuing phenomenal success of FURBY — including the introduction of five foreign-language editions, FURBY limited collector editions, plus adorable interactive FURBY BABIES — underscores the powerful combination of creativity and technology embodied by our 1998 acquisition of Tiger Electronics."

The 1999 annual report mentioned what in hindsight would prove to be one of the company's most important acquisitions: Wizards of the Coast. Wizards published science-fiction and fantasy literature and sold Magic: The Gathering trading cards, which had achieved cult status—and also Pokémon cards, which were in high demand.

Hassenfeld listed Pokémon as first among the new weapons Wizards of the Coast brought Hasbro, writing "We are now leaders in the fast-growing trading card game genre thanks to our acquisition of Wizards of the Coast and their incredibly popular POKéMON trading card game. Yet they bring us so much more, including game centers and great content such as MAGIC: THE GATHERING, which is played by more than six million people worldwide. Wizards of the Coast has retained its hobby roots while simultaneously extending the reach and popularity of trading card games to the mass market."

As events would prove, it would be Wizards, not Pokémon, that would be the real magic.

❧

Hassenfeld was not vindictive, but as he celebrated Hasbro's 1999 success, he shed no tears for his West Coast nemesis.

Mattel was reeling.

The company had reported an $82-million loss for the 1999 calendar year and CEO and chairman Jill Barad, who had succeeded Amerman in early 1997, had resigned, on February 3, 2000, just days before the start of Toy Fair. She blamed the full-year loss on what had turned out to be Mattel's disastrous $3.8-billion acquisition of educational software firm The Learning Company, in May 1999, described a year later by a columnist for London's *The Telegraph* "as one of the worst takeovers in recent history."

This was not hyperbole: when 1999 ended, The Learning Company division had lost $206 million, negating strong sales in other Mattel lines, notably Fisher-Price.

"There is nothing I can say to gloss over how devastating The Learning Company's results have been to Mattel's overall performance," Barad said during a conference call with analysts. "Because there must be accountability, I and the board agree that I must resign today as chairman and chief executive and from the board."

It was a stunning fall for Barad, whose success with Barbie had taken her to the corner office. During her first year as CEO, 1997, Barad had managed the company to a 6.6-percent sales increase and an earnings gain of 24.5 percent, but sales declined for the first time in a decade the next year and again in 1999. A share of Mattel stock traded at $45.625 in March 1998, but had dropped to under $12 the day Barad resigned.

"Ms. Barad is known as a keen marketer and brilliant presenter, but her critics have said she failed in important management areas, including financial matters and diplomacy," *The New York Times* reported. "Even after she became chief operating officer, she continued to keep close watch on the Barbie division, monitoring doll designs down to minor details on their faces. Sales began to trail off in 1994, as Beanie Babies and other toys began to nibble away market share, and in response, Mattel began producing thousands of Barbies from its collectors' line—angering collectors who had paid $50 to $100 for the dolls, believing that they were limited editions...

"Ms. Barad's tenure was tumultuous, with several important executives resigning over what one called the Jill Factor, an oblique reference to her volatile management style. Under the circumstances, the board had little choice but to appoint directors to manage the company after Ms. Barad's sudden departure."

Interviewed at Hasbro's New York showroom on the opening day of Toy Fair, Hassenfeld had kind words for Barad, calling her "a marketing visionary" and saying her resignation was "a shame." But he offered no such gentility for Hasbro's arch-rival, instead declaring that his company would capitalize however it could on the turmoil at Mattel.

"We will be as aggressive as we can," he said. "If there is any opening to be had, we'll take it."

As Hassenfeld had returned to health following his 1998 heart attack, he had begun to reflect more deeply on his own mortality and the future health of his company.

Verrecchia shared his reflections.

"Al would probably tell you the same thing," Hassenfeld later said. "It's amazing how fragile life is, in the sense that you can be running something today and tomorrow you're out of it. And nobody cares. Life goes on no matter how important you think you are. One day you're god, and the next day you're no longer there. And nobody cares. I see it all the time now."

The heart attack prompted him to ponder corporate succession at Hasbro and his own next chapter. When Hasbro followed the record year of 1999 with a disappointing 2000, Hassenfeld's thinking intensified.

"It woke me up to my own human frailty," he later said, "that if I really wanted Hasbro to continue, what was I going to? Then we had the '99, which was good, and then 2000, which was terrible. It really made me begin to think: *How long do you want to do this? What do you want to do?*" With the time left to him, that is.

Like Bill Gates, Michael Bloomberg and other wealthy individuals who have left the corporate world for philanthropy (and signed the Giving Pledge together with Warren Buffett, Elon Musk, Mark Zuckerberg, Priscilla Chan and others), Hassenfeld decided that eventually, sooner rather than later, he would work full-time for change.

"I had always wanted to be a catalyst for positive change, whatever it might be," he said. "I had at that point a fair amount of money; money was not an issue. What could I do to continue a family tradition and be a force in Rhode Island, be a force nationally and be a force internationally for positive change?"

Kindness and a degree of humility would help guide him. This was not a man who had back stabbed on his way to the top.

"I didn't alienate, on my way up, many people," he said. And he remained grateful for those who had supported his father and brother during the difficult period when the thought of Hasbro becoming a Fortune 500 company was laughable.

"Some people in our industry in the '70s when we weren't doing that well gave us a hand to try and get out of the mud rather than pushing our face into the mud," he said.

But not all.

"I've watched so many people in our industry be very successful one year, think they're god, and treat people like shit. And the next day, they're in the mud and nobody wants to help."

The lesson?

"Burn no bridges. And always remember where you came from. Too many people forget where they came from."

As the year 2000 progressed, Pokémon and Star Wars were crashing, a painful reminder that with rare exceptions, what goes up eventually comes down.

In 1999, Pokémon had brought in $900 million, Star Wars $500 million—but in 2000, Pokémon would net just $200 million, and Star Wars, a paltry $50 million. Hasbro overall would lose money for the year. The finance world began to lose faith.

"We had to go continuously back to the banks in the July, August, September, October time frame," Verrecchia would recall. "But the banks wanted nothing to do with us."

And there was a personnel crisis too. Hassenfeld had brought in Herbert M. Baum, chairman and CEO of Quaker State Corp., the oil company, to be president and chief operating officer—but Verrecchia had tired of working with him.

"At that point in time," the midpoint of 2000, Verrecchia said, "I told Alan I was probably going to leave the company, probably at the end of the year."

That got Hassenfeld's attention.

"We all have egos," Hassenfeld later said, "but in reality, the one thing I knew with Al is that whether he had an ego or not, he basically sweated and bled Hasbro blood. There was no one more loyal to doing the right thing for Hasbro."

And no one, Verrecchia believed, could have been a better partner than Hassenfeld.

"Alan and I would have been far less successful if we were apart from each other because we complemented each other," Verrecchia recalled. "Alan was always willing to pay a dollar more and I was always willing to pay a dollar less. There was enough of that tension and balance to make it all work."

Baum or Verrecchia?

For Hassenfeld, an easy choice. Baum left Hasbro.

Far from public view, other soul-searching discussions were taking place among Hassenfeld, Verrecchia and the board. They resulted in Hassenfeld in 2001 deciding that the last brother would begin the process of easing himself out of the corner office.

It's about time, Hassenfeld said. *I'm the greatest blockage this company has for its future. We have any number of talented young people but if they see no way of being able to move up, they'll leave. And what am I going to do, sit at my desk until I'm 70?*

"I knew I had become tired," Hassenfeld later said. "I didn't love it as much."

A succession plan was set: In 2003, Hassenfeld would become chairman and hand the CEO job to Verrecchia; together, the two would mentor Brian Goldner, who both agreed was best-suited to succeed Verrecchia when Verrecchia himself left the CEO job. When he did, he would replace Hassenfeld as chairman, although Hassenfeld would remain on the board.

But that was all in the future during the increasingly worsening year of 2000. The immediate task was to save the ship.

Hasbro's world headquarters, Pawtucket, R.I.

PART TWO: IN VERRECCHIA'S HANDS NOW

By August 2000, the price of a share of Hasbro stock had fallen from $18.94 at the start of the year to less than $11, a precipitous decline. With the departure of Baum, who left to run Dial Corp., Hassenfeld announced a shuffling of the executive deck.

This was the first step in his succession plan.

Goldner, it was announced, was promoted to president of U.S. toys, reporting to George Volanakis, who had been senior vice president of the international division and was now executive vice president. Volanakis reported to Verrecchia, who now became Hasbro's president and chief operating officer.

Having informed Verrecchia of Baum's departure in a telephone call to Verrecchia at home, Hassenfeld invited his long-time lieutenant to his Bristol home the next day for further discussion.

I want you to run the company, Hassenfeld said.

Verrecchia was interested, but insistent: he wanted his boss's assurance that Hassenfeld would not second-guess him if given the reins.

I want to be president and chief operating officer, Verrecchia said. *I want you to give me complete freedom to fix the company.*

You have it, Hassenfeld said. *You can do what you want, when you want, and how you want.*

Verrecchia knew Hassenfeld was a man of his word.

Publicly, Hassenfeld was effusive in discussing the new executive lineup.

"Al Verrecchia is one of the best and most experienced executives in our industry, and his appointment to president and COO is the natural next step for an individual who has contributed so much in his 35 years at Hasbro," Hassenfeld said.

"I'm just thrilled with the opportunity," Verrecchia told an interviewer. "Hasbro is in my blood. It's like Tommy LaSorda: he bleeds Dodger blue, I bleed Hasbro."

And his relationship with Hassenfeld, Verrecchia said, was tight.

"He knows when I bob, and I know when he weaves," the new second-in-command said.

But bobbing and weaving could not stop the accelerating declines in Pokémon, Furby and Star Wars sales. A golden era was ending, and Hassenfeld knew his new executive team faced significant challenges.

Still, as the summer of 2000 ended, there *was* something to celebrate: The Walt Disney Co. on September 20 named Hasbro its official toymaker, replacing Mattel, which had held the licensing arrangement since 1996. (Mattel did, however, retain rights to certain Disney properties, notably Mickey Mouse and Winnie the Pooh, licensing mainstays for decades.)

Hasbro won the rights to products tied to Disney movies, videos, and TV shows, and the right to place its brands at Disney theme parks and attractions. "Families that visit Walt Disney World Resort, Disneyland Resort and Disneyland's Paris Resort will see Mr. Potato Head side by side with Mickey and Minnie Mouse in theme park toy stores" and also a "human-sized Mr. and Mrs. Potato Head" at another resort, one report of the deal stated.

Wall Street applauded, with the consensus that all three companies would benefit.

"For Disney, the deals represent another step toward rebuilding the company's faltering consumer-products business," *The Wall Street Journal* wrote. "For the past 11 years, Disney has had a nearly exclusive relationship with Mattel. Andy Mooney, the new president of Disney Consumer Products Worldwide, said Disney split the business between the two toy rivals to take advantage of both Mattel's strength in preschool toys and branded toys and Hasbro's strength in movie-based programs.

"'They're two very strong companies, but in some aspects mirror images of each other in terms of their unique strengths,' Mr. Mooney said. He added that Disney expects the restructured licensing program will allow the company 'to significantly grow our toy share over the next three to five years.'"

Added analyst Krutick: "For Hasbro, the license will provide a steady revenue stream, build international sales and enhance its name recognition at Disney resorts."

Still, movie licensing is a volatile business that had stung Hasbro recently with its Star Wars and Pokémon licenses, as Krutick pointed out. In a research note, she said Hasbro would be teaming up with Disney's "strong track record of film successes." But "the company will continue to face the tricky issue of correctly forecasting licensed product sales," she wrote.

In Pawtucket, the celebration was short-lived.

On October 12, Hasbro announced it was cutting about 500 positions around the world, including in Pawtucket; operations in San Francisco and Napa, California, and Cincinnati, once home of Kenner, would be permanently closed. The fate of another center, Hasbro's Interactive division, which employed some 200 in Beverly, Massachusetts, but was hemorrhaging money was unclear, Verrecchia told analysts. Hasbro, he said, was "exploring strategic alternatives for this business. The goal is to stop losses."

In his discussion with analysts, Hassenfeld said Hasbro aimed to rely less on outside licensing and more on internal properties. "Core brands are our bread and butter," he said. "That's what we need to focus on to reduce risk and enhance shareholder value."

But outsiders feared that Hasbro's moves would fail to right the ship in time for a strong holiday fourth quarter, especially in light of other factors beyond Hasbro's control, including an industry-wide shortage of certain electronic parts; high oil prices, which inflated transportation and plastic-resin costs; an overall week domestic consumer market; and a strong U.S. dollar, which stifled sales in overseas markets.

And there was doubt that Hasbro really did intend to do what it said it would.

"Hasbro's always been reliant on the entertainment licenses," said Hayley Kissel, an analyst with Merrill Lynch Global Securities. "For as much as they say they're moving away, we've never really seen them do it."

The gloom was deepening.

On December 6, Hasbro announced that its full-year earnings would be "at best, break-even," with the potential for a loss of up to 20 cents a share. Layoffs, the company said, would reach 750 positions, not 500. Revealing the existence of some $75 million in unsold and now obsolete Pokémon inventory, Hassenfeld accepted much of the blame.

"Frankly, while Pokémon Trading Card Game cards are still selling well, we were too aggressive in our forecast following incredible demand in 1999 and 2000," he said.

He predicted brighter days ahead.

"While 2000 has been a very painful year, we are looking forward to returning Hasbro to profitability in 2001 and beyond," he said.

But first, he had to make it through the end of 2000. He did, joylessly.

When toymakers converged on New York for Toy Fair 2001, Hasbro was hurting. Hassenfeld delivered the bad news, reporting that in the final quarter of 2000, the company had recorded a net loss of $58.4 million, compared to earnings of $155.4 million during the same quarter in 1999; when after-tax charges from the sale of its Interactive division and the company-wide restructuring were factored in, the net loss for the full year 2000 was $144.6 million. Hasbro's sales dropped 10 percent to $3.79 billion, from the record $4.2 billion in 1999.

"We cannot change the fact that Pokémon, Furby and Star Wars are no longer the phenomenon they were in 1999 and early 2000," Hassenfeld told analysts. "2000 was an extremely disappointing year for Hasbro."

Verrecchia sought to reassure Wall Street, saying Hasbro's primary objective in 2001 was to become "leaner and consistently profitable for our shareholders."

At least the home state would fare well, Charness asserted.

"There's no change at all in Rhode Island," he said. "We said originally there would be some job loss in Rhode Island, but at the end of the day, there would be a net gain of jobs in Rhode Island because of folks transferring here to help the U.S. toy group."

Inside Hasbro, meanwhile, a restructuring rivalling Stephen Hassenfeld's own remaking of the company was underway. Verrecchia was engineering it.

He had begun shortly after being named president and COO, during a conversation with David Hargreaves, Hasbro's senior vice president for finance and deputy chief financial officer and a longtime associate and friend.

"David," Verrecchia said, "It's up to us now."

Up to them and a small group of executives, including Goldner, to devise a plan to "fix" Hasbro, as Verrecchia later described it. There was much to fix: at one point on December 7, 2000, the stock price had dropped to $8.38 a share, a modern low.

The fix would not be easy, fast or pain-free, as the layoffs demonstrated. In March 2001, Verrecchia gathered senior managers for an off-site meeting to plan what was next.

We have two choices here, Verrecchia said. *We can essentially lay off everybody and take all of our brands and license them out to other people and collect royalties. Or we can focus on our own core brands and try to rebuild this business.*

And there was a third, albeit unthinkable, option: sell the company. But with the stock still hurting -- $12.26 per share on March 23—a sale was unlikely to fetch a price reflecting the true value of the company.

The consensus at the off-site meeting: rebuild the company.

Verrecchia renegotiated terms with banks holding long-term debt, trimmed $200 million from expenses, and improved Hasbro's cash flow. He reduced Hasbro's global work force by about 4,000 positions, from some 10,000 to 6,000 jobs. He let Goldner and his team identify which of Hasbro's hundreds of brands were best suited to anchor the effort to recapture the company's golden touch. They came up with Play-Doh, Nerf, Transformers, Monopoly, Candy Land, My Little Pony, Littlest Pet Shop, Easy-Bake Oven, Tonka, and G.I. Joe.

The core brands would not simply receive amplified marketing: they would be incorporated into a broad play and entertainment spectrum that included a robust digital and screen presence intended for domestic and international consumers. They would be "intellectual properties," as Verrecchia called them, built on a foundation of storytelling. With the mantra of "reimagine, reignite, reinvent," Verrecchia, Goldner, and their people renewed or made new connections with Hollywood, fast-food chains, publishers, and digital services.

As the serious rebuilding commenced, Verrecchia did not want Hasbro employees to fall victim to rumor, so he began quarterly informational meetings with them at which no topic was off-limits, and no employee faced sanction for voicing opinion.

"I was dead honest with them," Verrecchia later said. "I put it up on the board. I said, 'hey, guys, this is it, we're in trouble. This is what we have to do.'"

The world at large initially knew nothing of this, only that some sort of dramatic change was underway at 1027 Newport Avenue to address the publicly reported numbers that continued to alarm investors.

"Hasbro reported yesterday that it lost $25 million in its most recent quarter as it struggled to manage the decline in popularity of the Pokémon trading card without a hot toy to replace it. It said revenue for the quarter plunged 40 percent," *The New York Times* wrote on April 24, 2001. "The quarterly loss was the second consecutive one for Hasbro, which before announcing a $180 million loss for the fourth quarter of last year had reported a string of profitable quarters since 1995. The company said it also expected second quarter results to suffer by comparison with the quarter a year earlier, when Pokémon sales were strong.

"But Alan G. Hassenfeld, chairman and chief executive, said sales should pick up by the end of the year, after new toys are introduced. The loss of 15 cents a share was more than double the 6 cents a share consensus estimate of analysts surveyed by Thomson Financial/First Call. But Hasbro officials said they had given warning and noted there was relatively little movement in the stock. The stock rose a cent, to $11.80. 'Hasbro is in the throes of a major transition,' Jill S. Krutick, an analyst for Salomon Smith Barney, said. Hasbro, based in Pawtucket, R.I., said it lost $25 million, in contrast to earnings of $15 million, or 8 cents a share, a year earlier. Revenue declined to $463 million from $773 million."

In *The Times* story, as elsewhere, Hassenfeld remained his company's cheerleader.

"Mr. Hassenfeld said he wanted Hasbro to focus on existing brands like Mr. Potato Head, PlayDoh, G.I. Joe and Tonka trucks," the newspaper continued. "Tonka sales were up 27 percent during the last quarter, thanks in part to new electronic versions of classic dump trucks, Hasbro officials said. Mr. Hassenfeld said the company would issue a new line of G.I. Joe toys later this year and would revive its line of Transformer robots. And even though Hasbro says it wants to wean itself from licensing toys from other companies, as with Pokémon, it is hardly going cold turkey. Last year Hasbro agreed to make toys for new Disney movies, after Mattel ended its relationship with the film company. This year Hasbro will be making Jurassic Park dinosaurs, Harry

Potter trading cards and a version of the Game of Life based on the movie 'Monsters Inc.'' from Pixar, the animation studio."

The story continued: "Wayne Charness, a Hasbro spokesman, said the difference was that Hasbro was emphasizing its old brands more, being more selective in choosing licenses and offering film companies smaller guarantees of toys sold than they have in the past. If the new strategy achieves a measure of success the company could be profitable even if Harry Potter cards fail to drive children to the same distraction as Pokémon. 'You won't get the up-20-percent years," Hayley W. Kissel, a Merrill Lynch analyst, said. 'But you won't get the down-40-percent quarters either.'"

In the year 2000, Hassenfeld had travelled with some of his employees to Pixar, in Emeryville, California, to pitch Hasbro's line of *Monsters Inc.* toys to Steve Jobs, who was then CEO and owner of the animation company. Jobs enthusiastically approved, Hassenfeld recalled.

"*Monsters* was just loaded with potential toyetics," Hassenfeld said. "Steve and I got along well." Hasbro won the license, beating Mattel.

Hasbro produced *Monster* plush toys, action figures, an electronic game, a movie version of The Game of Life, a unique Milton Bradley board game and other items. Opening the first week of November 2001, the movie grossed $240 million through the end of the year and the Hasbro line sold well during that holiday-buying period.

Under a separate licensing deal with distributor Disney, McDonald's gave away small, non-poseable *Monster* figures with its Happy Meals and the promotion was a runaway success. Hassenfeld estimated that consumers collected some 10 million of the figures with their food.

The Happy Meals toys "competed," Hassenfeld said, "affecting sales potential 'big time.'"

Nonetheless, Hasbro had done well enough by Pixar that Hassenfeld pitched a line for the studio's next major production, *Finding Nemo*, released in May 2003 on its way to a $339 domestic gross by year's end.

The script told "absolutely a wonderful, wonderful story," Hassenfeld would recall.

But from a manufacturing perspective, there was a problem:

"How do you take a beautiful story about fish and cross into the real world of toyetics?" is how Hassenfeld described it.

This was not the first time he had encountered such a conundrum: In 1999, Jeffrey Katzenberg of Spielberg's DreamWorks studio lobbied Hassenfeld to produce toys tied to *Chicken Run*, an animated feature about chickens plotting to flee their farm.

The script thrilled Hassenfeld—"it was *The Great Escape*, which is a movie I loved, but with *chickens*," he recalled.

I don't think we know how to make chickens heroic, which a boys' action figure has to be, Hassenfeld told Katzenberg. Hasbro passed, and *Chicken Run*, released in June

2000, did just $106 million domestically office before quietly disappearing that fall. Other companies did produce *Chicken Run* toys, but there was no stampede to buy them.

For the *Nemo* pitch, Hassenfeld recalled riding from San Francisco to the Pixar offices with his team for the presentation to Jobs wondering, half-jokingly, if they might find success with a compressed-fish toy that expanded into a bigger version when placed in water.

The presentation did not go well.

Hassenfeld was in Davos, Switzerland, for a meeting of the World Economic Forum a short while later when his hotel phone rang. It was midnight. Jobs was calling.

You're not being creative enough, Jobs said.

"I explained to Steve," Hassenfeld later recalled, "that one of the difficulties for me and our people was a combination of fish and water is not the best thing for parents." Too much mess. "And where a girl or a boy will sleep with a teddy bear, they'll sleep with a Snoopy, they'll sleep with Dumbo, not that many of them want to sleep with the fish."

Hassenfeld paused in the telling, laughing.

"My sense of humor did not win the day," he said. Jobs was not amused.

He did, however, let Hasbro sell a *Finding Nemo* playset, *Finding Nemo* versions of Guess Who? and Junior Monopoly, Finding Dory Play-Doh, and a Finding Dory version of Operation, but Hassenfeld's instincts had been true. The line would prove but a footnote in Hasbro history, although the Finding Dory Play-Doh was sufficiently popular that it remained on the market in 2019—$15.95 on Amazon for a "Dory cutter, Hank extruder, Nemo cutter, Bailey cutter, roller, and 5 cans of Play-Doh Brand Modeling Compound."

Jobs "was not happy" with Hasbro after *Finding Nemo*, Hassenfeld said, although he did give the company a piece of Pixar's next feature, 2004's *The Incredibles*.

And there the relationship ended.

"We pitched for *Cars* and lost," Hassenfeld said.

The full scope of the new focus on core brands was unveiled in February 2002, in New York at the 99th annual American International Toy Fair, when Hassenfeld accepted responsibility for over-emphasizing licensed products including Pokémon, Teletubbies and Star Wars to the neglect of in-house lines.

The timeworn risk, as Verrecchia explained, was that relying on "wonderful licenses that all of a sudden do a billion dollars" and then fade away left Hasbro with the question: "How do you replace that?" Not necessarily with another hot license, for such did not grow on trees.

"In the late '90s, I allowed us to neglect some of our children and our cores, and we were doing these licenses," Hassenfeld said. "Your children do not like to be forgotten. They like newness. They are alive."

And for 2002, they were rejuvenated, with fresh offerings of G.I. Joe, Transformers, Easy Bake Oven, Play-Doh, Monopoly, Tonka and other staples. Already, Hasbro declared, the new strategy had paid off, with sales of Joe rising 59 percent in 2001 compared to 2000, and fourth-quarter 2002 sales of Transformers up two-thirds over the prior-year period.

To keep on track, Hassenfeld said sales of core brands would have to increase annually by three percent to five percent, with earnings projected at six- to ten-percent annual growth. That contrasted with previous years, when expectations were that Hasbro would increase sales every year by ten percent.

"Not even God can do that over a long period of time," Verrecchia quipped.

The shift drew praise from analysts and the press.

"I think Hasbro's done a really good job in focusing on these lines. In integrating the toys that they have," toy-industry consultant Chris Byrne said.

"They're sharp people, they're not dummies," said *Playthings* magazine senior editor David Gerardi.

"Even though Hasbro's lineup at Toy Fair was familiar, with lots of G.I. Joe, Star Wars, Transformers and games, it represented a company that is much different from a year ago," a *Providence Journal* reporter wrote in a story headlined "Coming of Age: It's a brand-new game for Hasbro." The reporter continued: "There were fewer break-away products. Less risk. But still innovation. The toys Hasbro showed at Toy Fair are the products of a company wringing its talent's brains."

The reporter ended with a reference to future Hall-of-Fame quarterback Tom Brady, an unheralded sixth-round draft pick in 2000 who become the starter in 2001 with the injury of Drew Bledsoe—and who led the New England Patriots to their first-ever Super Bowl in 2002.

"It might not be a whiz-bang plan," the reporter wrote, "and the core toys in Hasbro's lineup this year may not have the sizzle once claimed by Furby and Pokémon. But Hasbro at least knows that its children deliver. As Verrecchia pointed out: 'The New England Patriots didn't have a star at the beginning of the year. What they did was win the Super Bowl.'"

There would be no Super Bowl for Hasbro in 2002, nor, halfway through the year, any strong public indication—beyond the assurances of Hassenfeld and Verrecchia, that is—that the company was headed toward glory. When the second-quarter numbers were released, the press was merciless.

"It is an earnings report that looks like Mr. Potato Head with his face on wrong," *The Providence Journal* wrote. "While Hasbro Inc. yesterday reported higher sales of Monopoly, G.I. Joe and Transformers, an unusual charge forced the toy maker to post an unexpected quarterly loss of $25.9 million. The event stymied what would have been an earnings report that beat Wall Street expectations, after 18 months of restructuring to make Hasbro a smaller but more profitable company."

The loss was related to a $28.6-million non-cash charge taken from a drop in the share value of video game firm Infogrames Entertainment SA. In 2001, Hasbro received 2.9 million shares of the company as part of the sale of Games.com and Hasbro Interactive, money-losers both. While the press did not applaud, analysts did, if softly.

"It's unfortunate that a portion of the payment Hasbro received for Hasbro Interactive had to come in the form of a risky stock," said Morningstar's Terrence Mackay. "[But] it does not affect our evaluation of the company because it's a non-cash charge. I focused more on the outlook than the results."

Some of those were promising. Sales rose year-over-year for the first time in nine quarters, from $511 million to $546 million, due in significant part to a stellar performance in Goldner's U.S. toy group: to $299.6 million, an 18-percent rise over the year before, bolstered by a nearly 50 percent increase in Transformers sales. International sales also rose, from $158.5 million to $174.3 million.

"The bottom line is we continue to be on track to achieve our financial goal for this year," Hassenfeld said. "We had a good quarter. The business is on track year-to-date."

It was, as the remainder of 2002 proved.

The full year closed with an operating profit of $219 million, up from $211 million in 2001; earnings rose from $96 million to $104 million. Revenues were down slightly, to $2.81 billion from $2.85 billion, but fixed costs and expenses were also down, and debt over two years had dropped 54 percent, to $684 million.

In Hasbro's jointly signed annual report, Hassenfeld and Verrecchia expressed satisfaction with the progress from the loss year of 2000 and quiet confidence for the future.

"Two years ago," they wrote, "we set out on a strategic course to make Hasbro a consistently more profitable company—one better positioned to deliver reliable and sustainable growth. To that end, we focused on improving our earnings, reducing our debt, strengthening our balance sheet, and investing in new product development geared towards growing our core brands. We are pleased to report that in 2002 we continued to make strides in all of these areas, in spite of a very challenging retail and economic environment."

Looking ahead, they wrote that "our focus in 2003 and beyond centers on generating revenue growth by emphasizing our powerful portfolio of core brands through increased advertising and promotional spending, in addition to creating new, innovative products. We remain committed to improving our earnings, reducing our debt, and strengthening our balance sheet."

Yes, there was a theme here, one that dated to Verrecchia's earliest days at Hasbro, when Hassenfeld was still in high school.

"The strategic course we set two years ago is still relevant today," the CEO and COO concluded, "and you can expect us to remain focused on delivering consistent profitability to you, our shareholder."

Surely, Henry, Merrill, and Stephen Hassenfeld would have approved.

PART THREE: EIGHTY YEARS IN, NO BROTHER, NO HASSENFELD

Those in Hassenfeld's inner circle knew what to expect when the company's annual share-holders' meeting began on May 14, 2003. Outsiders did not. But for everyone, Hassenfeld's announcement about the future of the company would make for an emotional day.

Hassenfeld opened the meeting at the cafeteria at 1027 Newport Avenue with his traditional overview of the previous year's financial performance, a prediction for the months ahead, and an introduction to Hasbro's new products.

Already revealed to buyers in February at Toy Fair, those included VideoNow, a recording device that played CD-cartoons of such as characters as SpongeBob SquarePants; Airtivity, a toddler's play table; Naknak, a stackable action figure game; and Thin-Tronix, a novel introduction from the Tiger Electronics division.

"In 2003, 'thin will be in' as Hasbro's Tiger Electronics brand introduces THIN-TRONIX, a revolutionary new line of fun, ultra-thin products sure to be a hit with tweens and teens alike," the company wrote. "From the hard-to-believe, fully functional Poster Phone and Poster Radio to the musical Electronic Stickers, from the cool styling of the LCD Watch Assortment to recordable Slap Message Bands, the THIN-TRONIX line offers energy, music, communication, and self-expression, in ultra-thin forms."

The line brought jobs to the country so important to Hassenfelds, as the copy stated: "At the heart of the THIN-TRONIX line of electronic stickers, watches and slap message bands are 'flat batteries' designed and developed by Power Paper Ltd., of Tel Aviv, Israel, enabling cool shapes and colorful designs through Power Paper's ultra-thin and micro-powered devices."

But the emphasis in 2003 was again on core brands, including innovations with Play-Doh, Spirograph, Easy-Bake Oven and Transformers.

Analysts applauded.

"This 2003 product line is the first one that's fully developed under a new focus," said Sean McGowan, of Gerard Klauer Mattison. "They're going to extend these existing brands... before going into a new direction."

In his prepared remarks on May 14, Hassenfeld re-emphasized the core-brand theme and hearkened to Stephen's games legacy, and his own, and the nurturing of both into 2003 and beyond. What Mattel had accomplished with Barbie, a single enduring brand, Hasbro had achieved with a rich library of timeless classics.

"We continue to be the leader in the games category," Hassenfeld said. "Our Milton Bradley and Parker Brothers brands have 97% and 96% awareness respectively among moms, and are known as the industry's 'gold standards.' Our Wizards of the Coast brand is known as the leader in hobby gaming. These three brands are among the most highly regarded in the game industry and have provided millions of people all over the world with countless hours of high quality entertainment.

"We maintained our leadership role in 2002 by growing our core brands and introducing many exciting new products. In 2002, we hit the jackpot with the number one selling new game in the U.S. in each of the preschool, children's family, electronic, and adult game categories! It was one of our most successful new product years in our Hasbro games division."

And it was after the formal remarks that Hassenfeld broke the news:

He was handing over the CEO job to Verrecchia, while remaining chairman of the board.

Some in the audience cried.

"For 80 years now Hasbro has been bringing smiles to children the world over," Hassenfeld said, but now it was time for a non-Hassenfeld to run the company. That someone was a man he referred to as an adopted family member, the man he jokingly called Al "Hassenfeld" Verrecchia.

"Since Stevie left us there's been only one person who, through thick and thin, has been there for us, for our shareholders, and for me," Hassenfeld said. "And that's Al."

Humbled, Verrecchia credited Hassenfeld's managerial changes two years before for the company's new direction. "Today is a day of tremendous pride for me and my family," he said. "Hasbro is on the move again and we will let nothing deter us in achieving our goal."

Alan Hassenfeld and Al Verrecchia, 2003. (Courtesy Providence Journal)

Already the engineer of Hasbro's turnaround, Verrecchia now had full throttle, and he used it to power the company's full return to Wall Street favor. The year 2003 ended with a $344 million profit, on revenues that rose from $2.8 billion in 2002 to $3.1 billion. Major successes were scored in games, with an 8.8-percent revenues increase; U.S. Toys, Goldner's domain, with an increase of 6.2 percent; and international, with a 22-percent rise in revenues, to $1.2 billion, another indication that Hasbro's own-brands strategy worked in markets beyond America.

"Our success in 2003 confirmed, once again, that our strategy of growing our core brands and developing new products through innovation is the right one," Verrecchia and Hassenfeld wrote in the 2003 annual report. "We have come a long way in improving our earnings, reducing our debt and strengthening our balance sheet. The good news is there is much more to come."

Shareholder satisfaction was evidenced at the annual meeting, on May 20, 2004. Only about 100 attended, a sign that shareholders had no gripes. The meeting ended in under an hour.

"The last three years have been about getting Hasbro back on track," Verrecchia said. "We finished the year a much stronger company."

A company, Hassenfeld told shareholders, that continued to exemplify the moral values of his family.

"Hasbro has a strong commitment to its code of conduct," he said. "We think we're doing an excellent job… to make it a better world."

Whether Hassenfeld could best continue his personal commitment to those values while still chairman of the company was a question weighing on his mind.

Two months after the annual meeting, a man who had little claim to bettering the world entered the Hasbro orbit—for the second time.

Once again, the name of real estate developer and now reality-TV star Donald Trump was on a Hasbro game.

The future president's debut had been in 1989, when he chose the Milton Bradley division to produce Trump: The Game, which *The New York Times* described as "not unlike Monopoly—the player with the most money wins."

Trump in 1989 told the paper that he had received offers from four companies to produce the game and chose Milton Bradley because "They're the Rolls Royce of game companies." Trump: The Game required a greater level of skill than Monopoly, where the roll of the dice was frequently the only deciding factor.

"I didn't want a game based solely on chance," Trump said. "I wanted a game based on talent. And I wanted to teach people if they have business instincts. It's great if they can learn that from a game instead of having to go out and lose your shirt."

Retailing for $25, and drawing from themes in his *New York Times* number-one bestselling 1987 book *The Art of the Deal*, Trump: The Game might have seemed little but an opportunity for narcissism: It was played with Trump cards, and Trump himself was the face of a fake $100 million denomination. But Trump portrayed it as not only fun self-help for aspiring entrepreneurs, but also a fund-raiser for worthy causes. He told *The Times* that profits, amounting to some $20 million real dollars, would be dedicated to research on AIDS, homelessness, cerebral palsy and other significant issues.

Profits of that magnitude never materialized, for the game sold poorly.

Nonetheless, Hasbro in July 2004 released an updated version keyed to *The Apprentice,* Trump's new TV series. The game bombed.

Reviewers of *The Apprentice* version of Monopoly were merciless, with *Time* in 2011 calling it one of Trump's ten worst business failures and noting that a year after its release, the 1989 version "was vastly underselling the predicted 2 million units he" and Hasbro had projected.

Mother Jones magazine, writing in the summer of 2015 as then-presidential candidate Trump was preparing for the Republican primary debates, savaged the 2004 reboot, with writer Tim Murphy recounting playing the game with magazine political reporters Molly Redden, Pat Caldwell, and Pema Levy.

"Afterwards, I asked our team of guinea pigs for their feedback," Murphy wrote.

" 'It's like Monopoly, but really dumb,' Pema declared.

" 'Nothing really happens,' Pat said…

" 'The thing about it is," Pema continued, "it's just a dumb game…'

Murphy's bottom line?

"Just don't ask any of us to play it again," he wrote.

So Trump: The Game, versions one and two, were not Game: The Bestseller. And Trump's claim of donating all revenues, however modest, to worthy causes would not be substantiated. A *Washington Post* investigation in June 2016, as Trump was on his way to the Republican presidential nomination, cast doubt on those claims:

"'The game was just nailed to the shelf,' said George Ditomassi, who was president of Milton Bradley at the time," *The Post* reported. "One problem, he said, was that customers were not told about Trump's pledge to give proceeds to charity. 'They felt perhaps this was going to be something that a millionaire would make some money on,' Ditomassi said.

"The TV commercial for the product was changed. 'Mr. Trump's proceeds from Trump: The Game will be donated to charity,' a new voice-over said at the end.

"It still didn't work. The game tanked.

"Still, Trump said he made $880,000 from it, and even more from 'The Art of the Deal. In 1987, the mogul started the Donald J. Trump Foundation to donate his royalties.

"But the proceeds didn't go straight to charity. They went straight into Trump's bank account."

Hasbro ended 2004 modestly, if in the black.

Revenues declined to just under $3 billion compared to 2003; profit was off, to $293 million. Verrecchia and Hassenfeld blamed "a challenging year for the toy industry both domestically and abroad" but emphasized that their response had protected the company while positioning it for greater gains when the retail market brightened.

"It was a year," the top two executives wrote in their annual report, "in which we continued to focus on expense reductions, generated good cash flow and delivered earnings per share ahead of last year, despite lower revenue." They described Hasbro's emerging corporate identity as a manufacturer of "lifestyle products," where innovation co-existed with tradition.

"In 1952, we were the first company to advertise a toy on television with Mr. Potato Head," Hassenfeld and Verrecchia declared. "In 1964, we revolutionized the toy industry with the creation of the action figure category by introducing G.I. Joe. We also were first to recognize the value of expanding our portfolio and created a new model for the modern toy company in 1984 with the acquisition of Milton Bradley and Playskool. Today that innovation continues…"

But 2005 did not begin with great promise. Shareholders arrived at Hasbro's annual meeting that May with the sting of a first-quarter loss, $3.71 million, the first such since the rebuilding effort had commenced. Hassenfeld opened the meeting with a crack about the release of the latest Star Wars movie, *Episode III -- Revenge of the Sith*, wondering how many in the mostly older audience had attended the midnight opening.

"I'm a little bit disappointed," he said. "I thought many of you would have been a little bit more bleary-eyed, having stood in line all night trying to get into the Star Wars movie."

Verrecchia attempted to assure shareholders that Hasbro was responding to changes in consumer preferences and buying habits: Increasingly, he noted, toys with an electronic component were in demand, and internet sales were rising.

"We need to be wherever consumers are shopping," Verrecchia said.

Just that month, Hasbro had launched its own web site, HasbroToyShop.com (now hasbropulse.com), to sell directly to consumers. The company was joining a revolution in consumer buying led by Amazon that would spell doom for many big-box retailers, including one that had been central to Hasbro and other toymakers for decades, Toys 'R' Us.

Three months after the annual meeting, on August 30, a bombshell was dropped.

Hassenfeld announced he was giving up his chairmanship in all but name; he would maintain an advisory role but remove himself from day-to-day involvement in Hasbro. Verrecchia henceforth would have responsibility at the top of the executive chain.

Starting immediately, it was announced, Hassenfeld would be the company's "non-employee chairman," a move that would further free him for his philanthropy and advocacy while setting the stage for Verrecchia to eventually and fully assume the chairmanship, although that transition was not mentioned publicly then.

Hassenfeld revealed his intent first in a message to employees: "I will move on to begin another exciting chapter of my life, one that is dedicated to the betterment of children and their families," he wrote.

Still, as non-employee chairman—a suitable if offbeat title—he would keep a hand in Hasbro affairs, with his seat on the board and as an ombudsman for the company and industry's global issues. He would, *The Providence Journal* reported, "travel the world as chairman of the International Council of Toy Industries CARE process -- the toy industry's ethical manufacturing program aimed at ensuring that companies maintain safe workplaces."

Hassenfeld would forego his $1-million yearly salary and other payments that had brought him almost $2 million in compensation in 2004, taking only $45,000 annually now for his "non-employee" duties, plus $1,500 per board meeting he attended.

"Certainly this is not goodbye, as you will still be seeing plenty of me in the office," Hassenfeld informed Hasbro employees.

Charness said that the move would not affect company performance. "For the day-to-day operations, we don't miss a beat," he said. "This is something that Alan has been thinking about for a while. This is really just a natural progression."

Unbound by the restrictions of the corner office, Hassenfeld would now enjoy more freedom to raise his voice on political matters. With his personal resources and the approximately 18 million shares of Hasbro stock he controlled—some ten percent of all stock, worth some $360 million on that August day, nearly half a billion dollars today—he would have the means to influence many causes. Having burned few bridges in his corporate career and having built enduring goodwill with a diverse network of other leaders, his phone calls would be answered.

CHAPTER EIGHT

A DIFFERENCE IN THE LIVES OF THOSE WE CARE ABOUT MOST

PART ONE: SOWING SEEDS

In due time, Hassenfeld closed his office at Hasbro and opened one for his Hassenfeld Family Foundation, incorporated in 2008, in Providence's historic Owen Building.

Completed in 1868 and listed on the National Register of Historic Places, the building—across the Providence River from College Hill and the Ivy League university he had generously supported for so long—was a survivor of an era when seafaring vessels and steam-powered textile mills brought great wealth to Rhode Island. It was all but certain that Hassenfeld's grandfather had been familiar with the Owen Building and perhaps even conducted business with the merchants and manufacturers who once occupied it.

Here on the fourth floor of this red-brick and granite building, Hassenfeld and his small staff went to work.

There was much work to be done, and Hassenfeld applied his restless energy to it. He had survived a heart attack, with the profound understandings such an experience brings.

"I always wanted to be a catalyst for positive change, whatever it might be," Hassenfeld said. "I had at that point a fair amount of money; money was not an issue."

The issue was: "What could I do to continue a tradition—and not only continue a tradition but be a force in Rhode Island, be a force nationally, and be a force internationally for positive change."

Change that brings happiness, that is: "I like to make people smile," Hassenfeld often said.

Many people did smile.

He and his foundation helped fund The Hummel Report, a web site and radio report that investigated wrongdoers and celebrated doers of good. An avid tennis player since youth, he donated to the International Tennis Hall of Fame. Appreciative of fine art, along with his wife, he supported the Bristol Art Museum, the Isabella Stewart Art Museum, Boston's Institute of Contemporary Art, and the Metropolitan Museum of Art. He and the foundation helped the Little Sisters of the Poor, Rhode Island Public Radio, the environmental group Save the Bay, the United Way, the Rhode Island homeless-service centers Amos House and Crossroads, the sexual assault and trauma center Day One, and several literacy, food-pantry and minority centers.

The Providence-based Institute for the Study and Practice of Nonviolence, a national model for peaceful resolution of problems, benefited from Hassenfeld generosity. The institute was founded in 2001 by Sister Ann Keefe and Father Ray Malm in the rectory of Catholic St. Michael's Church in South Providence. Embracing the principles of Dr. Martin Luther King, the nun and the priest sought to "to teach nonviolence to everyone, to increase a person's ability to see alternate solutions to potentially violent solutions," the institute declares.

Schools of many sorts also benefitted, including Brandeis University; Brown; Deerfield Academy, his high-school alma mater; Manhattan's Gillen Brewer School, for children with learning challenges; Columbia University; Hartford Seminary, a theological college in Connecticut; Harvard University; Johnson & Wales University; Massachusetts Institute of Technology; Moses Brown School; New York University; Middlebury College; Rhode Island College; Rhode Island School of Design; Salve Regina University; Sophia Academy, in Providence, for girls with as-yet-unattained academic potential; Tufts University; The University of California, Los Angeles and San Francisco; the University of Rhode Island; the University of Pennsylvania; and the Wolf School, in East Providence, which "inspires complex learners to discover confidence, compassion, and a love of learning to reach their full potential."

And many more causes, chronicled in an internal and unpublicized list that filled nine single-spaced pages.

Hassenfeld invested his time and resources most heavily in programs that would reap rewards starting now.

"Some people think they should wait to give their money away until after they die. They think that amount will be greater if they wait. How do you tell a starving child 'I'm sorry, there's nothing for you, just wait a couple of years?' " Hassenfeld wrote in the first chapter of *The Business of Changing the World: Twenty Great Leaders on*

Strategic Corporate Philanthropy, a book that also featured UPS founder Jack Casey, Dell founder Michael S. Dell, GlaxoSmithKline CEO Jean-Pierre Garnier, Salesforce CEO Marc Benioff, and singer Peter Gabriel.

"My passion for philanthropy definitely stems from my family," Hassenfeld declared, ascribing its origins to his Polish-immigrant grandfather and great-uncle. "During the Second World War, the village they came from, Ulanów, was almost completely destroyed. Even though they were safely in America, they never forgot where they came from, and they sponsored other villagers to come to America. We grew up with that."

Hassenfeld established and funded the Hassenfeld Social Enterprise Fund at Johns Hopkins University and the Hopkins-Nanjing Center for Chinese and American Studies. Also, the Hassenfeld Projects at Roger Williams University, to train and teach students participating in community-based social-justice and economic-development projects. "When students engage deeply in solving the hard problems facing society today, they are actually doing the work of building the future," Hassenfeld said of his $500,000 gift to Roger Williams.

The Hassenfeld Family Foundation established the Hassenfeld Emerging Markets Business Immersion Program at Brandeis and, with a $2.5-million gift, the Hassenfeld Family Innovations Center at its International Business School. "The groundbreaking research happening at Brandeis presents an exceptional opportunity to fulfill the deepest values of our university—changing the world through knowledge and action that serves the greater good," Hassenfeld said when announcing the center, in November 2014.

And his family foundation created the Rhode Island Public Service Fellowship, at Harvard's John F. Kennedy School of Government, with fellows having a choice of such programs as "Leadership for the 21st Century: Chaos, Conflict and Courage" and "Global Change Agents: Crossing Boundaries, Building Bridges and Leading Change."

And the crown jewel, as it were, of Hassenfeld's commitment to good government: The Hassenfeld Institute for Public Leadership at Bryant University, which opened in 2010 with a $1 million gift, followed by annual funding. The gift brought together Bryant president Machtley and Gary Sasse, the institute's director and former head of the Rhode Island Public Expenditure Council, a RightNow! partner.

"The Institute is a perfect fit for Bryant," Hassenfeld said at its opening. "President Machtley, who has served in Congress, understands the pressing need for ethical, effective leadership. Bryant's faculty and the Institute's founding director, Gary Sasse, have created a world-class program that can make a tremendous difference in Rhode Island's future."

Crediting Hassenfeld's "vision," Sasse would later speak of the institute's impact, beginning with its first efforts, a seminar for new mayors and a weekend "boot camp" for newly elected members of city and town councils and school committees.

"Since this beginning," Sasse said, "the Institute has conducted leadership programs for the Supreme Court and state judiciary, legislative staff, state cabinet agencies, regional planning organizations, school committees and municipalities, in addition to holding public policy workshops and publishing a quarterly public opinion survey on issues of interest to elected officials. For over a quarter of a century Alan Hassenfeld has been the face of good government in Rhode Island. He has been a tireless advocate and generous supporter of a myriad of initiatives to make Rhode Island government more accountable and effective."

More with his time than money, Hassenfeld after becoming non-employee chairman in 2005 intensified his commitment to international business, political, and human-rights concerns. He was further freed for these causes in 2008, when Verrecchia, passing Hasbro's president and CEO titles to Goldner, succeeded him as chairman—a move that gave Verrecchia more time for his own community service, including on the Lifespan and Wheeler School boards.

The Hassenfeld Family Foundation backed organizations including Afrika Tikkun, which serves disadvantaged children in South Africa; The Asia Society, which describes itself as "the leading educational organization dedicated to promoting mutual understanding and strengthening partnerships among peoples, leaders and institutions of Asia and the United States in a global context," with locations in Shangahi, Hong Kong, New York, Washington and elsewhere; the Dui Hua Foundation, whose "mission is to bring clemency and better treatment to at-risk detainees through mutually respectful dialogue with China"; the Brookings Institution; the Chicago Council on Global Affairs; the Japan-America Society of Rhode Island; the Landmine Survivors Network; and Relief International.

Plus, the Ploughshares Fund, which declares: "If you care about the future of our planet and humankind, if you believe everyone has a right to live safely and securely, if investing taxpayer dollars where they're most needed matters to you, then so does stopping a new arms race and reducing nuclear threats—wherever they come from."

And Refugees International, whose mission Hassenfelds had embraced since the dawn of the 20th century, an organization that today "advocates for lifesaving assistance and protection for displaced people and promotes solutions to displacement crises. We are an independent organization, and do not accept any government or UN funding."

And there were more such organizations in which the Hassenfeld Family Foundation was involved. Plus numerous pro-Israel and Jewish causes, domestic and foreign, in which Hassenfeld's close ally was his mother, whose pioneering work dated to the 1940s, when Merrill, like Merrill's father too, had become a leader of the local and international Jewish communities.

Rabbi Gutterman recalled the Hassenfeld philanthropy he discovered on his arrival in Providence in the early 1970s, when he became a friend of the family.

He recalled Merrill as "a big Teddy bear of a man with a lovely smile. Very sweet. I liked him very much." Gutterman attended, though did not officiate, at Merrill's funeral, and almost 40 years later he recalled the late Senator John Pastore who spoke then of the international flavor of the mourners—that when "a Jew dies in Rhode Island, the world takes notice."

Just as Merrill's commitments had sprung from his upbringing in the home of Marion and Henry Hassenfeld, Gutterman said, so too did Alan's commitments spring from his home.

"Some of these values in general are often caught rather than taught," the rabbi said. "Alan watched his parents give of themselves. Merrill was very rooted in the Jewish community and Sylvia was the first woman to head The Joint Distribution Committee, which is a very significant organization, sort of the social-service arm of world Jewry. Sylvia was very involved with that, as is Alan. It's a very big deal. The [early] locus of the Hassenfelds' concern was the Jewish community and then it ultimately spread out."

Gutterman said the world could be divided into takers and givers, with the Hassenfelds in the latter group. "It's their pleasure and it has been a pleasure to have made a difference for good in the world," he said. "That has a lot of support in Judaism, where the large question is not 'how do I save my soul?' but 'what do I do to make this world better than I found it? How do you take this broken world and help make it more whole by your actions and aspirations?' "

Gutterman found in Alan, as in his brother and parents, another desire.

"Recognition has been important to them. It has given them a sense of legacy. Particularly because Steve and Alan did not have children, there's a sense of leaving a good name, which is also rooted in Jewish tradition. So it then feeds on itself. It becomes 'what else can I do? Where else might I find a place to make a difference?' "

Alan's personality, Gutterman said, complimented that yearning.

"He has a very big heart. That's genuine. He has, ironically, a special soft place for children," and not necessarily because of Hasbro, Gutterman said. "He's boyish in a way and there is a certain childlike quality to him in terms of wonder and enthusiasm. Alan is sweet."

Hassenfeld also had the respect of fellow philanthropist Neil D. Steinberg, president and CEO of the Rhode Island Foundation, which had assets of almost $1 billion and annual giving that surpassed $45 million. Like Hassenfeld, Steinberg had a business background: he had been chairman and CEO of Fleet Bank Rhode Island, which later merged with Bank of America.

Steinberg knew many people of means, among them some who lived quietly off their wealth, the common good not concerning them. Not Hassenfeld.

"Alan is one of those role models for me," Steinberg said, "someone who didn't have to do it. It could have been, 'Hey, what's Alan Hassenfeld doing these days?' That's not the case. It's more 'Where is he in his world travels?' I still probably don't know the extent of his activities with different colleges and different countries, as well as being a voice here. There's a sense of giving back."

With his focus on Rhode Island, Steinberg particularly appreciated Hassenfeld's continuing allegiance to the state. "One of the things I admire about Alan is that while his company got bigger and his influence internationally got bigger, he's still committed to Rhode Island," Steinberg said. "There's no requirement for him to do that. There's no 'advantage' for him to do that. He does have the advantage of independence and part of that, candidly, is wealth. That gets him seats at the table—but even getting seats at the table, if you're not willing to step up and do something, you're just occupying another seat."

Like Hassenfeld, Steinberg's own road to philanthropy had been partly shaped by role models in the business world.

"It's a sense of appreciation for what you were given," Steinberg said. "Somebody gave us opportunities, somebody gave me knowledge, somebody took us under their wing at various times and we get a sense of, 'Hey, I need to do that too.' Paying it forward. You develop a sense of wanting to fix things. You see something and say, 'Hey, why can't this be better? Why can't we feed people, have housing, and educate people better?'"

Among his many causes, Hassenfeld kept health at the top of his agenda. So on that nine-page unpublished list, you would find financial and other support for Adopt a Doctor, the Alzheimer's Drug Discovery Foundation, the American Heart Association, Beacon Hospice, the Catherine Wilfert MD (pediatric AIDS) Fund, The Children's Brain Tumor Foundation, The Children's Burn Foundation, the Gift of Life Bone Marrow Foundation, Home and Hospice Care of Rhode Island, the International Rett Syndrome Foundation, the Juvenile Diabetes Research Foundation International, the New York Stem Cell Foundation, Operation Smile, the Perlmutter Cancer Center and the Providence (mental health) Center, among others.

You would see UCSF's Benioff Children's Hospital, Boston Children's Hospital, Brigham and Women's Hospital, Massachusetts General Hospital, Memorial Sloan Kettering Cancer Center, Miriam Hospital, NYU Langone Medical Center, Rhode Island Hospital, St. Jude Children's Research Center's affiliated institution in China, and even UCLA's Mattel Children's Hospital. Hasbro Children's Hospital, of course, and Women & Infants Hospital, for which Hassenfeld held special affection. He was, after all, born there.

On that unpublished list, you would also find references to seed money for women's health centers in Afghanistan and Darfur, and "Zambi, The Baby Elephant," the Hasbro's Children's Fund project benefitting Zambian children orphaned by AIDS. Hassenfeld spoke to those and related initiatives in 2010 at The United Nations during its "Engaging Philanthropy to Promote Gender Equality and Women's Empowerment" day. In introducing Hassenfeld, the organizing agencies stated that "Hasbro and Hassenfeld Family Foundation are focusing on the improvement of the emotional, mental, and physical health of disadvantaged children and the empowerment of women the world over."

And on that list, you would note the Hassenfeld Cardiovascular Scholars Program, which supports research by young physician-scientists at Mass. General and Harvard Medical School. The roots of that multi-million-dollar effort lay with Mass. General cardiologist Dr. Roman W. DeSanctis, who until his retirement in 2014 at the age of 83 had counted among his patients John Wayne, Henry Kissinger, legendary Boston Celtics coach Red Auerbach—and Hassenfeld.

"Roman and I just have a special bond," Hassenfeld joked. "He feels because I've tried to save the world, he's got to save me!"

In the Cardiovascular Scholars Program's 2016 report, several young women and men wrote personal letters to Alan and Vivien thanking them and outlining their latest research, which included studies of atherosclerosis, heart attack, stroke, genome engineering, venous thrombosis, aortic aneurysm and stenosis, valve replacement, heart failure during transplantation, and the possible application of the mechanisms zebrafish use to regenerate injured heart muscle to the damaged human heart.

Wrote Caroline Burns, one of the scientists in the zebrafish study: "Because of your vision, truly novel approaches to curing heart disease are being pushed forward in the laboratory instead of being stymied at the idea stage… Your contribution to our research program has already had long-reaching effects that we expect to ripple outwards for years to come. While the financial support has been vital to our operation, the validation of our ideas and the means to translate concepts to reality has been equally valuable."

And there was more: Hassenfeld's support of her group's work, Burns wrote, had already resulted in "a new research direction in the laboratory that we recently translated into over $500,000 of new funding."

To best feed the hungry, sow seeds.

The Hassenfeld family's 2015 gift to Brown University was sufficiently momentous that president Christina H. Paxson joined Rhode Island Governor Gina Raimondo at the State House to unveil it. The $12.5-million donation created the Hassenfeld Child Health Innovation Institute, which unites Brown faculty, staff and students and community partners. The university would match the gift to help realize the institute's promise.

"This new collaboration has my full support, especially as a mom of two young kids," the governor said. "Not only will this innovative institute help give kids a chance to be healthy and thrive, but it will also showcase our incredible relationships and talents across health care, universities, and government."

Said Paxson: "This is an unprecedented opportunity for cross-institutional collaboration to address critical health needs of a vulnerable population."

Opened in 2016, the institute was structured under an executive committee including Dr. Patrick M. Vivier, institute director, and Dr. Phyllis Dennery, pediatrician-in-chief at Hasbro Children's Hospital and the Sylvia K. Hassenfeld Professor and Chair of Pediatrics at Brown. Sylvia had died in 2014, and the professorship in her name was part of a family gift that included the Alan G. Hassenfeld Professorship of Pediatric Oncology endowment.

Speaking at the State House announcement, Dennery praised the initial focus on the three categories of autism; asthma; and healthy weight, nutrition and physical fitness.

"These initiatives are at the heart of pediatric health," Dennery said. "We have seen epidemics in all three areas and can attribute these in part to environmental factors facing vulnerable children and families. Clearly, the issues we have identified can be better addressed through targeted therapies and interventions. The institute will seamlessly coordinate our collective system-wide efforts to address these challenges."

Sylvia's son spoke of a desire she would have shared with him.

"My greatest hope is that when we look back 10, 20, 30 years, we will have created global solutions to alleviating some of these child health conditions," Hassenfeld said. "I know we can't remove them, but at least we can put the dollars behind research that will develop innovative approaches that help us truly move the needle in significant ways."

As he did the next year when lunching with the inaugural group of Child Health Scholars, Hassenfeld spoke of the debt his family and company owed.

"All of our incredible success is because of children the world over," he said. "We always have been a family that has tried to give back to our community, and to women and children around the globe."

The Hassenfeld family's deep connections with New York City long inclined Hassenfelds to support medical programs based in the city. So it was fitting that in 1990, the family had established the Stephen D. Hassenfeld Children's Center for Cancer & Blood Disorders at NYU Langone Medical Center—and that 21 years later, the family's largest gift ever would establish a new children's hospital in Manhattan.

Officials including mayor Michael Bloomberg attended the official announcement of the new Hassenfeld Children's Hospital, also part of NYU Langone, on October 2, 2011 at the Intrepid Sea, Air, & Space Museum—where, in 1994, Hasbro had celebrated 30 years of G.I. Joe. More than 1,000 attended, and Barbara Walters served as master of ceremonies.

"We've made enormous strides over the last ten years in improving comprehensive health services that will help more of our children enjoy successful, fulfilling lives," Bloomberg said. "With the generous help of the Hassenfeld family, NYU Langone Medical Center will create a state-of-the-art pediatric facility that makes a difference in the lives of those we care about most."

"The well-being of children is one of our great passions," said Sylvia, a longtime NYU Langone Medical Center trustee. "The first toys Hasbro made were doctor and nurse kits. I like to think that, with those, we inspired some youngsters who are now practicing pediatric medicine at NYU Langone. This gift is special to me, and to my family as it ensures our commitment to children's health and well-being for generations to come."

Opened in June 2018, the 160,000 square foot Hassenfeld Children's Hospital at NYU Langone hospital incorporated many of the elements of Rhode Island's Hasbro Children's Hospital: "More than 400 doctors from 35 specialties provide inpatient and outpatient care for common and complex childhood conditions, including a Pediatric Intensive Care Unit and Congenital Cardiovascular Care Unit; surgery services; cardiac catheterization, electrophysiology, and bronchoscopy labs; positive and negative pressure isolation units; procedural and surgical services; and the KiDS Emergency Department," NYU states.

The Hassenfelds' "extraordinary gift," $50 million, said Dr. Robert I. Grossman, dean and CEO of NYU Langone Medical Center at the 2011 announcement, "begins a new era of children's health care in New York and helps ensure bright futures for countless children, our most precious patients, and their families."

One afternoon in October 2015, Hassenfeld walked into Hasbro's world headquarters, where 40 employees participating in the annual "Hasbro U/Experiencing Hasbro" conference awaited him in The Tank, the fabled auditorium where, during his executive years, he had passed untold thousands of hours in research, design, sales and marketing meetings. During those, he sat at the top row of seats in the back, where he could best watch presentations and the reactions of the assembled crowd. This had been Stephen's spot, too. But today, Hassenfeld would be center-stage on the main floor, facing the assembled employees.

The Hasbro U participants, like Hasbro itself, were diverse. They were of many ages, and of Asian, African-American, Hispanic and white descent.

The group included Sharon, a field test coordinator and product archivist had been employed since 1973, when, according to the corporate biography she provided for the Hasbro U catalog, she had worked "assembly lines after school." It included

Ramya, a global consumer insights manager, who had previously worked at Nielsen and Daimler Chrysler. And Huma, a Monopoly brand manager, who had worked in Pakistan. Rosanne, a digital specialist, who had worked as a civilian employee of the Navy. Finance manager Mike had worked at Disney. Tara had served in the Coast Guard, and Jonathan had been with NESN. Debbie, an associate manager at Hasbro's kids-research division FunLab, had been a kindergarten teacher. Eder had come to Hasbro from Wells Fargo Bank.

And others had arrived at Hasbro from CVS Health, Coors, Reebok, Adidas, Rhode Island-based Chow Fun Food Group, Progressive Insurance, Toys 'R' Us, *Cape Cod Life* magazine, Apple, Frito Lay, General Mills, 7-Eleven, and the Solomon R. Guggenheim Foundation. One employee had been a theater-company stage manager and lighting designer. Hasbro welcomed many talents, which together sparked creativity and passion.

The chatter inside The Tank stopped when Hassenfeld entered. Everyone knew who he was, even though some had never met him.

Hassenfeld began with a joke for Sharon, the Hasbro employee for more than 40 years. Someone, like him, who had lived some of the long company history he would discuss.

"Sharon, are you here for remedial training?" Hassenfeld said.

"I might have missed something!" she shot back.

The laughter settled and then Hassenfeld conducted an hour-long seminar on good business practices, corporate leadership, social justice, and philanthropy—after which he answered every question asked of him, which added another half hour.

If he seemed a bit scattered, he said, forgiveness was in order.

"I'm a little bit dyslexic today because in the last three weeks I've spoken in England on human rights, I've spoken in Stockholm with the Nobel group, I've been in Amsterdam, I've been in Shanghai, I've chaired a conference on Chinese-European economic policy in Lisbon and then I was in Madrid for one on co-existence. I came back last night, so I'm all over the place."

The story of Hasbro was the first story Hassenfeld told.

"Too often, we forget about history," he said.

With a quip about nepotism, he related the journey of his grandfather and great-uncle, who traveled from Manhattan to buy scraps from textile mills.

"They literally were rag merchants," Hassenfeld said. "You had New England: the economy was around the rivers. With the rivers, they took the seconds and thirds from the mills and they made hat liners. And from hat liners they ended up making, believe it or not, pencil boxes. And then from pencil boxes, we got into the doctor-kit business."

Hassenfeld spoke of the leadership of his father, then his brother and then him, and of "passing the baton" to Verrecchia, who in turn had passed it to Goldner. The transition to Verrecchia, he said, began in the late 1990s when he began to seriously consider the fact that there was no fourth-generation Hassenfeld waiting in the wings. Given his last name, he said, the matter had never been presented formally to the board.

"The only person for many years who was untouchable was me," Hassenfeld said. "And I finally went to the board, and I said, 'You know, we're really not creating the future and the person we've got to get rid of is me.'"

The Tank was silent.

"They said, 'Have you lost your mind?' And I said, 'Yes.'"

Laughter.

"My mother thought so too, but we won't go there."

More laughs.

"After a while," Hassenfeld said, "you have to begin to think about passing the baton. You get fresh thinking, fresh ways of dealing with things."

And, in his case, Verrecchia, who rescued Hasbro from Pokémon.

"Maybe there are other companies, but I have never seen in a family company where the baton passes outside of the family and is passed as cleanly," Hassenfeld said. "I think it's mainly because of the culture. We are a 'We' culture, not a 'Me' culture. We're very different than almost anyone else, I think, in the toy business."

Hassenfeld got in a dig at Mattel, recalling the 1996 hostile takeover attempt.

"A couple of you remember that we had a Barbie-Q," he said.

The memory was unpleasant.

"It was a very difficult time for me," Hassenfeld said, "especially when your own mother picks up the phone and says, 'You know, son, they offered this much money and do you realize how much it is for the family? I've decided I'm calling the hospitals in Rhode Island. Maybe I took the wrong baby home from the hospital.'"

Hassenfeld had a bit more to say about Hasbro's West Coast rival: "I can remember Mattel about seven years ago saying, 'Oh we're the best in the industry! We have 600 years of intellectual property!' Well, we have about *6,000* years of intellectual property. So you say, 'He's dreaming, he's doing something.' No. If you take how old G.I. Joe is, how old Playskool is. Game of Life is 125 years. Or Ouija. You take everything and add it up, it's amazing."

Hassenfeld made only a mention of an organization he had helped build that had bettered the lives of many: the International Council of Toy Industries' Caring, Awareness, Responsible, Ethical process, or ICTI CARE as it was familiarly known. The only fair-labor organization of its kind, ICTI CARE describes itself as "the ethical supply chain program for the global toy industry," providing intensive audits to ensure employee health and safety, "a robust ethical certification scheme," and "worker well-being programs" that include a free helpline, a program that keeps migrant workers connected to their children back home, and support services addressing emotional needs of all workers and their children.

More than 1,200 toy factories, many in China, employing hundreds of thousands, are ICTI CARE certified. Passing muster are Hasbro, Mattel, Lego, Crayola and another approximately 1,500 toy companies, retailers and licensors including Disney, WalMart, Nickelodeon, Hallmark, McDonald's and Viacom.

"For two years, I crisscrossed the world getting our industry on board and raising $5 million to fund until we could become sustainable," Hassenfeld later said. "Speaking around the globe about 'one industry, one standard' and trying to explain to NGOs that yes, we were the fox guarding the hen house but we were vegetarian foxes."

No Hassenfeld toy talk could end without mention of Pot Head. Despite his Hasbro U catalog disclaimer—"Favorite Brand: They are all my children, I am not allowed to play favorites"—it was clear that in fact, he did place one first among equals.

With reservations.

"Potato Head has been a problem for me. All my life," he said, to laughter again. "There are about four years difference in age between Potato Head and myself but Potato Head believes that he was in the ground five years before they took him out."

Hassenfeld was on a roll.

He mentioned Pot Head's role with the League of Women Voters campaign, the presidential fitness program featuring Schwarzenegger, and the run for mayor of Boise, Idaho, "not something I'm that proud about," he said.

Shortly before the voting in Boise, Hassenfeld said, someone from the election board called him.

"Mr. Hassenfeld, we have a problem," the person said.

"What's your problem?" Hassenfeld replied.

"Well, you know there are five candidates right now. Potato Head is running second—but the polling is now showing that he could win. Is there any way we could get you to withdraw him as a candidate?"

When the laughter subsided, Hassenfeld dead-panned: "Since that day, Potato Head and I have not talked."

And then there were the drug smugglers, another favorite Hassenfeld tale.

"I'm sure you all read that three or four years ago the Mexican cartel decided that Potato Head had a rear end and they decided to stuff their stuff in Potato Head's rear end and cross the border. Potato Head became a mule! The stories I could tell could go on forever."

Hassenfeld opened the floor to questions.

Should Hasbro invest in educational products beyond its Playskool offerings? an employee asked.

"Educational products are important," Hassenfeld said, but he cautioned against overuse of technology in them. It was a recurring theme with him: children and adults being sucked into their devices. He told the story of a recent lunch at a Boston restaurant when he saw "four Chinese girls from university who for 45 minutes didn't say a word. They were just texting. I really believe they were texting each other."

The story drew laughter, but it was a serious issue for Hassenfeld.

"I beg the teachers: 'Please teach your kids at a young age how to play with one another, how to socialize with one another.' If we can educate them that way, I'm excited."

Disturbed was his reaction to recent trends in public elementary and secondary education.

"One of my passions obviously is I don't like what has happened in our schools, especially Rhode Island. The first place that we have a tendency to cut money is in the arts, is in music, and is in physical education. Why do we have little kids with so much of the obesity issue today? Well, if you don't let kids run around and burn off their energy, it's going to happen."

What is your favorite part of the day? A model-shop worker asked.

"When you're able to see dreams become reality. Hasbro Children's Hospital was a dream and it became a reality. Hassenfeld Children's [in New York] is a dream which will become a reality. The new institute to study autism, asthma and obesity—that's a dream for me."

But, no, he said, he could not single out one favorite time of his day, only name "special" times: "When I'm with little kids and all of a sudden where there's been a tear and you see the smile and the sunshine come out."

What would you say is your favorite brand? another employee asked. Perhaps Hassenfeld's earlier comments had been unclear.

"I have this love-hate relationship obviously with Potato Head," he said, but went no further. "I'm just proud of whatever we have been able to put together."

Another employee asked about Hasbro's commitment to remaining in Rhode Island when surely other states with could offer attractive tax breaks or other incentives.

That was a good opening for a joke.

"First of all, when my grandfather got off the ship, I really wish he hadn't come to Rhode Island," Hassenfeld said.

Turning serious, he spoke of the thousands of jobs Hasbro had created and kept in his home state over almost a century without seeking government help. "The one thing that I'm very proud of is all that we've done for the state of Rhode Island—and we've never asked for anything," he said. No hand out to a politician, ever.

Paraphrasing Will Rogers, who said "a statesman is a man that can do what the politician would like to do but can't because he is afraid of not being elected," Hassenfeld said statesmen were rare in the world today. German Chancellor Angela Merkel was one exception, Hassenfeld said—but her policies welcoming immigrants and refugees were bound to bring her trouble at a time when much of the rest of the West was closing borders, and presidential candidate Trump in his June announcement had vowed to build a wall on the Mexican border. Trump had since doubled down on that vow and said in an incendiary CNN interview: "You have people coming in, and I'm not just saying Mexicans, I'm talking about people that are from all over that are killers and rapists and they're coming into this country."

That kind of sentiment infuriated Hassenfeld.

Save for Native Americans, Hassenfeld said, "we're all immigrants. Or we all came from immigrant or refugee stock."

After an hour and 20 minutes, Hassenfeld ended his talk with Hasbro U's class.

"In closing," he said, "I think that you're in the most wonderful business in the world. I find that anyone who comes into this business doesn't like to leave this business. Because it's one of the few businesses where you're truly—most of the day, anyway—young at heart."

His final words: "Remember, you have to give back to your community. Don't take where you are today for granted. Remember those who became before you. Thank you for not falling asleep!"

Like Hassenfeld's stories about him, Potato Head seemed destined to go on forever. The character's resurgence with the release of *Toy Story* in 1995, six years into Hassenfeld's tenure as chairman and CEO, had continued as the 21st Century dawned and the sequel became a box-office giant again.

Released over the 1999 Thanksgiving holiday, *Toy Story 2* grossed $245.8 million domestically, with another $251.5 million overseas, and brought Mrs. Potato Head, voiced by Estelle Harris, onto the big screen with her husband, voiced again by Don Rickles. Dressed in black tie, the Potato Heads joined Buzz Lightyear and Woody on stage during the 2000 Academy Awards ceremony for a spoof, and in another confirmation of Pot Head's continuing relevance, Potato Head threw out the first pitch at Wrigley Field at a Chicago Cubs game.

The year 2000 was also when Mr. Potato Head was inducted into the Toy Hall of Fame, which acknowledged many landmarks in the toy's history: first toy advertised on TV, a 1950s promotion in *Life* magazine, the transition from actual vegetable body to plastic body in 1964, and the first two *Toy Story* movies decades later, which "gave the big spud a new life on key chains, mugs, ball caps, Christmas ornaments, and boxer shorts."

Another indicator of Potato Head's place in the culture came in 2001, when Garfield cartoonist Davis launched a Mr. Potato Head comic strip with longtime collaborator Brett Koth. Nationally syndicated, the strip was collected the next year on the 50th anniversary of the toy's birth in *Mr. Potato Head Unplugged*, a book published by Andrews McMeel.

"He is the man, the myth, the legend...the potato," the publisher wrote in the catalog copy, which described the life not of "a lone spud," but of a tuber living with his wife, daughter and son. "The four deal with such typical family follies as sibling rivalry, office issues, and chores, plus other unique challenges that come with being a large-headed tuber in the new millennium. Mr. P., as he's affectionately referred to by Davis, is a total couch potato when he's at home. His wife is a bit more ambitious as the author of her own gardening column, 'Ask Mrs. P.' *Mr. Potato Head Unplugged* is sure to sprout rib-tickling laughs with readers of all generations, from young children discovering this much-loved spud for the first time to baby boomers who remember the toy as the first one ever advertised on television."

With Mr. Potato Head of grandfather (if not great-grandfather) age now, the AARP marked the toy's 50th birthday in 2002 by issuing a membership card and sponsoring a contest benefiting Operation Smile. And as the new millennium continued to unfold, Mr. Potato Head found new venues. A 529-pound, 43-foot-tall balloon version appeared in Macy's Thanksgiving Day parades. Hasbro also granted rights to advertisers who wanted to feature Mr. Potato Head in commercials, including Bridgestone Tires.

Broadcast during Super Bowl XLIII in 2009, the Bridgestone ad depicted Mr. Potato Head racing a yellow sports car along a mountainous road. Mrs. Potato Head sits in the passenger seat, and she is not amused.

"Slow down, slow down! What's the hurry! You're driving like a maniac!" she says.

Pot Head keeps a lead foot.

"Are you listening?" his wife says. "Are you listening! I can't stand it when you ignore me. This wind is mussing up my hair."

"Don't give me that look," Mr. Potato Head says.

"Watch the road."

The car rounds a corner and nearly hits a flock of sheep. Pot Head slams on the brakes. Mrs. Potato Head's red lips fly off her face and tumble down the mountain, as her fading voice says: "Great, now look what you've done. I told you not to drive so—" before going silent.

Mrs. Potato Head swaps her sweet eyes for a set of angry ones, her husband's moustache twitches, and the announcer closes the 30-second spot with: "For drivers who want to get the most out of their cars, it's Bridgestone or nothing."

Great art, it was not; a throwback to the era of the toy's birth, when wives were expected to be subservient to their husbands, it was.

With its presence on YouTube, the spot generated more laughs (and a few misogynistic remarks) than controversy. But such was not the case with a 30-second spot for Lays potato chips broadcast in 2014 and created by Chicago's Audio Producers Group for ad agency Energy BBDO Chicago.

In it, Mr. Potato head walks into his house after a day's work and calls out: "Sweetie, I'm home."

We hear the crunching of a potato chip being eaten somewhere. Startled, Mr. Potato Head walks from the living room to the kitchen, where he discovers a pot of water boiling.

More crunching, still off-screen.

"Hello?" Mr. Potato Head says.

He walks into the pantry—an old-fashioned, '50s sort of pantry—where he discovers Mrs. Potato Head sneaking Lays chips from their distinctive yellow bag.

Caught, red-handed.

"But you're a *potato*," her husband says.

"The light, crispy taste of Lays potato chips," the announcer says. "One taste, and you're in love."

The commercial closes with Mrs. Potato Head tempting her husband with a bite.

"Our little secret, OK?" he says as he swallows one.

Many found the ad funny. Others read darkness into it, and it sparked a social-medial firestorm rife with conspiracy theories and bizarre allegations. On YouTube, where it was watched millions of times, viewers had their say.

A point of contention was cannibalism: some viewers maintained that the spot condoned, even promoted, it. True, two cartoon potatoes did indeed eat (cooked) potatoes—but some saw a subliminal message involving *homo sapiens*, not *solanum tuberosum*.

"This is actually horrifying, imagine coming home to find your wife eating slices of salted human," wrote one person.

Another wrote: "'our little secret' promoting cannibalism. Why? because rich tards have been doing it for a long time and one of the reasons they're so wack. causes spongiform encephalitis (holes in the brain) like mad cow disease when a cow would eat another dead cow. rich people thought it kept you young. only recently found out it pretty much makes you nuts. one reason why the world is the way it is."

Such reactions prompted creator Audio Producers Group to disable comments, though the commercial remained online and had, by summer 2019, been viewed more than 22 million times on the APG channel. Numerous other individuals had also uploaded the spot to their channels, making for a viewership of at least 23 million. The culture continued to churn, and Potato Head continued to play a role.

Approve or disapprove of the Lays spot, no one could dispute that Mr. Potato Head was permanently ingrained in Americana. You needn't be a girl to appreciate it, as was true with Barbie; or be a boy, as with Transformers; or even be a child. Unlike G.I. Joe, which remained popular with adult collectors but had largely left the collective consciousness of boys in the contemporary era, the Potato Head line in 2019 included almost three dozen offerings. The classic Mr. and Mr. Potato Head toys continued to sell, as did the Spudette, Pirate, Disney/Pixar Toy Story 4, Mash Mobiles, Chew-Bake-A, Star Wars, and other versions.

Much of the character's staying power could be attributed to Hasbro's commitment since 1952 to refresh and reimagine the toy to follow the ever-shifting winds of consumer interest. Over the years, Hasbro brought a Homer Simpson Potato Head to market. A Kiss Potato Head (honestly). A Friday the 13th Jason Potato Head. Ghost-busters. Spider-Man. A Breaking Bad (honestly again) Mr. Potato Head. The Hulk. Wolverine. Doctor Who. Captain America. Green Goblin. Iron Man. Falcon. Thor. Hawkeye. Transformers. Super Spud. A string of Star Wars Pot Heads, many named with a traditional pun: Luke Frywalker, Darth Tater, Spudtrooper, ArtooPotatoo, Frylo Ren, Chewbacca, Yoda.

The *Toy Story* movie franchise helped fuel Potato Head longevity. *Toy Story 3,* produced with a $200-million budget and released in June 2010, topped $1 billion in worldwide box office and earned two Oscars, for Best Animated Feature and Original Song, Randy Newman's "We Belong Together." Its success ensured production of *Toy Story 4,* which opened in June 2019 and had grossed $991 million worldwide by the middle of August and was still in theaters.

The fourth installment featured the voices of Keanu Reeves, Tom Hanks, Jordan Peele, Laurie Metcalf, Tim Allen—and Rickles, who voiced Mr. Potato Head in *Toy Story 3* and died in April 2017. In *Toy Story 4,* his voice was sourced from archival recordings.

"Of course we loved Don obviously, and after he passed, his family contacted us and asked if there was any way that we could create a performance using the recordings that we had," *Toy Story 4* director Josh Cooley told *Entertainment Weekly.* "Now, he had signed to be in Toy Story 4. Unfortunately we did not get a chance to record him for the film. But we went through, jeez, 25 years of everything we didn't use for Toy Story 1, 2, 3, the theme parks, the ice capades, the video games — everything that he's recorded for Mr. Potato Head. And we were able to do that. And so I'm very honored that they asked us to do that, and I'm very honored that he's in the film. Nobody can replace him."

In an article a few years before he died, at age 90, Rickles spoke of an irony in his Potato Head role, which came near the end of a decades-long career.

"You're the voice of Mr. Potato Head in the *Toy Story* movies," an interviewer for *Maxim* magazine asked him. "Are you a fan of those?"

"Well, sure," Rickles said. "I busted my bird for 60 years in the business, but my grandkids only know me as Mr. Potato Head."

In England, a writer for the BBC knew Potato Head as the first major step in creating what was sometimes called "pester power" there and the "nag factor" in America.

In an April 2012 column marking the 60th anniversary of the toy's launch, Jon Kelly wrote that "with his bulbous nose, perpendicular ears and rictus grin, he makes for an unlikely-looking business trailblazer. And yet an industry worth millions owes its very existence to the synthetic, tuberous figurine that is Mr. Potato Head."

Kelly stated the importance of the 1952 Potato Head commercials, writing that they were "an innovation that, by pitching directly to the product's juvenile target market, ushered in a post-war era in which children were specifically targeted as a consumer demographic. In doing so, however, Mr. Potato Head would pave the way for complaints from generations of parents that children were being urged to pester them for countless commercially available treats…"

Watching the early ads for Potato Head, Kelly wrote, "it's striking how old-fashioned and cumbersome they appear today… But according to Paul Kurnit, a New York-based advertising executive who has helped promote toys like G.I. Joe, My Little Pony and Mr. Potato Head, the campaign was wildly radical for its time. The very concept of promoting brands in 30-second slots was still a new technique, he says. And previously, toy adverts in newspapers and magazines had generally been pitched at those paying for them - parents - rather than the children themselves. 'The idea of putting adverts to children on television was a brand-new concept,' Kurnit says. 'It was revolutionary…'"

Those seeking confirmation that Potato Head still held currency with younger generations could point to 24-year-old singer/songwriter Melanie Martinez, whose sensational career began on *The Voice*. "Mrs. Potato Head," a cut on her 2015 hit album *Cry Baby*, was a haunting exploration of the unrealistic beauty expectations placed on American women, and the cost and potentially disastrous consequences of the plastic surgery some seek trying to meet them. In the music video, a man hands the woman struggling with body-image issues a note reminding her of an appointment for a facelift as Martinez sings: *Sexual, hey girl if you wanna feel sexual, You can always call up a professional, They stick pins in you like a vegetable.*

The video had drawn more than 86 million views by August 2019, and its power lay with its polished production and haunting lyrics:

> Oh Mrs. Potato Head tell me
> Is it true that pain is beauty?
> Does a new face come with a warranty?
> Will a pretty face make it better?
> Oh Mr. Potato Head tell me
> How did you afford her surgery?

PART TWO: 'NOW AND FOREVER'

At Hasbro, change had become the new normal. The culture and industry simmered with the acceleration of the Digital Age, and Verrecchia and the board, with Hassenfeld still holding a seat, had decided that Goldner, 42, soon would be master.

The next-to-last step in his ascension to CEO occurred in January 2006, when Verrecchia named Goldner Chief Operating Officer, reporting only to him. When the two arrived at Toy Fair the next month, they were greeted warmly.

Chris Bryne, a toy industry analyst, applauded Goldner's management style. "I think he's a guy who surrounds himself with people who know things he doesn't," said Bryne. "When I've been up there, his people are really happy to see him and they enjoy working with him."

Said Ryan Beck & Co. analyst Margaret Whitfield: "He seems like he's the heir apparent."

He was, and he would claim his inheritance two years later.

A native of Huntington, New York, Goldner was the son of Norman Goldner, an electrical engineer who specialized in the stealth technology of electronic warfare, and Norman's wife, Marjorie, daughter of a man who headed the Mississippi State University's journalism department. Marjorie was working for UNICEF when she married Norman, in 1961, and she was teaching school when son Brian was born in 1963. Their other child, Brad, was born five years later.

Marjorie and Norman had no toy-company connections, but the Goldners imparted in their sons a commitment to giving back, something that would influence the future executive's corporate philosophy at a company where it had been a bedrock principal since 1917.

"That was an important element of who I was as a child," Brian Goldner recalled decades later.

Goldner's mother still kept a yellowed clipping from the local newspaper with a photograph of her older son at about the age of six selling lemonade and candy with a neighborhood friend to raise money for Huntington Hospital, a cause suggested by Marjorie, who still supported her former employer UNICEF, the United Nations Children's Fund, which provides developmental and humanitarian assistance to vulnerable mothers and children in developing nations.

JUNIOR PHILANTHROPISTS, the photo caption began.

"The campaign of the Huntington United Fund got off to an unexpected early start this week. Two enterprising young men, Bryan [CQ] Goldner of 50 Turtle Cove Lane, left, and Kenneth Katz of 9 Henhawk Lane, set up a lemondade and candy business. Their proceeds, donated to the Huntington United Fund, became the first contribution to the campaign, which is schedule for September 15 to October 30."

Philanthropist. Enterprising. Business. Words that foretold Goldner's future.

The Goldners also participated annually in the "Trick-or-Treat for UNICEF!" campaign, which raises money utilizing distinctively branded cardboard collection boxes.

"I had always understood what orange boxes meant at Halloween," Goldner said. "That was an important element in our family." In their home, the Goldners also trained dogs for the visually impaired, "one of my favorite things that we did," he recalled.

During his teenage years at Huntington High School in the late 1970s and early 1980s, Goldner gravitated toward the outdoors, pursuing hiking and sailing and, one year, completing a 370-mile whitewater canoe journey from Maine into neighboring New Hampshire.

"I found it interesting to go out with a group of people and sort of test your mettle," Goldner later said. "To build those personal skills, being outside without those creature comforts, I found that very helpful to my development."

Dartmouth College, located between the White and Green Mountain forests, attracted the teenager and he enrolled there after graduation from high school in 1981. He majored in government, but his passions ran to deejaying at college station WFRD and public speaking. "I liked debating," he said, "taking a topic and understanding it and being able to present it in a really compelling way."

He liked, too, the breadth of a liberal-arts education.

"Dartmouth was an amazing education," he said. "College to me taught you how to learn something and taught you to learn it at a pace. It was really more about the discipline of learning."

Having accumulated sufficient credits to graduate by the end of his first semester in senior year, Goldner took a job as a marketing assistant with a Long Island healthcare company and after that, went to Leo Burnett Advertising, founded by the man responsible for some of the 20th century's most famous brand campaigns, including The Marlboro Man, Charlie the Tuna, Tony the Tiger and the Maytag Repairman. He stayed in Chicago with Burnett from 1985 to 1990, when he left for a position with Walter Thompson Advertising, which counted Ford, Kraft Foods, Toys 'R' Us, Kellogg's and Nestlé among its clients. Goldner worked in the agency's offices in Chicago and Los Angeles, home of Hollywood. By then, he had married Barbara Genick, a social worker and nurse he had met at the Long Island healthcare company. They would have two children: a son and a daughter.

Goldner was a rising marketing and advertising star, but he sought a different test of mettle in 1997, when he left Thompson to become president of Bandai North America, the U.S.-based branch of the giant Japanese toy company that sold a line including the popular Digimon and Mighty Morphin Power Rangers video games. He stayed two years before becoming executive vice president and chief operating officer of Tiger Electronics, which Hasbro had acquired in 1998. In 2000, Goldner went to Pawtucket, as president of U.S. Toys.

"Coming to Hasbro was a natural fit on many levels," Goldner said years later, when he was CEO. "Obviously a deep desire and need for a new strategic direction for the company—a reassertion of the power of our brand. A new philosophy that was more contemporary and more fast-paced to keep up with the evolution of consumer behavior and play behavior globally—but also the idea that we could create a purpose within our business strategy and objective of making the world a better place for children and their families."

Tikkun Olam.

Recognizing the momentous nature of Goldner's eventual inheritance—he would be the first former outsider to run Hasbro—the hometown *Providence Journal* devoted much of a business-page cover story in the Sunday, February 19, 2006, edition to him. Readers learned that he liked boating, biking, skiing, and running, and that he lived with his wife and children in Barrington, an affluent town on the east shore of Narragansett Bay that was a short drive from Bristol, where Hassenfeld kept his summer home.

Readers also learned about Goldner's management style, which was team-oriented with a captain who set a clear direction. "Everybody on my team knows what the play is," Goldner said.

Until he became CEO, Goldner himself would have but one captain, Verrecchia, whose faith in him was absolute; he had seen the results. He praised Goldner, telling the Journal writer he "has been at the forefront of Hasbro's drive to bring innovation and growth to the toy industry and his tremendous experience and entrepreneurial spirit will serve him well in his new role." Goldner, in turn, pledged continued fealty, saying that "I think that Al and I have very complementary skill sets." Which they did; the financial married to the product and marketing as Hasbro continued to develop its brands, while being more selective about licenses.

Two years passed, and Hasbro continued to prosper with Verrecchia as CEO, Goldner the COO, and Hassenfeld non-employee chairman. Hasbro saw revenues rise from $3 billion to $3.1 billion in 2006, as operating profit rose almost $66 million, to $376 million. Revenues rose more dramatically in 2007, to $3.8 billion, with a correspondingly big jump in operating profit, to $519 million and a basic net earnings of $2.18 per share of stock, a company record. When the results were announced in February 2008, a share of stock was selling for more than $27. Wall Street once more was smiling on the Rhode Island company, and there would be bigger smiles in the years ahead as the stock climbed toward and then surpassed $100, numbers once unthinkable for a toy firm.

The birth of what was destined to be one of the biggest movie franchises of all time would deserve a fair degree of credit.

The first *Transformers* movie, with Goldner and Spielberg as executive producers, grossed $709 million worldwide after its July 2007 release. Box office-wise, that was merely a tease, albeit a big tease. With Goldner continuing as executive producer, the first of several sequels, *Transformers: Revenge of the Fallen,* which hit screens two years later, would hit $836 million worldwide. *Transformers: Dark of the Moon*, third in the series, would open in June 2011with a sizzling $97.8-million domestic weekend box—*Jurassic* and *Star Wars* territory—and go on to bring in $1.1 billion worldwide. And the series wasn't done yet.

"It is the big pendulum swing from being a manufacturer of toys to being an owner of entertainment properties," Goldner said on the eve of release of the first *Transformers* movie.

Thus was Goldner cloaked in success when he assumed the corner office at the annual meeting on May 22, 2008. Hassenfeld praised him as "a dynamic talent," the right man for the future. "The entire board has confidence in his ability to succeed," the last brother said.

It was an emotional gathering for Hassenfeld and Verrecchia, as the longtime partners assumed new, less powerful positions (with day-to-day management, at least) at the company where their combined service totaled nearly a century—more, if you factored in Hassenfeld's childhood and youth as the grandson of Henry, son of Merrill, and brother of Stephen.

The day began with a breakfast meeting in the executive dining room of Hasbro's board of directors: Hassenfeld, Verrecchia and Goldner joined former McDonald's chairman and CEO Jack M. Greenberg and Alan's mother, 87, an emerita member and leading stockholder. The directors then joined a larger assembly in the main cafeteria at 1027 Newport Avenue.

As he left the chairmanship, turning it over to Verrecchia, Hassenfeld said of the retiring CEO: "There has been one person, through thick and thin, who has been there for us." Hassenfeld then handed Verrecchia—who he called an "adopted Hassenfeld"—a silver light saber, the totemic *Star Wars* toy. In return, Verrecchia announced that a playground in Providence, where Hassenfelds had lived and worked since 1915, in Alan's honor.

"Anyone who knows Alan knows of his love of children and his home state of Rhode Island," Verrecchia said. "They also know that Alan has always resisted naming opportunities that featured the Hassenfeld name, preferring instead to let the company take the lead.

"Well, in honor of his incredible service to both children and this state, the city of Providence is going to rename the beautiful Roger Williams Park Boundless Playground that we dedicated in August of 2001 to the Alan G. Hassenfeld Boundless Playground. Now and forever in his home state, Alan's name will be affiliated with children, fun and play."

In one of his final duties as CEO, Verrecchia reviewed the 2007 results, a rewarding vindication of the brand-centric strategy that he implemented following the painful reorganization required by the crisis year of 2000, when Pokémon so threatened Hasbro. Hasbro stock earlier in May had reached a record of $37.19 a month. Verrecchia's job was largely done.

Chairman still, he left his office to Goldner and for the first time in 43 years would no longer be a daily presence at Hasbro—deliberately. He did not intend to mess with Goldner's management, explaining his rationale with another of his sports metaphors: "Retired ballplayers go to the owner's box, not the dugout."

Financially secure and then some, he and Gerrie would move from their waterfront home in Warwick to a nicer waterfront home in Narragansett, near the home of Thomas M. Ryan, retired CEO of CVS Health and a fellow University of Rhode Island graduate. Verrecchia would continue with his responsibilities as chairman of the board of Lifespan, which included among its entities Hasbro Children's Hospital and Bradley

Hospital, the nation's first psychiatric hospital for children. He would continue, too, as a board member of FM Global, a commercial-property insurance company, and Old Stone Corp., a brokerage firm. He would remain, for a while, chairman of the Toy Industry Association.

He and Gerrie would travel, and they would savor the fruits of his long labor.

"The wonderful thing is, I don't have to have a plan," he said, "just get up in the morning and decide what we want to do. I want to enjoy all the hard work I've done over the last several years. As a friend of mine said: 'You don't want to be the richest guy in the cemetery!' "

He had no inkling of the health challenge he would face—one similar to Hassenfeld's own years before. One from which he, like his friend, would recover, having found fresh perspective.

Goldner took the reins with a veteran Hasbro team that had supported Verrecchia during his time as CEO: David Hargreaves, who replaced Goldner as COO and kept his position as Chief Financial Officer; John A. Frascotti, appointed chief marketing officer; Duncan Billing, named global development officer; and Dolph Johnson, who became senior vice president for human resources.

Goldner began his first speech as CEO by thanking the board and Alan, who "has been an incredible source of inspiration over the years. I am especially happy to know that he will still be active and engaged as a member of Hasbro's board of directors."

He thanked Al, declaring that "it has been your unwavering, steadfast leadership in both the toughest times and best of times that provided all of us at Hasbro with the roadmap to success. You have demonstrated an excellence in leadership and I am so pleased that you will be part of the leadership team going forward."

After thanking many others, Goldner outlined his corporate strategy, which broadened the course Verrecchia had charted. "At the heart of our objective to be the best toy and game company in the world is our relentless drive to re-invent, re-ignite, re-imagine, and grow Hasbro's world class brands," Goldner said. "We will also create exciting new brands."

Beyond brand-building, the new CEO vowed to "expand and drive Hasbro's brands into digital gaming"—a vow he would keep, with dramatic results for the bottom line. A new era in electronics was dawning: the original iPhone had been released the year before, the iPad was just two years in the future, flat screens were sending cathode-ray ones to the recycling grave, and game developers for all platforms were frantically creating the play patterns of a new age, patterns desired by entertainment-seeking individuals of all ages and on all corners of the planet.

Goldner emphasized the proven strategy of integrating winning brands into as many platforms as possible.

"We will continue to make our brands meaningful by bringing them to life via lifestyle licensing and publishing," he said, citing *Transformers* as the model. More than ever, he said, consumers drove the business, not the other way around. The days of a company—any company—forcing their products on buyers had ended. The internet, among other factors, had made that era as antiquated as one of Henry Ford's Model Ts.

"We will work to expand and contemporize our brands by delivering the right entertainment and immersive experience for every consumer and audience," Goldner said. "We understand that consumers today are in the driver's seat and want to experience brands when they want, where they want, and in any form or format they want. We will inspire play and play experiences for consumers of all ages across our deep portfolio of brands."

Goldner described 2007 as a "strong" year, which it had been, and said he expected momentum to continue in 2008, which it would.

"I believe we are still in the early innings of our opportunity to evolve and further develop Hasbro as a brand-driven, consumer oriented global company," he concluded, "a company that can continue to consistently grow revenues and earnings for our shareholders over the long term." These words were the proverbial music to investors' ears. Verrecchia and the last Hassenfeld brothers had themselves spoke similarly during their turns at the helm.

In his address and in an interview, Goldner also summarized some of Hasbro's recent achievements, including regaining the global rights to Trivial Pursuit, which would be the basis for a TV show, *Trivial Pursuit: America Plays,* which aired from September 2008 to 2009. He noted transactions that returned to Hasbro ownership of nearly 1,000 episodes of TV programs featuring toys including Transformers, G.I. Joe, and My Little Pony. He mentioned buying Cranium Inc., a Seattle-based board-game manufacturer founded by two former Microsoft executives, in January for $77.5 million, and the license deal with the license with Electronic Arts Inc. for video and digital games based on Scrabble, Tonka, and Yahtzee.

He spoke of the six-year deal with Universal Pictures to produce four or more movies based on properties such as Candy Land, Ouija, Monopoly and Stretch Armstrong, and the recent creation of Cake Mix Studios, Hasbro's own production facility in Pawtucket. Had he mentioned it, no one should have been surprised to learn that Goldner owned an iPhone, an iPod, BlackBerry, a Nintendo Wii and a PlayStation 3, from Sony Interactive Entertainment.

Born in conversations involving storyboards Hasbro employees drew during early pre-production of the first *Transformers* movie, Cake Mix Studios was a video and still-photography shooting and editing facility for commercials and internet clips of Hasbro products. The name incorporated Goldner's conception of how the company's products should translate into all traditional, new and emerging formats, building on each other to create a seamless brand experience the new CEO likened to a "seven-layer cake." Cake Mix had been built inside a cavernous space on the lower levels of Hasbro's main headquarters building, the converted factory where Merrill, Stephen and Alan Hassenfeld had kept their offices in a long-gone era.

Merrill might never have imagined such a thing, but Stephen and Alan surely could have.

Brian Goldner. (Courtesy Providence Journal)

Business experts following from afar approved of the latest transitions at Hasbro, and of the quickened pace, if not sense of urgency, since Verrecchia had become CEO.

"I always say leaders have to be looked at in the context of the period in which they're going to lead," said Vijay Govindarajan, a professor of strategy with the Tuck School of Management, Dartmouth College, Goldner's alma mater. "This is a watershed appointment for Hasbro. To me, Brian Goldner is perfect."

Govindarajan, who met Goldner when he returned to Dartmouth for a Tuck School leadership program, said the fit was perfect in more than just a managerial sense.

"Hasbro is more than product, it is about culture," he said. "This is a company with a strong emotional infrastructure. That is how Alan Hassenfeld built this company; the emotional bonds are very important. Brian Goldner has that in his blood."

Five months after the 2008 annual meeting, nurse Debbie Beck lifted four-year-old Dante Pendleton from his wheelchair and lifted him onto a swing at the Alan G. Hassenfeld Boundless Playground, new name for the Roger Williams Park Boundless Playground after a months-long renovation paid for by the Hasbro Children's Foundation.

Dante, a special-needs child born with holoprosencephaly, a severe brain disorder, could not talk or walk. He had never ridden solo on a swing before.

Beck pushed, and young Dante "beamed, captivating those around him," wrote *The Providence Journal.* "The corners of [his] mouth curled up into a broad, bright smile."

One of those around him at the park's reopening was Hassenfeld. Another was Verrecchia, who told the crowd that "I know of no gentler, kinder, or more compassionate individual than Alan Hassenfeld. Alan, I can't think of a better way to recognize your commitment. … You are Hasbro's kid."

Hassenfeld read a poem about remembered childhood, when girls and boys build "castles in treetops," sprinkle pixie dust and play games.

"And then something happened," the poem ended. "We grew up."

Hassenfeld looked over the place he was dedicating, with its fresh paint, new toddler area and slides, and what *Journal* reporter Kate Bramson called its "labyrinth of walkways, slides and climbing structures" —and, to no one's surprise, "a Mr. Potato Head who greets children of all ages as they enter the park."

Said Hassenfeld: "May this playground be a place of boundless opportunity for all, a place where no one ever grows up."

That was Kid Number One speaking. Or perhaps it was Pinocchio.

PART THREE: LEGACY

Until her last days, when illness slowed her, Sylvia Hassenfeld worked energetically for her many causes, often hand in hand with the son who liked to joke that perhaps she had taken the wrong baby home from the hospital. Sylvia's earliest philanthropic endeavors had involved Israel and Judaism, and they remained in the forefront until she passed in her Manhattan penthouse, on August 15, 2014, at the age of 93.

In its obituary, *The New York Times* called her "the matriarch of the founding family of Hasbro, the maker of G.I. Joe, Mr. Potato Head and the Transformers, who became a path-making philanthropist and one of the first women to head a major international Jewish aid organization," the American Jewish Joint Distribution Committee. *The Times* noted that during her four-year tenure as the relief organization's first female president, she also became its first head to expand crisis assistance to people of other faiths.

A longer obituary in *The Providence Journal* listed some of the many awards she was given in honor of her "diplomatic skills and her role in protecting human rights, promoting religious freedom, influencing social policy and assuring services to children in need," and singled out her Honorary Citizenship of Jerusalem and the American Jewish Historical Society's Emma Lazarus Statue of Liberty Award for "contributions to improving the human condition."

Eulogists who spoke during funeral services at Providence's Temple Beth-El, not far from the home where Sylvia and Merrill raised their sons, spoke of a woman who touched countless lives.

"This woman meant so much to so many," said Rabbi Gutterman during the ceremony, attended by hundreds.

Jehuda Reinharz, former president of Brandeis University, spoke the longest in a 15-minute eulogy that summarized her many achievements and firsts and imparted a strong sense of her no-nonsense, if generous, personality. He spoke with candor and respect—and a sense of marvel that one of Hassenfeld's final wishes was that he eulogize her.

"It is the only time in our 20-year friendship that Sylvia made a request of me," Reinharz said. "I wish I could have told her in person how much this request means to me."

Reinharz said he knew about Hassenfeld before meeting her in 1994, when he assumed the presidency of "a university with a lackluster board, among a long list of other problems"—and was told that if he could convince Sylvia, by reputation "a dynamo," to join the board, many of those problems would begin to be resolved.

So taking a deep breath, he telephoned her.

"Come to see me next week at 4 p.m. at my apartment" in Manhattan, she said.

"I was served the customary Sylvia specialty of a small cup of coffee and two cookies," Reinharz recalled. "And I made my case."

He had never met any potential donor, Reinharz said, who was "as straightforward as Sylvia. She did not play coy."

Who was on the board? she asked. *Who will survive and who will be sacrificed? What would my role be?*

"She was not going to be a decoration or a symbol of gender diversity," Reinharz said. "I told her I expected her to make financial contributions and help me build up the rest of the board. Sylvia agreed on the spot with the following brief sentence: 'I will join the board and I will support you.' And she was true to her word. So began a most wonderful relationship between one of the most remarkable women of our generation and a grateful new university president."

Hassenfeld's many philanthropic passions impressed Reinharz. "Her energy was boundless," he said. "I was incredulous about the traveling she did."

Echoes of Alan.

"Yes, she also lived very well," Reinharz said. "She loved to dress well, eat well, laugh at good jokes, and she could have fun playing bridge with the best of them. On the other hand, she disliked pretentious people who took themselves seriously."

Reinharz drew knowing laughter in his descriptions of Hassenfeld's manner-isms and style. "Despite her endless travel schedule," he said, "Sylvia never missed a board or committee meeting. She sat at the meetings like a queen, never wearing the same outfit twice. She had read all the materials sent to her beforehand, was well in-formed, and had a no-nonsense attitude."

He related how Hassenfeld and fellow board member Ann Richards, former governor of Texas, formed a powerful duo in accomplishing his agenda. Before meet-ings, he said, "I would tell them exactly what I wanted, and they would literally intim-idate the board into passing my agenda. Sylvia simply said, 'Here is what I think. And here's what needs to be done.' And Ann Richards would chime in and say immediately afterwards, 'I totally agree, let's vote.' And that was it... No one on the board wanted to cross these two women."

Laughter filled the temple.

In closing, Reinharz put humor aside for respectful tribute.

"Obviously, Sylvia was a woman of great wealth, who, like many of her gen-eration, could have spent her life in leisure activities, writing the occasional large check and feeling good about it," he said. "But Sylvia chose a different path. She did not just write checks. She did the work. She got involved in every aspect of the organizations she worked for; talked to everyone, rich and poor; prime ministers as well as the most powerless and vulnerable people in our society. She traveled tirelessly throughout the world trying to improve the lives of less fortunate individuals and communities."

He could have been describing her son.

"She teaches us that with privilege come obligations and opportunities," Rein-harz said. "Not many people can say that they have changed the world for the better. I believe Sylvia is one of those who truly has. We will all miss her very much. May her memory be a blessing."

Hassenfeld at mother Sylvia's funeral. (Courtesy Providence Journal)

One day a year after Sylvia was laid to rest alongside Merrill and Stephen in Lincoln Park Cemetery, a documentary film crew visited Alan Hassenfeld in his Providence office.

They were shooting a movie about the history of the toy industry as part of festivities surrounding the 100th anniversary of the founding of the Manhattan-based Toy Industry Association. The anniversary celebration would begin with the upcoming September 17, 2015, ribbon-cutting for the National Toys Hall of Fame new 5,000-square-foot exhibit space at The Strong National Museum of Play in Rochester, New York.

Hassenfeld had been a driving force behind the Toys Hall of Fame, which for the first time formally combined The Strong's National Toy Hall of Fame with the Toy Industry Association's Toy Industry Hall of Fame to create what was described as "a cutting-edge, state-of-the-art museum installation that recognizes iconic toys and the people who make them," The Strong stated. Financial backing came from The Hasbro Children's Fund, the Hassenfeld Family Foundation, the state of New York, the National Endowment for the Humanities, Lego, Radio Flyer, Toys 'R' Us, the Dutch-owned Pressman Toy Corporation, and former Mattel chief Thomas J. Kalinkse and his wife, Karen, among other sources.

The documentarians put Hassenfeld on camera in his main conference room, which is decorated with items confirming the front-row seat to toy history he had occupied virtually from birth—nearly 70 years by then.

A poster of a Special Forces-like character signed by friends and reading "To Alan Hassenfeld, the Original G.I. Joe, Happy Birthday!" hung on a wall. A Junior Doctors Kit shared space on a shelf with several early Mr. Potato Heads, all in their original boxes. A sideboard served as a place of honor for other sentimental favorites: A Japanese doll case Bandai presented him on Children's Day in Japan some four decades before; a Chinese figurine representing longevity; a porcelain Potato Head; and a New York Jets helmet signed by legendary quarterback Joe Namath, who wrote: "Hey Alan, It's great to be on the same team, pal! Good Luck." Namath had been featured as a Kenner Starting Lineup figure.

"Be the Change," a poster with an image of Barack Obama commemorating his January 20, 2009 inauguration, graced a wall, and next to it were books stacked in a pile reaching almost to the ceiling. Many were about the toy industry, including *Inside Santa's Workshop, Toyland, The Game Makers*, and the hard- and softcover editions of *Toy Wars*. Others spoke to Hassenfeld's philanthropy: *The Business of Changing the World, Ten Rules for Strategic Innovators*, and *Building Better Boards*—as in trustees or organizations, not games.

Hassenfeld also kept a large statue that had been his father's on the sideboard. "I am not sure where he got it, but it was in his office forever and it reminds me that he is watching over me," his son said. Hassenfeld had other reminders, too, in the conference room: sepia-toned photos of the 1946 and 1947 annual Hassenfeld Bros. Christmas parties.

Alan Hassenfeld in his Providence office (Miller photo)

Dressed in his signature collarless shirt, jeans and brown penny loafers without socks, and wearing his rubber bands, Hassenfeld was on camera for more than an hour.

What is your role in the worldwide toy business? the documentary director asked.

"We have many global issues that we in the industry must come together on in order to meet global standards, whether it's in safety, whether it's in advertising," Hassenfeld said. "One of the things that I'm very active in is the human rights for the factory workers that make the wonderful toys."

What was the early history of regulation in the United States?

The first governance, Hassenfeld said, was through the federal Food and Drug Administration; regulation later shifted to the Consumer Products Safety Commission. Advertising standards were a result of the private sector working with the government, Hassenfeld said, but it was long work, and not always easy—and while he did not mention it, consumer advocates and Congressional champions had been a factor, too.

How has the industry changed over the years?

"One of the great changes has been consolidation," Hassenfeld said. He recalled his earliest years in the industry, when Parker Brothers, Milton Bradley, Tonka and other companies later acquired by Hasbro and Mattel were independent. But there was a sense of camaraderie, even among these long-ago competitors, Hassenfeld said. The Barton family, which owned Parker Brothers; Jim Shea at Milton Bradley; the Handlers and Ray Wagner at Mattel; his father and brother at Hasbro—these "giants of the industry," as Hassenfeld called them, all shared wisdom and friendship.

"You were able to pick up the phone and call them for advice," Hassenfeld said. "We were very fortunate in our industry to have great leaders, great mentors, that were willing to help teach us how to deal with customers, how to do things differently in the Far East."

Memories of long-ago Toy Fairs surfaced.

"Can I say we were all fishermen?" Hassenfeld said. "We all told fish stories, 'I caught a fish that was this big or this big or THIS big.' We always exaggerated. But there was a special warmth: Anyone who came into the toy industry never wanted to leave the toy industry. To be honest with you, no matter how important we thought we were, our job was really to think like a seven-year-old. I used to tell people 'Ninety percent of my job is being a seven-year-old and playing with toys. Ten percent I have to wear a suit and deal with bankers and people like that.'"

Was this not the storyline of the 1988 film *Big*, starring Tom Hanks and Penny Marshall?

What do you consider the biggest accomplishment of the industry over the last century? the documentary director asked.

"To speak with one voice on many of the governmental issues that faced our industry, a lot of that having to do with quality standards, a lot of it having to do with foreign trade, a lot of it having to do with advertising, and I think very importantly, talking about play," Hassenfeld said.

"We all forget as we get older that we were once children," he continued. "We forget that we used to chase the wind as little kids when we were flying kites. Most importantly for me is making sure that we explain to all people: Never forget that you were once a child. More importantly, a child's work is a child's play. Because children when they are playing are socializing with one another, interacting with one another, learning dexterity, learning so many things. Too often we think play is frivolous but it's not."

The director closed with the obligatory question: *What is your favorite toy?*

"If you've been in this business as long as I have, they all become your children," Hassenfeld said, then made a familiar crack: "Is it right to say which child you prefer?!"

The crew laughed.

"I have an argument all the time with Potato Head," Hassenfeld said, though it was unclear if the director and his cameraman understood what he meant. "I love G.I. Joe—he put me through college. I love Transformers. I love My Little Pony. Again, it's very hard."

Hassenfeld was planning to lunch with a writer at Capriccio, on the bottom level of the Owen Building, where Hassenfeld had his office.

Among the finest restaurants in a city distinguished for its culinary excellence, Capriccio was a Hassenfeld favorite. He savored not only the food (and convenience), but also the banter with longtime owner Vincenzo Iemma and his staff, and the company of the politicians, businesspeople and others who frequented Capriccio. Hassenfeld's father may have preferred furtive fare at a wiener joint, but Capriccio, with its white linen and exquisite wine selection but cozy ambiance, was more Hassenfeld's kind of place. It was *so* Rhode Island, in business for decades. And the double espresso always helped power Hassenfeld through his busy afternoons.

But first, as the documentary crew packed their equipment, Hassenfeld went to his desk, where he checked his email on his iPad and conferred with Lori Holland, his personal assistant and secretary of the Hassenfeld Family Foundation board of directors who had worked directly for Hassenfeld for 16 years and for Hasbro before that starting in 1986.

But there were no pressing matters, and Hassenfeld had a rare moment of free time.

If the conference room were a sort of ode to Hasbro icons, Hassenfeld's office would qualify as a miniature Toy Hall of Fame—mostly Hasbro toys but with several manufactured by others, including an antique metal racecar and locomotive. Lit by tall windows that afforded views of Providence's East Side—home of Moses Brown School, Brown University and, from 1920 to 1940, the headquarters of Hassenfeld Bros.—the items on Hassenfeld's bookshelves and red-brick walls chronicled a life of interwoven play and philanthropy.

Hassenfeld displayed G.I. Joes, among them a "Japan Limited Edition Two Figures Set Sports Joe Father & Son." He had Hasbro games, including the generic Game of Life and the Rhode Island Monopoly special edition. And a Barney plush toy. Babe Ruth, Honus Wagner, and Ty Cobb Starting Lineup figures. A Hungry Hungry Hippo.

And, naturally, Potato Head drawings, cartoons, and toys, including a large clear-plastic Potato Head that contained his stock of rubber wristbands.

There was a "Laugh Your Face Off!" *Toy Story* poster with a Potato Head image and quotes from reviews, including "One of the year's best!" There was a trophy of Potato Head wearing shirt and tie commemorating Hassenfeld's induction into the Toy Hall of Fame on February 18, 1994, six years before the toy itself was inducted, and ten years before G.I. Joe was enshrined. And figures of Star Wars droid C-3PO high-fiving a Mr. Potato Head, inside a glass case with a plaque proclaiming: "Lucas Film and Hasbro, Hand in Hand into the New Millennium, Alan Hassenfeld."

Hassenfeld displayed the HH-11 Rhode Island license plate that had been his grandfather's and then his father's; the grandson had used the Potato Head Help End Hunger version on one of his own vehicles. He kept a photo of himself with Stephen, and one of Merrill taken shortly before his death surrounded by Hasbro toys of the late 1970s, including Potato Head, Mickey Mouse, Raggedy Ann and Digger the Dog. And a framed 1950s Hasbro brochure, "The Guide to America's Top Ten Toys!", with Mr. and Mrs. Potato Head, "the joyful toy of 1001 faces," surrounded by Doctor and Nurse Kits and Junior Miss Cosmetics Kits.

Hassenfeld had a Hasbro Children's Hospital tile with his name, and in a place of prominence, an award plaque from the National Conference for Community and Justice, formerly the National Conference of Christians and Jews. It quoted "Underneath We're All the Same," a poem written in the 1990s by 16-year-old student Amy Maddox and reproduced in *Teaching Tolerance*, the 1995 book:

> He prayed—it wasn't my religion.
> He ate—it wasn't what I ate.
> He spoke—it wasn't my language.
> He dressed—it wasn't what I wore.
> He took my hand—it wasn't the color of mine.
> But when he laughed—it was how I laughed,
> and when he cried—it was how I cried.

Bubble-wrapped citations and awards awaiting placement took up space on the floor. Others hung from a wall in the kitchen area of the Hassenfeld Family Foundation suite. There, you would see his honorary degrees, a plaque from the China Toy Association, the 2002 Rhode Island March of Dimes Citizen of the Year award, and a print of photos taken at the 2003 groundbreaking of the Afghan Women's Development Centers in Jalalabad and Talaq, which Relief International, Hasbro, and the Hassenfeld Family Foundation helped build to further literacy, improve health and promote participation in civic affairs for women and children in Afghanistan. "With deepest gratitude on behalf of the women of Afghanistan," the print declares.

Even among these acknowledgments of achievements, the playful side of Hassenfeld maintained a presence. Hassenfeld had framed and mounted "Toy giant aims to march in step with fickle kids," lead story of the business section of the April 23, 2005, *Irish Times*, a cover piece illustrated with an impish depiction of Hassenfeld and Mr. Potato Head riding in a Monopoly car. Even NASDAQ, the stock market on which Hasbro shares were listed, had a bit of fun when it saluted Hasbro in a full-page ad during Hassenfeld's tenure as CEO and chairman.

"Play is universal. So we're turning America's best-known toys and games into global brands. From Mr. Potato Head and Tonka to Monopoly and Nerf," Hassenfeld says in the ad.

Overlaid on the ad was a photo of Hassenfeld, with a Potato Head nearly the size of his own head floating next to him.

Memories stirred by the documentarians, Hassenfeld reminisced—first, about his father.

He recalled the cigars Merrill loved, how he habitually chewed on them while at work after he had quit smoking, having been persuaded by his family's history of heart disease that smoking elevated his own risk of cardiac trouble—a tragic irony, in light of what killed him.

"Dad would have a wastepaper basket right here by his desk, and I don't know why, but he could never find it!" Hassenfeld laughed. "You always knew where my father was because he dropped these chewed-off cigars."

He recalled Merrill's love of golf and food and friends, and his discomfort with Sylvia's stern discipline when he and Stephen were kids. Seeking to please his wife, Merrill occasionally—and reluctantly—would take a belt lightly to the Hassenfeld brothers' bottoms.

"It hurt him more than it hurt us, trust me when I say that. He hated it," Hassenfeld said.

His mother, on the other hand, believed that to spare the rod was to spoil the child. *He did wrong, teach him a lesson,* was her message to Merrill when Stephen or Alan transgressed.

Merrill's discomfort reflected his nature, his son believed: "I don't think my Dad had a mean bone in his body," Hassenfeld said. "He was truly one of those incredibly special people. There are very few times that I don't remember him smiling; he had that twinkle, he was made for the toy business. He loved people. He loved giving back, believed totally in living charity—giving while alive to things that can bring a smile."

Merrill's company, Hassenfeld said, carries on the spirit. "There have been a lot of changes at Hasbro," he said, "but the one thing we have done our best—Brian does it very well and Al passed it on—is the culture. The culture of caring, the culture that people are not a number. And that no company is anything without its people."

Hassenfeld spoke with pride of another business that his grandfather, father, and uncle had opened in Israel shortly after it achieved statehood, in 1948: The Jerusalem Pencil Company, first factory built in that city after independence, he said. Memories of Hassenfeld's grandfather elicited memories of Henry's wife, Marion, Alan's paternal grandmother. Alan Hassenfeld was only 11 when she and Henry died, but he still recalled her warmth and the visits to the summer home in Narraganset that she and Henry owned.

Lunch neared, but Hassenfeld found time to recall his first infatuation for Potato Head—when he was a young boy who hated one of the servings Sylvia forced on him and his brother at dinner every night. The toy, he joked, "was great for kids like me who didn't like vegetables! To try and get rid of all the vegetables we didn't like."

There was more to it than that, needless to say.

"It was magic," he said. "And when I say magic, it was a play pattern that was whimsical, it was humorous, it got kids to use their creative skills, their artistic skills.

And it was funny! And this is how Potato Head took on the life it has and why it's stayed in pop culture so long."

Summer was nearly over when Hassenfeld traveled to Rochester for festivities at The Strong museum marking the September 17, 2015, opening of the Toy Halls of Fame and kickoff to the 100th-anniversay celebration of the Toy Industry Association's founding.

He arrived amidst pomp-and-circumstance, courtesy of the The Strong museum team, which chronicled the scene, writing that "the atrium of The Strong was packed with television crews, reporters and dignitaries from across the state, all gathered for a press conference announcing the opening of the Toy Halls of Fame. Thanks to a partnership between TIA and The Strong launched in 2013, the exhibit underwent a $4 million reno-vation and emerged as a state-of-the art installation that honors America's favorite classic toys alongside the industry luminaries who helped to bring those toys to life."

Three Hassenfelds and two other Hasbro employees ranked among those lu-minaries.

Merrill was an inaugural inductee into the Toy Industry Hall of Fame in 1985, along with Herman G. Fisher, Jerome M. Fryer, A.C. Gilbert, Marvin Glass, Nathan Greenman, and Louis Marx. "It was under the leadership of Merrill Hassenfeld, then-president of Hassenfeld Brothers (now Hasbro), that Mr. Potato Head, the first toy to be advertised on television, and G.I Joe, the industry's first male action figure, were born," the Hall of Fame citation declares.

Stephen was inducted posthumously in 1991, and his declaration immortalizes him:

"Stephen Hassenfeld devoted his life to the firm founded by his family, build-ing Hasbro into the largest toy manufacturer in the world. With vision, dedication and a gift for managing the talents of others, he expanded the company's broad product spectrum through astute acquisitions and bolstered new toy lines with unrivaled mar-keting expertise.

"Hassenfeld took control of Hasbro after the death of his father in 1979. In an eight-year time span, Hassenfeld increased Hasbro's profitability from $102.3 million to $1.3 billion. Forbes Magazine rated Hasbro number one in a thousand-corporation survey of increased value during the first half of the 20th century. Hassenfeld also over-saw the acquisition of Milton Bradley in 1984. A passionate believer in giving back to the community, in 1983 he established the Hasbro Children's Foundation and Hasbro Charitable Trust, helping to improve children's quality of life for generations to come."

Alan, inducted in 1994, is recognized not only for his corporate stewardship but also his philanthropy, like his bother:

"With a firm commitment to corporate social responsibility, Alan Hassenfeld has led the successful family business he grew up into new heights. Hassenfeld officially began his career at Hasbro in 1970 and proceeded to work his way up the ranks of the business established by his grandfather.

"As former chairman and CEO of Hasbro, Hassenfeld has diversified the company's portfolio of companies and expanded international operations while initiating a singular brand of corporate activism designed to improve the lives of children. He is co-chair of the Hasbro Children's Hospital Advisory Council, has served as chairman of Families First, and has led joint efforts by corporate executives and elected officials to end childhood hunger. His vision and enthusiastic support of industry, community and charitable causes has set a standard of leadership for generations to come."

Verrecchia, inducted in 2011, was similarly recognized for his corporate acumen and advocacy of safe toys:

"Al Verrecchia is known for his industry leadership and his role in harnessing success at Hasbro. He began his toy industry career in 1965 as an accountant at Hasbro, and rose through the ranks to become CEO in 2003. While at the helm, Verrecchia was one of the prime architects of a strategy to leverage the company's portfolio of brands in categories beyond traditional toys and games. Prior to his tenure as CEO, Verrecchia held a range of executive positions, including CFO, president of manufacturing services, and executive vice president of global operations, among other key roles. In 2008 he became chairman of Hasbro's Board of Directors.

"Verrecchia has also assumed many leadership roles in the industry. He has served on the TIA Board of Directors, was chair of both the Finance Committee and the Budget Committee, and served as a member of the Investment Committee and the Audit Committee. While on the board Verrecchia helped manage the overwhelming changes taking place with the Consumer Product Safety Commission and the Consumer Product Safety Improvement Act. He worked closely with TIA staff and board members to ensure that the industry's safety record and self-assessments were brought to the government's attention." Verrecchia, board chairman from 2008 to 2010, was a member of the Advisory Committee in 2017.

And there was George Ditomassi: "Throughout his four-decade-long career at Milton Bradley and its parent company Hasbro, George Ditomassi demonstrated his commitment to bringing what have become household brands to worldwide prominence," his inscription read.

The Hasbro inductees kept elite company in the Hall of Fame. Among the other members are Walt Disney; George Lucas; John Lasseter; Muppets creator Jim Henson; Wal-mart founder Sam Walton; Charles Lazarus; Robert A. Iger, chairman and CEO of The Walt Disney Company; Mattel founders Ruth and Elliot Handler; Amerman, Barad, Kalinske and Wagner, former Mattel heads; Frederick August Otto Schwarz, FAO Schwartz; Herman G. Fisher; Milton Bradley; Binney & Smith, of Crayola Crayons; and Ole Kirk Christiansen, LEGO founder, and his grandson, Kjeld Kirk Kristiansen.

The festivities at The Strong included a ribbon-cutting, cocktail party, formal dinner, a screening of the centenary tribute video in which Hassenfeld appeared, a cutting of the centenary cake, and a dessert reception.

Hassenfeld delivered an admonition in his dinner address.

"Too often in this nano-second world, we have a tendency to forget history," he said. "It is imperative that we do not forget those who came before us—pioneers that created through incredible diversity the path we walk and which we have truly expanded upon."

Hassenfeld applauded those who established the Toy Halls of Fame. "To all who have lent their creativity, energy, passion and finances to this wonderful marriage, I say thank you."

And then he turned poetic, literally, reciting favorite verses that he also had read at the opening of Providence's Alan G. Hassenfeld Boundless Playground.

"My sister told me that someone once wrote:

> *We all knew magic once.*
> *We saw fairies where there were fireflies*
> *We talked to animals and we sang to birds*
> *We believed in pixie dust and red capes*
> *We built castles in treetops*
> *We raced clouds*
> *We flew on carpets*
> *We traveled to the stars*
> *And then something happened...*
> *We grew up.*

Hassenfeld ended his remarks by saying: "Promise me do not grow up and never forget that you once chased the wind."

CHAPTER NINE

RESPONSIBILITY

PART ONE: CIVICS

Just as Sylvia Hassenfeld had, Al Verrecchia also sometimes remarked that Alan Hassenfeld wanted to save the world. It was an allusion not to grandiosity but to the unflagging optimism that underlay Hassenfeld's beliefs, despite the discouragement found daily in the news.

The world, Hassenfeld believed, cried for salvation.

The job, he knew, was beyond a single savior, so he embraced opportunities offering possibilities to change individual lives. Children's hospitals, for example. Educational and research programs. And while no single person could save the world, one person in a democracy could influence politics. Hassenfeld had demonstrated with RIghtNow!

As the second decade of the 21st century unfolded, politics continued to compel him.

Hassenfeld donated to candidates of any party whose beliefs matched his, and he occasionally hosted fundraising events, including one at his Bristol home for Hillary Clinton in September 2008 to help pay the campaign debt she had accrued in her primary run against Barack Obama. He became involved in Republican Brendan Doherty's 2012 Congressional campaign, saying at Doherty's formal announcement, "He is an American's American. He is in it for all of us to make that ethical and unselfish difference." Doherty, former superintendent of the Rhode Island State Police, lost to incumbent David Cicilline, the former mayor of Providence who in Congress has become a fierce critic of President Trump.

Hassenfeld also brought his voice to the public arena through interviews with journalists who sought his opinion, and with regular op-ed columns in *The Providence Journal*. Government ethics remained of paramount interest to him.

On the eve of the November 8, 2016, election, Hassenfeld penned an op-ed piece beseeching Rhode Islanders to approve referendum Question Two, a constitutional amendment that would restore the Rhode Island Ethics Commission's jurisdiction over state lawmakers, with authority to investigate and punish unethical behavior. The Commission had such power from 1987 to 2008 but lost it in 2009 when the state Supreme Court ruled in favor of former Senate president William Irons, who had challenged it.

"In layman's terms," Hassenfeld wrote, "the court ruled that the speech in debate clause gives legislators immunity from the Ethics Commission. Since the Irons decision, there has been no such entity policing the General Assembly and punishing a lawmaker who uses his or her office to enrich him or herself."

That was wrong, Hassenfeld argued. And voters had the power to change it.

"Voting to approve Question 2 will not change our history, and it won't prevent greedy people from trying to make money from public service, but it will send a message: Rhode Islanders care about ethics and expect their elected officials to as well. I have spent much of my adult life advocating for policies and laws that will make state government more transparent, more effective and more able to serve the people who rely on government to make their lives better. This year you have an opportunity to take a giant leap forward and put the Ethics Commission back on the front lines. Please vote to approve Question 2. It's your turn to make Rhode Island government better — and this year you can."

The time seemed ripe for voters to approve Question 2. In a stunning fall from grace that recalled the worst corruption cases in state history, House Speaker Gordon D. Fox, Rhode Island's most powerful politician, had resigned in March 2014 after a State Police raid on his State House offices and home on the East Side of Providence. A year later, Fox pleaded guilty in federal court to wire fraud, bribery and filing false tax returns.

"In other words, it is all true?" U.S. District Court Judge Mary M. Lisi said as he accepted a plea agreement that would result in Fox serving three years behind bars.

"It is, your honor," the disgraced former speaker said, trying not to cry. With him was his lawyer, William J. Murphy, House speaker prior to Fox.

As Fox headed to federal prison, John Marion, head of Common Cause Rhode Island, beseeched legislative leaders to pass legislation enabling what became Question 2.

"This is a sad day for Rhode Island; this situation is unacceptable," newly elected Governor Gina Raimondo said. "Elected officials must always uphold the highest ethical standards—people deserve honest government."

In the General Assembly, at least, they did not get it.

Less than a year after Fox began serving his sentence, House Finance Committee chairman Raymond Gallison, arguably the most powerful politician in the House after the speaker, abruptly resigned his seat after word of a federal investigation of his activities became public. The May 3, 2016, end of Gallison's tenure stunned even lawmakers who had witnessed Fox's departure from the scene.

"I am shocked," said Jamestown Representative Deborah Ruggiero. "It shows poor decision making ... A lot of what I am hearing goes against my moral compass."

Representative J. Aaron Regunberg, who took over Fox's seat, said "Folks in my neighborhood are going to be upset because they expect and deserve a higher standard."

Gallison eventually pled guilty in federal court to nine felony counts of fraud and theft and faced a prison sentence of up to 111 years. He received four years and three months for swindling almost $678,000 from the estate of a dead man, stealing from a taxpayer-funded non-profit organization where he had once been employed, and robbing a disabled woman's trust.

"The defendant was a scoundrel who engaged in dishonest, unscrupulous behavior," prosecutor William Ferland said. "He's a tax cheat... He stole for greed... Plain and simple."

The time for new reform indeed was ripe and voters in the November 2016 general election responded, approving Question 2 by a landslide, with 78 percent of those casting ballots in favor.

Phil West had joined Hassenfeld and many others in the campaign, and Common Cause head Marion was among those applauding. "Because of this victory," said Marion, "once again our lawmakers will be held accountable for any conflicts of interest, and citizens will know that legislators are serving the public interest, not their own self-interest."

In March 2017, as Rhode Island's unemployment rate dropped below the national average for the first time in more than a decade, capping a long painful period, Hassenfeld penned another op-ed piece that struck the same theme, arguing that "there is a culture of corruption in Rhode Island that is holding the state back from a broader economic recovery."

Hassenfeld praised measures that the General Assembly had passed and the governor signed into law, including campaign finance reform, an online voter registration system, and elimination of the so-called "master lever," which gave Democrats an unfair advantage in the ballot booth. He thanked voters for approving Question 2, but work remained, he said.

"Businesses do not want to move to a state where you need to 'know a guy' to succeed," Hassenfeld asserted. "If Rhode Island's economic recovery is going to continue, we need to be an attractive place to do business. The more attractive and ethical — the more one will have an incentive to invest, innovate, and give back. It's time to take action to improve the integrity of government in Rhode Island. If the state's economic comeback is going to succeed, it needs to be paired with reforms to create an open, transparent, and accountable state government."

Among other new reforms, Hassenfeld urged adoption of a line-item veto, to permit the governor to "remove wasteful spending from the state budget."

"The General Assembly should act quickly to pass these proposals," he concluded. "We have strong momentum on good-government reforms, and we must continue that momentum this year. Rhode Islanders deserve a modern and efficient government. Our continued economic success depends on it. Gandhi once said, 'The world has enough for human needs, but not enough for human greed.' Here in Rhode Island, let us focus on human needs."

The legislature listened, to a degree: Not every reform Hassenfeld supported passed, but the General Assembly did vote to create a commission to study the line-item veto, and to allow customers at the Department of Motor Vehicles to register to vote, a convenience that would draw more citizens into the democratic process.

Behind the scenes—in person, by telephone and by email—Hassenfeld voiced his opinions directly to Rhode Island's members of Congress, the governor, mayors, and other elected and non-elected officials. He maintained an aggressive interest in his home state's healthcare system and in the universities with which he was most closely associated: Brown, Bryant, and Roger Williams. He spoke regularly with education and healthcare leaders, sometimes on issues they might rather avoid. Hassenfeld was not shy about criticizing polices he believed were misguided or self-centered.

The December 14, 2012, massacre of 20 children and six adults at Sandy Hook Elementary School in Newtown, Connecticut, shook most Americans like few other events in the nation's long history of gun violence. A month had yet to pass when, on January 8, 2013, *The Providence Journal* published one of Hassenfeld's most impassioned columns.

"We have just witnessed one of the most horrific acts of violence that Americans have ever seen," Hassenfeld began. "Little children and their teachers executed mercilessly at a school. It did not happen in a war zone in the Third World, but in a quiet town in the wealthiest state, in the wealthiest and most powerful country in history. It has shaken us all, and once again the debate has surfaced on mental health, violence and gun control. We must act now."

Hassenfeld urged renewed funding of Rhode Island's Institute for the Study and Practice of Nonviolence, which had been forced to lay off workers after cuts in government funding. Among the Institute's novel programs affected by the cuts were its "Streetworkers," who intervened with young men whose response to violence is more violence.

"The Streetworkers respond 24 hours a day to shootings and stabbings," Hassenfeld wrote. "They have formed a partnership with Rhode Island Hospital and Hasbro Children's Hospital to immediately engage with victims of crime, their families and friends. They counsel and support the victims and assess quickly the nature of the conflict and what should be done to stop it from further escalation into a cycle of retaliations."

Hassenfeld wrote that improved access to mental health care "is part of the solution."

And so, too, he wrote, is tighter control of guns:

"Strengthening the gun laws is not the only solution, but let's get serious about gun regulation: banning bullets that can pierce a police officer's bulletproof vest, or insanely big bullet clips that let dozens of rounds be fired. This enabled the Newtown massacre of children! We must get serious about background checks, and yes, we must get rid of the semi-automatics... Let Dec. 14, 2012, be remembered in America as the culmination of insanity that for the past decades has willingly brought us to a place where small children are being executed in the confines of a safe school, not in a war zone, not in a poor and desperate neighborhood, but in healthy, thriving Anytown, America. It is a matter of life and death."

This was not the first time Hassenfeld had waded into the gun debate, nor would it be his last. And it would make legislation that he supported the target of the NRA, Tea Party members, and others who opposed gun control.

Their wrath was aroused anew beginning in 2015, after that year's General Assembly had recessed without passing what advocates called "common-sense" gun control legislation that included a maximum 10-round magazine, no guns in schools from kindergarten through grade 12, and no guns for anyone convicted of a domestic-violence misdemeanor. The killing of 14 people in San Bernadino, California, on December 2, 2015, prompted Hassenfeld to join veteran Democrat presidential adviser and fundraiser Mark Weiner in a new effort, RI For Gun Safety, which supported bills to keep firearms out of the hands of domestic abusers.

"My main goal is not to recruit politicians to talk about it," Weiner said. "My main goal is to recruit people in the community and get them involved, because so little happened after Newtown.... Everybody talks about all this stuff for like a month or two, and then it goes by the board, and then you have something that happens ... and now everybody is talking about it again for another couple of days, and all the politicians are holding press conferences and stuff... It's got to be more than that."

Weiner pledged "a couple of hundred thousand dollars" to the cause, and Hassenfeld pledged almost $100,000.

"You have a partner," Hassenfeld told Weiner. "Financially, I am there for you."

Communicating with *Providence Journal* reporter Katherine Gregg, Hassenfeld elaborated: "Would love to see RI take a lead and some legislator have the gumption to propose ... [making] RI safest state in America," he wrote. "Is there anyone in our RI government with courage or are they cowards?"

Some who learned of RI For Gun Safety spewed venom anonymously on social media.

"They are a traitorous group to the American People," one spelling- and grammar-challenged person wrote. "...ALL a bunch of Jews BTW, all want our guns. History shows this jewish inlfuence will be the downfall of this country. They (jews) look upon all of us as Goyim, wake up folks. This is not anti-semitism, this is truth. Just look up Talmudic Jews and realize that RI politics is totally infiltrated."

Another commenter declared, with apparent ignorance of the fact that Hasbro, not Alan and his family, made toys: "If the Hassenfelds want to try to be the R.I. Version of Mikey Bloomberg maybe it's time to organize a boycott of their products!"

The 2016 General Assembly session passed no significant gun-control measures, prompting the NRA to congratulate its local association, the Rhode Island 2nd Amendment Coalition, for its lobbying efforts in "another successful year." In a media release, the national organization wrote that "problematic bills that included misdemeanors and temporary restraining orders failed to pass because of the due process considerations and rights restoration concerns we highlighted. Despite being constantly attacked by well-funded anti-gun groups, your NRA and the Rhode Island Second Amendment Coalition worked gavel-to-gavel this session against determined anti-gun politicians and the groups supporting them."

But the NRA urged continued observation of the likes of Hassenfeld and others who vowed to renew the fight when the General Assembly reconvened. "Far from being complacent, gun owners in Rhode Island will have to remain vigilant in 2017 as anti-gun groups have already pledged to return and continue their assault on the Second Amendment next January," it wrote.

Despite the gun lobby's pressure, Hassenfeld nonetheless achieved a victory in 2016. Two, actually.

Having contributed $87,500 to RI for Gun Safety, Hassenfeld was credited with helping to defeat two entrenched pro-gun legislators in the September primary elections: House Majority Leader John DeSimone and Representative Jan Malik, both endorsed by the National Rifle Association Political Victory Fund, lost to candidates sharing Hassenfeld's views on weapons.

DeSimone, a state legislator for a quarter of a century, went down blaming "special-interest money" that "manipulated the voters of my district" for his loss to Marcia Ranglin-Vassell, a special-education teacher and native of Jamaica. "They spread false claims and they came into my district and distorted the election results," DeSimone said.

DeSimone vowed a write-in campaign, which prompted Ranglin-Vassell to respond that she ran "because for too long we've had politicians who only help themselves and their well-connected friends. I believe we need a government that actually fights for all of us. The voters spoke in September and made it clear they want change. I'm disappointed that John is ignoring their will but I will run my campaign on the issues that defined the primary: the need to raise our minimum wage to $15 an hour so families can provide for themselves, the need for ethical oversight of our government to fight corruption and restore trust, and the need to implement common-sense gun reform to help make our streets safe and to protect our children..."

This was a woman Hassenfeld happily supported. DeSimone's write-in candidacy failed, and in November, Ranglin-Vassell was elected state representative for Rhode Island District Five, which includes three predominantly working-class neighborhoods of Providence.

And there was a larger message Hassenfeld had sent with the defeat of DeSimone and Malik, who also mounted an unsuccessful write-in general-election campaign. He wanted the General Assembly to know that "you've got to come to grips with this, you can't keep pushing it down the road," he later said. He wanted certain legislators in positions of power to understand that "I could have gone after them and I didn't."

But without progress on gun control, he might.

Hassenfeld did not mention names, but an observer of Rhode Island politics could infer that he meant the state's most powerful politician, House Speaker Nicholas A. Mattiello, who held an "A+" rating from the NRA.

Marking the four-year anniversary of the Sandy Hook massacre, some 100 people attended a vigil on December 15, 2016, at Providence's First Unitarian Church, near Brown University's main campus.

Rabbi Alan Flam, former chaplain and Hillel head at Brown, told the gathering that children in Japan, Canada, and Germany are exposed to the same level of media violence as American kids, "but they don't kill people afterward." He placed the blame on "the prevalence of our guns and the cowardice of our politicians." Declaring that "our gun-flooded society has turned weapons into idols," Flam said the only proper response is "sustained moral outrage."

Congressman Cicilline, who held an F-minus rating from the NRA, said he did not blame the organization for thwarting gun control. "I blame my colleagues, in Congress, he said. He joined Governor Raimondo and Providence Mayor Jorge Elorza in urging citizens to work for "sensible gun violence prevention on a state and federal level."

The vigil was organized by the Rhode Island Coalition Against Gun Violence, which claimed more than 120,000 supporters through 77 partner groups.

Said the Rev. Eugene Dyszlewski, chairman of the Religious Coalition for a Violence-Free Rhode Island, "Who would ever imagine that it would be so difficult to sell something so sensible?"

But it was, and when the General Assembly opened its new session in January 2017, the NRA and like-minded groups and individuals were ready for the next round.

It went again, mostly, to the NRA and allies. By the final days of the session in late June, proposed bills to limit carrying of firearms on school grounds to peace officers, outlaw the possession or sale of high-capacity magazines, require applicants for a license to carry firearms to undergo a national criminal background check, require minors possessing a firearm to be in the presence of a guardian or parent at all times, among other Senate and House measures, were "held for further study," the kiss of death in Rhode Island, at least for the current legislative year.

That left just one measure still before the General Assembly: the Protect Rhode Island Families Act, latest version of the oft-introduced legislation limiting access to firearms by an individual under certain types of domestic protective or restraining orders.

With the measure seemingly headed for approval and certain signature by Raimondo, the NRA went red-alert.

"Anti-gun groups are bombarding senators with text messages, emails and phone calls, urging them to support" the legislation, the organization wrote in a "Take Action" release. "As previously reported, this gun confiscation bill masquerading as 'domestic violence' legislation has cleared hurdles on the House side and is nearing final passage in the Senate."

The NRA continued: "As we have repeatedly stated, domestic violence is an abhorrent crime, but this bill doesn't protect domestic violence victims. Current federal and state laws are in place to make sure convicted violent abusers cannot possess firearms, and this bill is as dangerous as it is unnecessary... The stakes could not be higher for the Rhode Island firearms community. Anti-gun groups have co-opted domestic violence organizations simply to notch a victory that they can use as momentum for their larger gun ban agenda. It's absolutely vital that Rhode Island gun owners make their voice heard on this legislation."

They did, and so did citizens in Hassenfeld's camp. When the General Assembly reconvened on September 19 after a summer recess to conclude business left unfinished in June, it voted overwhelmingly to approve the legislation.

"A cheer went up from gun-control advocates and past victims of domestic violence, watching from the House gallery, as the lawmakers passed — and sent to the governor — a long-sought bill to remove guns from batterers," *The Providence Journal* wrote.

"For far too long survivors of domestic violence and families torn apart by violence called upon this legislature for help," said Representative Teresa Tanzi, one of the legislation's sponsors. "Today they get their answer."

"This is common sense… Abusive people should not have access to guns," said Jennifer Boylan, a volunteer for Moms Demand Action, whose members wore red tee shirts and carried red "Protect Rhode Island Families" signs as they watched debate before the historic vote.

Raimondo signed the bill into law on October 30 during a State House ceremony. But the gun-control work was not complete, and Hassenfeld and his allies would be back. They would push, again in 2018 and in 2019, for more changes including legislation prohibiting a person legally licensed to carry a concealed weapon from entering as school with a hidden gun.

"In Rhode Island, you can't take it into a federal building, but you can take it into a school," Hassenfeld said. His concern, heightened by Sandy Hook, was those rare individuals who give no outward signs of violent inclination but then abruptly turn.

"I don't know what makes people 'flip,' I haven't been challenged like that," he said. "But you can be normal, I can be normal, and all of a sudden something triggers."

For the moment, though, Hassenfeld was weary.

"I still have to fight that one, but let me rest up a little bit," he said.

During these many battles, Hassenfeld contemplated seeking office himself. Others encouraged him to run.

They and he viewed the U.S. Senate as the body where he might best make a difference on the major issues that preoccupied him. With his financial resources and the goodwill he'd engendered, he could wage a credible campaign.

A possible opening surfaced in February 2011 when the Raleigh, North Carolina, polling firm Public Policy released results of its Rhode Island Senate 2012 survey. The poll presented respondents several scenarios about possible challengers to then-freshman Senator Sheldon Whitehouse, a popular Democrat with a 49-percent approval rating in the poll. Respondents gave Buddy Cianci little chance of beating Whitehouse were he to run, and former governor Don Carcieri, a Republican, fared no better. Warwick mayor Scott Avedisian, another Republican, well-liked in his city and state, fared best, although Whitehouse would get 47 percent of the vote to his 37 if that matchup materialized.

Hassenfeld's name was not polled, but having heard the stories circulating about a possible candidacy, a reporter contacted Alan. Would he be throwing his hat in the ring?

"I am interested, but at this point, I'm not sure if it's the right thing for me," Hassenfeld said. "The question is where can I make the most difference? I'm not sure if being in D.C. has too many roadblocks. One of the real issues I have with Washington in general is the cacophony of voices going on. At the end of the day, we are all Americans and it is about time we're united and we stopped this absolutely vicious type of dialogue."

This was 2011, but the situation would only worsen.

Were Avedisian to run, Hassenfeld said that would seal his decision. "He's been a very, very good mayor and he is someone that I've worked with before and respect greatly," he said. "Right now, I'm really looking to see who is going to run. I want to take my time."

"Just what we need, a multi-millionaire, spoiled rich kid who helped destroy the RI economy by shipping jobs out of RI," one reader commented, but his opinion was the exception. And more public support for a Hassenfeld bid was soon to come, following a letter to the editor Hassenfeld wrote, eviscerating the Washington establishment.

"I am a third-generation immigrant from a family where the first two generations set the table for the third," he wrote, in a letter published on August 1, as the debt-ceiling crisis was nearing its end. "In my immigrant family, we were taught the Pledge of Allegiance - with our right hand over our heart: 'I pledge allegiance to the Flag of the United States of America, and to the Republic for which it stands, one Nation under God, indivisible, with liberty and justice for all.'

"Today, I hear about pledges for no immigrants, no abortion, no guns, no revenue (tax) increases; and our 'leaders' in Washington sign on the bottom line to these pledges. I ask them to choose to pledge their allegiance to their country... Will Rogers once said the difference between a politician and a statesman is that a politician thinks of the next election and the statesman the next generation. If only leadership in Washington could become statespeople rather than political hacks. If only they could see themselves as we see them.

"Washington and America - wake up! Compromise means both sides give something substantial, unless your pledge to a special interest trumps your allegiance to all America. To do what is right is not difficult. Our country, because of your insane bickering, is on a precipice, and I only hope it is not too late. Remember, you and I pledge allegiance to our country, not to our state, district or campaign financers."

Hassenfeld was piqued, writing more scathingly in "Stop fiddling, you pols, and return to Washington now," an op-ed column published three weeks later as Congress remained on vacation. In it, Hassenfeld painted legislators as self-centered brats interested only in ego, and raising the obscene amounts of campaign funding they needed to stay in power.

"Never, at least in my life, has there been more acrimony, cacophony, dyslexia, pettiness, and, dare I say, hatred in my capital," Hassenfeld wrote. "As individuals, many of you in Congress are bright, but when you get together, you become cackling geese. Look how America regards you: 14 percent approval rating (CNN opinion research, Aug. 1)... Never have I heard more blithering rhetoric. Jobs, jobs, jobs. Yet our Congress fiddles while jobs burn. Members of Congress are home for a five-week vacation, while Washington burns. Forgive me; they are working hard at fundraising for their next election."

Hassenfeld expressed the wish that representatives and senators pledge not to accept or raise money for campaigns until they cut the federal deficit by $4 trillion— necessary, he said, to ensure the nation's financial future. He suggested that Congress establish a commission headed by Warren Buffet; former commerce secretary and billionaire philanthropist Pete Peterson; and Rutherford Institute president John Whitehead, "three of the wisest people I know," to set a new national direction toward solvency and decency.

"Our greatness as a country has been and is deteriorating, and it is you, Washington, we turn to," Hassenfeld ended. "Are you capable of being as you were born: American? You were not born Republican or Democrat, or whatever; you were born American. As friends of mine say, 'no labels.' Help us to regain our greatness. Please remember that it is said that our greatest natural resource is our children. Please transcend your pettiness. Do not squander their future for your next election. Get back to Washington and put the fire out. Do your job!"

Hassenfeld's words inspired some Rhode Island residents to urge him to finally run.

"Mr. Hassenfeld's article represents what many of Americans feel," a woman wrote in a letter to the editor. "We are sick of the bickering and back-stabbing and want our Congress and president to work together for the survival of our country. Mr. Hassenfeld should run for president! Or, at least, head that 'dream' committee he mentioned."

Another woman agreed, chiding Hassenfeld in another letter to the editor for not stepping up .

"Alan Hassenfeld's Aug. 22 Commentary piece was another sobering commentary by the retired chairman and chief executive of Hasbro," she wrote. "His request that Congress do its job was clear, concise and true. Hassenfeld has noted that the difference between a statesman and a politician is that the latter thinks about the next election and the statesman thinks about the next generation. Both of his concepts are stunningly simple and easy to understand. What I do not understand is why Mr. Hassenfeld would not become a statesman and run for office. My advice, Mr. Hassenfeld, is do not continue to fiddle and run for office."

In the end, he decided he would not. One day shortly after the 2016 election, which had stunned him and many others, he explained his rationale. The paralysis that the Donald Trump presidency would bring to Washington further confirmed the wisdom of his decision.

That wisdom had come at the cost of losing faith.

"Growing up, the people that you looked up to were obviously your president, your senators, your Congress people," Hassenfeld said. "And we had some great ones in this state."

He listed the late Democrat John O. Pastore, Rhode Island governor before serving 26 years in Congress: the son of immigrants who grew up on Providence's Federal Hill, home to many newcomers to America, he was the first Italian-American to serve in the U.S. Senate, and was known for his liberal social policies and flamboyant oratory. Also on Hassenfeld's list were Ron Machtley, Republican representative before becoming president of Bryant College, and the late Senator John Chafee, an environmentalist and social progressive who supported abortion rights and opposed school prayer, the death penalty, and the ban on gays serving in the military. Chafee was also one of the rare Republicans who backed tighter gun control.

Chafee's heart was close to Hassenfeld's: "I would call my family New England moderate Republicans who are fiscally conservative but liberal on social issues," is how Hassenfeld described his political leanings.

In that long-gone era of crossing the aisle in Washington, bipartisan cooperation had been a key to legislative accomplishment. Hassenfeld had observed in the 1970s, '80s and '90s as the late Republican senator Chafee worked with the late Democrat Senator Claiborne Pell, father of the National Endowments for the Arts and Humanities and Pell Grants creator. He saw Republican Representative Claudine Schneider cooperating with the late Democrat Fernand St. Germaine, Machtley's predecessor, on issues advancing the common good.

"As I got older and saw the games being played, I became somewhat disillusioned," Hassenfeld said. "I watched Washington shuddering in the early days of George Bush Junior and Cheney, and then I watched our Congress basically for the last decade doing nothing—or thinking they were doing something but actually not doing anything. I also was a little bit jaded even with our own senators and Congresspeople here in Rhode Island."

One difficult lesson had come in the early 2000s, when he, Warren Buffett, Vidal Sassoon, and Jerome Kohlberg Jr. met with then-Senate Whip Mitch McConnell to discuss their support for the Bipartisan Campaign Reform Act of 2002, popularly known as McCain-Feingold, for its chief Senate sponsors, Republican John McCain and Democrat Russ Feingold. Congress eventually passed this act regulating campaign financing and Bush signed it into law, but McConnell and the NRA were fiercely opposed. They brought a challenge to the Supreme Court.

"Pinkos" was the word McConnell used to describe Hassenfeld, Buffet, Sassoon, and Kohlberg, Hassenfeld recalled.

"I basically shook my head and said, 'fight some other battles,'" Hassenfeld said. "But we got McCain–Feingold. And then it obviously was overturned in Citizens United. And then it became a game: How much money you could give through the PACs, through this or that."

Hassenfeld's disillusionment intensified. Were he to run and be elected, *What would I be able to accomplish?* he asked himself.

Time weighed on him, too.

"As you get older, you get more impatient," he said.

He was two years shy of 70 when he said that, with a joke: "Sixty-eight today is yesterday's 48, so leave me alone!"

But 68 was not 48 biologically, as he knew. Mortality prescribed limits.

"You want to make a difference quickly," Hassenfeld said.

And he was, albeit not in the nation's capital.

"I sit on a global platform, doing things nationally, locally, and globally," he said, "and I felt that I could make a greater difference outside of Washington than in the cacophony that Washington has become."

Hassenfeld closed his reflection with a favorite proverb.

"They say one of the greatest things you can do is plant a tree under whose shade you will not sit," he said. "I want to make a difference today in helping to create the future."

Hassenfeld at R.I. State House on another public-policy campaign.
(Courtesy Providence Journal)

Given Hassenfeld's long reach, large heart, and deep pockets, it was perhaps inevitable that eventually someone would take advantage of him. That someone was Dan Doyle, whose background included jobs as an assistant Brown basketball coach and promoter of boxer Sugar Ray Leonard.

Doyle was a charismatic man who dreamed on a grand scale and preached a mission of enriching young lives. In the 1980s, he founded the Institute for International Sport, a center on the University of Rhode Island's main Kingston campus that hosted the World Scholar-Athlete Games, which attracted thousands of young people from across the globe.

During its heyday in the 1990s and 2000s, the non-profit institute hosted guests and speakers including Bill Clinton, Colin Powell and The Beach Boys.

"The Institute for International Sport has become a Rhode Island jewel," Bill Reynolds, the region's leading sportswriter, declared in 2001. "It routinely brings people into this state who wouldn't be here otherwise. For 15 years now it's been a unique and innovative part of the sports culture in this country, whether by running seminars that deal with the hot-button sports issues of the day, or by using sports to bring disparate people together."

Doyle's institute taught diversity and cultural understanding. Children and young people benefitted. It was a program that Hassenfeld could support.

He did, by agreeing to be chairman of the World Scholar-Athlete Games, succeeding honorary chairman Bill Bradley, professional basketball Hall-of-Famer and former U.S. senator, after meeting with Bradley, Doyle and Senator John Chafee in Chafee's Washington office.

Hassenfeld's name lent the Games further credibility, and he also agreed to co-sign and guarantee $425,000 in loans to keep the institute operating while Doyle sought state and federal grants (loans that Hassenfeld eventually paid himself). Separately, Hassenfeld also pledged to contribute $500,000 for construction of a new institute building. He was not the institute's only supporter: Many others gave, including former Mastercard CEO Russell Hogg and prominent Rhode Island philanthropist Alan Shawn Feinstein, who has devoted his adult life and wealth to children and young people. Rhode Island was so proud of Doyle's achievement that it mounted signs on highways into the state proclaiming it the home of the World-Scholar Games.

But unknown to the public, according to law enforcement, Doyle was taking more than $1 million from institute coffers and using it for, among other things, cosmetic eye surgery for himself, a $100,000 contribution to his college alma mater, college tuition for his three daughters—and for one of the three, a wedding rehearsal dinner.

Hassenfeld testifies at Doyle's trial. (Courtesy Providence Journal)

After a state audit concluded in February 2012 determined that the institute could not thoroughly account for its use of a $575,000 state grant, State Police and the state attorney general began investigations, as did a *Providence Journal* team of award-winning journalists Kathy Gregg, Tom Mooney and Mike Stanton. On May 2, 2013, a state grand jury indicted Doyle on 18 counts of obtaining money under false pretenses, embezzlement of more than $1 million, forgery, and filing and counterfeiting false documents.

Among them were documents on which Hassenfeld's name had been forged.

Doyle's Superior Court trial began on September 22, 2016, with one prosecutor saying Doyle had used the institute, defunct by then, "for his own piggy bank."

Called by the state as a witness, Hassenfeld took the stand on September 29 for two days of testimony, telling jurors that initially, he delighted in Doyle's work.

"It was incredible," he said. "I couldn't be more proud of the years spent with the World Scholar-Athlete Games."

A state prosecutor showed Hassenfeld the institute's 2009 state non-profit corporation annual report, which listed International Olympic Committee member Anita DeFrantz and former Penn State Football Coach Joe Paterno, since disgraced, as board members. It listed Hassenfeld as institute president and bore his alleged signature.

It wasn't his.

"I did not authorize anyone to put my name on the document," he said.

When he brought this to Doyle's attention, Hassenfeld said, Doyle was "surprised."

Hassenfeld testified: "Dan said he would immediately try and figure out how [the] name was signed."

But, Hassenfeld said, "No one got back to me."

In January 2016, as he had been preparing his defense for his upcoming trial, Doyle had issued a strong statement of innocence.

"When I am fully exonerated, which I surely will be," he said, "where should the members of my family, my many loyal friends who have anguished over this witch hunt, the thousands of kids who have been prevented from participating in the World Scholar-Athlete Games… where does everyone go to reclaim the lost hours, months, and, in many cases, years, embezzled from us by the state of Rhode Island and a few misguided individuals who have been unfair?"

But jurors convicted Doyle on all 18 counts and ordered him to repay the Hassenfeld Foundation $550,000. Superior Court Judge Melanie Wilk Thunberg sentenced him to 15 years in prison, with seven to serve.

"The number of people you let down is innumerable," the judge said. "In short, Mr. Doyle, you played a dirty game."

Doyle offered no apology and expressed no remorse.

"I'm in essence a coach," he said.

Doyle said he would appeal.

PART TWO: CHANGES ON THE COASTS

Emotion filled the Hasbro cafeteria once again on May 21, 2015 as the final step in the transition from the Hassenfeld/Verrecchia era was completed. At the company's annual meeting that day, Verrecchia retired as chairman, passing that title to CEO and president Goldner.

The meeting featured the usual presentations, but the tributes to Verrecchia and the displays of the many Hasbro products and properties that he had played a key role in bringing to success — and to shareholder profit — stole the show. A new Verrecchia Scholarship was announced. Hugs and handshakes abounded. And when the ceremony concluded, employees by the hundreds lined the central corridor to give Verrecchia a standing-ovation send-off.

In the days leading up to the annual meeting, Hassenfeld, Goldner and Verrecchia had taken a walk down memory lane, each of them reflecting on the outgoing chairman's half-century-long career at Hasbro. Verrecchia had started in 1965 on a part-time basis for $1.75 an hour, becoming full-time two years later with a salary of $165 a week. He was a wealthy man now, his legacy as a corporate leader and community philanthropist secured.

Goldner viewed him as a savior.

"Were it not for Al," he said, "I'm not sure Hasbro would be here."

"Having Al as a partner — you never had to look behind you," said Hassenfeld. "He was always there if there was a problem, if there was a good time, if there was a bad time. Al was a tower of strength. I don't think much ever fazed him except a couple of his product ideas when they got rejected."

Then Hassenfeld made a crack one might expect from kid number one.

"No one talked to you about Flush-and-Brush Cabbage Patch, did they? It was one of Al's ideas."

Verrecchia said he found satisfaction in more than the financial stability he infused into Hasbro after the crisis year of 2000 and the rebirth that had followed. He could have passed a successful but quiet career with some accounting or banking firm, but he had experienced the excitement of the entertainment industry, with its Hollywood flavor.

"I enjoyed what I was doing," Verrecchia said. "It was fun and one of the reasons why it was so much fun is the need for new product each and every year ... You're not just showing this same jar of whatever day after day after day."

Verrecchia said that Hasbro had managed to meet shareholders' expectations while remaining true to the values first established by Hassenfeld's grandfather and great-uncle.

"Sometimes companies can become very mercenary," he said. "We didn't want that to happen. I think Hasbro has always had a style of doing business that relates back to their family traditions, being leaders in the community, recognizing responsibilities. Alan is the prime example of that. He's very involved in the community—not just philanthropically, but expressing his opinions and funding things he hopes will benefit the community."

More emotion at the annual meeting was found in the tribute video that was shown. Recorded in Cake Mix Studios, it mixed gentle humor with genuine appreciation for the executive that many of those present credited with rescuing their company.

"Al really helped in the most desperate of times to save Hasbro and to keep the company in business at a time when keeping the company in business was the most important thing we could do," Goldner said on camera. "Al was really the architect of coming up with a strategy that would save the company."

Asked by the video director to give a single word to describe the outgoing chairman, executives who had worked for him came up with "loyal," "driven," "solid," "tough" and "grounded," Hassenfeld's choice. His son, Michael, who had recently left his job at Hasbro to begin a new chapter of his life in California, chose "integrity." Michael expanded later in the video, saying "whether it's as a dad, certainly as a husband, and now as a grandfather, he's very much about doing things the right way."

Video participants poked fun at Verrecchia, noting what one called his always "button-up" attire and another his "perfect CEO hair" at a company where sneakers and jeans were the preferred look, even often with Goldner.

"Always together, never a hair out of place," said Karen Davis, Senior Vice President Global Philanthropy & Social Impact.

"I used to wonder, 'How does that all work?' " said his son. "From about the age of two and a half, that's how his hair was"

"He could have been The Godfather," quipped CFO Deb Thomas.

Verrecchia's last day as chairman. (Courtesy Providence Journal)

Verrecchia's four grandchildren had sweet messages for Verrecchia. Executives and board members who served with him offered thanks and answered the question: If Verrecchia were a Hasbro toy, which would it be?

G.I. Joe, a Transformer or Mr. Monopoly were among the answers.

"Al, I can't thank you enough for everything that you've done for the company, you've done for the family, but you've done especially for me," Hassenfeld said. "We are truly indebted for everything that you've done for this company called Hasbro."

Star Wars creator George Lucas topped the bill.

"Congratulations on a half century with Hasbro," he told the camera. "Our groundbreaking deal with Lucasfilm has inspired the imaginations and the playtime of generations. Not a bad legacy. Welcome to the retirement club."

In his final formal address as Hasbro chairman, Verrecchia thanked everyone he had worked with since joining the company a half century ago, singling out Merrill and Sylvia Hassenfeld and their two sons.

"It's been a privilege to be a part of this amazing company and to have worked with so many wonderful people," Verrecchia said. "Although I will miss Hasbro, I leave knowing that the company is in terrific hands and I'm excited about the future because I believe Hasbro's best days are yet to come."

Said Goldner: "We are so indebted for all you have done for the company and for me and for my management team."

Chairman now, Goldner summarized the strategy behind Hasbro's ambition to "achieve and create the world's best play experiences." Storytelling and brand-building, he reminded the audience, were central, as market research had confirmed.

"The key theme that emerged from many of these interactions with our consumers was the power of story and storytelling," he said. "Using great stories and great characters is driving innovation in all that we do and is an important strategic differentiator. Story also allows us to drive our consumer-products licensing business."

The proof, Goldner said, was already in the pudding.

"Over a 10-year period, Hasbro has outperformed all publicly traded toy companies," he said, a point the late Stephen would have appreciated. "At the beginning of 2005, both Hasbro and Mattel were trading around $20. Today, Hasbro is over $70 a share while Mattel is under $30. For Hasbro this translates to a 10-year total shareholder return of 14 percent, which is nearly two times the total shareholder return of the S&P 500."

Hasbro had achieved sales of $4.28 billion in 2014, and closed the first quarter of 2015 with $713.5 million in revenues, a 5-percent increase. When the market closed on May 21, 2015, Hasbro stock was trading at $72.61. Mattel was going for $26.08.

The California company that once was so mighty that it assumed it could acquire Hasbro, regardless of what the Rhode Island firm wanted, wasn't that mighty now—and not only as measured by the stock price, though that was a telling measure.

Mattel had placed its biggest bets on licensing and its comparatively small library of core brands—Barbie, Hot Wheels and Fisher-Price among them—but the strategy was not exciting investors. The September 2000 decision by Disney to grant it rights to certain properties including Mickey Mouse and Winnie the Pooh while naming Hasbro its official toymaker, with rights to screen properties, had not favored Mattel: the lovable rodent and bear had charmed past generations of children, but not so much the present one. In the social-media age, Mickey and Winnie were, one might say, your grandmother's and grandfather's toys.

And while flagship brand Barbie had hardly been retired, the heart of Mattel since the doll's introduction in 1959 was encountering generational difficulties too. The company invested resources in new versions with diverse looks and more realistic body types, but the daughters of Millennials did not clamor for the doll as children of an earlier time had—and Millennial parents' buying habits were not those of their counterparts with the Gen X and Boomer generations, who almost reflexively thought *Barbie* when Christmas and birthdays rolled around. Many Millennial parents found a better role model in the superhero of the 2017 film *Wonder Woman,* helmed by director and screenwriter Patty Jenkins

Even the name "Barbie," for Barbara, worked against Mattel: When the Social Security Administration compiled its top 200 female and male names given to babies born from 2000 through 2009, neither Barbie nor Barbara made the female list (the top ten girls' names were Emily, Madison, Emma, Olivia, Hannah, Abigail, Isabella, Samantha, Elizabeth, and Ashely). Perhaps small consolation could be found in Barbie's long-time male friend, Ken: Kenneth was 121 on the top male baby list during the decade. But Ken would become the butt of a new round of jokes in 2017, when Mattel contemporized him, too.

Mattel suffered another blow in September 2014, when Disney pulled its license for *Frozen* and awarded it to Hasbro, beginning in 2016. The 2013 movie featuring the voices of Josh Gad and Kristen Bell had earned $1.2 billion worldwide, with a $400 million domestic box office—a blockbuster performance certain to be repeated with the release of the sequel in November 2019. Disney also granted Hasbro rights to its popular Princess line, which included Little Mermaid and Cinderella, timeless classics with continued appeal to the latest generation.

In reporting the deal on September 24, 2014, even Mattel's hometown newspaper, *The Los Angeles Times,* lauded Hasbro, calling the deal "a coup for the toy maker as it expands its offerings for girls."

The quest for a smash girls' doll line had long been Hasbro's Holy Grail, having haunted Merrill and bedeviled Stephen Hassenfeld. Now, it seemed, Hasbro finally had found it.

Disney was happy they had.

"We are excited about our collaboration with Hasbro on the Disney Princess and Frozen franchises and the expansion of a robust partnership that has already yielded tremendous results across our Star Wars and Marvel properties," said Bob Chapek, Disney Consumer Products president. "Hasbro's focus on quality, innovation, and market-leading products designed for today's consumer, makes them the best choice to grow one of the world's most popular girls brands."

In El Segundo, California, home of Mattel, that stung. In Pawtucket, Rhode Island, Goldner celebrated.

"Our strategic-thought leadership and innovation has led to the steady growth of our girls business over the past several years demonstrating that we have a true understanding of girls globally and how today's girls want to play," he said. "The entire Hasbro team is looking forward to providing consumers with inventive new play experiences based on the beloved Disney Princess and Frozen characters and stories."

Added Hasbro Chief Marketing Officer John Frascotti: "Our industry-leading design and marketing teams are looking forward to delivering to consumers around the world wonderful play experiences based on these magical Disney properties."

Mattel did its best to put a good face on things. Spokesman Alex Clark reminded *The Los Angeles Times* that the company held licenses for another two holiday seasons during the "arc and apex" of *Frozen's* popularity among children. He also pointed to Mattel's other doll brands, including Barbie and Monster High. 'We are naturally disappointed,' Clark said. 'But we are confident in our portfolio moving forward.'"

Always competing: Hasbro's My Little Pony and Mattel's Barbie in a Target store.
(Miller photo)

The *Frozen* deal was particularly distressing for Mattel CEO Bryan Stockton, who just two months before, in reporting a nine-percent drop in overall second-quarter sales (with a 15-percent drop in sales of Barbie), had said "the star of the portfolio in the quarter was our line of products supporting Disney's *Frozen*, and we are continuing to chase demand here."

The chase was destined to end. So was Stockton's job.

In January 2015, he was fired.

Wall Street had not seen numbers it wanted on his watch, and no sprinkling of fairy dust could change them. Mattel recorded net sales of $6.4 billion in 2013, but that dropped to $6 billion in 2014. Net income also slid: from $903 million in 2013, to $498 million in 2014. Operating income also slid, from $1.1 billion in 2013, to $653 million.

The years 2015 and 2016 brought no relief under Stockton's successor, Christopher A. Sinclair. Net sales slid to $5.7 billion in 2015 and to $5.4 billion in 2016; net income declined to $369 million in 2015 and to $318 million the next year.

In its 2016 annual report, the company declared that "Mattel is a creations company that inspires the wonder of childhood. Our mission is to be the recognized leader in play, learning, and development worldwide."

But Sinclair acknowledged the difficulties still facing Mattel. "We knew 2016 was going to be a particularly challenging year, and as I look back, I believe we executed well against our key strategic priorities and made significant progress on resetting the Company's foundation for growth," the company wrote in its 2016 annual report.

One "resetting," which followed a disappointing fourth quarter 2016 performance, was naming Google executive Margaret H. Georgiadis to succeed Sinclair as CEO, effective February 8, 2017. Sinclair kept the company chairmanship.

Observers hailed Georgiadis' record at Google and her prior positions at Groupon, Card Products, Discover, and McKinsey & Company, but the task facing the Harvard Business School graduate was formidable—not only in the corner suite, but on Wall Street. Regardless of hopes for the future and spin that might be put on the situation, bad results invariably generate bad press, to which investors pay attention.

To wit:

"The El Segundo, Calif.-based toy maker saw its shares plummet nearly 18 percent after it reported weaker-than-expected Q4 earnings, in which revenue declined 5 percent year over year," wrote Investopedia, edited by financial-news veteran Caleb Silver, on March 11, 2017. "While former Chief Executive and current executive chairman Christopher Sinclair blamed the slowdown on industrywide challenges, in the same quarter, Hasbro posted worldwide sales up 11 percent. The Pawtucket, R.I.-based company outran its competition by transforming into something greater than a toy business, rather, a firm determined to create 'play experiences.'"

Investopedia flagged what arguably was the most critical issue facing Mattel: Barbie.

"Before Georgiadis," Investopedia declared, "it seems as though Mattel had been reluctant to jump on the innovation train, instead focusing on reviving declining businesses and pursuing dead-end markets. For example, take Mattel's Barbie doll, launched this week in 1959.

"Once one of America's most popular toys, Barbie sales have been on the decline for years. As Barbie turns 58, analysts say it may just be time for her to retire. The company has failed to transform the doll in order to boost sales, despite a revamp of the toy line with new body shapes and skin tones. Closely following the rebrand, Barbie sales declined 3.4 percent in the first quarter of 2016. In Mattel's most recent fourth-quarter earnings report, Barbie sales fell another 2 percent in North America."

The decline continued in the first quarter of 2017, with worldwide sales for Barbie dropping 13 percent quarter-to-quarter, from $141.1 million to $123.4 million. The news was also disappointing for another core brand, Fisher-Price, with worldwide sale dropping nine percent quarter-to-quarter, from $272.6 million to $246.9 million. Total girls and boys brands declined 16 percent, from $527.9 million to $441.1 million.

Investors continued to sour on Mattel's once high-flying stock. And more management changes were in the wind. Georgiadis would soon follow Stockton out the door.

Mattel stock hit a nearly four-year high of $47.08 on July 12, 2013—but it had dropped to $20.02 on July 31, 2017, when *The Motley Fool* published its latest analysis.

With a headline of "Mattel Struggles as Barbie Gets Dumped: Another quarter of tepid growth and declining margins saw investors growing impatient for Mattel's stock makeover to materialize," *The Motley Fool* had chilly words for the southern California firm.

"Investors have been waiting for industry-leading toymaker Mattel, Inc. to pull Barbie and friends out of an ongoing slump," the story began. "The stock had already fallen 23 percent this year, after the company disappointed investors with less-than-stellar post-holiday results, and then announcing that it would cut its dividend to fuel a turnaround. After detailing plans to get the company back on track last month, investors had hoped for signs that the carnage was over and Barbie was back on the road to recovery. When the company reported its financial results for the recently completed quarter, investors' hopes were dashed and the stock fell another seven percent. What is going on?"

Not the "strength at retail" that Georgiadis described in a statement.
"That 'strength at retail' failed to translate into positive results for Mattel's core brands," *The Motley Fool* declared. "Worldwide gross sales for Barbie fell 5%, while American Girl sales were off six percent from the prior-year period. Fisher-Price and Power Wheels didn't fare much better, with sales declining three percent from the prior-

year quarter. Sales of Monster High and Ever After High were the big losers, plummeting 28 percent year over year."

The publication did note some potentially positive developments, including investments in the fast-growing China market and a 58-percent increase in the company's entertainment division, largely due to the success of the movie *Cars 3,* which would reach a worldwide box office of $350 million by September 10, when it had disappeared from most theaters.

But two weeks later, Mattel's stock had dropped further, selling for $17.42 when NASDAQ, where it traded, published an article from independent investment-research firm Zacks that called Mattel "The Bear of the Day," hardly an enviable description.

"Mattel's adjusted loss of 14 cents per share was worse than the Zacks Consensus Estimate of a loss of eight cents," the research firm wrote. "Also, revenues of $974.5 million while up two percent year over year missed our estimate. While worldwide gross sales were up one percent, North American gross sales declined two percent. Worldwide sales for Mattel Girls & Boys Brands were up 10 percent, but Fisher-Price sales were down three percent, and American Girl doll sales declined six percent.

"Estimates have also plunged after the report. Zacks Consensus Estimates for the current and the next year have fallen to $0.79 per share and $1.00 per share from $0.95 and $ 1.16 respectively before the results. The company has missed in three out of last four quarters, with an average negative quarterly surprise exceeding 47 percent. Shares fell after the report and are now down over 39 percent year-to-date. In June, the company announced that it is slashing its quarterly dividend to $0.15 per share from $0.38 per share earlier."

The bottom line, according to Zacks?

"Mattel has seen weak sales for the past many quarters as they struggle with kids' rising preference for videogames and smartphone applications."

These were areas where Hasbro excelled, which Zacks understood.

"Additionally," the firm wrote, Mattel was "losing in competition with Hasbro after Disney selected Hasbro for the Disney Princess and Frozen franchises."

The firm gave Hasbro strong recommendations on two of its key measures, writing "Hasbro currently has a Zacks Rank #2 (Buy) and VGM Score of A." The score stood for Value, Growth and Momentum, "based on academic research which has proven that stocks with the best value, growth, and momentum characteristics outperform the market," the company stated.

Mattel on September 12, 2017, when its stock was trading at $15.73 (and Hasbro was at $95.66) had a Zacks Rank 5 (Strong Sell) and VGM of F, failing.

Could Ken help save the day?

Mattel hoped so, and in June 2017, the company unveiled a makeover of the male doll. Ken was now available in original broad and slim body types, and seven different skin tones reflecting a diverse world. Consumers could choose from a selection of new hair colors and styles, including a man-bun Ken. Attire options included athletic and casual wear.

The rollout followed Mattel's 2016 introduction of the similarly diverse Fashionistas Barbie line, which had landed the new look on the cover of *Time* magazine with the headline "Now can we stop talking about my body?" Mattel aimed not only for better sales, but an end to years of criticism of its dolls' unrealistic anatomical proportions and what critics asserted was their negative effect on the minds of growing girls.

That criticism found support in science.

A paper published in 2006 in *Developmental Psychology*, a peer-reviewed publication of the American Psychological Association, had concluded that "girls exposed to Barbie reported lower body esteem and greater desire for a thinner body shape than girls in the other exposure conditions... early exposure to dolls epitomizing an unrealistically thin body ideal may damage girls' body image, which would contribute to an increased risk of disordered eating and weight cycling."

The new Ken drew praise—and some favorable headlines. Mattel itself trumpeted new Ken and the new Fashionistas line, Tweeting with an abundance of emoji:

"Meet the New Crew: @Barbie Fashionistas' most diverse lineup yet! Includes new body types & hairstyles (hello, #manbun 👱) for Ken."

But the launch also was met with ridicule. In today's viral world, Man Bun Ken was quickly a laughingstock.

The Washington Post, no less, described the scoffing in a June 21, 2016, article by staff writer Sintia Radu. "Let's face it," Radu wrote. "Few women out there date just one hunk throughout their lives, so we're still not sure why Mattel waited till now to give Barbie a few more options. Yet after the doll-maker announced it's releasing 15 new Ken dolls that come in different looks and body types, there seemed to be one man-Barbie who stood out. Introducing 'Man Bun' Ken."

In her story, Radu included several of the many Tweets that had greeted the doll's debut.

They were not handsome.

"#Manbun? How very 2013 of you. Can we just call him Uncool Hipster Ken?" read one.

"I'm already tired of hearing about his study abroad to Amsterdam where he just "fell in love with the culture". #manbunken," read another.

Not cited in *The Washington Post* were replies to Mattel's initial Tweet. Many were no more kindly.

"Jeez youre a little late. Man buns were so last year!" read one.

Read another: "It's only about $$$$$ Mattel cares nothing about the persona they present about any gender!"

And another, which drove to the heart of the challenge facing a company trying to reinvent a fashion doll that was rooted in a bygone era: "Maybe you should have one with a typewriter and 8" floppy disk. Or perhaps a dial up modem. #BarbieIsSoLastCentury"

Georgiadis, as it developed, was last year. Brought in with fanfare, she re-signed in April 2018 (to take the chief executive position at ancestry.com) with the Mattel reins going to American-Israeli businessman Ynon Kreiz, Mattel's fourth CEO in four years. Kreiz had cut his teeth in the toy industry with Haim Saban, the billionaire media mogul behind Mighty Morphin Power Rangers and other smash hits.

Kreiz, it seemed, would need superhuman powers to restore Mattel to glory—and Wall Street confidence.

As *Bloomberg News* reported: "Mattel Inc. seems to change CEOs about as quickly as kids cycle through favorite toys."

The *Frozen* coup was not the only notch on Goldner's belt. It could even be deemed an ancillary achievement, given the harvest Hasbro was reaping from the home-brand strategy that had emerged from the reorganization under Hassenfeld and Verrecchia in the early 2000s—the company's answer to the painful Pokémon period at the turn of the millennium.

The 2016 annual report testified to the success of the strategy, and to Gold-ner's helmsmanship. The first complete year under his full command, the CEO and chairman wrote in his six-page introduction, "was a very good year for our company."

It was.

Net revenues grew 13 percent over 2015, from $4.4 billion to $5.019 billion—Hasbro's first-ever $5-billion performance. Operating profit increased from $691 mil-lion to $788 million, and assets also rose, from $4.7 billion to $5 billion. Cash dividends of $2.04 were declared, up from $1.84 in 2015. And cash and cash equivalents on hand rose 37 percent, to $1.1 billion, a number Verrecchia especially appreciated. He would never forget the days of holding onto Hasbro checks so they wouldn't bounce in order that Merrill Hassenfeld could make payroll.

The chart eight pages into Hasbro's 2016 annual report told a telling story.

It depicted the five-year total Hasbro shareholder return, from 2011 through 2016, compared to the S&P 500 Index and the Russell 1000 Consumer Discretionary Index, two leading stock market indexes. Assuming an investment of $100 at the end of 2011, the S&P 500 rose to $199 in 2016; the Russell 1000 also rose, to $221. But that same $100 invested in Hasbro common stock at the end of 2011 would have brought $282 in 2016. When the annual report was released in February 2017, a share of Hasbro stock was trading at close to $100.

By contrast, that same $100 invested in Mattel in 2011 would have brought $123.62 in 2016.

"Over the past ten years," Goldner wrote in the 2016 report, Hasbro "assembled an exceptional team with the capabilities to execute our Brand Blueprint with excellence. The blueprint has remained a constant, our North Star, guiding our strategic decisions and investments while we built an organization with differentiated brands, capabilities and approaches to the consumer. The investments we are making and the cultural mindset we are instilling are not only delivering improving results but also creating strategic differentiators for Hasbro. Through our consumer insight and story-led brand focus, we are creating innovative play and compelling entertainment to successfully operate as a global play and entertainment company and enhance long-term shareholder value..."

Additional charts and bar graphs affirmed Goldner's conclusion. Net revenues in girls, boys, games and preschool, Hasbro's four product categories, all rose from 2014 to 2016, as did net revenues in each of the firm's three sales segments: entertainment and licensing, international, and the U.S. and Canada. In the increasingly global world, the international growth was particularly encouraging, as those markets, together with domestic, were Hasbro's future.

"We grew in major developed economies including the U.S., U.K., France, Germany and Canada," Goldner wrote. "Revenue also increased in Brazil, Russia and China. In total, revenues in the emerging markets grew approximately 12 percent in constant dollars. Hasbro's growth in 2016 outpaced the overall market and we gained share in almost every country we track. This includes share gains in the U.S., U.K., Brazil and Russia. We finished the year strong. Hasbro was ranked number one in market share in the industry for the month of December. We grew to become the top market share company in the Brazilian market for the year, and, after taking over the number two position last year in Europe, we gained share across the region and were the top company in Spain."

"Making the World a Better Place" was the title of the page that closed Goldner's introduction to the 2016 annual report. On it, the CEO summarized Hasbro's continuing devotion to charity, through gifts of its money and employee time. Hasbro workers qualify for four hours of paid time off every month for volunteering with causes that benefit children, and they annually participate in the day-long holiday-season Global Day of Joy, another volunteer program that was a Goldner brainchild.

"Hasbro has the best people in our business, or any business, driving our strategy, creativity and results," Goldner stated. "Every day, they are inspired to achieve our purpose of making the world a better place for children and their families. In 2016, 93 percent of our employees gave a total of 67,000 volunteer hours through our Team

Hasbro program. Over the past year, Hasbro provided $14 million in total philanthropic support, impacting more than three million children worldwide."

Hasbro's "strong corporate social responsibility mindset," as Goldner phrased it, extended beyond philanthropy. "Product safety continues to be one of our highest priorities and we maintained our outstanding product safety record with no consumer product recalls in 2016," he wrote. "We continue to take ambitious steps to reduce our environmental footprint, including the use of renewable energy for 100 percent of our U.S. electricity consumption. In 2016, we launched Hasbro's Sustainability Center of Excellence marking the next phase of our sustainability journey to drive our environmental strategy across the global organization. We also work closely with our suppliers to ensure ethical sourcing in our supply chain."

If there seemed to be a touch of boastfulness to Goldner's words, he could be forgiven: Hasbro's long record of corporate social responsibility had been recognized by many outsiders as among America's best.

In 2017, *Corporate Responsibility Magazine*—which evaluated a firm's policies on climate change, the environment, human rights, philanthropy and employee relations, among other factors—ranked Hasbro first on its 100 Best Corporate Citizens List, ahead of Intel and Microsoft. The company placed fifth on the list in 2018 and 13th in 2019.

For the seventh consecutive year in 2017, Hasbro ranked as one of the Ethisphere Institute's World's Most Ethical Companies, an honor it repeated in 2018 and 2019.

In 2017 and 2018, it again made The Civic 50, a program run by Points of Light in partnership with Bloomberg LP that "recognizes the 50 most community-minded companies in the nation each year as determined by an annual survey."

And in 2016, for the second consecutive year, it was one of America's most reputable companies on the U.S. RepTrak 100 List, compiled by the Boston-based Reputation Institute, which calls itself "the gold standard in the science of reputation." Hasbro would repeat on the list in 2017, 2018, and 2019.

PART THREE: WHAT MATTERS

Al Verrecchia was home getting ready for bed the night of Monday, October 26, 2015, when he felt pain in his chest. He thought it might be heartburn. The pain passed, and he slept well. The next morning, he went to Boston for a board meeting of Iron Mountain, the data-management and shredding company. Tuesday passed uneventfully.

He was in bed in his hotel Wednesday night when he broke out in a sweat.

"I was soaking wet in almost an instant," Verrecchia would later recall.

He felt fine again on Thursday, but when he returned home that evening, he mentioned what had happened to his wife.

"You've got to go see the doctor tomorrow morning," Gerrie said.

That Friday morning, Verrecchia called Dr. Timothy J. Babineau, president and CEO of Lifespan, parent company of Rhode Island, Miriam, Hasbro Children's, Bradley and Newport Hospitals. The men knew each other well: Verrecchia had chaired Lifespan's board for a decade.

"You need to get here right away," Babineau said.

Tests were run when Verrecchia arrived.

"You had a cardiac event," a doctor said.

"What the hell is a cardiac event?" Verrecchia said.

"A heart attack. The good news is there's been no damage to the heart."

Further testing determined the course of treatment.

"You need open-heart surgery," Verrecchia recalled being told. "You've got several blockages and they're in a position where it would be very difficult to do a stent." Even if they succeeded with a stent, odds were Verrecchia would be back in a year or two for further surgery.

Surgery was scheduled for the morning of Sunday, November 1. Verrecchia spent Halloween, October 31, in a bed at Rhode Island Hospital. Dr. Frank Sellke, chief of cardiothoracic surgery at Rhode Island and Miriam Hospitals and a professor at The Warren Alpert Medical School of Brown University, was scheduled to operate on Verrecchia.

The operation was successful, and with Gerrie staying with him around the clock and his children and Alan Hassenfeld visiting daily, Verrecchia began to improve. By midweek, Sellke was looking to discharge him on Thursday afternoon or Friday morning, with Verrecchia expected to fully return to health after going home. He had been lucky: heart disease kills some 610,000 Americans every year, according to the Centers for Disease Control and Prevention.

On Thursday afternoon, Gerrie and daughter Lisa Verrecchia Montes were alone with Verrecchia, who was sitting quietly in a chair. The stream of visitors had subsided.

Verrecchia's attention was not on his wife and daughter. He appeared to be listening to someone else and concentrating on how he would respond.

"Dad looks like he's in 'meeting mode,'" Lisa said. "He looks like he's going to get up and get out of his chair and just start walking or something."

"Are you OK?" Gerrie asked her husband, again and again.

"I can't find the words," he finally said.

And then he returned to the imaginary meeting.

"Cabbage Patch kids are going to be good," he said. "Cabbage Patch are going to be OK."

Once, Hasbro had owned the Cabbage Patch license, and Verrecchia had been deeply involved in the battle to keep the license when it was up for renewal. Mattel's Barad also was aggressively seeking it and Verrecchia had led a delegation to the Georgia home of creator Xavier Roberts to make Hasbro's case. In the end, Barad had won.

It was a loss for Verrecchia and then-CEO Hassenfeld, but not a big one: Cabbage Patch had not generated any profit in the four years Hasbro made it.

That was more than two decades before Verrecchia's imaginary meeting.

"Go get the nurse," Gerrie said.

But Lisa had just flown in from Brazil the night before and didn't know which nurses had her father's care. So Gerrie went.

"We gotta get it on the Internet," Verrecchia said.

And then: "I don't know what the hell I'm saying."

"It's OK, Dad," Lisa said. "You've had a big surgery and you're on a lot of medication. Mom is getting the nurse. It's OK."

The nurse came, and then more nurses and doctors. They began treatment.

Verrecchia had suffered a stroke.

By evening, Verrecchia could answer diagnostic questions correctly: where he was, what day it was, who was U.S. president. Likely because professionals had intervened so quickly, Verrecchia had sustained no cognitive impairment. In days to come, he would wonder what his fate would have been had he not been in a hospital.

Mild impairment of his right-side peripheral vision, which would not affect his life, would to be the only potentially long-lasting effect of the stroke. As he later reflected on a multitude of "what-ifs," Verrecchia would count blessings.

"You think about what could have happened—how fortunate you were that you had the stroke in the hospital, as opposed to at a basketball game or somewhere," he later said. "You're fortunate in that you had a heart attack but there was no damage to the heart. If the only impact was I'd lost some peripheral vision, I'll sign up for that any time."

Verrecchia went home, his care entrusted to his family and visiting nurses. His energy slowly returned, along with the stubbornness—and gritty humor—that had been his hallmark during a half century of helping build, then rescue, Hasbro.

In relating the story of that autumn of 2015 over lunch one day at a restaurant on Providence's Federal Hill, which held many cherished memories for generations of his and Gerrie's families, Verrecchia laughed recalling his first travels in a car after being discharged to home. While Gerric drove, he sat in the back seat, a large plush heart cushioning his chest from the seat belt. The surgeons had split his sternum to reach his heart, and until the bone healed fully, it needed soft protection.

"Here I am in the back seat of the car, my wife's driving, and I'm sitting there with this frigging pillow," he said. "We pull to a red light. A guy looks in and I'm sitting there like this."

He held an imaginary pillow between him and the table. The image was ridiculous.

Eventually, the visiting nurses came less regularly, and Gerrie was free to leave the house for short periods of time. As soon as she did, Verrecchia, against doctors' orders, took the keys to his car and cruised around Narragansett. He snuck out again the next day, and days after that for about a week, until he confessed to Gerrie.

During that lunch on his beloved Federal Hill, Verrecchia, who would turn 75 in 2018, mused about mortality in general and the additional insights the fall of 2015 had brought.

"I try to take better care of myself," he said. "I make sure to spend more quality time with my grandkids, but that's not so much because of the heart attack as it is that, no matter how you slice it, more of your life is behind you than ahead. I'm not somebody who is saying 'Gee whizz, the end could be near, let's take a trip' or 'this could be our last Christmas.' I don't think that way. But I do think, 'OK, if something does happen, is my family ready to deal with that? What do I have to do to make sure that I don't leave things complicated for them' and that sort of thing. To me, it's more about what matters and what doesn't matter."

Verrecchia was finishing his heart-healthy lunch: Caesar salad with grilled salmon. It tasted good, but Verrecchia would have been OK if it hadn't.

"At the end of the day, if the piece of salmon I had today wasn't cooked the way I liked it," he said, "life's too fucking short to worry about it."

CHAPTER TEN

FEARLESS AND KIND

PART ONE: LOVE WHERE THERE IS HATRED

As the year 2016 began and the fight for the Republican presidential nomination turned increasingly ugly, sickening Hassenfeld and many other Americans, Hassenfeld shared his views with the editor of the *Providence Business News*. Hassenfeld had taken heat for moving his primary residence to Florida, where his late mother kept a house— and where taxes were lower than in his native state, prompting an increasing number of Rhode Islanders to flee—and he took this opportunity to explain his rationale.

The move was not for personal gain, Hassenfeld said; with his wealth, saving a few million dollars was inconsequential.

"I moved to Florida after my mom died because of her estate, because I want to give the money away," Hassenfeld told the *Providence Business News*. "I want to do my philanthropy to study autism, asthma, and obesity, I want Hasbro Children's Hospital to grow. Just trying to be a catalyst."

Money saved from lower taxes was more money available for worthy causes. That was simple math. Hassenfeld's policy on donating it, however, had evolved over the years.

"More and more, I'm directing the gift the way I want to," Hassenfeld said. "You can't come to me and say, 'Alan, I'd like you to give a million dollars to Brown.'"

Hassenfeld wanted to sow seeds.

He gave the example of Massachusetts General Hospital, where he underwent surgery after his heart attack. "I knew Mass. General would want a large gift from me,"

Hassenfeld said. This was an occupational hazard of the philanthropy job: someone always seems to want something, although in the case of the Boston hospital, it was something a grateful survivor was happy to give.

"I went to my doctor and I said, 'Let's you and I create what you want to move the hospital forward,'" Hassenfeld said. "And we decided we would give out three research awards of $50,000 a year for two years at Mass. General to heart researchers. I'm so proud because at the American College of Cardiology convention, one of my researchers from two years ago who got $50,000 from me now has been granted $2 million from them because of that research that we started."

Experience had also prompted Hassenfeld to change his rules on giving.

"Our foundation believes we can give to something for three years running and then we go dark for at least a year or two, because we don't want to be like the drug addict, where they always come back for their next [fix]," he said. "We want them to be able to stand up on their own. And *I've* changed."

How have you changed? the *Providence Business News* asked.

"One of the things I'm doing with my philanthropic work is to try and be a catalyst for good change," Hassenfeld said. He cited the Hassenfeld Institute for Public Leadership at Bryant and the leadership-training program he had funded at Harvard's Kennedy School of Government. "And then I decided I couldn't do more at Harvard," he said. "But what I wanted to do for Rhode Island was to take town councils and school committees—because many times people get into public service that way—and have training for them, not telling them how to vote, but giving them the skill sets to understand what it meant to be on a school committee, what a contract looks like."

Hassenfeld's dream?

"Make the United States united once again," he said. "And stop the gamesmanship."

If he could, how would he rewrite federal tax law?

"Stop the loopholes for the wealthy," he said. "Stop the loopholes for the corporations that don't pay anything. I can tell you right now, almost every American company would bring their money back from overseas if the tax rate was about 17 percent or 18 percent. Not the 35 or 36 or 38 that it is now."

His personal ambition?

"Be a positive change agent, and have fun doing it. How do you be a positive change agent for good? I don't have skin in the game anymore, in a sense. I don't want anything from anybody, except to make sure every dollar I give away works as hard as it can."

Hassenfeld talked of wisdom accrued with aging.

"When I was in my 20s or 30s, I had an answer for everything," he said. "Everything was black and white. Today, everything is gray to me. When people come wanting advice, I say, 'no, I can't give you advice. I'll make you ask yourself questions, but it's a different world today.' I would like to be a catalyst for positive change, that's all.

I want to be an honest broker. I chair the Jerusalem Foundation. I believe in coexistence. I took that on because I wanted to be part of the peace process. Look where we are. But my future is partly here. There are also any number of places I want to go."

Well, where haven't you been?

"Haven't been to Tibet," said Hassenfeld.

Only read about it, beginning in his youth.

Hassenfeld didn't make it to Tibet in 2016, but in late September, he travelled to Israel to participate in three days of celebrations marking the 50th anniversary of the Jerusalem Foundation, which the Hassenfeld family had supported since former Jerusalem mayor Teddy Kollek founded it. If any organization encapsulated the Hassenfeld commitment to Jewish causes—and their commitment to philanthropic causes in general—the foundation was it.

"Since before the unification of Jerusalem in 1967, the Jerusalem Foundation has worked toward the beautification, modernization and enhancement of the city for *all residents regardless of race or religion,*" the organization wrote in announcing the celebrations. "The foundation has raised upwards of five billion shekels [$1.4 billion in 2019 dollars] for over 4,000 projects ranging from parks and gardens to community centers to educational programs and more."

Among the "flagship projects" the foundation supported were the Max Rayne Hand in Hand School for Jewish-Arab Education in Jerusalem; the "Gan Hashalom" Erna D. Leir Peace Kindergarten for Jewish and Arab Children at the YMCA; the Central Arab Library, for Arab schoolchildren in the old city; the Center for Children at Risk, at Hebrew University; the Jerusalem Shelter for Battered Women; the Yellow Submarine Music Center; the Jerusalem Symphony Orchestra; an archaeological gardens; a film archives; a theater; a school for the deaf; a center for the deaf and hearing impaired; science laboratories and a science museum; the Golden Era Comprehensive Center for the Elderly; the Sheikh Jarrach Health Center; and the Zichron Menachem Day Care Center for Children with Cancer and their Families.

"All my life I have been involved with toys and children's entertainment," Hassenfeld said during the 50th-anniversary celebration. "Some say I think like a child, so close your eyes for a moment and pretend with me what we children would say: Starlight, star bright, first star I see tonight, wish I may, wish I might have the wish I wish tonight."

Hassenfeld said his wish was for Kollek's dream to be fulfilled: "A wish of community co-existence and culture, a wish of east and west, old and new, coming together in unity and sharing together hand-in-hand the future of this eternal city." That future, he said, is not something that is entered at some later date, but rather created beginning today.

He closed with a quote from Eleanor Roosevelt about the future belonging to those who believe in their dreams, and a paraphrase of the Peace Prayer of Saint Francis:

"May we bring love where there is hatred; healing where there is pain; harmony where there is discord; light where there is darkness; hope where there is despair; peace where there is strife. May this world be a better place and let it begin with us, making Jerusalem the most special of cities, as Teddy envisioned."

The 50th anniversary visit was not Hassenfeld's first to the Jerusalem Foundation, which his family had backed from its earliest days. He had been there with his mother just three years before, in the spring of 2013, for the dedication of a new park built in Mamilla, what in Kollek's time had been a no-man's land—"a largely neglected and sorry-looking spot" near the Old City's Jaffa Gate, as Ilene Prusher, a novelist and writer for newspaper *Haaretz,* described it.

This was the view the late Kollek had seen looking from his mayoral office, Prusher wrote, "and so it stands to reason that as some of Kollek's family, friends, and favorite philanthropists gathered here Thursday night to inaugurate a park in his name just outside the Old City walls, they felt Teddy was looking down and smiling."

Hassenfeld and his mother, 92, certainly were smiling, along with the crowd that turned out to celebrate the opening of the park with the nighttime lighting of the Sylvia Hassenfeld Family Fountain, a majestic, if unconventional, creation dedicated to the memory of Kollek that allows children to run across its flat surface as streams of water shoot gently into the sky.

Writer Prusher had harbored reservations when she read the announcement of its impending public debut.

"The fountain, my press release told me," she wrote, "is like the Barcelona Magic Fountain, The Bellagio Fountains in Las Vegas, and the musical fountains in Prague, Moscow, Geneva and Singapore, with computerized water performances set to light and music composed especially for the show. I've been to many of these cities, but somehow didn't remember being particularly impressed by any of their fountains—and the idea of a fancy water-spouting monument in a country with persistent water shortages didn't grab me."

Then she saw it.

"Watching the show is something akin to seeing columns of water perform The Lord of the Dance or Stomp," she wrote. "The water takes on a personality of its own, sometimes dancing ballet, sometimes zumba, sometimes a jig. Sometimes it literally seems to be on fire, lit up as the fountain is by some 1,500 bulbs that are used intermittently. And, quenching some of my concerns, it will all work on recycled water."

It would reflect the beauty of kids—Arab, Jew, Orthodox kids—playing together.

Hassenfeld told the crowd at the fountain's inaugural performance that its prominence in the new park helped proclaim Jerusalem as "a must-see, magical destination for inspiration." He expressed his hope that the park would become a crossroads "between East and West, for secular and ultra-Orthodox, Jews and Arabs, Christians, Muslims…that it be a meeting place for everybody, for peace and hope."

Prusher later interviewed the philanthropist, who said the fountain's state-of-the-art design had been a hard sell: "We wanted to do something for Teddy. I said, 'It can't just be another park, it has to be a destination.' I think I drove people crazy, mostly Israelis, trying to get them to realize the power of this concept. The idea was a fountain like the one at the Pompidou in Paris, or like Anish Kapoor's Cloud Gate in Millennium Park in Chicago. I want this to be Cloudesque."

The interview closed with a comment by Hassenfeld that would take on deeper meaning three years later in the U.S.

"Anywhere you go today, there is polarization," he said, addressing racist events in Jerusalem at that moment in 2013. "We see more of it in America, too. But if you believe in coexistence and peace, you need to be a change agent."

Hassenfeld had started his Hasbro career spending much of his time abroad, and with its opportunity for adventure with the work, he treasured it. But his executive responsibilities as Stephen's second-in-command in the 1980s and as CEO and chairman the 1990s and early 2000s had necessarily restricted his visits to foreign shores. Leaving the corner office had freed him to resume his worldly travels.

On his many missions since stepping down as CEO, Hassenfeld had journeyed to Argentina, Brazil, Canada, China, Cuba, Cyprus, England, France, Germany, Hong Kong, India, Israel, Ireland, Italy, Japan, Korea, Laos, Latvia, Malaysia, Mexico, Montenegro, the Netherlands, Panama, Portugal, Spain, Singapore, Slovenia, Switzerland, Taiwan, Thailand, Turkey, and Vietnam.

His foreign travels in 2016 brought a degree of respite from alarming developments at home. Donald Trump was moving toward his party's presidential nomination on a campaign of insult, exclusion, misogyny, xenophobia, racism, and falsehood that horrified Hassenfeld and millions of others but energized a base including Christian evangelicals whose values Hassenfeld did not comprehend.

As Trump secured the GOP banner during the party convention (that saw his wife delivering a plagiarized speech) and readied his campaign against Hillary Clinton, Hassenfeld watched in a state of mixed disbelief and anger—and the hope that come Election Day, voters would reject the reality-show host's message.

Surely, he thought, *Americans are better than this.*

And this was before the general public fully learned of Russia's efforts to throw the election to Trump—an effort allegedly involving Trump insiders that the FBI, Congress and Special Counsel Robert Mueller would investigate.

Trump's victory on November 8 stunned Hassenfeld.

"Still licking my wounds from the election," he wrote in an email a few days later.

"I don't know what's going on, I don't know where they're going," he said on the day before Trump's inauguration as the 45th president, January 20, 2017. "It's like having all of the pieces of a jigsaw puzzle but the puzzle is defective, they don't fit together."

Starting with his first trip to Japan, Hassenfeld had always held special affection for Asia; it was the source of many memories, including meeting his wife. Hong Kong and China topped the list of his favorite destinations, but Thailand—where he and Vivien often vacationed during the American winter—was home of one of the most innovative changemakers that Hassenfeld had ever met, and whom he had long supported.

And so, in February 2017, during an escape from the political turmoil unfolding at home, he and Vivien visited that innovator and friend.

Mechai Viravaidya, 78 years old in 2019, was respectfully known in his native land as Khun Mechai—but in the rest of Asia and the world, he was more familiarly known as "Mr. Condom." It was not a nickname one might have wanted, until you learned its meaning.

Son of a Thai father and Scottish mother, both doctors, Viravaidya in 1974 founded the non-governmental organization Population and Community Development Association, which promoted family planning—with the use of oral contraceptives and condoms—to cities and rural regions, where knowledge and resources were scarce. His work with condoms was credited not only in controlling population but reducing the incidence of AIDS.

Among other ventures, Viravaidya founded a chain of restaurants called "Cabbages & Condoms" where diners can receive a free condom with a meal. "Not only do the restaurants offer excellent food," the chain declares, "but they also promote the health and safety aspects of condom use in a fun and amusing manner. All proceeds from the restaurants are used to fund the social development programs of PDA."

Those were several.

From family planning, Viravaidya had expanded his mission to include The Village Development Partnership, which empowered rural communities to lift themselves from poverty; The Bamboo School, which provides an education to children who might otherwise not receive one; the Mechai Viravaidya Foundation, which promotes youth philanthropy; the Business for Rural Education and Development (or BREAD), "a new type of business enterprise with the objective of utilizing profits for improving the quality of life for people in rural Thailand"; and the Green Village Toy Library, a program enabling urban children with their parents and grandparents to donate toys to rural children, as they "extend their hands in friendship and generosity," the Library stated. In the process, all involved children participate in community service, leadership, environmental stewardship, and philanthropy.

Taken together, Viravaidya asserted, these efforts would "create a new generation of good citizens who recognize the 'Joy of Doing Public Good.'"

If the hand of Hassenfeld and the flavor of Hasbro were detected, it was no coincidence. Hassenfeld had long supported Viravaidya with ideas and donations, and their bond—like Hassenfeld's to another prominent Asian, Hong Kong philanthropist Li Ka-shing—was strong.

Hassenfeld's involvement with Viravaidya began on his first visit to the Bamboo School, also known as Mechai Pattana School, in rural Buriram Thailand, some five hours by car northeast of Bangkok near the Cambodian border. What he witnessed—children learning entrepreneurial skills that might lift them from poverty—awed him.

There, in a region so poor that some homes lack electricity, Hassenfeld said, "they were literally teaching kids how to make ethanol from sugar cane in the classroom, in the second and third grade, and then, they were selling it." They were extraordinarily resourceful with other materials as well. "They use anything and everything: as I say about Mechai, anything that's not nailed down. I don't stay there long because they'd take my body parts and make something out of them!" Hassenfeld laughed.

The Bamboo School was a revolutionary concept for that part of Thailand. More than educating a new generation of entrepreneurs, a laudable mission in itself, it today "promotes environmental protection, poverty eradication, philanthropy and integrity, as well as democracy and gender equality," according to the Thai school directory site sataban.com.

In Viravaidya, Hassenfeld had found a sort of soulmate.

And there was another aspect of the school that aligned with Hassenfeld's core values. Students were not charged tuition or any other traditional costs, but rather, according to the Thai school directory site, "the students and parents have to plant 365 trees and pay their fees with 365 hours of community service."

Hassenfeld found further appeal at the Bamboo School's toy-lending library that Viravaidya had opened before meeting Hassenfeld.

"Mechai would get used toys from wealthier families in Bangkok or wherever and send them to some of the villages that had been adopted," Hassenfeld said. "I remember meeting with five kids, eight to 12 years old. They had diaries of every toy they had loaned out. Before you could get the toy for a week you had to do community service, which might mean picking up empty bottles or picking up trash or planting a tree or walking grandma through the snake- infested rice paddies or something like that. I loved it."

Hassenfeld funded additions to the main toy library and satellite branches, financed continuing improvements to the school, established scholarships, and built a pool to teach children to swim. "Many times, kids were drowning," Hassenfeld said; instruction might prevent that. He also arranged for some children of Hmong hill tribes to attend the Bamboo School.

Beyond philosophy, Viravaidya and Hassenfeld also shared a quirky humor.

In a 2010 TEDxChange talk, Viravaidya spoke of how he had mined American culture in labeling some of the condoms he distributed.

"One says, 'Weapon of mass protection.' We found—you know—somebody here was searching for the weapon of mass destruction, but we have found the weapon of mass protection: the condom. And then it says here, with the American flag, 'Don't leave home without it.' But I have some to give out afterward. But let me warn you, these are Thai-sized, so be very careful."

The crowd roared.

Viravaidya brought in his own culture, saying, "in Thailand we're Buddhist, we don't have a God, so instead, we say, 'In rubber we trust,'" to more laughter.

Then he turned serious, describing the role his condoms helped play since he began giving them away in reducing the incidence of a deadly disease: "According to the U.N., new cases of HIV declined by 90 percent, and according to the World Bank, 7.7 million lives were saved. Otherwise there wouldn't be many Thais walking around today. So it just showed you, you could do something about it."

Something could be done also about poverty and Viravaidya closed his TED presentation with a brief tour through his own efforts in sowing seeds. "Poor people are businesspeople who lack business skills and access to credit," he said. "Those are the things to be provided by the business community. We're trying to turn them into barefoot entrepreneurs, little businesspeople. The only way out of poverty is through business enterprise. So, that was done."

His TED talk has been translated into 31 languages and been viewed more than a million times online, impressing many, including Melinda Gates, who wrote on *Impatient Optimists*, the Bill and Melinda Gates Foundation's site:

"My hope is that when TEDxChange is said and done, everyone who watched and participated in the event will leave feeling moved to action. For me, Mechai Viravaidya is an inspiration, showing what business savvy, creativity—and a great sense of humor—can accomplish."

The Gates Foundation honored Viravaidya with its 2007 Gates Award for Global Health, one of many such recognitions he has received. His native land bestowed one of its highest honors on him in 2009: The Prince Mahidol Award for Public Health, a prize established in honor of His Royal Highness, Prince Mahidol Adulyadej, father of the late Bhumibol Adulyadej, King of Thailand from 1946 until his death in October 2016.

Hassenfeld's February 2017 visit to Viravaidya was a welcome antidote to more ugly sentiment back home when, in his first month as president, Trump issued an executive order banning travel to the U.S. from certain Muslim countries—a ban that had been red meat to his nativist base, but an affront to American values in the opinion of many others, including Hassenfeld, grandson of a refugee immigrant.

"My kids were incredible," Hassenfeld said after his return from Thailand. "When we were there, even I was awed and my Hmong kids made us cry when we left. Mechai is a one-machine creator of everything good with the most incredible team."

PART TWO: POINTS OF LIGHT

Two weeks before Christmas 2016, Hasbro employees gathered in their global headquarters cafeteria for one of the highlights of their professional year.

It was the morning of December 15, the company's fourth annual Global Day of Joy, when Hasbro gives all of its workers worldwide a paid day off in return for performing acts of charity and community service. Hasbro employees in the earlier time zones of New Zealand, Europe and elsewhere had already started their day.

From the podium, Goldner reminded the crowded cafeteria of Hasbro's and its workers' commitment to do what they could to "make the world a better place for kids and their families. And it's just so gratifying that each of you are participating, along with 93 percent of the rest of our company. We love the fact that we take out a day in one of our most important times of the year to demonstrate what our real commitments are. Which is to our communities, to the people that we love, and to the children that need our help around the world."

Hasbro Brands President John Frascotti, whom Goldner two months later would promote to companywide president, tallied the numbers. "Today we're going to actually, in a 24-hour period, do about 250 projects in over 40 countries," Frascotti said. "It will actually be over 23,000 hours of volunteer service, which is more than two years when you do the math."

Wearing green-and-red elf hats and blue Team Hasbro tee shirts, employees filled bags with games and toys for distribution to nearly 5,000 children in Pawtucket schools, with more gifts headed to schools in Central Falls and Providence, where the company began.

Goldner himself filled some bags and then walked Hasbro's central corridor, its storied "Main Street," to conference rooms where he briefed members of "Dohvengers," "Equestria Bots," "Optimus Pie" and "Potato Blasters," the four teams competing in the 2016 Kindness Challenge. The teams headed into the community on a scavenger hunt in which they scored points for completing acts of charity such as buying food for needy families. Their progress was updated on Kindness Leaders screens at the end of Main Street, near the main headquarters entrance. The winner would award a $1,000 community grant to a recipient of their choice.

Leaving Pawtucket, Goldner visited Providence's Roger Williams Middle School, in the city's economically disadvantaged and racially diverse South Side, where dozens of his company's employees attired in "Power of Service" tees were busy cleaning, painting, refurbishing bathrooms and installing new furniture in the school's community center. Other employees, meanwhile, engaged students in games designed to encourage empathy and kindness.

Brian and Barbara Goldner at Global Day of Joy, Frascotti on right. (Miller photo)

Abroad, Hasbro employees in Italy had volunteered at a camp for children with serious illnesses. Employees in Peru had been renovating Clínica San Juan de Dios, a pediatric orthopedic rehabilitation center for children with physical disabilities. Hong Kong employees had engaged children with disabilities in cookie decorating, city tours, and playing board games. Netherlands employees hosted a game day for children with autism.

"What's great about this day is that we're all part of something much bigger," Frascotti said while commencing the Rhode Island effort.

In the weeks leading up to the Global Day of Joy, Hasbro had propelled empathy to the top of its social-responsibility agenda with the launch of its Rules of Kindness campaign, in partnership with generationOn, the youth division of Points of Light, the nonpartisan, international organization founded by former president George H.W. Bush to help mobilize volunteers and resources to address pressing social problems. Running from September 1 through October 17, the campaign invited kids and teens to create their own "rules of kindness" and plans to put them into action.

Four weeks into the campaign, Delores Morton, Points of Light's president of programs, wrote of its relevance in a presidential race that had witnessed candidate Republican Donald Trump publicly mock a disabled person and also the mother of an American Muslim solider who died in service to his country in Iraq; ridicule Vietnam War veteran Senator John McCain, a member of Trump's own party and a prisoner of war for five and a half years by declaring, "he's a war hero because he was captured. I like people that weren't captured, OK?"; denigrate women based on their looks and menstruation; tell repeated lies; accuse media outlets that exposed them of being worthless purveyors of "fake news"; have only good things to say about Russian President Vladimir Putin; deny that he knew "anything" about supporter David Duke or white supremacists in general; brag about his looks and the size of his penis; question that climate change was real; describe Hillary Clinton as "nasty," as "crooked," and many other things as supporters chanted "lock her up!"; question Supreme Court Justice Ruth Bader Ginsberg's cognitive functioning, declaring in a Tweet that she "has embarrassed all by making very dumb political statements about me. Her mind is shot - resign!" and calling Mexicans "rapists" while vowing to force Mexico to build a wall he could never force it to build.

And that was the short list of items Points of Life's executive Morton found objectionable.

"With just weeks to go in perhaps one of the most heated election cycles our country has had in a long time, our nation has reached a heightened point of divisiveness," Morton wrote. "We find ourselves in a time of both political and social unrest, with intense debates taking place not only on TV between candidates, but also on social media, in communities and in homes. A recent article from [online parenting community] TODAY described a situation where even young children are repeating the rhetoric they hear and getting into political debates.

"We voice our opinion loudly, and across many different platforms, but it seems we rarely take time to listen. So how can we combat this self-centric, divided path that we're on and work together to become a more unified, supportive nation?"

Morton's answer?

"With kindness and empathy. We need to step in and work to develop young changemakers who have empathy, compassion and kindness, who will work to bring our world closer together and celebrate our commonalities, rather than move us farther apart."

Rules of Kindness inspired more than 110,000 youth from eight countries to share their rules and action plans, and then, if they chose, write their guidance on the online Story Wall, the sort of wall Hasbro was happy to build.

Many children did. Wrote a girl from Indiana:
1. *Help those in need*
2. *Forgive*
3. *Stay positive*
4. *Be humble*
5. *Accept others as they are*

Wrote a boy from Sacramento, California:
1. *Be Kind.*
2. *Be Safe.*
3. *Be Clean.*

From boys and girls in a Louisiana school:
1. *Be Inclusive*
2. *Be Kind*
3. *Smile at Others*
4. *Show Empathy*
5. *Help others just because*

From an elementary school in Central Falls, Rhode Island:
1. *Honesty*
2. *Caring*
3. *Respect*
4. *Responsibility*

From students at New York City's High School of Arts and Technology:
1. *Create good karma*
2. *Inspire others*
3. *Provide nurturing*
4. *Dedicate yourself to kindness*
5. *Practice selflessness*

From the mouths of babes, as it were, wisdom that if practiced more assiduously by more adults in positions of power would make the planet the better place that Hasbro, Goldner, Verrecchia, and Hassenfeld continued to believe was possible.

As the Rules of Kindness campaign entered its sixth week, a Category-5 storm punished the Caribbean. Before dissipating over the North Atlantic in mid-October, Hurricane Matthew had killed more than 600, including 546 in Haiti, where tens of thousands were left homeless.

As it had many times before in response to natural disasters, Hasbro stepped up, with donations of cash and toys. Through its Children's Fund, it gave $25,000 to

SOS Children's Villages USA, a global organization that provides family-based care for abandoned and orphaned children, to fix damage to one of its Haitian villages and support children who lost parents in the hurricane. It gave a $75,000 grant to Partners in Health, an NGO operating in Haiti, to fight pediatric malnutrition. Hasbro employee volunteers packed games into shelter kits as part of the company's Play Relief program, a partnership with Good360, the organization that connects generous corporations to worthy causes. "The Play Relief program is designed to help provide a distraction and some sense of normalcy for children staying in emergency shelters when a disaster strikes," Hasbro said in a media release.

"Our thoughts are with everyone who has been affected by Hurricane Matthew," Hasbro Senior Vice President Global Philanthropy & Social Impact Karen Davis said in announcing the efforts. "We hope these funds will help SOS Children's Villages and Partners in Health provide much-needed care to families in Haiti recovering from the storm."

Ten days after the Rules of Kindness campaign ended, Hasbro launched Be Fearless Be Kind, its largest philanthropic venture ever. The program offered a variety of tools to children, parents, educators and others designed to teach empathy, compassion and inclusion, and the courage to stand up to others who practice the opposite: bullies, for example. Its creation generated extensive interest, with stories in *The Street, Yahoo Finance, Toy News, Toy Book, Kidscreen, Sustainable Brands, Bloomberg*, and numerous newspapers.

The principal portal into the campaign was through BeFearlessBeKind.com, where participants find empathy resources including books, videos and school programs; links to partner organizations embracing inclusion and diversity, including UNICEF's World's Largest Lesson, No Bully, and generationOn; and guided meditation with Awaken Mindfulness & Resilience Training head Katherine McHugh and her friend Serena, the cartoon frog who lives at the Peaceful Pad in an online video.

"Scientists have found positive changes in the brain for those who practice mindful meditation," was the word from the Peaceful Pad. "These changes correlate with a renewed sense of overall good health, feelings of inner peace; a better ability to focus and self-regulate; and an increased capacity for compassion and kindness towards others."

The Be Fearless Be Kind campaign recognized children between the ages of five and 18 who had become community volunteer leaders through Hasbro's existing Community Action Heroes program, which awarded scholarships to the winners. Through its partnership with Special Olympics' Unified Schools program, the company would begin bestowing a Hasbro Kindness Award "for extraordinary empathetic leadership" in areas where it maintained offices: Miami, Los Angeles, Seattle and Rhode Island. And with generationOn, the company would sponsor its seventh annual Joy

Maker Challenge, which encourages children "to spread joy and kindness to people in need during the holidays" through such means as bake sales, coat and food drives, donations of decorations to nursing homes, care packages for troops, and toys for other children. For every child participating, Hasbro donated a game or toy to Toys for Tots, the Marine Corps Reserve's program, up to $1 million. By the 2016 Joy Maker Challenge, children and adolescents had completed nearly a million acts of service.

"We recognize that empathy is a critical social skill that impacts our youth and our world," Goldner said in debuting Be Fearless Be Kind. "Hasbro has always been committed to standing up for children, and we are pleased to be using our resources to help address this important issue."

Said Davis: "We know the amazing difference kids can make by putting empathy into action through service, and we've seen how that work changes them, giving them confidence and a greater sense of purpose." The goal of Be Fearless Be Kind, Davis said, was "creating a generation of kids who include everyone, appreciate differences, and experience the feeling of fulfilment that comes with making a difference."

Be Fearless Be Kind traced its lineage to the summer of 2015, when Hasbro, in partnership with the city of Pawtucket, introduced a "No Bully" program into all 17 of the city's public schools. The effort employed the techniques of the San Francisco-based non-profit No Bully organization, www.NoBully.org, which had proved effective elsewhere in combating in-person and cyber bullying, pervasive problems with sometimes severe consequences for the physical and mental health of young people.

"Supported by Hasbro's long tradition of empowering children and as part of the company's ongoing effort to promote peace and kindness," the company said in announcing the program on August 31, 2015. "Pawtucket is the first district in New England to adopt the No Bully program department wide and declare itself a 'Bully Free' city."

Nicholas Carlisle, No Bully founder, claimed that the organization's "non-punitive No Bully system has a 90-percent success rate, creating bully-free campuses for over 120,000 students nationwide."

It was a claim Davis accepted.

"We are excited to take a proactive step in the national fight against bullying to help create positive environments for the children that live in our hometown of Pawtucket," she said. "Our purpose is to make the world a better place for children and their families, so we look forward to introducing the right tools and resources to teachers and students so they can become part of the solution in preventing bullying in our community."

The program worked: At the start of the school year, 54 percent of students reported being bullied, but by the end, that had dropped to 20.

Just before the June 21, 2017, release of *Transformers: The Last Knight,* fifth film in the franchise, Goldner granted an interview to a *Hollywood Reporter* writer. The story was illustrated with photographs of Goldner in his office, which he had decorated with photographs of family, friends and company employees; a Mr. Potato Head (how could he not); a Darth Vader figure; a football signed by Joe Namath, a sort of analog to the signed helmet Alan Hassenfeld kept in his office; and a snowboard with a Transformers logo and American flag made by Gilson Snowboard CEO Nicholas Gilson. It was one of only two in the world. *Transformers* director Michael Bay owned the other one.

The Hollywood Reporter writer was interested in the new Hasbro movie and future ones, and the relationship of the toy industry with Hollywood.

On the latter, Goldner gave an answer from Entertainment Business 101.

"The movie business is increasingly important to the toy and game business and to global consumer products overall," he said "The movies create incredible events to help elevate the interest in those brands globally. Television and streamed content help the fans learn about new stories over time. We're looking at an all-screens strategy because each element of that content deployment does different things for the audience."

He was more revealing when asked about the Disney Frozen and Princess deals.

"Our partner brands, of which Disney is a major piece, represent on any given year 25 to 28 percent of our revenue," Goldner said.

But he was less revealing in responding to the question: "Would you ever buy a studio? There's always one for sale."

"Owning and controlling the calendarization of your properties, the storytelling and the economics of the engagement of a global audience and consumer are all very compelling," Goldner said, and left it there.

The reporter drilled in, asking about gossip that Hasbro had considered buying DreamWorks Animation.

Goldner was even more tight-lipped.

"We didn't comment at the time, and we certainly wouldn't comment now," he said. "It's not surprising that it was a rumor. We worked closely with them on *Trolls.* It was a great partnership."

Rumors have long been a part of the fabric of the toy and entertainment industries, so the one that took life in February 2017 should have come as no surprise. It was a juicy one.

What began to spread was so-called "informed opinion" that Hasbro and Mattel were engaged in merger discussions. It generated predictable if tired headlines, for such speculation had periodically surfaced starting in 1995 and early 1996, when Alan Hassenfeld rebuffed Mattel CEO John Amerman's merger advances and Amerman shifted to hostile-takeover mode. From a pure narrative point of view, the prospect of the two long-time rivals finally reaching the altar was as enchanting as a Disney storyline.

"Will Barbie Say Yes to GI Joe?" read the headline on a February 10, 2017, story in *Seeking Alpha*, a crowd-sourced financial-news publication.

Wrote InvestorPlace: "Leonard Sherman, Columbia business school professor, believes that Mattel, Inc. and Hasbro, Inc. may be ready for a merger. He notes that HAS may be better at managing MAT than its own team is."

And so it began, the rumor spreading globally, with business publications including *The Malaysian Reserve* analyzing a possible merger from Disney's point of view.

"Hasbro has resuscitated Transformers and My Little Pony with films and TV, turning them into licensing forces," the paper wrote. "Analysts have criticized Mattel for not doing enough to boost its brands, and teaming with Hasbro could help them with that, posing a bigger competitive threat to film and TV studios. For instance, a movie based on Mattel's Barbie, a rival to Disney Princess and Frozen, has been in development for years."

But Disney, *The Malaysian Reserve* concluded, "might have an objection to the wedding of Barbie and G.I. Joe," since the company would no longer be able to pit one company against the other for the best licensing deals.

Even *The Los Angeles Times* reported on the rumor—but it, too, injected a note of reason.

"A merger would create a formidable company, combining Mattel's dominance in girl toys with Hasbro's traditional focus on the boys' aisles, although Hasbro has been expanding its girl's business with brands like My Little Pony," the paper wrote. "Industry analysts noted that rumors of a Mattel-Hasbro marriage have surfaced repeatedly and then faded in the 20 years since Hasbro resisted a formal $5.2-billion purchase bid from El Segundo-based Mattel."

Still, *The Times* quoted Jim Silver, editor in chief of Toys, Tots, Pets & More, or TTPM, a research and review firm, in essentially debunking the speculation. "I don't know if there would be a benefit, and I think that's why it hasn't happened yet," Silver said.

"Could Hasbro's Blowout Earnings Reignite Mattel Merger Talks?" asked Mad Money host Jim Cramer's site *The Street*.

Citing similar rumors of merger discussions in February 2016, *The Street* attempted an answer. "After Hasbro reported strong 2016 full-year and fourth quarter results on Monday morning and Mattel posted disastrous 2016 fourth quarter results last month, those talks may surface again, although if they persist, the companies will face several obstacles," *The Street* wrote.

"For one, antitrust issues would be a hurdle for a tie-up as Mattel and Hasbro represent the largest toy companies in the industry. Another may be that the companies, headquartered on opposite sides of the country - Hasbro in Rhode Island, Mattel in

California - would have a tough time combining management." The Street concluded its analysis with a quote from TTPM's Silver, who said there was a "one in a zillion chance" of a merger actually happening. Another TTPM analyst, Christopher Byrne, author of the definitive *They Came to Play: 100 Years of the Toy Industry Association,* published in 2016, did not opine on the rumors.

But history had demonstrated that Hasbro/Mattel rumors die hard.

As late as the summer of 2017, *Seeking Alpha* was repeating this one, albeit with less zeal than in February.

"Mattel-Hasbro Merger Getting Improbable," read the headline on a July 3 story. "With the recent contrasting developments at Mattel and Hasbro, it seemed to me that an oft-touted merger between the two names has become unlikely," stated the writer.

In any event, Mattel had other pressing issues. On the last day of summer, its stock hit a five-year low of $14.52. A share of Hasbro stock was trading at $96.14, nearly seven times more.

Goldner had no comment on the persisting rumors. He, too, had other things on his mind.

During an overall lackluster summer of 2017, *The Last Knight* became the least successful of the four *Transformers* movies, grossing $130 million domestically and $605 million worldwide by the time it left theaters. Still, that was no small potatoes, and the next film in the series, *Bumblebee* (technically a *Transformers* prequel spinoff), slated for a Christmas 2018 release was into pre-production and planning was underway for a 2019 release of *Transformers 6,* a working title. The biggest market for *The Last Knight* had been China: a $228.8-million box, down from the $320 million gross from 2014's *Age of Extinction,* which did $1.1 billion globally, but still a healthy return.

Attention inside Hasbro, meanwhile, was turning to a public celebration of its brands that it planned for early September. Comic Cons had proliferated across America and it was time for the company to stage one of its own.

As the first year of the Trump presidency unfolded, few in Washington seemed to hold much passion for the well-being of the people who mattered to the Goldners and Hasbro, and to Verrecchia and Alan Hassenfeld, for whom the November election had been so unsettling.

Even abroad—perhaps especially abroad—Hassenfeld could not escape Trump.

By the summer of 2017, the president had announced his intention to withdraw from the Paris Climate Accord, assailed the Iran nuclear deal, further alienated China and Mexico, questioned America's participation in NATO, and dismissed or ridiculed many heads of state, with the notable exception of Vladimir Putin. And more, much more.

Hassenfeld was so besieged by foreigners asking him to explain the president's zigzag-ging actions, statements, and Tweets that he threw up his hands and stopped trying.

Hassenfeld's angst surfaced publicly overseas in late May 2017, when he spoke in Portugal at the Horasis Global meeting, an annual assembly of global business, government, political, and thought leaders that in 2017 he co-chaired. Founded by Ger-man-born Frank-Jürgen Richter and headquartered in Zurich, Horasis calls itself "a global visions community dedicated to inspiring our future" that seeks to foster coop-eration between emerging markets and developed nations. Sowing seeds on a grand scale, one could say.

Speakers at the 2017 meeting in Cascais, a seaside resort town west of Lisbon, included leading citizens of Russia, China, Japan, Spain, Portugal, England, Mozam-bique, Nigeria, Afghanistan, Egypt, Finland, the U.S., India, Brazil, Turkey, Sweden, Finland, Belgium, South Africa, the United Arab Emirates, Bahrain, Estonia, Australia, Israel, Canada, Argentina, Vietnam, Hong Kong, France, Germany, Ghana, Jordan, An-gola, Luxemburg, and other countries. There was a current prime minister, four former prime ministers, a Vatican cardinal, a confidante of the Archbishop of Canterbury, a Mormon elder, the president of the Lisbon Islamic Community, the Russian State Duma deputy, the vice president of Time Inc., a sculptor, the chairman of an Indian pharma-ceutical firm, two Nobel Peace Prize winners, and the National Geographic Society's chief scientist.

On the second day of the four-day conference, Hassenfeld appeared on the "Plenary: World Economic Outlook" panel with a Canadian banker, the CEO of a Rus-sian sociology research firm, a Chinese official, and Robert Friedman, a senior editor with Bloomberg News.

Their topic: *The world economy changes at an unprecedented pace as a result of hyper-connectivity and external shocks. What are the risks and opportunities at the top of the global economic agenda in 2017-2018? Which trends can participants of the Horasis Global Meeting discern? Which trends might enhance togetherness?*

Not Trump, that much was certain.

Hassenfeld spoke about the administration, with conference comments that were reported internationally by Reuters. The news service began a story from Cascais with this broadside:

"Confusion surrounding the trade policies of U.S. President Donald Trump's administration means U.S. companies no longer know the rules of the game, a board member and former CEO of toymaker Hasbro told an international conference on Mon-day."

The Reuters reporter quoted Hassenfeld on international business. "We thought, you know, if you run a business today you would like to know what the rules of the game are," he said. "Right now in America we don't know what the rules of the game are. They are changing constantly… Right now we don't know whether we are friendly with Mexico, whether we are friendly with Canada, whether we are friendly with China, whether we are friendly with Russia."

Hassenfeld attributed the confusion to the "white noise and smoke coming out of the White House... Right now, our Congress and in some cases our courts, are caught up in trying to figure out what they are going to do with the executive branch. So right now, we are in that—almost twilight zone—that we are really not sure where things are going."

Could Trump deliver on his promise to bring more jobs back to America?

"Even if they did come, we've all learnt how to automate, we're all spending money to innovate," Hassenfeld said. It was a true assessment of 2017, when advancing technology was among the factors determining how and where things were made.

Reuters sent the story worldwide and American television carried it, with blowback from the White House reported on TV.

"I remember watching CNBC when I got home that night from Portugal and there was a group from the White House that was attacking Hasbro for buying in China," Hassenfeld recalled. "And there was another group that was basically saying, 'Excuse me, anything and everything that Mr. Hassenfeld said is the truth. What *is* our economic policy?'"

Hassenfeld did not want to get drawn in further, so he stopped taking calls temporarily.

"I went underground for two days!" he said.

He understood how those crossing the president could be torched, and Hasbro did not need to pay that price, even if these had been his personal remarks, not official company policy. In 2017, such distinctions could be lost on Washington.

PART THREE: CAMARADERIE

That Rhode Island was no stranger to strangeness was irrefutable. Its founder, contrarian Roger Williams, was deemed so strange for his time that Puritans would have burned him at the stake had he not fled south from Massachusetts. Edgar Allan Poe had lived in Providence, and H.P. Lovecraft had spent most of his life there. More recently, Providence had been the setting for the first World Fantasy Convention, in 1975, and three subsequent ones. In the new millennium, Rhode Island Comic Con and Necronomicon, a celebration of Lovecraft's work, had become fixtures on Providence's fall calendar.

Even against that backdrop, the scene inside the Rhode Island Convention Center on the morning of Friday, September 8, 2017, stood out.

Governor Gina Raimondo, Secretary of State Nellie Gorbea, and Providence Mayor Jorge Elorza joined Hasbro's Goldner, Frascotti, and CFO Deb Thomas to cut the ribbon officially opening the first-ever HASCON, a convention devoted entirely to Hasbro brands. Standing with them were human-size Mr. and Mrs. Potato Heads, a similarly outsized Play-Doh, and a ceiling-tall character from the Transformer franchise, Bumblebee. Also, two human-size My Little Ponies, Pinky Pie and Rainbow Dash, and four Planeswalkers characters from Magic: The Gathering.

Gorbea and Raimondo, left; Goldner, Thomas and Frascotti, center. (Miller photo)

Rhode Island—strange indeed: Pot Head with the governor, secretary of state, and the mayor of Providence, where Hasbro was born. It may have been a first for Gorbea and Elorza, but it was not the first time Raimondo and the spud had been together: The head of state and the state's iconic character had taped a promotional video for HASCON, which attracted thousands of fans whose spending was a boon to the local economy, and whose attendance at HASCON, magnified by mainstream and social media, amounted to valuable tourism advertising.

HASCON had unofficially opened Thursday evening with a private party for Hasbro employees and their children and families—partly in celebration of the company and its lines, and partly as thanks for the hundreds of workers who volunteered thousands of hours of their time in manning the exhibits and shows inside the Convention Center and the adjacent Dunkin' Donuts Center, affectionately known as The Dunk.

There was much to manage: booths and activity sessions involving all of Hasbro's major brands; a performance by Grammy-winning songwriter and singer Daya; a presentation of the upcoming animated series "Stretch Armstrong and the Flex Fighters," which was Hasbro Studios' first original Netflix show; panel discussions with the creators of many Hasbro products and shows; and appearances and autograph sessions by comic legend Stan Lee, actor Mark Wahlberg, Red Sox future Hall-of-Famer David Ortiz, and teen acting and dancing sensation Maddie Ziegler, who could boast of more than 1.4 million Twitter followers.

Also, "Chewbacca Mom," the real-life 38-year-old Candace Payne, whose Facebook Live selfie-video of her hamming it up in a Star Wars Chewbacca mask designed by a Hasbro team had gone crazily viral, with more than 170 million views, and millions more on YouTube and elsewhere. The video's message, "the simple joys," moved not only internet viewers but also publishers and a movie producer, who offered deals to Payne, a Texas mother.

Payne explained the popularity of her video to a newspaper columnist.

"People love raw unfiltered moments that connect us," she said. "I think that video was purely that—a moment people identified with. Maybe a long-lost laugh they had forgotten."

Payne said her upcoming book, *Laugh It Up: Embrace Freedom and Experience Defiant Joy,* would explore the importance of such moments through her experiences.

"It's about how I had to defy my circumstances to find joy," she said. "I've struggled with poverty. Depression. A suicide attempt. And abuse."

Her secret to overcoming those challenges?

"Hope is the main thing," she said. "Everyone wants joy, but I've never met anyone who's hopeless who had joy."

At about the time on Saturday morning that Chewbacca Mom was greeting fans, Al Verrecchia arrived at HASCON with his grandson Austin. They found their way to the Mr. and Mrs. Potato Head booth, along a back wall of the Convention Center. My Little Ponies, Transformers, Monopoly, Disney's *Frozen*, Nerf, Magic: The Gathering, and other Hasbro brands occupied larger and more prominent real estate, but Pot Head's Playskool corner saw a steady stream of visitors. The human-size characters patrolled the room, drawing attention and requests for photographs.

Al Verrecchia with Mr. Potato Head. (Miller photo)

Speaking to a writer, the retired CEO and chairman recalled playing with Potato Head when he was a child.

"It was a bag of plastic parts that had sharp points," Verrecchia said. "My mother would give me a potato and I would push the parts into the potato or a cucumber. It was great. You'd pull a potato out and you'd go in a corner and you could make faces. That would keep you busy for a couple of hours."

Today, Verrecchia said, "I don't know if there's a brand that has more awareness. It's not a high-dollar-volume brand because of the nature of the toy, but no matter where you go, Potato Head is well-known. It's an icon."

Grandson Austin, 22, remembered the toy he owned decades after his grandfather had played with the original.

"Whether it was a Darth Vader one or a Transformers one, so many different brands that Hasbro already had," he said. "They were combined into one legacy."

Frascotti, who had worked for Verrecchia, expressed warm feelings, too.

"I love Mr. Potato Head. And Mrs. Potato Head," he said. "It's amazing the number of people who come to Pawtucket, park, come out, and take pictures with their kids. It's one of those things that is so unique in the world that people come from all over just to get their picture taken with Mr. Potato Head."

Hassenfeld did not get to the Convention Center until Sunday morning, but he did make it to Providence Friday evening after having flown back from a board meeting in San Francisco for a lunch with the president of Brandeis University and the dean of the Brandeis Business School. There in a Renaissance Providence Hotel ballroom, G.I. Joe collectors and fans had gathered to celebrate the 35th anniversary of the 1982 relaunch of the toy. Hassenfeld, who often quipped that the original Joe had put him through college, was the guest speaker.

Hasbro Global Brand Management vice president Derryl DePriest introduced Hassenfeld. DePriest had taken an intriguing path to Hasbro: he held a bachelor's degree in psychology and a master's in neuroscience, and he had worked at Atari. Hasbro had long valued diverse backgrounds, having learned that cookie-cutter thinking stifled innovation

Hassenfeld, DePriest said, "is the most self-effacing gentleman I know. His charitable work—it would take 50 people to do what Alan does because of his passion and commitment to causes, especially Hasbro Children's. Your work is phenomenal. Thank you very much."

Dressed in his usual loafers, jeans, and collarless shirt under a vest, Hassenfeld took the stage. Being diehard collectors, the mostly middle-age crowd—including several former Hasbro employees who had been on the 1982 Joe relaunch team—knew about the latest controversy surrounding the true inventor of G.I. Joe.

It had been sparked by the death of licensing agent Stan Weston, who had played a role in bringing the toy to market but was not its inventor, not the man who really had "introduced the world to the heroic G.I. Joe, one of the most popular toys ever produced," as the May 11, 2017, *New York Times* obituary, later corrected, stated. In truth, that was the late Larry Reiner, who had worked with Weston and later, at Hasbro, the late Don Levine, a research and development executive. Like Westin, Levine had sometimes exaggerated his real role in the success of G.I. Joe. As Hassenfeld had told *The Washington Post* in its May 25, 2014, obituary: "Don Levine and his team took it from a good concept to a great concept."

After DePriest's introduction, Hassenfeld began on a somber note, asking the audience to think of the victims of recent hurricanes Irma and Harvey and "wish any and all of our fellow Americans the very best."

Then he joked, with a version of a line he used every autumn: "There are 108 shopping days between now and Christmas. What are you doing here?"

When the laughter subsided, Hassenfeld said that he had talked to Goldner today, as he regularly did. "He said, 'Promise me you won't do one thing. Don't come up with a new inventor of G.I. Joe.' So tonight I thought I'd really tell you."

Hassenfeld opened his vest to reveal… a Mr. Potato Head tee shirt.

The ballroom roared.

Then Hassenfeld spoke truth. "Honestly, if we hadn't had Potato Head, maybe we wouldn't have been able to do G.I. Joe."

During the next hour, Hassenfeld told many stories, starting with his own early employment at Hasbro.

"How did I get the job?" he said. "The magical word called 'nepotism.'"

The night was vintage Hassenfeld, a mix of history and humor with a dash of advice—and candid answers to pointed questions. Upmost in the minds of many at the Renaissance was this one, posed by a collector from Connecticut:

How could Hasbro market G.I. Joe so it would appeal to today's children. Put another way, *how could Joe be relaunched yet again?*

"If I had the answer, Hasbro would be paying me," Hassenfeld said.

When the laughter had subsided, Hassenfeld said "the most important thing is the story." But he did not profess to know what that story should be as the second decade of the new millennium neared its end and the Internet of Things and the millennial generation had so dramatically transformed global culture.

Hassenfeld did not mention Trump, but the president's failure to unite a sorely divided nation and lead a world beset by war and poverty might have been read into his words when he said:

"I personally would love to get back to the Real American Hero, but again, how do we do it? Just know how passionate I am about keeping Joe alive—but meaningfully."

Still, as he acknowledged, Hassenfeld's ability to shape product decisions was limited.

"Just remember, I'm only the chairman of the executive committee at Hasbro," he said. "Now that's a very important title, but what does it really mean?"

There was more laughter as Hassenfeld explained that in essence it meant his committee acted only as directed by the full board and made no product decisions, although its voice found receptive ears in Pawtucket and gave Hassenfeld additional credibility on the global stage. Nonetheless, as Hassenfeld sometimes joked, "it's like running a cemetery. There are a lot of people underneath you but nobody's listening."

Kid Number One did make an appearance at the Renaissance, with an allusion to a movie franchise in which Hassenfeld's alter ego, Mr. Potato Head, had starred.

"Every toy has a story and they do come to life at night," Hassenfeld said.

Hassenfeld was humbled and awed on Sunday morning, when he visited the Convention Center before HASCON opened to the public.

"There are a few times when one has an epiphany moment," he said.

He cited his trip with Goldner for a premiere of *Transformers* in Moscow's Red Square as one of them. And now this.

"If only my grandfather, father, and Stephen could see what they had started and where it is today—never would they believe," Hassenfeld said. "As I walked through The Dunk and Convention Center, it was another of those epiphany moments. It was incredible and emotional but what was most important was the camaraderie, the Hasbronians—all volunteers—working hand in hand to bring smiles to so many."

Henry, Merrill, and Stephen—"the culture they started has endured and will endure," Hassenfeld said. "This was a win for Rhode Island, for children, and for Hasbro. Not often one can check all the boxes. I am so proud especially for our toys which came to life because of our greatest asset, our people."

Hassenfeld left HASCON as new challenges faced the company whose board's executive committe he chaired: on the eve of the holiday buying season, Toys 'R' Us filed for bankruptcy. A heavy debt load and competition with Amazon, Walmart, and Target, among other factors, had brought the once-might toy retailer to its knees.

In reporting Hasbro's third-quarter results, which showed increases in both revenues and earnings, Goldner said "as a result of the Toys 'R' Us bankruptcy filing in the U.S. and Canada, there was a negative impact on our quarterly revenues and operating profit." Goldner expressed optimism heading into the critical final quarter, but Hasbro stock took a hit, dropping from $98.19 to $89.75 on the news. It quickly recovered, however, rising to $97.14 four days later.

Other developments reflected Hasbro's confidence that the core-brand strategy Hassenfeld and Verrecchia had set following the Pokémon debacle remained sound. Just days after third-quarter 2017 results were released, Goldner and new Paramount Pictures chairman and CEO Jim Gianopulos announced an exclusive five-year partnership that continued the relationship that had already produced the Transformers franchise. The new deal covered live-action and animation properties on the big screen and TV.

"Storytelling, in its many forms, is revolutionizing our business and differentiating Hasbro in all sectors where we operate," Goldner declared.

More tantalizing was the report on November 10 in *The Wall Street Journal* that Hasbro was seeking to acquire Mattel—a twist on the recurring rumors that the rivals would merge.

"Hasbro Inc. has made a takeover offer for rival Mattel Inc., according to people familiar with the matter, a potential combination that would unite the two biggest U.S. toy makers and put Barbie and G.I. Joe under the same roof," the paper reported. "Hasbro's approach to Mattel was made recently, one of the people said. The terms of any possible deal couldn't be learned, and the approach may go nowhere."

Despite the fact that executives at both companies declined to comment, the report sparked days of speculation and analysis in financial, industry and mainstream publications around the globe.

And this rumor seemed to have credibility, given key numbers: As *The Wall Street Journal* noted, Mattel's market value was about $5 billion, less than half of Hasbro's, which was greater than $11 billion. Little dog, big dog.

"The company has made a push into getting the rights to television and movie franchises such as Disney's 'Frozen' and 'Star Wars,' and its results have outperformed those of Mattel," *The Wall Street Journal* wrote. Hasbro's longtime rival, the paper continued, "has been struggling with losses and weak sales, forcing it to suspend its dividend and outline plans to slash costs and scale back new product launches." Mattel stock benefitted from the report, rising from a five-year low of $13.04 on November 2 to $18.54 on November 14.

Hassenfeld meanwhile grappled with the president's issuance of a third travel ban targeted mostly at Muslims and the backdrop of Trump's involvement in deepening investigations by Congressional committees and Special Counsel Mueller, who would indict 34 people before his nearly two-year probe ended in 2019. Washington remained gridlocked on many major issues facing America, including gun violence, despite new mass shootings in Las Vegas and Texas. In Rhode Island, the gun-control and good-government battles would continue, a new election cycle would near, and politics would remain a passion for Hassenfeld.

New needs continued to arise.

Five days after HASCON ended, Hassenfeld met with Governor Raimondo and Meghan Hughes, president of the Community College of Rhode Island, to determine how he might help make a difference there. Raimondo recently had initiated a free-tuition program at the school, which served thousands of diverse students—many of them working parents—who saw the school as the key to better-paying jobs and advancement to four-year bachelor's- degree-granting colleges, which could lead to entry into the middle class.

But neither free tuition from Raimondo's Promise Scholarship program nor federal Pell Grants would cover other education-related expenses such as transportation and food.

To help fill that gap, Hassenfeld established the Rhode Island Promise Plus program with a $650,000 gift, largest in the school's 53-year history. The program motivated students to graduate through a series of incentives including, at Hassenfeld's insistence, a requirement to perform community service. A second-year Rhode Island Promise Plus student could fulfill the requirement by mentoring a fellow student in her or his first year, among other ways.

"When young people do community service," Hassenfeld said, "the beauty is that almost instantaneously, they see the change. They know they can be a change agent."

When the gift to the Community College of Rhode Island was announced on September 27, 2017, Hassenfeld traced its roots to a meeting he had several years before with students at another school who were receiving financial aid.

"All of them explained the difficulties of working with the office of financial aid, but their greatest problem was that aid did not include the costs of food, books, or daily life," he said. "Three of them, I remember, were living by eating rice twice a day."

Hassenfeld helped those students then, and hundreds more now.

"This gift was my remembering the past and trying to aid students who achieved certain goals to be able to live a better educational life without more burden," he said.

Paying back. Paying forward.

One day the next week, just hours after Trump on a visit to hurricane-devastated Puerto Rico tossed paper towels into a crowd and bragged on Twitter of his "great day" on the island, a jet carrying doctors, nurses and 11,000 pounds of food, water, clothing, medication and other supplies lifted off from Miami.

They were on a relief mission that Hassenfeld and his foundation had financed and arranged with Natalia Denegri, an activist, actress and host of the popular Spanish-language Mega TV show *Corazones Guerreros*, or *Warrior Hearts*. Hassenfeld and Denegri produced the show, which she described as "stories of children's self-improvements and overcomings. Children who, despite their physical and psychologial limitations, have been able to overcome and go ahead in life."

Denegri flew on the mission and helped coordinate the return flight, which transported several seriously sick Puerto Ricans to mainland hospitals for treatment.

"We brought many elders, babies and young people on the plane," Denegri said. "I slept only two-and-half hours, but my heart is happy."

In an update to Hassenfeld, Denegri said "it is a difficult situation there. A senator told us they lost communication with many towns and they do not know if the people are dead or alive. There is a lot of pain and anguish on the faces of people who have lost everything.

But, she said, "the people we brought and the parents of the babies said you are an angel who saved their children."

A person accompanying a patient with kidney disease asked Denegri to convey a message to the Hassenfeld foundation.

"Thanks, thanks very much," the person said. "She will have dialysis today. You saved a life."

A week later, as island residents still suffered from the devastation of Hurricane Maria, Hassenfeld flew to Miami to assist in a second relief mission. His sister, Ellie, flew on it, as did her daughter and grandson.

"My family and the way I was brought up always believed that you should try and bring sunshine where there is darkness," Hassenfeld said in *Hope*, a short video of the relief effort that Denegri helped produce. "Really because of your phone call to me, asking us to try and help the children and many of the senior citizens and maybe bring that smile where there's a frown—that's what this is all about."

A packet of letters awaited Hassenfeld when he returned from Florida. Students at Mechai Viravaidya's Bamboo School had written from Thailand to thank him, Vivien and his foundation for their support. The letters provided evidence of young lives changed—and a new language, English, learned.

Fifteen-year-old Piyapat wrote "I am very happy to be in this school because this school teaches me many things, for example, agriculture, business, life skills, and I learned how to play ukelele and I can swim, too. I feel very proud when I do activity. I would like to thank you for your scholarship to support me. I will study hard and I will be a good person in the future."

Attaya, 17, wrote with gratitude for Hassenfelds' "kindness" and about her background as a hill tribe member, although "I don't have a nationality." A Hmong student thanked Hassenfeld for a schooling that imparted "life skills," and another Hmong youngster appreciated a place where he learned "skill to help society"—and had the opportunity to develop a talent for drawing. One student was grateful for the chance to develop "a public mind." Several said that one day they, too, would provide scholarships for children.

In an especially moving letter, eleventh-grade student Phisid wrote of teaching villagers "to do agriculture with new innovation" and of the lessons he himself had taken from Mechai Viravaidya's programs. "The Bamboo School teaches us about creative thinking, self confident discipline, occupation skills and learning to live with people like family," Phisid wrote. "My idol is the Hassenfeld family and the director of our school. He give us everything.

"Finally, thank you again.

"I promise I am going to be a good person, share my experiences to social, and go back to develop my hometown.

"I wish you be happy, be healthy and get everything you want."

CHAPTER ELEVEN

REACH FOR THE STARS

PART ONE: RIP. ICE.

For the company that Hassenfeld's grandfather and great-uncle had founded a century before, the year 2018 had dawned with reason to smile: When Hasbro announced full-year 2017 results on February 7, it reported a four-percent rise in net revenues from 2016, to $5.21 billion for the year, another Hasbro record. The balance sheet was rosy.

Said CFO Thomas: "Over the past five years, we added over $1 billion in revenues to our top line, growing revenues four consecutive years, while meaningfully increasing operating profit, net earnings and generating significant cash flow. Hasbro is in a strong financial position with the cash and profitability to invest in growing our business for the long term."

In his remarks, Goldner emphasized the vigorous performance of what he called Hasbro's "franchise brands," My Little Pony, Nerf, Monopoly and Transformers among them. The crown jewels had produced net revenues of $2.56 billion, a ten-percent increase over 2016.

"Hasbro's global team's execution of our Brand Blueprint drove revenue gains in Franchise Brands, Hasbro Gaming and Emerging Brands, including immersive brand experiences across consumer products and digital gaming," Goldner said. "Our strong performance ranked Hasbro number one across the G11 markets for the full-year 2017."

Entertainment and licensing revenues had increased eight percent, to $285.6 million, generating a robust operating profit of $96.4 million, almost double 2016. For the full year, revenues in gaming, driven by the popularity of Magic: The Gathering, hit $893 million, like Hasbro's franchise brands, a ten-percent jump over the prior year.

The results beat Wall Street expectations, and Hasbro stock closed at $102.22 a share the day they were revealed.

But clouds were moving in.

The double trouble of overall slowing consumer demand and the September 2017 Toys 'R' Us bankruptcy filing had played Scrooge for Hasbro's critical holiday fourth quarter: in October, November and December 2017, net revenues had declined to $1.60 billion from $1.63 billion in 2016. And no one could predict the once-mighty toy chain's future. Toys 'R' Us had secured $3 billion in financing as it tried to restructure its debt, but whether that could save the company was dubious. Just two weeks before Hasbro reported its 2017 financials, Toys 'R' Us had announced it was closing about a fifth of its U.S. stores. Could the remaining 80 percent hang on? Likely not: in this real-life Game of Life, Toys 'R' Us was spinning losing numbers. Wal-Mart, Target and Amazon were driving the giant into oblivion. Sears was among the once-mighty retailers that knew this story well.

Goldner made no predictions about the fate of Toys 'R' Us in a conference call with analysts, but he assured the Street that Hasbro was prepared for the worst.

"Our team has built a plan for the right sizing of the Toys 'R' Us business," he said. "We have continued to grow the number of doors and continued to grow our revenues outside of Toys 'R' Us. We continue to be supportive of them, but most importantly, we continue to manage our risk and inventory as they streamline the amount of inventory they can take. And we are prepared for any eventuality. Obviously, the more time we have the better it is..."

As it would develop, Hasbro and the entire industry had less time, not more.

Toys 'R' Us was a ticking time bomb.

For Mattel, the clouds were dark and raining. When the company reported its 2017 results, on February 1, surely there was anguish in El Segundo.

CEO Georgiadis, the third head of Mattel in as many years, attempted cheer by declaring:

"We have taken aggressive action to enter 2018 with a clean slate so that we can reset our economic model and rapidly improve profitability. We are optimistic about stabilizing revenue in 2018 anchored by our key power brands, entertainment partnerships and exciting new launches. We continue to gain momentum toward the medium-term goals..."

But sunny words cannot change reality. For the full year, Mattel's net sales were down 11 percent, contributing to an operating loss of $342.8 million and adjusted loss per share of $1.08. And while not penny stock, those shares were trading in the

$15 and $16 range, continuing the long slide from late 2013, when they had traded as high as $47.58.

The fourth quarter of 2017 had been even more brutal to Mattel than Hasbro, with net sales off 12 percent and an operating loss of $252.8 million. And the Toys 'R' Us effect was only just beginning—for both companies, and many others besides.

The bomb burst on March 14, when New Jersey-headquartered Toys 'R' Us told its employees it would sell or close all its U.S. stores and likely all it owned elsewhere in the world.

"We're putting a for-sale sign on everything," CEO David Brandon told employees.

Some 33,000 American jobs would be lost—and for toy manufacturers of all size, a coast-to-coast outlet that had been at the center of their retailing for decades would disappear. And the harm to manufacturers would extend further. When the chain had filed for bankruptcy six months before, it owed Mattel $136 million, Hasbro $59 million, and Lego, the world's largest toy firm, $32 million, money the firms might never see.

Whether the end was a factor in another passage will never been known, but on March 22, eight days after Brandon's announcement, Toys 'R' Us founder Charles Lazarus died at New York's Mount Sinai Hospital of respiratory failure. He was 94.

Closed for good. (Miller photo)

In its obituary, *The New York Times* described the chain's closing as "a painful denouement for a company that Mr. Lazarus founded 70 years ago in Washington, D.C., and that grew into a global toy seller with thousands of stores in locations stretching from the United Kingdom to Asia." Lazarus would be remembered as "an aggressive entrepreneur" who "steered his company through decades of growth and several years of financial turmoil," the *Times* wrote.

"There have been many sad moments for Toys 'R' Us in recent weeks, and none more heartbreaking than today's news about the passing of our beloved founder, Charles Lazarus," Toys 'R' Us said in a statement. "We will forever be grateful for his positive energy, passion for the customer and love for children everywhere."

Once a game-changer, Lazarus and his company had lost in a new game of toy retailing.

RIP, Geoffrey the Giraffe.

The end for Georgiadis at Mattel came less than a month later, when the company announced she was leaving "to pursue a new opportunity in the technology sector" after 14 months in El Segundo. The new opportunity was as CEO of Ancestry.com, the Utah-based genealogical company, a better fit for the considerable talents of the former Google executive.

Naming former Fox Kids Europe chief Ynon Kreiz its new CEO and chairman, Mattel wished Georgiadis well. "We thank Margo for her service and many contributions to Mattel," outgoing chairman Christopher Sinclair said in a statement. In its coverage, the *Los Angeles Times* noted her focus on Barbie, American Girl and other core brands and "streamlining its operations and slashing costs to match its lower sales."

Her efforts had not sufficed to right a listing ship. Nor was her departure and replacement necessarily seen by Wall Street as the move that would. As *The Los Angeles Times* noted, "after the announcement of Georgiadis' departure, Mattel's stock closed at $13.45 a share, down three percent on the day. The stock has tumbled nearly 50% since she became CEO."

No champagne was uncorked in Pawtucket when the first-quarter 2018 numbers had been tallied: with the death of Toys 'R' Us in the U.S., it seemed a curse had been cast. How long it would hold was a question without an immediate answer, Goldner's preparations for "any eventuality" notwithstanding. This retail Lazarus would not rise from the grave, nor would it rest quietly for some while yet, either. The collateral damage would be widespread.

"We are working to put the near-term disruption from Toys 'R' Us behind us," Goldner said in a statement on April 23.

Disruption indeed: From January through March, Hasbro's revenue dropped from $849.7 million in 2017 to $716.3 million, well below forecasts, contributing to a loss of $112.5 million, or 90 cents a share. From a year-to-date high of $102.22 a share, stock on the day first-quarter results were announced had dropped to $86.12.

Hasbro's West Coast rival announced its first-quarter numbers three days later, and new CEO Kreiz did his best to find a silver lining.

"Mattel delivered positive sales growth in the first quarter, excluding the impact of the Toys 'R' Us liquidation," Kreiz declared. "And we continue to see strong momentum in our key Power Brands, with Barbie and Hot Wheels each up double-digits. While Toys 'R' Us will present a near-term challenge, our transformation plan remains our focus, as we work to deliver improved profitability and return Mattel to its leadership position as a high-performing toy company."

But the numbers were not industry-leadership caliber: from January through March, net sales were down seven percent in constant currency compared to the first quarter of 2017 and the operating loss was $276.6 million, or 90 cents a share. The stock closed at $13.98 on April 26, nothing to cheer about, albeit better than the year-to-date low of $12.80 on March 21.

Disappointing though the U.S. demise of Toys 'R' Us was for Hasbro, the company could find comfort in other developments in the first half of 2018. One was Saban Brands' decision, announced in February, to choose Hasbro (and not Mattel) as the toy licensee for its Power Rangers line. In May, Hasbro paid $522 million in cash and stock to acquire Power Rangers and other Saban properties, including "My Pet Monster," "Popples," "Julius Jr.," "Luna Petunia" and "Treehouse Detectives."

And Hasbro was honored yet again by several groups for its corporate ethics, starting in February, when the Ethisphere Institute selected it as one of its World's Most Ethical Companies, the seventh consecutive year Ethisphere had named Hasbro. That spring came word that CR Magazine named the company fifth on its 2018 list of 100 Best Corporate Citizens, and word that Hasbro once again made the list of America's Most Reputable Companies, compiled by the Reputation Institute.

In marking that honor, Goldner waxed eloquent.

"We challenge ourselves daily to look beyond Hasbro's own interests for opportunities to do what's right and create an enduring, positive impact within our industry and our world," he said. "We could not have achieved this honor without the passion, dedication and ingenuity of our employees, and their commitment to our shared purpose, to make the world a better place for children and their families."

Goldner did not foretell the fate that awaited some employees in the fall, when the full impact of Toys 'R' Us's demise would be felt.

As board member, stockholder and friend of many Hasbro executives and employees, Hassenfeld, per usual, was following corporate developments closely in the new year.

But his causes continued to be all-consuming and at his age, he was aware of the passage of time—of the fact that he had outlived his father and brother. Critically, 2018 was an election year, with potentially significant ramifications for the country, Rhode Island, and Florida, where he now owned a condominium in Miami.

For Hassenfeld, as for many in Rhode Island and beyond, January had brought another chilling development. Against the backdrop of a nativist president who was bent on building walls and punishing immigrants and refugees, ICE agents had seized a Providence wife and mother of two young women and imprisoned her in Boston—without, at first, informing her family where she was or what had happened to her. The story of Lilian Calderon-Gordillo, 30, a native of Guatemala who entered the U.S. with her parents at the age of three, enraged Hassenfeld and many others. It seemed to echo of Somalia or North Korea, not America.

And did it ever echo of Kishinev.

These were the facts of the case, which made national headlines:

Lilian crossed with her parents from Mexico to the U.S. in 1991, but her father's asylum request was denied and in 2002, the U.S. Board of Immigration Appeals issued a final order of removal for the family. Six years later, the board denied a petition to reopen the case. In 2016, Lilian applied for Deferred Action for Childhood Arrivals, or DACA, status, but the government denied the request, claiming she had not provided sufficient evidence that she had lived continuously in the U.S. That same year, Lilian married Luis Gordillo, a U.S. citizen and a man she had known since high school. The couple had two children by then.

Hoping the government would verify their marriage, which would make Lilian a lawful permanent resident, the couple on January 17, 2018, visited a U.S. Citizenship and Immigration Service field office in a Providence suburb.

A trap had been set.

"Calderon said immigration agents spoke with them separately, first her husband and then her," *The Providence Journal* would later report. "Everything went smoothly at first, she said. Her husband came out of his brief meeting and she went in. An immigration official told her their marriage had been verified and was considered legitimate—the first step in seeking lawful permanent residency.

"But a moment later two other immigration officials entered the room and swept her away without even the chance to speak to her husband, Luis Gordillo.

"'They just put handcuffs on me and said I had to go with them, and I can't see him, I can't speak to him. I can't even tell him what happened,' Calderon said."

The story became public two weeks after agents had imprisoned Lilian, and friends, supporters, and a Unitarian Universalist minister had organized a protest and hired a lawyer. When Hassenfeld learned of the case, after *The Providence Journal* published the first of its several stories, he immediately offered to cover the couple's legal bills and help in any other way he could, including relocation expenses should Lilian be deported, the worst-case scenario.

But he sought no public attention, preferring to quietly help another needy family, albeit not with ordinary need.

Hassenfeld was not alone in caring for these strangers thrust suddenly into the public discourse. A GoFundMe campaign quickly surpassed its $8,700 goal and the #FreeLilian hashtag trended on Twitter. Gabriela Domenzain, then the director of the Latino Policy Institute at Roger Williams University—herself the daughter of Mexican immigrants—helped organize protest.

"We know that the United States is detaining, imprisoning, and taking the rights away of thousands of people like Lilian. It's shattering our communities and it's shattering our families and how we as a state and community react to these situations matters," said Domenzain, a former journalist, Democratic Congressional Campaign Committee aide, and staff member of the National Council of La Raza, now known as UnidosUS.

And the American Civil Liberties Union joined the cause, filing a petition to free Lilian.

"I believe her case demonstrates from the beginning until today we are dealing with a federal agency that is continuing to inflict pain and sorrow on immigrant communities for no good reason," said Steven Brown, executive director of the American Civil Liberties Union of Rhode Island. "Real people, real lives are being affected in real profound ways by this administration's aggressive and indiscriminate immigration enforcement policy."

For four weeks, Lilian remained imprisoned with only an occasional, brief phone call with her husband, who was caring for five-year-old Natalie and two-year-old Noah, children who could not understand why their mom had suddenly disappeared. But the ACLU and Martin Harris, lawyer for Lilian and her husband, prevailed and the mother was released as the legal fight to keep her in the U.S continued—and the ACLU field a class-cation lawsuit against Trump and officials with ICE and the Department of Homeland Security.

More harsh language from the ACLU accompanied that filing.

"The Trump administration has relentlessly pursued detaining and deporting as many immigrants as possible, no matter the costs to family unity and civil rights," said Carol Rose, head of the group's Massachusetts branch. "In all of the quotas, the raids, and other cogs of the Trump deportation machines, there are human beings."

The initial response from ICE was in language as cold as its acronym.

"Ms. Lilian Calderon Jimenez Gordillo is a Guatemalan national who has a final order of removal issued by an immigration judge," a spokesman told *The Providence Journal.* "ICE arrested her Jan. 17 based on that final order of removal… The agency does not target those who may be seeking immigration benefits. Any suggestion to the contrary is baseless and without merit… The individuals targeted had previously ignored the aforementioned removal orders and will now be held in ICE custody pending removal. As ICE Deputy Director Thomas Homan has made clear, ICE does not exempt classes or categories of removable aliens from potential enforcement. All of those in violation of the immigration laws may be subject to immigration arrest, detention and, if found removable by final order, removal from the United States."

Cold, and also partly a lie.

Emails released in the ACLU's class-action lawsuit confirmed that not only were individuals such as Lilian targeted, they were snatched in carefully planned and executed actions that had the flavor of a dark operation from a CIA playbook.

"As far as scheduling goes," read one email from an ICE agent to a Citizenship and Immigration Services employee, "I would prefer not to do them all at one time as it is not only a strain on our ability to transport and process several arrests at once, but it also has the potential to be a trigger for negative media interest, as we have seen in the past. If you have the ability to schedule one or two at a time and spread them apart, that would work best for us."

Domenzain, left, with freed Lilian and Luis. (Courtesy Providence Journal)

Said Brown: "The government's actions in this case are truly despicable. Essentially, they waved the carrot of permanent legal status before unsuspecting immigrants with the intent of arresting, detaining and deporting them. The devastating effect of these machinations was to unnecessarily and cruelly tear families apart."

A month after she was imprisoned, Lilian was released. "I am so happy to see my husband and children again and to be out of immigration detention, which was a terrible ordeal for our family," she said in a statement by the ACLU. "What the government is doing to my family, and to so many others, is simply wrong."

❦

The year 2019 would bring more developments in Lilian's case. That May, a federal judge ruled that her class-action suit could proceed—and that other immigrants like Lilian in New England, perhaps numbering in the thousands, could join it. The ACLU praised the judge's decision.

"The family separation crisis—whether on the southern border or in New England government offices—is the direct result of the Trump administration's policy choices, driven by the view that immigrants deserve nothing but cruelty and punishment," said Rose, ACLU of Massachusetts head. "This class certification is about ensuring that families stay together."

Hassenfeld hailed the ruling, too—and also the decision by the U.S. Consulate in Guatemala, which granted Lilian a visa to return to her homeland to continue on a path to U.S. citizenship. She and her husband travelled there almost immediately.

Recalling a tradition of assisting immigrants and others in need that began with his grandfather and great-uncle, Hassenfeld said "my family has always been involved in helping those who have been forgotten or dismissed or persecuted by powerful institutions and leaders. To paraphrase Don Quixote, against imposing odds, truth and justice have prevailed with Lilian. Quixote fought the unrightable wrong. We did, too, and we won."

On her return from Guatemala in late May, Lilian was a legal permanent resident of the United States. She and Luis appeared at an emotional press conference arranged by Domenzain.

"It feels like a total weight has been lifted off our shoulders," Lilian said. "Just amazing, an amazing feeling."

Lilian recounted her experiences with ICE and the 26 days she had just spent in her native land, awaiting a decision on her application for permanent residency.

"Guatemala is a beautiful country but within its beauty lies a very sad country," Lilian said. "I met people from all walks of life during my time there but the people that will stay with me for the rest of my life are the children and the elderly. The children that have no other option but to forgo their studies and start working at such a very young age just to be able to survive and the elderly that continue working because they don't have any other option. They might never have the opportunities that all of our children here have to be free, happy and simply enjoy their childhood and that to me is just very sad."

Lilian thanked journalists who had covered her story, her attorney, the ACLU, Senator Jack Reed and his staff, the many Rhode Islanders who had supported her, her husband, Domenzain and one other individual: "The next person we haven't thanked publicly before but without whose support we wouldn't be here today."

That person, Hassenfeld, had deliberately stayed in the background, with the rationale that in this, as with much of his work, "some people do it for recognition, but I do it because I can make a difference. That's what makes you smile."

At her press conference, Lilian said that Hassenfeld, "who read about our story because of [local] journalism, has supported my family since day one, and he has also become part of our family. In the year it took for our situation to be resolved he has consistently been there for us and for that we will be eternally grateful."

Lilian and Luis pledged to help others facing immigration struggles. Asked what they would say to someone who failed to comprehend what their family had been through, Lilian declared: "Take a look at everyone around you and at the end of the day we're all human. We all hurt. We all cry. We go through emotions and we're all just trying to do our best, just like everyone else."

"Don't shut the doors on anybody," her husband said.

PART TWO: TRANSFORMERS

Although he no longer ran Hasbro or served on the board, Verrecchia in retirement continued his own tradition of giving back. On April 10, 2018, he and Gerrie celebrated the opening of the Verrecchia Clinic for Children with Autism and Developmental Disabilities at Bradley Hospital, part of the Lifespan healthcare system, whose board Al had once chaired. Located in East Providence, Bradley was nationally renowned for its services for children and adolescents.

Michele Levy and her husband Chris Levy, Gerrie and Al,
their daughter Melisa Verrecchia and fiancé Andy Marr.
(Photo by Al Weems, reprinted with permission of Lifespan)

"The service is a crucial one and timing couldn't be better," Bradley wrote in a post to the Lifespan site. "Estimates show one in 59 children will be diagnosed with autism. And children with developmental disabilities are more than four times as likely to experience behavioral and psychiatric issues."

Made possible by what the hospital called Gerrie and Al's "extraordinary million-dollar gift," the new clinic, Bradley wrote, "works collaboratively across the Lifespan system, including the Children's Neurodevelopment Center at Hasbro Children's Hospital" and would allow "the hospital to build on its legacy of autism research and breakthroughs for the future."

"Children have been very good to us," Al Verrecchia said.

"And because we have been so fortunate, it's important to us to give back to the children in our community," said his wife.

Two of the Verrecchias' own children, Michele Levy (with husband Chris) and Melisa Verrecchia (with fiancé Andy Marr) joined them at clinic opening.

Hassenfeld was not one to seek sympathy, so when he prepared for his own visit in the spring of 2018 to a hospital—for upper-spine surgery at Massachusetts General, where he had gone under the knife 20 years before following his heart attack—he did not bring attention to what he faced. He faced a risky operation to repair nerve damage that was causing debilitating pain in his right shoulder and arm. Likely caused by decades of his passion for tennis, a sport he now could not play, the damage was so severe that he could no longer even raise his arm.

Privately, Hassenfeld kept friends informed. Cheerful optimism was his message.

"Tomorrow will be fine," he wrote in an email to a writer who had sent best wishes the day before the surgery.

Publicly, Hassenfeld in the months before (and after) his surgery was intent on the November 2018 midterm elections. In Rhode Island, one U.S. Senate seat would be contested, as would the Providence mayoralty and all seats in the General Assembly. Nationally, the midterms would in part be a referendum on the Trump presidency. Hassenfeld had a dog in many of these fights, and as always, he was investing words and money in desired outcomes.

In deciding to back independent Dianne "Dee Dee" Witman for Providence mayor with a $50,000 campaign contribution, Hassenfeld was rejecting incumbent Jorge Elorza, who, he and others believed, had failed to solve the capital city's considerable financial difficulties. In an interview with *Providence Business News* two years before, Hassenfeld said the city was in worse trouble "than anyone comprehends" and bankruptcy might be the best solution.

"Someday the plug will get pulled in Providence," Hassenfeld said. "I'm not sure, and this will shock you, I'm not sure if we shouldn't pull a Detroit or Central Falls and level the playing field and start all over." Both the Motor City and Central Falls had emerged successfully from bankruptcies, their finances returned to stability.

On another issue—one he'd advocated for some while—Hassenfeld in an op-ed piece co-written with prominent businessman Robert Manning argued for a referendum that would ask Rhode Island voters to approve the line-item veto, which would give the governor greater control over state spending. All but six states had such a provision, Hassenfeld noted.

"Sometimes things that greatly harm Rhode Island get traction in the House or the Senate, and the go-along, get-along culture of Smith Hill makes it hard to derail them before they get baked into the budget," the op-ed declared. "A line-item veto review by the governor is the perfect check on this kind of thing."

Much of Hassenfeld's time—and his $10,800 in campaign contributions—was spent, largely behind-the-scenes, on the U.S. Senate candidacy of Robert Flanders. Hassenfeld served as a sort of unofficial adviser to Flanders, a Republican, much as he had in 2012 for unsuccessful U.S. House candidate Brendan Doherty.

Former Associate Justice of the Rhode Island Supreme Court and the court-appointed receiver who had steered Central Falls out of bankruptcy, Flanders enjoyed the respect of Democrats and Republicans alike. Many said he would make a fine governor—but his odds against incumbent Gina Raimondo, who was seeking a second term, were long. In any event, he wanted to be in the U.S. Senate, which, he maintained, had become bitterly partisan at the expense of the nation.

There, too, he faced long odds: in November, he would be facing off against the two-term Democrat Sheldon Whitehouse, a leading champion of strong policies to address climate change and a ferocious critic of Trump, as were fellow Rhode Island senator Jack Reed, U.S. Rep. Cicilline and Hassenfeld. But Hassenfeld had concluded that Flanders, being Republican, might have more influence in the Republican-controlled Senate.

Speaking when Flanders announced his bid, in November 2017, Hassenfeld had struck that theme. "These truly are trying times," he said. "I call it the twilight zone. We don't know what is going to happen from one day to the next. There's a lack of certainty, a lack of execution, a lack of high moral purpose."

"Like many of you I'm dissatisfied with the hyper-partisanship that we see down in Washington, D.C., these days," Flanders said. "The entrenched politicians who are there—there's too much finger-pointing and not enough handshaking going on. We need problem-solvers." Flanders acknowledged his party affiliation but called himself "an independent-minded Republican." He mocked Whitehouse's patrician upbringing, referring to his opponent as "Silver Spoon Sheldon." It was time, Flanders said, "to stick a fork in all the arrogance, the prosecutorial pomposity, and the climate-change bullying that have characterized his tenure."

Flanders chose Central Falls, the city he had helped save, for his announcement. The mayor of the small municipality, Democrat James Diossa was not at

Flanders' side. But he was on Hassenfeld's mind. Just 32 years old, this son of immigrants from Colombia was Central Falls' first Latino mayor. In his second and final term, he would be seeking new directions when he left office. Impressed by his civic leadership, Hassenfeld would offer to assist him.

Hassenfeld's affinity for the Latino community, which dated to Hasbro's early days in Central Falls and Pawtucket, which each had large Hispanic populations, had strengthened in recent years. With his support for TV star and producer Natalia Denegri, who had organized the relief missions to Puerto Rico after Hurricane Maria that Hassenfeld and his sister had underwritten, Hassenfeld's philanthropy now extended to the commonwealth and to southern Florida, where he had his new residence—and to South America, where Denegri was born and where a humanitarian crisis was unfolding in Venezuela.

In 2018, Hassenfeld philanthropy included continued financial backing for Denegri's television show featuring inspiring stories of Hispanic children and families, *Corazones Guerreros*. "Thanks to Alan's support and his family, we can bring happiness and smiles to many families," Denegri said.

Hassenfeld also supported Trinitus, Denegri's film-production firm which made *The Truth*, a documentary released in 2019 about contemporary Venezuela.

"It all began with a dream. They wanted to bring a child into the world," says the narrator of the film's trailer, which opens with images of a smiling couple and their newborn. "And then they realized this child was born in Venezuela."

The smiling images then dissolve into footage of police firing on protesting citizens, which fade to photographs of the dead and dying.

"If we don't take care of our children," the narrator says, "what's going to happen to our future?"

The words "power... corruption... forcing millions of people to suffer" roll across the screen, and the narrator declares: "What are we going to do to make a difference?"

Lori Holland kept friends apprised of Hassenfeld's spinal surgery.

"Just wanted to let you know that Alan is in recovery," she emailed a writer late the afternoon of the operation.

Early the next morning, which happened to be Good Friday, she wrote: "He called me a little while ago. Sounded better than I expected. He couldn't talk long. Was so nice to hear his voice!"

Not long after, Hassenfeld himself was emailing.

"They finally have let me out, but I'm not very pretty. Talk to you later," he emailed. In the same message, he expressed appreciation for a story about a four-year-old girl born with a severe abdominal defect whose life had been saved and made normal during multiple stays at Hasbro Children's Hospital. The occasion for the story was little Paige Alston being named the Children's Miracle Network Hospitals' Rhode Island Champion.

"Wonderful article, and it brought a smile to my addled brain," Hassenfeld wrote.

Paige Alston with surgeon Francois Luks. (Courtesy Providence Journal)

Hassenfeld's surgery proved successful, and after some post-operative complications, one requiring readmission to Mass General, Hassenfeld returned to his office for a few hours two weeks after the surgery. He was wearing a neck brace, which he would for several more weeks, and he tired easily. But there was work to do, and no one else to do it.

The second quarter of 2018 brought no relief for Hasbro, nor for Mattel. Hasbro's revenues decline seven percent for the April-through-June period, and net earnings were off; international revenues dropped 11 percent, resulting in a 99-percent decline in operating profit in that sector, to $200,000. Still, the company had on hand $1.2 billion in cash—and, Goldner proclaimed, reason to expect "profitable growth in 2019 and beyond" with investments "in innovation, entertainment and a modern global commercial organization."

His prophecy would prove true, but not until after more pain.

Goldner said "2018 is unfolding as expected as our teams manage the liquidation of Toys 'R' Us in many markets and address the rapidly evolving European retail landscape... We are focused on moving beyond the near-term disruption of losing a major customer, with a clear path forward including new retailer activations to meet the consumer demand made available by the Toys 'R' Us departure."

Mattel also cited Toys 'R' Us when reporting its abysmal second-quarter performance, on July 25, two days after the Hasbro numbers were announced. Revenue was down by almost 14 percent compared to the prior year, resulting in a net operating loss of $189.2 million. Such trends were unsustainable, and Mattel announced that it would lay off more than 2,200 employees and sell its factories in Mexico. Mattel stock on July 25 closed down, at $16.29.

But there were bright spots, CEO Kreiz said, including "continued strong performance by Barbie and Hot Wheels." The company, according to Kreiz, was "in a turnaround."

It seemed he was right: when Mattel on October 25 reported its third-quarter results, the numbers were promising. On net sales of $1.44 billion, operating income had increased by nearly 50 percent, the first time in two years it had scored year-over-year growth. Based on point-of-sale information from toy retailers compiled by market research firm NPD, Mattel could once again claim to be the "the number one toy company globally in each of the last four months through September," Kreiz said. "We were also the number one toy company in the U.S. and Latin America year-to-date through September," he added.

Earnings per share, the West Coast company reported, were two cents. No bragging rights there—until one remembered that in the same quarter of 2017, Mattel had posted a loss of $1.75 per share. Wall Street did remember. The stock closed up on October 25, at $13.84.

CNBC was one of several media outlets that approved.

"Mattel shares leaped 6 percent after hours Thursday after the company reported a third-quarter profit ahead of the all-important holiday season," the financial network said. "Although its third-quarter results fell short of projections, they signal Mattel's progress on profitability."

Even the often-ornery *Motley Fool* offered praise, writing:

"It's been a long road for toy maker Mattel. The trouble began several years ago, as demand for the company's flagship Barbie faltered and it lost the coveted Disney Princesses and Frozen doll business to archrival Hasbro. The coup de grace came with the demise of Toys 'R' Us, the last remaining big-box toy-centric retailer, which hit Mattel's financials worst of all. Some thought this might be the end of the House That Barbie Built and anticipated that it would be swallowed up by Hasbro.

"After enduring quarter after quarter of disappointment, Mattel investors went into the company's third quarter holding out little hope for signs of improvement. They were in for a surprise when Mattel posted an unexpected profit."

In Pawtucket, the ground was moving as the third quarter ended and Hasbro tallied its numbers. The Toys 'R' Us collapse continued to exact a toll—and more was happening. With the digital revolution still transforming entertainment and play, plastic toys no longer prevailed in a world of electronic devices that children virtually from birth owned or were exposed to.

Hasbro had navigated the transition with considerable success, but it could not yet declare mastery. No toymaker could. A parallel could be found in Hollywood, where Hasbro's presence was large, in the difficulties traditional studios and broadcast networks were experiencing with the rise of Netflix, Amazon, Hulu, and other digital content-creators.

There were other issues for Hasbro, and they related to Hollywood. The company's long involvement with movies and TV had demonstrated time and again that the screen world can be a two-edge sword—and the current era seemed a reminder of that lesson.

Exhibit Number One was Hasbro's *Transformers* series, the crown jewel.

The first film in the contemporary line, *Transformers*, released in 2007, had done $319 million domestically and $709 million worldwide (the 1986 *Transformers: The Movie* barely registered at the box office). The first sequel, 2009's T*ransformers: Revenge of the Fallen,* had done even better, with $402 million in the U.S. and $836 million worldwide. But domestically, the next three in the series, *Transformers: Dark of the Moon,* $352 million; *Transformers: Age of Extinction,* $245 million; and *Transformers: The Last Knight,* $130 million, had all trended down. The overseas box office had trended up for the first two of these three, but down with the last, *Transformers: The Last Knight,* which had done $475 million foreign, bringing the worldwide box to $605 million. Hardly peanuts, but only about half of what the king of the series, *Transformers: Dark of the Moon*, had done worldwide: $1.12 billion.

In December 2018, Paramount released *Bumblebee*, a *Transformers* spinoff, and the advance hype was strong. But in May, the studio had canceled plans for what had been called *Transformers* 7 (*Bumblebee* being 6).

Entertainment site *Collider* was one of many fan-oriented outlets that took note. "The news isn't particularly surprising after *The Last Knight*, which fizzled out at the domestic box office," the site wrote. "The film fared better overseas, but the final sum tallied 'only' $605.4 million, an impressive sum no doubt, but a long fall from the billion-plus days of *Dark Side of the Moon* and *Age of Extinction.* For his part, long-time director Michael Bay, who helmed the first five films in the Transformers franchise made no bones about the fact he was done directing *Transformers* films during the *Last Knight* press tour."

But the next film seemed to offered salvation.

Bumblebee opened with glowing reviews and what Hasbro described as "highly positive social sentiment," scoring a near-perfect 93 percent on the Tomatometer and receiving the site's "Certified Fresh" seal. "Bumblebee proves it's possible to bring fun and a sense of wonder back to a bloated blockbuster franchise—and sets up its own slate of sequels in the bargain," read the Critics Consensus. The movie grossed $468 million at the global box office and performed particularly well in key international markets including China, Southeast Asia, Latin America and the United Kingdom.

Directed by Travis Knight, who helmed 2016's *Kubo and the Two Strings*, *Bumblebee* starred Hailee Steinfeld and John Cena. Hasbro attributed its success "among families across age and gender" to what it described as "it being part action-packed adventure and part heartwarming story of friendship." Importantly, the company said, "the goal of *Bumblebee* was to re-establish the *Transformers* films as an all-family franchise where males and females of any age can connect with strong stories and characters. The team behind the film positioned *Bumblebee* to bring heart, humor, and fun back to the franchise, while laying the foundational roadmap for the next decade of *Transformers* entertainment and storytelling."

But Hasbro was not betting it all on future *Transformers* properties. And so, the company looked to Hasbro Studios, a wholly owned subsidiary headquartered in Burbank, to carry some of the water. The *My Little Pony* and *Littlest Pet Shop* TV and movie franchises continued their hold on girls, and four major motion pictures were confirmed in development from Hasbro Studios division Allspark and Paramount: *G.I. Joe: Ever Vigilant*, *Micronauts*, a *Dungeons & Dragons* film, and an untitled project.

There were other projects as well, including *Monopoly*, *Clue* and *Furby*, that had been announced, but whose status was uncertain: *Furby*, for example, which The Weinstein Company in 2016 had announced it would produce. A year later, *The New York Times* and *The New Yorker* in stories that won both the Pulitzer Prize exposed Harvey Weinstein as a sexual predator. The Weinstein Company went out of business in July 2018, two months after the disgraced studio boss was charged in New York with rape and sexual assault, leaving *Furby* in limbo.

Except perhaps for the most astute observers of the toy and entertainment industries, few outsiders foresaw the news that broke the morning of October 17, 2018, when media outlets responding to tips prompted Hasbro to respond to rumors of impending workforce reductions.

"While not explicitly confirming that layoffs are taking place, Hasbro Inc. said Wednesday that 'difficult' changes are underway that affect 'a single digit percentage' of the toy company's global workforce of 5,000 employees," *The Providence Journal* reported. But Hasbro "refused several requests for further specifics on the number of layoffs that are apparently taking place," the newspaper reported.

Company spokeswoman Julie Collins Duffy took no calls but did email a statement. "As part of Hasbro's ongoing transformation, we continue to make meaningful organizational changes," it read. "While some of these changes are difficult, we must ensure we have the right teams in place with the right capabilities to lead the company into the future... We continue to add new capabilities based on our understanding of the consumer and how our retailers are going to market, while evolving the way we organize our business across our Brand Blueprint."

Duffy said the "changes" were unrelated to news the day before that the law firm of Pomerantz LLP on behalf of investors was investigating "whether Hasbro and certain of its officers and/or directors have engaged in securities fraud or other unlawful business practices." The claims, Duffy said, "have no merit and we intend to vigorously defend against them."

Four days later, Hasbro reported its performance for July, August and September. "Well short of third-quarter expectations," wrote the Associated Press. Net revenues decreased 12 percent, to $1.57 billion—less than the $1.71 billion that Wall Street had expected. At the end of the day, Hasbro shares fell to $95.01, from $98.04 the previous trading day.

But beyond those numbers were others that enabled Goldner to put shine on the quarter.

Hasbro earnings were $263.9 million, or $2.06 per share—lower than expectations and slightly lower than the year before, but still satisfactory, given the continuing impact of Toys 'R' Us' demise, which Goldner in his prepared remarks emphasized.

"The global Hasbro team is effectively managing our business forward through a very disruptive year," he said. "The lost Toys 'R' Us revenues are impacting many markets around the world, notably the U.S., Europe, Australia and Asia." But, he added, "a growing array of retailers are now ramping new programs to take share this holiday season and we are well positioned to meet their demand."

Hasbro and Goldner made no mention of layoffs in the third-quarter report, but insight was found in the long conference call with him and CFO Thomas that followed the financials release. Goldner did not discuss specifics—no numbers, positions or locations of employees let go—yet reading between the lines, perceptive followers of the industry could conclude that the layoffs involved more than balancing a balance sheet hurt by the passing of a retail pillar.

Just as Hassenfeld and Verrecchia in the 1990s had remade Hasbro for a new age, Hasbro now was transforming itself with ambition to fully exploit the digital era.

"Reinventing and reimagining," is how Goldner phrased it during the conference call. Many of the reinventors and reimaginers were of a new generation, adults now, parents of children who found through a device the same excitement children decades before had found with a plastic Barbie or G.I. Joe. Old thinking had no place anymore.

"Recognize that half of our employees to date are new to the company over just the last six years," Goldner said in the call. "And these new experts are increasingly leading across design and development, storytelling, marketing, data analytics, social listening, and other new areas like shoppable social content. So we felt—given the current environment, we felt there was an opportunity to make a step change in our organization and to go faster. And yes, there are some cost savings. But this also allows us to continue to invest in our team, in our brands and our capabilities… This is all part of a comprehensive plan to return to growth in 2019 and beyond. And so, we had a strong commitment to diversity in our teams globally, a strong commitment to female leadership across the company."

In the city of Pawtucket, birthplace of the American Industrial Revolution, panic set in. The layoffs had breathed new life into rumors that Hasbro wanted another location for its world headquarters—a new place that suited its team approach, in which employees from all departments freely interacted, the exchange of ideas not hampered by the siloes and cubicles that had arisen inside the meandering corridors, corners and floors of a retrofitted old factory building.

And it was true that once you got off the fabled Main Street with its glittering displays of product, you really had gone down the rabbit hole. What ideally should be an environment for idea incubation and execution—cross-pollination being an operative theme—in reality was more akin to the set of a Tim Burton movie. Magical and glittering, maybe, but no creative wonderland.

Would Hasbro find another location in the city where Stephen Hassenfeld had engineered a small toy company into a Fortune 500 firm? Or would it go elsewhere, perhaps Providence, "The Creative Capitol," where it already had leased quarters in downtown? Would it leave Rhode Island altogether? Opportunity might beckon across the state line in Massachusetts, whose economy was humming. Tax credits dangled by the Bay State might be alluring.

Massachusetts was paying attention, as would become public in April 2019.

"State economic development officials in Massachusetts are considering trying to lure Rhode Island-based toy company Hasbro across the border," the Associated Press reported on April 19. "Colleen Arons, a spokeswoman for the Massachusetts Office of Business Development, tells The Boston Globe for a story Friday that the agency is 'working to establish a dialogue' with Hasbro. Pawtucket-based Hasbro Inc., which employs more than 1,000 people in Rhode Island, has made no secret of the fact it is in the process of evaluating several options for its corporate headquarters."

Already stung by the recent decision by the Pawtucket Red Sox, the Boston Red Sox' AAA farm club, to relocate to Worcester, Pawtucket mayor Donald Grebien on November 7, the day after the 2018 midterm elections, called a press conference at City Hall. Joined by Central Falls mayor Diossa, Pawtucket municipal leaders and members of the General Assembly, Grebien asked the help of state officials including the governor in an "urgent" effort to keep Hasbro in his city.

"This is where they started, this is where their history is and we want them here," the mayor said. Some 1,200 of Hasbro's total workforce of more than 5,000 worked in Pawtucket.

Grebien said city officials for several months had been engaging in discussions with Hasbro executives, but "they haven't really told us what direction they're moving; it changes ... They're a private company and [play it] very close to the vest."

In a statement released on the day of the mayor's press conference, Hasbro shed no new light. "We are in the process of evaluating several options for contemporizing our corporate headquarters, including finding a new corporate campus in the vicinity of our current headquarters," Duffy said. Hasbro, she added, was "committed to delivering a fully updated, connected and flexible workspace for all of our employees, and want to find the right solution that will ultimately create the best corporate headquarters for Hasbro into the future."

Two days after Grebien's press conference, Governor Raimondo and Rhode Island House Speaker Nicholas Mattiello publicly declared their commitment to persuade Hasbro to remain in the state, though not necessarily in Pawtucket.

"It's my job. I'm going to do everything I can to convince them to stay in Rhode Island," Raimondo said. "I'm in constant contact with the CEO to say that you better not think about leaving Rhode Island. You're a part of Rhode Island, and we need you to stay."

"We will do our best," Mattiello said. "Hasbro is a world-class company, and they're in a headquarters that's very dated right now. I certainly hope they stay either somewhere in Pawtucket or in Rhode Island, [or] Providence somewhere."

And so once again, Hasbro was thrust into the maelstrom of Rhode Island politics.

This one, however, the last Hassenfeld brother sat out. He was no longer an executive with the firm, and he had more than enough already on his agenda.

But he could not stop others from bringing him into the fray. Humorist Charlie Hall did just that, if indirectly, with a newspaper cartoon that depicted a man with Raimondo asking "Governor, Hasbro wants to leave Rhode Island, how can we keep them here?" in one panel.

On the other: a Mr. Potato Head atop the State House, in place of the real-life statue of the Independent Man.

PART THREE: STARFISH

One evening in late November 2018, Hassenfeld welcomed an audience to a room in the Rhode Island Convention Center, scene of HASCON the year before.

The crowd had answered the call of the Rhode Island Foundation, which was launching its new Pioneers podcast series. Coming later would be Rabbi Gutterman; Angel Tavares, the first Hispanic mayor of Providence; Amanda Milkovits, a *Providence Journal* crime reporter whose coverage of sex trafficking had won awards; and Julie Nora, director of the International Charter School in Pawtucket, a dual-language elementary school for Latino children whose mission was "to integrate the diverse languages and cultures of the communities it serves...and helping children develop an appreciation of other cultures."

But Foundation head Neil Steinberg wanted Hassenfeld first, and his crew had engineered a sellout by posting a public invitation to hear from "a pioneer in improving the lives of children through toys, as a child health advocate, and a civic leader."

As the audience took their seats and the sound technicians prepared to record, Hassenfeld and Steinberg chatted on the stage. Hassenfeld had placed a Mr. Potato Head on the table in front of him, and those who knew him well expected him to have a bit of fun with it. Which he did, once they were rolling.

Alan Hassenfeld, Mr. Potato Head, and Neil Steinberg. (Miller photo)

Although Steinberg was the host, he had left interview duty to Mary-Kim Arnold, a writer, poet, visual artist and visiting lecturer in English at Brown University. Adopted from Korea and raised in New York, Arnold had headed the Rhode Island Council for the Humanities and then worked at the Rhode Island Foundation before devoting herself entirely to her art.

"So our audience and listeners likely know of your role with Hasbro, but maybe don't know much about its founding," Arnold began. "I wonder if you would tell us a little bit about how Hasbro got started."

"Wonderful question to start with," Hassenfeld said. "But first, many of you are probably wondering why Potato Head is sitting here. As you know, Potato Head was one of the first advertised toys, back in 1952. But today the management of Hasbro does not let me speak without a handler and someone who watches over what I'm going to say. So Potato Head is here and if he says something crazy, it's because I've said something wrong."

The audience laughed.

"The other thing, as I've already told Neil," Hassenfeld continued, "is there are only 28 more shopping days to Christmas, so please support your local toymaker." Some jokes never die.

Hassenfeld told of his grandfather and great-uncle coming to New York and then Rhode Island, and of their early business as rag merchants. "When I say rag merchants, I don't mean the clothing business," he said. "They literally took the seconds and the thirds from the mills that were producing textiles and they first made hat liners. And then they made pencil boxes because we were also in the pencil business. And then all the sudden pencil boxes became doctor kits and doctor kits gave birth to Potato Head."

Arnold asked Hassenfeld what he had learned from his family's "immigrant experience."

Not as much directly from his grandfather and great-uncle, he said, because he was young when they died. But the story had been passed to his mother and father, from whom he had learned. Henry and Hillel, members of what he called "the first generation," were Hasbro's first pioneers, Hassenfeld said; his father and uncle, the second generation.

And he and his late brother belonged to the third—in the Bible, the cursed generation, "the ones who supposedly waste everything," Hassenfeld joked. "Somehow I was able to remove myself from Hasbro in time before everything went south!" It was a reference to the aftermath of the Pokémon disaster, when Verrecchia stopped the hemorrhaging.

The conversation turned to Hassenfeld's earliest days at Hasbro, when he came into the company on his terms and spent most of his time in the Far East. There, he said, he began to embrace a philosophy that had guided him ever since: do not attempt to impose American values on other cultures. He could have cited many examples, but he chose to tell the story of the establishment of the Afghan Women's Development Centers.

It began by gaining the trust of the matriarchs, a process that involved not challenging certain Afghan traditions that Westerners might have found offensive, Hassenfeld said. "We had learned that we needed the community to be a part of the program, especially the women's community," he said. "And the only way you make change happen is from within."

Arnold asked Hassenfeld to discuss the guiding principle behind his contemporary philanthropy.

"That's easy," he said. "Any time any of us sees a child who's not smiling, who's going through problems—if we're able to turn that grimace into a smile, that makes your heart just absolutely feel so good. What makes me happiest is trying to be creative in philanthropy and trying to make sure that we're making a difference because too often I think we give but we don't think necessarily what the end goal is going to be. And so for me, the end goal is how do we bring sunshine where there's darkness."

As summer had faded, voters had tuned in more closely to the September 12 primary and November 6 general elections. Hassenfeld was busy, on the local and national fronts.

Flanders trailed against Whitehouse in polls, but Hassenfeld stuck with his candidate, who beat his primary opponent with more than three-fourth of the vote. With a $1,000 donation, he backed Republican Steven Frias in his general-election contest against House Speaker Mattiello. Hassenfeld "supports me because I believe in government reforms like line-item veto and stuff like that," Frias told a reporter.

And Hassenfeld gave $40,000 to the Rhode Island Coalition Against Gun Violence, which opposed Mattiello and was itself part of another organization, "Citizens for a Corruption-Free RI," which also included the state chapter of the National Organization for Women.

But Mattiello won re-election, and Flanders and Providence mayoral candidate Witman both lost.

Still, Hassenfeld found encouragement on the national scene with the Democrats taking back control of the U.S. House.

"I see huge hope in the House," he said after the election.

But when, if ever, he wondered, would Republican senators rebuke Trump?

"I wonder if you would speak to some of the qualities that you look for in a leader," Arnold asked Hassenfeld as the Pioneers Podcast recording reached the halfway mark.

The first quality, he said, was one he had learned from his wife: "From listening comes wisdom," Hassenfeld said.

Next, he said, was surrounding oneself with "wonderful, talented people."

What were his views on today's young people?

Hassenfeld answered by recounting a recent visit he took to Wentworth Institute of Technology, where he talked to students.

"Their biggest concern today is mental-health issues," he said. "We're seeing at universities an incredible amount of problems in our younger people today. Is it because of social media? Because they're turned on all the time." He cited a study that found, as he put it, that "kids today are spending eight to ten hours on electronic media."

With eyes glued to screens—people engaged with machines, not people—is something essential disappearing? Hassenfeld mused.

"I'm scared because I don't know if we're losing humanity," he said.

Hassenfeld spoke of Brown University's Hassenfeld Child Health Innovation Institute, headed by Dr. Patrick M. Vivier, who was in the audience, and the institute's work on autism, asthma and obesity.

Nearing the end, the session turned playful.

"When we spoke earlier you perhaps made the mistake of mentioning that you were a creative writing major," Arnold said. "I'm a writer and I teach creative writing. So I'm going to take you back in time," to when Hassenfeld was in college studying a favorite author.

"So we're back in your dorm room and you're reading Dickens, writing your English Lit papers. What do you tell your younger self about the life ahead?"

"I basically say be like David Copperfield, be a picaresque character willing to go on the road and never, never fear," Hassenfeld said. "If the door is open, try and walk through it and see what's on the other side. And, very much like Copperfield, as you're walking down a path, don't be afraid of taking the left fork or the right fork. At least don't remain stationary. Too many people, I think, fear change. For me, change is good. And you if you're going to be successful, you have to try and change within the times you're in."

The session was drawing to a close.

"As we wind up," Arnold said, "is there any answer that you have or a question that I had to get past?"

Hassenfeld shared one of his favorite quotations: "Problems are like ice cream cones. If you don't lick them quickly, they become very messy… My other favorite quote is one from Gandhi. One of the things that I am somewhat worried about nationally is greed. But Gandhi once said 'there's enough in this world for human need not enough for human greed.' And I think we're living in a time where there's a lot of greed."

Arnold closed with what she called the lightning round—quick questions to elicit a quick response.

"What word or phrase do you most dislike?" Arnold said.

"It can't be done."

"What is your idea of perfect happiness?"

"Everybody's smiling and working in harmony together."

Eleven days before, Hassenfeld had marked turning 70 with a small gathering of family and friends. He wanted no lavish party, no public celebration. He knew what he and his family had accomplished, and that was sufficient for him.

Vivien had prepared a short video to be shown at the get-together, and she had asked her husband to write and narrate the montage of images of him and significant people and moments in his life that the video featured.

"Once upon a time, there was a wise man who used to go to the ocean to do his writing," Hassenfeld began. "One day, he was walking along the shore. As he looked down the beach, he saw a human figure moving like a dancer. He smiled himself to think of someone who would dance to the day. As he got closer, he saw that it was a young man and the young man wasn't dancing but instead he was reaching down to the shore picking up something and very gently throwing it into the ocean.

"As he got closer, he called out 'Good morning, what are you doing?' "

"The young man paused, looked up and replied, 'throwing starfish in the ocean.'"

"'I guess I should have asked, why are you throwing star fish in the ocean?'"

"'If I don't throw them in, they'll die.'"

"'But young man, don't you realize that there are miles and miles of beach and starfish all along it. You possibly can't make a difference.'

"The young men listened politely and bent down to pick up another starfish. And he threw it into the sea and said, 'it made a difference.'"

Images crossed the screen: of Hassenfeld with his brother, father, mother and wife; with celebrities including Michael Eisner, Steven Spielberg, Hillary Clinton and Muhammad Ali; dressed in Monopoly and Star Wars costumes; presenting the Dalai Lama with a plush panda bear; with many different Mr. Potato Heads; at Toy Fairs past; and with many, many children.

From the 70th birthday video. (Courtesy Alan Hassenfeld)

"Isn't it strange that princes and kings and common people like you and me are builders for all eternity," Hassenfeld said. "To each of us is given a bag of tools, a piece of clay in a book of rules. And each must fashion. Their life has flown a stumbling block or steppingstone.

"What lies before us and what lies behind us are tiny matters compared to what lies within each and every one of us. We have to remember we were once children too and how quickly we forget what it was like to be a child.

"We do not stop playing because we get older. We get older because we stopped playing. No matter what they tell you, never stop playing—especially with toys!

"Wherever you see a tear on a child's face and you can bring sunshine while you're living and you see the difference you've made, that's important.

"We have all been gifted with the ability to make a difference. And if we can become aware of that gift and we gain through the strength of our visions the power to shape the future, we must each find our starfish. And if we throw our stars wisely and well, the world will be blessed."

As the year 2018 drew to a close, Hassenfeld prepared his annual New Year's greeting to those in his many circles. It consisted of a quote from Harriet Tubman, the African-American abolitionist and activist, and a request from him:

"Every great dream begins with a dreamer. Always remember, you have within you the strength, the patience, and the passion to reach for the stars, to change the world.

"In this New Year, please reach."

CHAPTER TWELVE

SANTA'S ELVES

Just five shopping days remained until Christmas when Hassenfeld stepped out of a car in front of Hasbro Children's Hospital. Gerrie and Al Verrecchia and grandson Austin were waiting inside for him, along with Karen Davis and hospital officials. Gurneys piled high with toys were ready for distribution, and the Hasbro chef had baked dozens of his finest cookies.

An annual tradition begun in 1994—when Hassenfeld and Verrecchia had first played Santa, to no press or publicity, the ground rules still—was about to commence again.

"I pinch myself when I leave here," Hassenfeld said, "just sort of wanting to say to anyone who complains, 'Get off your rear end and look around. Whether it's the children's hospital or the food bank or social workers or whatever, understand the incredible work some people do and the incredible hardships some endure.'" Perspective, he called it.

Hassenfeld and the Verrecchias took an elevator to a patient floor, first stop on a nearly three-hour visit that brought them to every ward and the busy emergency room. The hospital was accustomed to celebrated guests—among them recently Superbowl-winning New England Patriots and Rhode Island summer resident Taylor Swift, who spent five hours on an unpublicized visit in 2014—and staff had been told to expect this entourage. But they may not have expected its size, or two former heads of a $5-billion company in such a merry mood.

Before visiting patients, Hassenfeld and Verrecchia stopped at the nurses' station, to offer cookies.

"Are you the head of Hasbro?" a nurse said.

"Well, we used to be," Hassenfeld said.

Verrecchia began selecting toys while Hassenfeld peeked into a conference room, where staff members and Brown University medical residents were meeting.

"Would you like a heart-healthy chocolate chip cookie made at the real Hasbro?" Hassenfeld said.

The women and men laughed. They didn't recognize Hassenfeld, either.

"The real Hasbro?" someone said.

"Oh, wow!" said someone else.

"Thank you very much!"

Hassenfeld and Verrecchia began their patient rounds, checking first with staff and parents on possible food allergies before offering cookies, and allowing parents and children their choice of toy.

"Hi, how are?" Verrecchia said to a girl. "Just wanted to come by and wish you a happy holiday."

"Where are the chocolate-chip cookies?" Hassenfeld said, heading toward a boy's room. "I need the cookie man. I don't need Cookie Monster, I need cookies! Where is the cookie tray?"

When they finished with that floor, everyone headed toward the elevators. As they waited, a hospital photographer took a shot of them by a gurney that carried Hasbro's oldest toy, among many newcomers. Hassenfeld seized the opportunity for a joke.

"I really didn't want Potato Head in the picture!" he said.

The entourage went to the fifth floor, where Hassenfeld stopped before entering a room. The seven-year-old boy inside was non-verbal and developmentally delayed. He lay on his side, his face on the brink of a smile.

"What's his name, Karen?" Hassenfeld said to Davis, who carried a list.

"Ryan," she said.

Ryan Hebert, son and oldest child of Jeanne and Michael Hebert.

Hassenfeld went in. Verrecchia followed with a tray of cookies,.

"This is for Ryan!" Hassenfeld said. He held an R2-D2 Bop It toy, which played the sounds of the Star Wars droid.

"Look at that," said his mother, Jeanne Hebert. "That's awesome! Thank you so much."

"Do you know if Ryan wants R2-D2?"

"That seems like something he might really like!" said Jeanne.

Hassenfeld handed the toy to the mother, who activated it. Her son lit up.

"That's a smile," Hassenfeld said. The toy would go home with Ryan.

"Are you sure?" Jeanne said.

"Oh, please, for Ryan? Yes!"

"Yes, he does like R2-D2."

"By the way, I do, too."

"His dad does, too, so maybe they can watch it together. Pretty cool, huh, Ryan?"

"You forgot to ask us," Hassenfeld said, pausing before the punch line. "We don't know how to shut it off."

"If he smiles like this every time," Jeanne said, "I will not mind."

"Great," Hassenfeld said. "Bye, mom. Merry Christmas. Have a good holiday."

"Thanks for the visit."

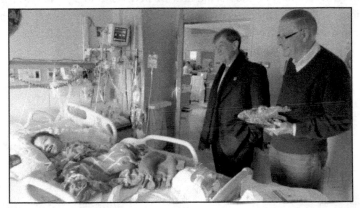

Ryan Hebert, with visitors Hassenfeld and Verrecchia. (Miller photo)

Born four months premature at Women & Infants Hospital, Ryan spent the first six months of life in that hospital's Neonatal Intensive Care Unit. In need of continuing care from what Jeanne called "an amazing team of medical specialists that help us keep him healthy and thriving," Ryan had later spent many more days and nights at Hasbro Children's Hospital.

As the volunteer coordinator for the Rhode Island Community Food Bank and the mother also of a young, healthy girl, Jeanne and her husband deeply appreciated Hasbro Children's.

"Having a child with complex medical needs can be very stressful—emotionally, physically and certainly financially," Jeanne said. "Hasbro Children's Hospital, in more ways than we can count, alleviates much of that stress for our family. Having top pediatric specialists so close to home means we don't have to travel to Boston or even further away, nor are we pulled away from work and the support of family and friends. We have said many times how very lucky we are to have one of the nation's top pediatric facilities right in our backyard."

Jeanne did not know who Hassenfeld was until he was introduced, and she did not learn much about him until after his visit, when she looked into his and Hasbro's philanthropy.

"I was awestruck by how far-reaching their philanthropic efforts go and incredibly moved to find that all of their efforts give back to children and families," she said. "It did not surprise me to learn that Mr. Hassenfeld ranked at the top of the list of Rhode Island's Wealthiest and Most Influential or that the Hassenfeld Family Foundation's annual giving falls in the millions. What surprised me was that the man that we had the privilege of meeting that day at Hasbro Children's Hospital was so genuine, unpretentious, and generous with his time.

"As a parent, as a mother to a boy who struggles with so much, it was incredibly heartwarming. Ryan doesn't understand how Mr. Hassenfeld's philanthropy and charitable giving has helped him in so many ways, but he certainly appreciated a man that took a few minutes to play with him and laugh with him.

"As a parent, I recognize that type of giving is the greatest of all."

EPILOGUE

For Hasbro, the new year brought developments confirming that Goldner had successfully steered the company past the Toys 'R' Us era—and deeper into the digital family-entertainment business, no longer the wave of the future but the now.

When the first-quarter results were released on April 23, 2019, the numbers were positive: net earnings came in at $26.7 million, compared to a net loss for the first quarter of 2018 of $112.5 million; net revenues rose two percent to $732.5 million, versus $716.3 million for first-quarter 2018. Hasbro had a healthy $1.2 billion in cash on hand and paid $79.3 million in cash dividends to shareholders.

The market responded with a strong vote of confidence: On the first day of the trading year, January 2, Hasbro stock had closed at under $80 a share and it had remained largely in the $80 range until the first-quarter numbers were announced, when it shot past $100. As the spring unfolded, the trend continued upward.

"The global Hasbro team is executing very well and delivered a good start to the year," Goldner said on April 23. "Our long-term investments in new platforms provided a meaningful contribution from our digital and e-sports initiative, Magic: The Gathering Arena, as well as growth in Magic: The Gathering tabletop revenues. In addition, Monopoly, Play-Doh, and Transformers were among the brands posting revenue gains this quarter.

"We are beginning to see improvement in our commercial markets, notably in the U.S. and Europe, and operating profit was driven by high margin revenue growth and our cost savings activities. With most of the year ahead of us, we remain on track to deliver profitable growth for the full-year 2019."

Mattel's first-quarter results were mixed. Net sales declined three percent versus the first quarter of 2018, to $689.2 million, and the company reported an operating loss of $131 million. Still, that was significantly less than the $276.6 million loss in the first quarter of 2018—and the company's so-called legacy brands, led by Hot Wheels and Barbie, enjoyed impressive growth, suggesting that the iconic fashion doll might flourish with a new generation after all.

In announcing results on April 25, Mattel chairman and CEO Kreiz was justified in declaring that "the positive momentum exiting 2018 has continued and is reflected in our operating results. While we are in a multi-year turnaround, we remain on-track to achieve our goals to restore profitability and regain topline growth in the short-to-mid-term..."

But Mattel stock remained a fraction of Hasbro's, trading at $13.32 the day after first-quarter results were released and dropping to under $11 by the end of May. Hasbro stock traded at $102.59 the day after announcing first-quarter numbers, then dipped to $95.14 on May 31 before climbing to a near-record $107.46 on June 14. "Near" would become "new" just weeks later.

During the first quarter of 2019, Goldner was welcomed into the elite club whose members included Verrecchia, the Hassenfelds, and other industry icons when he was inducted into the Toy Hall of Fame during a February ceremony in New York during Toy Fair. The late Stan Lee and Joe Mendelsohn, former president of Kenner, which Alan Hassenfeld brought into Hasbro when he was CEO, were Goldner's fellow inductees. In the toy business, this was sacred ground indeed.

"You almost feel superheroic to be inducted alongside the legendary Stan Lee, a dear friend we at Hasbro got to know so well through our Marvel partnership, as well as Joe Mendelsohn, a luminary in our industry and member of the extended Hasbro family through our Kenner acquisition," Goldner said in his acceptance speech. "This is a true honor, and I am very grateful."

Goldner praised earlier inductees, saying "we all stand on the shoulders of giants—from Alan and Stephen Hassenfeld, to Walt Disney, Bob Iger, Bob Bakish, Haim Saban, Kathleen Kennedy, Brian Robbins, and so many others who have pioneered great storytelling and play experiences throughout the years."

He closed with an ode to the final Hassenfeld brother, offering "a very special thank-you to Alan Hassenfeld for your friendship, and your trust in me to lead Hasbro for the last 10 years."

Given the values Hassenfeld had instilled in Hasbro, Goldner was further honored three months later when the company was named again to *Corporate Responsibility Magazine's* 100 Best Corporate Citizens—this time, ranking 13.

"Corporate social responsibility is fundamental to how we operate our business," he said when the 2019 list was announced in May. "We believe that by fulfilling our purpose to make the world a better place for children and their families, we are also doing the right thing for our shareholders and key stakeholders. We're proud that the Hasbro logo is a trust mark for consumers around the world and appreciate that our global teams are achieving success the right way: by living our values and building long-term value."

There was more such recognition to come of Hasbro's role in furthering the common good: In June, the company again was named to The Civic 50. It was one of only 11 companies that have been included on the list every year since the volunteer-recognition program began in 2012.

"We firmly believe every child deserves a world where they can experience hope, kindness, and joy," Goldner said, "and we are grateful to our outstanding philanthropic partner organizations and passionate employees who generously give their time and talents to help make the world a better place for children and their families."

Goldner's business expertise was held in such high regard that when CBS Corporation sought to regain its footing after the departure of chairman, president and CEO Les Moonves following allegations of sexual harassment, Hasbro's chief was named one of six members of CBS's independent board, in September 2018. And Goldner was rumored to be on the short list of permanent replacements for Moonves, though that would not come to pass. As *The Wall Street Journal* soon reported, "Mr. Goldner's contract with Hasbro expires in 2022, and a noncompete agreement prevents him from moving to an entertainment company that is primarily directed toward children and families."

As the Fourth of July holiday passed, Hasbro was crunching the second-quarter numbers, for which analysts held high expectations, given the growing momentum of January, February, and March.

The expectations were not realized when the results were announced the morning of July 23—they were beaten. Six analysts surveyed by Zacks Investment Research had estimated sales of $966.8 million, but actual sales were $984.5 million. The analysts had expected earnings of 51 cents per share, but Hasbro earnings per share came in at 78 cents.

Wall Street responded with exuberance, pushing the stock price to $119.31 a share, a company record. Mattel's stock price on July 23? One-tenth Hasbro's. When Mattel reported its second-quarter results on July 25 with a narrower-than-expected loss

($108 million) and a modest increase in overall sales including a nine-percent rise in Barbie, investors gave Mattel stock a bump, with the price rising from $12.50 at the opening bell to as high as $13.40 in after-hours trading.

Figuratively speaking, that was still peanuts compared to Hasbro, the East Coast company Mattel had tried to acquire in an unsuccessful hostile takeover attempt on Alan Hassenfeld's watch. And the enthusiasm for Hasbro continued into July 24, when its stock closed at $121.83 a share, another record. The day after that, Mattel's long rival hit still another record in early-morning trading, $123.56. And on July 26, Hasbro stock rose in mid-morning trading to $124.33, another record, before falling to $123.69 a share at the close.

In a conference call with investors when the second-quarter numbers were released, Goldner cited continued growth in Magic: The Gathering tabletop and digital game-playing as first among the brands responsible for Hasbro's strong performance. Magic: The Gathering remained another of Alan Hassenfeld's legacies, a brand he brought to Hasbro in 1999 when the company acquired Wizards of the Coast. Pokémon trading cards, which had proved to be a sort of Achilles's heel for Hassenfeld, also came with the acquisition.

In the whirlwind world of the toy and entertainment business, that of course was ancient history two decades later. A much longer history, however—one dating to 1952—remained very much alive in the summer of 2019.

With the release of *Toy Story 4* on June 21, Pot Head once again rode high.

Hasbro celebrated by bringing to market several Mr. Potato Head Disney Pixar Toy Story 4 toys including the Buzz Lightyear Mini Figure, Woody's Tater Roundup Figure, Andy's Playroom Potato Pack, and the Bo Peep Mini Figure.

Hasbro did not disclose sales figures for the latest Potato Head line, but box-office numbers were publicly reported—and they suggested robust sales. During its first weekend, *Toy Story 4* grossed $120.9 million on 4,575 screens domestically, the biggest opener of the franchise. Worldwide, the movie had grossed more than $1 billion as of mid August, matching *Toy Story 3*, which also had topped $1 billion. Together, the four movies were closing in on a $3-billion box office worldwide, putting the franchise in the rarefied company of Marvel blockbusters.

During the conference call, Goldner pointedly mentioned Hasbro's recent presence at the San Diego Comic-Con, said by *Forbes* to be the largest convention of its kind in the world. Hasbro had shifted its convention efforts there after postponing its second HASCON, originally planned for September 2019, to an unspecified date.

"This past weekend at San Diego Comic-Con, we had a major show presence that we also shared with fans through social media live from the show floor with interviews, behind-the-scenes information, news around upcoming product and preorder launches," Goldner said.

Looking ahead, the CEO said: "Hasbro's investments in brand-driven story-telling uniquely positions us to monetize content-to-commerce experiences across online platforms."

As stockholder and Executive Committee chair, Alan Hassenfeld was delighted with Hasbro's first-half 2019 and the prospects for continued success predicted by the man he and Al Verrecchia had selected to succeed them.

Contemplating the future prompted the last Hassenfeld to reflect on the past.

"I'm so proud of what my brother started in the sense of buying up content, which I continued and Al and Brian have continued," he said as he sat in his office one July morning between calls to politicians and beneficiaries of his philanthropy.

Regarding his grandfather and father, Hassenfeld said "I don't think they could comprehend where we are as a company and in the field of both toys and children's entertainment. I don't think they could comprehend how we have continued to be a catalyst for philanthropic giving. But I think that they would be awed because many times when passing the baton to the next generation things don't always go so well!"

He laughed, then turned serious discussing his family's "ethical beliefs that started so many decades ago," beliefs that have endured for more than a century.

"It's as if the past generations would be looking and really would be smiling because Hasbro is a company with heart and soul," Hassenfeld said.

The nation in 2019, not so much, he said.

"I'm not as optimistic as I have been only because of the dialogue that's going on in our country right now," he said. "What I really abhor is the denigration of other human beings that we're allowing to take place. I don't understand how Lindsey Graham could have stood next to the president after he had maligned his best friend John McCain without really speaking out."

Two penniless refugees escaping the slaughter and persecution of fellow Jews in their native Europe in 1903 came to mind.

"America was founded on equality and immigration," Hassenfeld said. "We need immigrants. We need to stop basically claiming that we're not immigrants—you know, that we're purebloods."

Kid Number One, however, did not lack hope.

"I am optimistic that there are people that are willing to take on causes and fight the good battle," he said. "But the good battle also means listening to the other side and desperately trying to find a way of bringing things together for the common good of America. Not Republicans, not Democrats, not Trumpians, not Pelosians. Just for our own society."

AUTHOR'S NOTES

GENERAL NOTES

Alan Hassenfeld and I began discussing a sequel to *Toy Wars* more than a decade ago during one of our regular get-togethers that followed my long immersion at Hasbro with him and Al Verrecchia during the reporting and writing of that book, a three-year project in total. Al and I also had stayed in close touch since those days, and he, too, agreed a sequel was in order. So much had happened at Hasbro, in their worlds, and in the world generally since 1997, the end point of *Toy Wars*.

Some while after deciding to write this book, I visited Alan at his Rhode Island residence to discuss my ambitions. As we sat on the veranda of the home which he had shared in the 1980s with his late brother, Stephen, Alan tossed out some ideas. They were in sync with mine and so, once again, a storytelling journey began.

"This isn't meant to be about accomplishments," Hassenfeld said on that day, although *Kid Number One* appropriately chronicles many of them. "I want it to be a wonderful story, about a family-thinking company where people matter. A fun read, with some of the escapades that went on." With the philosophy of Tikkun Olam as a foundational theme.

During the long gestation of this book, Hassenfeld, who sometimes calls himself Kid Number One—and, more playfully still, Pinocchio—often asked me: "Are you having fun?"

I was. I did!

Not every book is thus. Nor does every book tell an inspirational and uplifting story, but that, too, is my hope for *Kid Number One*: That in these deeply troubled times when so many individuals with power indulge narcissism, not humanism, people on stages small and large will know they can make a difference. Collectively, that could change the world.

Now, some writerly nitty-gritty:

I have included certain references within the main text and have not repeated them here.

The online archives of *The Providence Journal* and *The New York Times* were invaluable and saved an incredible amount of time that was unimaginable when I began writing books in the 1980s, and had to rely on hard copies and microfilm for most sources.

Christopher Byrne's *They Came to Play: 100 Years of the Toy Industry Association,* published in 2016, is a wealth of information, wonderfully illustrated, and it lists Hall of Fame inductees with photos and brief bios: www.toyassociation.org/App_Themes/tia/pdfs/events/centenary/theycametoplay.pdf

Timeless Toys: Classic Toys and the Playmakers Who Created Them, by Tim Walsh, Andrews McMeel Publishing, 2005, was also an excellent reference.

Jack the Toyman: Takes Road Champs to the Finish Line... and Wins!, by Jack Robbins, BMR, 2016, is a lively memoir of the toy industry from 1945 to 1997.

I relied on Pinterest, Instagram, eBay, Google Images, Hasbro and Mattel catalogs and other sources to see images of original product, packaging and instructions for many of the hundreds of toys and games mentioned in *Kid Number One*. Photographs for long-gone products especially were useful for detail.

The searchable Strong National Museum of Play online collections, organized by toys, dolls, games, video and more, proved useful: www.museumofplay.org/online-collections/

For movie grosses, production budgets, casts and crews, and other details of Hollywood entertainment, I relied on Box Office Mojo, www.boxofficemojo.com, the authoritative industry source and a division of the equally vital IMDb, www.imdb.com, originally called the Internet Movie Database, now owned by Amazon.

Many cartoon reference sites exist, but I found the most comprehensive and accurate to be the Big Cartoon DataBase, BCDB for short: www.bcdb.com/

Similarly, there are many doll reference sites on the web, but I found Doll Reference, www.dollreference.com/index.html, comprehensive and current, including for Barbie.

Many good sites for G.I. Joe also exist, but I have found that Yo Joe!, www.yo-joe.com, cannot be beat for thoroughness and accuracy.

Hasbro annual reports and proxies dating to 1998 are at http://investor.hasbro.com/annuals.cfm, with other financials at http://investor.hasbro.com/financials.cfm. Today's products are at www.Hasbro.com.

Mattel annual reports dating to 1998 are at http://investor.shareholder.com/mattel/annuals.cfm. Today's products are at www.Mattel.com

Conference calls for both companies (and many others) are archived at https://seekingalpha.com/

In 2014, *Time* magazine named "The 13 Most Influential Toys of All Time," http://time.com/3089384/influential-toys. Six past and/or present Hasbro brands/products made the list: G.I. Joe. (3), Nerf (4), Easy Bake Oven (6), Super Soaker (7), Star Wars (9), and Cabbage Patch (13). Lego was number one, followed by Barbie, at 2.

According to Blitz Sales Software, June 2016, Mr. Potato Head, Easy-Bake Oven, Transformers, G.I. Joe, Super Soaker, Star Wars are among the 15 best-selling toys of all time. Barbie tops that list: nowblitz.com/blog/15-best-selling-toys-in-history/

While writing *Toy Wars*, I spent hours at the Hasbro archives compiling a master list of toys and products, with descriptions and other details, from annual reports, catalogs and other primary sources from the years 1953 through 1994. This list was invaluable in writing this book, as were photographs, videotapes and other materials from that 42-year-period, and recorded interviews now archived at the University of Rhode Island Robert L. Carothers Library & Learning Commons' Special Collections. I relied on those archives to include in *Kid Number One* some events and details that did not make it into *Toy Wars*, or to provide a more compressive presentation in this book.

Two U.S. editions of *Toy Wars* were published: the hardcover by Random imprint Crown Business in 1998, and the softcover by Adams Media in 1999.

Several photographs in *Kid Number One,* including the cover shot, were taken by the author.

For more photographs, videos, stories and more, visit www.KidNumberOne.com and on www.facebook.com/KidNumberOneBook. Follow on Twitter: @kid_number

CHAPTER NOTES

FOREWORD: TIKKUN OLAM

This lunch scene took place on August 18, 2016.

Brown University's Hassenfeld Child Health Innovation Institute: www.brown.edu/initiatives/child-health/

More than once in writing *Kid Number One*, I visited Lincoln Park Cemetery in Warwick, Rhode Island, where Sylvia, Merrill and Stephen Hassenfeld are buried; and also Alan's grandfather, Henry J. Hassenfeld and his wife, Alan's grandmother, Marion L. Hassenfeld; Alan's great-unce, Hillel Hassenfeld; Alan's great-grandfather, Osias Hassenfeld (1860 – 1933); and Herman, Pessel and other Hassenfelds. Through a curious twist of fate, I live within walking distance of their final resting places.

Transformers, Star Wars, Disney *Frozen* and *Princess* licenses: www.providencejournal.com/news/20160214/bulls-eye--nerf---and-60-year-old-play-doh---are-brightest-stars-in-hasbros-galaxy

In writing about Mr. Potato Head, I relied on past and present Hasbro catalogs; the recollections of Alan G. Hassenfeld and others; *Mr. Potato Head: Celebrating 50*

Years of One Sweet Potato! by Gilbert King, Running Press, 2002; and the 1952 TV ad, www.youtube.com/watch?v=fBGxCJQkNUc, and elsewhere on YouTube.

Also, Victoria and Albert Museum of Childhood, www.vam.ac.uk/moc/collections/mr-potato-head/; and the Wikipedia entry, https://en.wikipedia.org/wiki/Mr._Potato_Head

In their desire to impact lives today while also sowing seeds for tomorrow, Hassenfeld and his family are representative of a new class of wealthy philanthropists depicted in "Philanthropy In Their Lifetimes," a *New York Times* story by David Gelles that ran on front page of the October 22, 2017, business section. George Soros, Bills Gates, Michael Bloomberg and Mark Zuckerberg top that class of individuals who are "increasingly willing to take on hot-button social and political issues—on the right and left—that thrust them into the center of contentious debates… Plenty of billionaires are still buying sports teams, building yachts and donating to museums and hospitals. But many new philanthropists appear less interested in naming a business school after themselves than in changing the world."

CHAPTER ONE: 'IN THAT DIRECTION LIES HOPE'

Historically, many spellings of Kishinev have been used. Today, Chișinău is the largest city and capital of the Republic of Moldova.

The Voice of America on Kishineff, edited by Cyrus Adler, The Jewish Publication Society of America, 1904, provides a wealth of detail on the Europe from which Henry and Hillel fled. Digital versions are available at multiple sites on the internet.

A Proclamation Inciting a Pogrom of the Jews, Easter, 1903 [excerpted from *Readings in Modern European History*, James Harvey Robinson and Charles Beard, eds., vol. 2 (Boston: Ginn and Company, 1908), pp. 371-372]

The Times, 13 August 1903, "The Kishineff Outrages", testimonial from the British vice-consul in Odessa, from: Seder Olam - Revisted, "Generation 48: Hebrew Years 5640 to 5760 (1880 – 2000 CE)" http://www.seder-olam.info/seder-olam-g48-sion.html

Pogrom: Kishinev and the Tilt of History, by Steven J. Zipperstein, Liveright, 2018, provides and exhaustive account of the Easter 1903 barbarianism.

Although not specific to Kishinev, *Anatomy of a Genocide: The Life and Death of a Town Called Buczacz,* by Omer Bartov, Simon & Schuster, 2018, provides great insight into the psychology of victims and perpetrators of a 20th-century East European pogrom.

Lower East Side Memories: A Jewish Place in America, by Hasia R. Diner, Princeton University Press, 2000, depicts Manhattan when the Hassenfeld brothers arrived in 1903. The memories of "an elderly man of Italian heritage" are contained therein.

Touro Synagogue: www.tourosynagogue.org/history-learning/synagogue-history

Bruce Sundlun: Interviews I conducted in the summer of 2006 while writing "Bruce at 86: Former Gov. Bruce Sundlun lived a life few people ever will," *Providence Journal,* Nov. 19, 2006. The tape recordings are archived at the University of Rhode Island's Special Collections.

*****

Period photographs and a wealth of detail about the history of West Warwick are at: www.preservation.ri.gov/pdfs_zips_downloads/survey_pdfs/west_warwick.pdf

"The Pawtuxet Valley Railroad Company was a ten-mile branch of the New York, Providence & Boston which ran from Hope to the junction with the NYP&B at Auburn (Cranston)... The line served a number of mills...": http://bit.ly/2MBwB0G

West Warwick City Directories for the period during which David Frank was in business are kept at the West Warwick Public Library.

*****

South Providence Jewish life at the time of Henry's relocation to Rhode Island: "Old Bottles, Rags, Junk!" by Eleanor F. Horvitz, *Rhode Island Jewish Historical Notes,* V. 7, No. 2, November 1976, pp. 189 – 257. The issue also has several detailed articles about Jewish life over the years in other parts of the state, including Newport, home of Touro Synagogue. www.rijha.org/wp-content/uploads/2013/01/7-2-Nov-76.pdf

South Providence synagogues: https://broadstreetsynagogue.com/home/stories/shaare-zedek/mr-b/

Bradner's article: *A Modern City: Providence, Rhode Island and its Activities,* ed. by William Kirk, University of Chicago Press, Chicago, 1909.

*****

The first mention of a Hassenfeld in *The Providence Journal* was on August 24, 1913, page 20, "To Announce Bethrothal." [CQ] The story read: "The announcement of the bethrothal of Miss Marion L. Frank, daughter of Mr. and Mrs. David Frank of Phenix, to Henry Hassenfeld of New York, will be made according to the rites of the Jewish faith at a gathering to-day at Pythian Hall, Phenix."

The next mention was on January 16, 1916, page 33, a brief story: "Mr. and Mrs. Henry Hassenfeld of 151 Somerset Street announce the birth on Thursday of a son." The son was Harold.

I wrote a history of Hasbro's early days for *Toy Wars,* but it was incomplete, as my research for this book demonstrated. I devoted many hours for my account here, which I submit is the most thorough and authoritative history of the company by anyone to date.

The 1917 Providence City Directory listing of "Hassenfeld Brothers" is the first known reference to the company by that name, although Henry and Hillel were in business together for several years prior to that date, initially in New York and then in Rhode Island. Until and if further research finds an earlier, authoritative reference to "Hassenfeld Brothers"—later shortened to "Has(senfeld)bro(thers)," of course—1917 can serve as Hasbro's establishment.

The April 14, 1919, incorporation of The Leatherite Company is on file at the Rhode Island Secretary of State archives: "I, J. Fred Parker, secretary of state, hereby certify that Isaac Green, Henry Hassenfeld and Helal Hassenfeld, have filed in the office of the secretary of state, according to law, their agreement to form a corporation, under the name of Leatherite Company, for the purpose of engaging in the business of manufacture of novelties and frames of all kinds and descriptions as well as buying and selling at wholesale and retail of said articles and the doing of all things incidental thereto; also the manufacture of cloth and leather merchandise, and with the capital stock of three thousand dollars; and have also filed the certificate of the general treasurer that they have paid into the general treasury of the state the fee required by law."

Additional detail on the incorporation is found in "Providence Trade Conditions," *The Jewelers' Circular,* Volume 78, Issue 1, April 23, 1919, p. 84: "A charter was granted to the Leatherite Co. the past week by Secretary of State Parker, for the purpose of manufacturing leather novelties. The corporation will be located in the city with a capital stock of $3,000. The incorporators are Isaac Green of Manchester, N.H.; Henry Hassenfeld and [Hillel] Hassenfeld of this city, and Isadore Green of Lowell, Mass."

The identities of Isaac and Isadore Green are unclear, as are the roles they played in the 1919 incorporation. I found reference to an Isaac Green being granted a $30 peddler's license in 1913 in "1913 Reports presented to the General Assembly," http://bit.ly/2WgSsiA

An Isaac Green paid $10 for a peddler's license a decade earlier, according to "Acts and Resolves passed by the General Assembly of the State of Rhode Island and Providence Plantations, May Session 1894," http://bit.ly/2VVa0vt

I find references to an Isadore Green, with ties to Lowell, Mass., and Manchester New Hampshire, in *History of Lowell and Its People*, by Frederick W. Coburn, Lewis Historical Publishing Company, New York, 1920. This Isadore Green, Coburn wrote, was a principal in a five-and-dime chain and also a prominent real-estate dealer. He was born "in Russian Poland, December 20, 1880," and immigrated to the U.S. at a young age after his mother died. "He has long been active in the Young Men's Hebrew Association, filling the office of president of the Lowell Association, and is a member of the Independent Order of B'nai Brith," Coburn wrote.

*****

I found the longer story of David Frank's relatively short life compelling. Sons Jacob and Harry joined him in his businesses, which came to include a prominent dry-goods store in a building that still stands (it's a Pentecostal church now). He had a third son, and three daughters: Marion Hassenfeld, and Florence and Dorothy Frank, later Dorothy Frank Fox, one of my sources for *Toy Wars*. Frank was a founding member of Ahavath Shalom Congregation. He died of an apparent heart attack at the age of 55 in December 1929. His obituary in the *Pawtuxet Valley Times* stated that "Although he had been in failing health for a long time, his untimely death came as a sudden shock to all who knew him. He was at his store shortly before seven o'clock and from there walked to his home about an eighth of a mile from the establishment. Shortly after he reached home, he was stricken with what proved to be a fatal attack."

Frank was buried at Lincoln Park Cemetery in Warwick, the first to be interred at the Hassenfeld lot, which is located on Hassenfeld Avenue. Osias followed in 1933; Hillel at the age of 57 in 1943 after "a long illness," according to his obituary; and Herman in 1947.

*****

Israel Cohen's statement to The New York Times: "Jews give reports of Polish pogroms; Answer Denials of Information Bureau Here with Press and Other Statements. Reply by Nathan Straus." *New York Times,* May 27, 1919, page 6.

Harry Marshak's story and the history of the Sons of Jacob Synagogue is at www.preservation.ri.gov/pdfs_zips_downloads/national_pdfs/providence/prov_douglas-avenue-29_sons-of-jacob-synagogue.pdf

Textile World, 1920, volume 58, part 1, July 3, 1920: "PROVIDENCE, R.I. – Hasssenfeld Brothers, Cotton Goods, have completed plans for the erection of a new two-story brick building 45 x 100 feet, at North Main and Bowen Streets. Harry Marshak, Strand Building, is architect."

Maps and details about the North Main Street district and Roger Williams' home are in *Cultural Landscape report for Roger Williams National Memorial*, by John Auwaerter and Karen Cowperthwaite, Olmstead Center for Landscape Preservation, National Park Service, Boston, 2010.

For inflation conversion of dollars throughout this book, I have used the authoritative https://westegg.com/inflation/#

Marketing in 1922: *The Modern Stationer and Book-Seller A Business Magazine for the Retail Stationer and Department Store Buyer,* http://bit.ly/2wqRQY2

Geyers Stationer, V. LXXIII, January 5, 1922, no. 1825, and subsequent issues in 1922. A weekly publication, published from Fifth Avenue New York, "The

Authoritative Weekly of the Stationery, Office Supply, Engraving, Greeting Card and Allied Trades," published weekly since 1877, http://bit.ly/2W7cITs

During their early years in Rhode Island, Henry and Hillel Hassenfeld first worshipped at the Orthodox Congregation Sons of Jacob Synagogue, near the Rhode Island State House; the temple opened in 1906 and is today designated a National Historic Site. Congregation president Harold Silverman gave me a tour. The families also worshipped at what is today known as the Broad Street Synagogue, initially Temple Beth El, at 688 Broad Street, near an early Hasbro factory. In 1958, the Herman Hassenfeld Talmud Torah, an addition including a Hebrew school and a mikveh, or ritual bath, opened. "The addition is named after a member of the Hassenfeld family, the founders of Hasbro," according to https://broadstreetsynagogue.com/

Merrill Lloyd Hassenfeld was born February 19, 1918, in Providence.

Also on Hasbro origins: Providence Business Directory, Sampson & Murdock Co., Providence, R.I., 1919. https://archive.org/stream/providencedirect79brow/providencedirect79brow_djvu.txt

And: www.rijha.org/wp-content/uploads/2013/01/6-2-Nov-72-262-308.pdf

Move to Central Falls: www.rijha.org/wp-content/uploads/2013/01/6-2-Nov-72-262-308.pdf

A Handbook for Air Raid Wardens, from the Office of Civilian Defense http://www.idaillinois.org/cdm/ref/collection/isl3/id/10981

*****

As indicated in the acknowledgments, Cheryl Fishbein, Aaron Ginsburg, Joshua Jasper, Kate-Lynne Laroche and Harold Silverman provided great assistance in my research of Hassenfeld family history. Other information was found in the following:

Herman and Pesche (Pessel) Hassenfeld and their children: www.geni.com/people/Pessel-Hassenfeld/6000000027816816916

This listing for Osias Hassenfeld is listed on Find A Grave, an ancestry.com division, www.findagrave.com/cgi-bin/fg.cgi?page=gr&GRid=175559936. It appears to be substantially accurate, with the exception of his year of birth, engraved as 1860 on his tombstone:

Birth: 1859, Poland. Death: May 5, 1933

Husband of Bella (Koller), and a son of Joseph and Rose (Geitzholtz) Hassenfeld. His previous wife Chaya (Reich) died before Osias left Poland. He arrived in 1920 with his wife Beile and son Herman (Hirsch) and his family, and youngest son Israel.

Spouse: Beile Meyerstein Hassenfeld (1870 - 1930)

Children:

Herman Hassenfeld (1882 - 1947)*

Hillel Hassenfeld (1886 - 1943)*

Esther Hassenfeld Oelbaum (1894 - 1947)*
Israel Hassenfeld (1904 - 1982)*
*Calculated relationship

Inscription:
Here Lies an upright and honest man ...
r. Yeshia ben r. Yosef Baruch
d. 9 Iyar 5693
May his soul be bound up
in the bond of eternal life

This listing for Beile Meyerstein Hassenfeld is also listed on Find A Grave, www.findagrave.com/cgi-bin/fg.cgi?page=gr&GRid=96004386, and includes what appears to be two more children from this second marriage, but I could not verify that:
Birth: 1870
Malopolskie, Poland
Death: Nov. 3, 1930
Manhattan
New York County (Manhattan)
New York, USA

Family links:
Spouse:
Osias Hassenfeld (1859 - 1933)*
Children:
Ida Hassenfeld (____ - 1959)*
Israel Alter Hassenfeld (1904 - 1982)*
*Calculated relationship

Inscription:
Beile bas Yisroel

Burial:
Mount Carmel Cemetery
Glendale
Queens County
New York, USA

JewishGen, www.jewishgen.org, an affiliate of the Museum of Jewish Heritage, has a page on Osias Hassenfeld (under "Isaiah" Hassenfeld) with additional background. The page, http://kehilalinks.jewishgen.org/kolbuszowa/Ulanów/ancestor. html, was no longer active in October 2017: Isaiah Hassenfeld & his wife Chaya Sheindel Reich Hassenfeld; Hillel Hassenfeld (born 1886 in Ulanów); Henry Hassenfeld (born 1889 in Ulanów); Herman Hassenfeld (born 26 Aug 1882 in Ulanów, marriage ca 1899 in Ulanów) and his wife Pesche Laufer Hassenfeld and their children: Jean Hassenfeld Blasbalg (born 18 Oct 1900 in Ulanów); Esther Hassenfeld Gold (born 14 Aug 1903 in Ulanów); Jack Hassenfeld (born 12 Jun 1904 in Ulanów); Ruth Hassenfeld Oelbaum (born 19 Apr 1906); Josef Hassenfeld (born ca 1912 in Ulanów; died ca 1914 in Ulanów; David Hassenfeld (born 19 Sep 1914 in Ulanów; Edith Hassenfeld Reich (born 29 May 1910 in Ulanów, married 15 Mar 1936 in Ulanów). Esther Hassenfeld Oelbaum (Benjamin Oelbaum's 2nd wife)

CHAPTER TWO: AN AMERICAN FAMILY

The first Mr. Potato Head commercial is found at this site (and many others): www.youtube.com/watch?v=fBGxCJQkNUc

Sarasota Herald-Tribune story: www.heraldtribune.com/news/20150518/ walt-disneys-idea-man-turning-100

*****

More from the era:

In 1953, Hasbro also offered a selection of school supplies; scrapbooks; Junior Miss Cosmetic kits; doctor and nurse cases, kits and bags; Toyville Medical Bags; Luggage Style Junior Doctor Kits; Luggage Style Dolly Nurse Kits; and the Ukulele Pencil Case ("Strum up volume sales with this best seller."). The Let's Play series included Let's Play School, Let's Play Mailman and Let's Play Conductor. Buyers might want the Teach-a-Toy cartoon set, the Teach-a-Toy plastic map of the U.S., or the Teach-a-Toy circus set. There were travel arts sets, an alphabet set, oil and finger and by-the-numbers paint sets, stencil and blackboard sets.

Also, Jolly Hobby Play Clay and a related product that was apparently the first keyed to real and fictitious scientific developments that would soon become an enduring hallmark of the Hasbro game plan: Rocket Patrol Play Clay, announced with a declaration that described a fascination of the Baby Boom generation and generations to follow. "There is no subject that stimulates the young mind of today more than that of conquering space," the 1953 catalog declared. "Modeling Clay has for generations been the tool of imaginative expression."

Introduction of Rocket Clay and associated Hasbro products—the Rocket Patrol Pencil Case, the Rocket Patrol and American History pencil case, the Rocket Whiz and Safety First set —was inspired by the publication the year before of the first in a widely-read series of magazine articles by rocket pioneer Wernher von Braun and others. Lavishly illustrated by some of the finest artists of the time, the *Man Will Conquer Space Soon!* series, first published on March 22, 1952, and continuing into 1954, tantalized the American public. Backed by credible science, the pieces depicted the path by which the fiction of Jules Verne and H.G. Wells could come true. Further proof of the magazine series' popularity would be found in three books that resulted: *Across the Space Frontier*, 1952; *Conquest of the Moon*, 1953; and *The Exploration of Mars*, 1956. Three episodes of a Disneyland TV anthology also were produced from the Collier's articles: *Man in Space*, 1955; *Man and the Moon*, 1955; and *Mars and Beyond*, 1957.

The Man Will Conquer Space Soon! series was not merely scientists extrapolating on Verne and Wells, although there was some of that. By the first installment, the real-life groundwork had been laid for space travel. Air Force test pilot Chuck Yeager had broken the sound barrier over the Mojave Desert on October 14, 1947, and the National Advisory Committee for Aeronautics, precursor to NASA, was conducting research influential in the development of jet-powered aircraft, military and civilian. www.rmastri.it/spacestuff/wernher-von-braun/colliers-articles-on-the-conquest-of-space-1952-1954/

In the issues it raised and the events it predicted, the first installment in the *Man Will Conquer Space Soon!* series proved prescient. That March 22 edition feature articles including "Crossing the last frontier," by von Braun; "What are we waiting for?" and a Space Quiz, by the editors; "The heavens open"; "A station in space"; "This side of infinity"; and two pieces that posed two intriguing questions.

The first was: "Who owns the universe?"

The answer, law professor and United Nations legal counselor Oscar Schachter, concluded after a long argument, was—or should be—everyone.

"Beyond the airspace, as already noted," he wrote, "we would apply a system similar to that followed on the high seas; outer space and the celestial bodies would be the common property of all mankind, and no nation would be permitted to exercise domination over any part of it."

Dr. Heinz Haber, of the Department of Space Medicine in the Air Force School of Aviation Medicine, posed the second question: "Can we survive in space?"

His answer was a resounding yes.

"Man is extremely hard to please in his demands," Haber wrote, "but the engineer can lick the problem and supply the crew of a rocket ship or space station with all the necessities for survival. Neither rocket ship nor space station will have the snug comfort of Mother Earth, and flying through space will be a rough job that will call for healthy, tough and physically well-trained individuals. But it can be done."

*****

Merry Milkman play: The rules indicated that two, three or four children could play. "Players, by a series of spins, perform the duties of a milkman," was the object of the game. "All the necessary steps are included-loading trucks with dairy products and making delivery of orders to houses. First player to complete deliveries is the winner." The game also doubled as a toy, according to the instructions: "The young child and his friends will enjoy MERRY MILKMAN as a toy, as well as a game. He can set up the houses and deliver the dairy products. MERRY MILKMAN is made to provide the greatest possible play value for the youngster, while it aids him in developing further finger dexterity, recognition of shapes, and recognition of colors. As both a toy and a game, it is adaptable to almost any play area. MERRY MILKMAN is a creative toy-game for the young child." www.skooldays.com/blog/merry-milkman-rules/

Mickey Mouse Club Loony-Kins: In its catalog pitch to buyers, Hasbro forwent modesty: "We predict this to be one of the hottest toys in 1956. Assemble the famous Mickey Mouse Club characters in 3-dimension and they stand in front of the Clubhouse in the most hilarious off-balance positions you can imagine. Seldom does a toy have so much appeal for children 5 to 15."

Captain Kangaroo and Bob Keeshan: www.nytimes.com/2004/01/24/arts /bob-keeshan-creator-and-star-of-tv-s-captain-kangaroo-is-dead-at-76.html

Also in 1958: Hasbro sold Disneyland and Mickie Mouse Club Paint-by-Number sets; the Mickey Mouse Club Pencil-by-Number set; the Donald Duck Doctor Kit; the Walt Disney Minnie Mouse Nurse kit; and Disney Zorro oil Paint-by-Number, tied to the new ABC TV hit. Hasbro's Popeye license was used for another Paint-by-Number set, extending the line beyond a lighthouse, woods, a sailboat, "winter wonderland" and more in the primary line; and flowers, dogs, birds and horses in the miniature line. "The success of oil painting by numbers lies in the 'pride of achievement,' " the catalog stated. "To assure this, Hassenfeld commissions only recognized contemporary artists to produce the originals." Merrill took special pride in the Beaux Arts Miniature Paint-by-Numbers "drawn by French artists."

*****

More from the era:

NASA put the first U.S. animals safely into space, with safe return, on May 28, 1959; the animals, Rhesus monkeys Able and Baker, became national celebrities, with their photo gracing the cover of Life. The next year, America launched the first solar and lunar probes. President John F. Kennedy on May 25, 1961 told a joint session of Congress that America would "catch up and overtake" the Soviet Union—and would send an American to the moon before the end of the decade.

*****

Radio and TV host Art Linkletter's popular *House Party* television show was broadcast from 1952 to 1969. Its "Kids Say the Darndest Things" segment became the basis of two books illustrated by *Peanuts* cartoonist Charles Schulz. In 1960, the centennial year of The Game of Life, Milton Bradley hired Linkletter to lend his name to the game and his likeness appeared on $100,000 bills and the box cover, with the slogan: "I heartily endorse this game." www.toyhalloffame.org/toys/game-life

Moon Rocks: "Complete with magic moon rocks, magic solution that makes them grow, plastic moonscape, dome, interplanetary man, and rockets," the catalog said.

World Heritage Encyclopedia's "Hassenfeld Brothers" history provided some useful details. http://self.gutenberg.org/articles/hassenfeld_brothers#History

CHAPTER THREE: ASIA CALLING

Merrill Hassenfeld's obituary was published in *The Providence Journal*, reproduced here: https://arealamericanbook.wordpress.com/2014/03/10/merrill-hassenfeld-obituary-1979/ A short obituary was published on Page 37 of the March 22, 1979, *New York Times*.

Lost Horizon, by James Hilton, 241 pages, Harper Collins, 1933.

Li Ka-shing: *The Miracle: The Epic Story of Asia's Quest for Wealth,* by Michael Schuman, HarperCollins, 2009; also, www.forbes.com/billionaires/#1398c492251c

Harvard Business School Case Study: "Li Ka-Shing," by Nitin Nohria and Bridget Gurtler. Harvard Business School Case 405-026, August 2004. (Revised December 2005.) https://www.hbs.edu/faculty/Pages/item.aspx?num=31390

West Coast longshoreman's strike: *New York Times,* Feb. 22, 1972, page 73.

Romper Room: http://people.com/archive/romper-room-takes-its-own-advice-do-bee-the-longest-running-kids-program-on-u-s-television-vol-9-no-5/;and "Hasbro, Inc." http://www.encyclopedia.com/social-sciences-and-law/economics-business-and-labor/businesses-and-occupations/hasbro-inc

Confronting the Child Care Crisis, by Stevanne Auerbach, Beacon Press, 1979.

*****

Social and political backdrop during Romper Room era:

Further enticement for Hasbro to enter the daycare business came in August 1969, when new President Nixon announced his Family Assistance Plan, an overhaul of the federal welfare system that promised a minimum stipend for all families in poverty, including, in a dramatic reform, those with heads who held jobs. Within certain limits, work dollars would not be at the loss of welfare income, presumably an incentive for more mothers (and fathers) to find employment–and require daycare for their children. The plan also promised subsidies for daycare centers.

Congress did not pass the F.A.P. www.nytimes.com/books/98/10/04/specials/moynihan -income.html

There was another decisive factor which Merrill and Stephen did not anticipate: The watchdog organization Action for Children's Television, founded in Newton, Mass., in 1968 by activist Peggy Charren. Among ACT's first targets was the Boston-produced Romper Room, starring "Miss Jean," a former schoolteacher. Charren criticized the Boston production for its in-program promotion of branded toys and threatened it with the possibility of sanction by the Federal Communications Commission. Hasbro kept selling Romper Room toys into the early 1980s, even broadening the line with Snoopy, Mickey Mouse, Weebles and Hugabees extensions. Charren: www.nytimes.com/2015/01/23/arts/peggy-charren-childrens-tv-crusader-is-dead-at-86.html?_r=0

*****

Galloping Gourmet and Graham Kerr: www.encyclopedia.com/social-sciences-and-law/economics-business-and-labor/businesses-and-occupations/hasbro-inc; www.emmys.com/shows/galloping-gourmet; Sarasota (Fla.) *Journal*, July 24, 1972, page 5-B.

Hypo-Squirt Giant Hypo Water Gun: www.pbs.org/wgbh/pages/front-line/shows/drugs/cron/

Jarts and other banned toys in 1970: *New York Times*, Dec. 19, 1970, p. 19; *New York Times,* Dec. 22, 1970, page 15.

Loomis: www.rebelscum.com/loomis.asp; *New York Times*, June 6, 2006, page C-13

International Licensing Industry Merchandisers Association's Licensing Hall of Fame members: www.licensing.org/about/licensing-hall-of-fame/members/

Fred Kroll: *The Palm Beach Post*, August 5, 2003, page 53.

CHAPTER FOUR: KIDS NO MORE

Stephen Hassenfeld gaining confidence: "Possibility of acquisition raised at Hasbro meeting," *Providence Journal*, May 13, 1982, page D-04.

"Charles M. Schulz, 'Peanuts' Creator,' Dies at 77, by Sarah Boxer, *New York Times,* February 14, 2000.

Stephen transformed: "Hasbro does turnaround in recession's face," by Hamilton Allen, *Providence Journal,* September 19, 1982, page F-01.

Transformers, GoBot competition: *People*, December 3, 1984.

Leibowtiz, Rothman, and Stephen Hassenfeld on Shea's departure: "Hasbro setting sights on No. 1 Milton Bradley purchase, hot toys put Pawtucket firm near industry's top," by Hamilton Allen, *Providence Journal*, December 23, 1984, page F-01.

"Marketing makes magic of Hasbro," by Gwynne Morgan, *Providence Journal,* December 18, 1984, page B-01.

"Dramatic earnings": "Hasbro earnings rocketed to a 245% gain in 1984," by Jan Brogan, *Providence Journal*, February 13, 1985, page C-09.

"Santa Claus good to Hasbro," by Hamilton Allen, *Providence Journal*, December 22, 1985, p F-01.

Here and in other passages about Transformers products, J.E. Alvarez's *The Unofficial Guide to Vintage Transformers: 1980s through 1990s,* Schiffer, 2017, was helpful.

The Fortune 500 archive lists Hasbro's placement on the lists from 1985 to 2001: http://archive.fortune.com/magazines/fortune/fortune500_archive/letters/H.html

Zartan: TOY MAKER TO REMOVE 'SCHIZOPHRENIC' LABEL, Associated Press in New York Times, December 6, 1984; also, www.therobotsvoice.com/2013/03/ the_top_ten_most_controversial_action_figures.php

*****

"The Eyes Have It in Idaho, Where Mr. Potato Head Is Running for Mayor of Boise," *People*, November 4, 1985. http://people.com/archive/the-eyes-have-it-in-idaho-where-mr-potato-head-is-running-for-mayor-of-boise-vol-24-no-19/

Guinness Potato Head records: the Guinness World Records, 2008; www.guinnessworldrecords.com/world-records/fastest-marathon-dressed-as-a-mr-potato-head

Potato Head Kids TV show: Intro, www.youtube.com/watch?v=lBaurKSyIrk; Potatolympics, https://www.youtube.com/watch?v=CawLbfjSe2Q

Kissyfur, Foofur, etc.: Rob Bricken, a knowledgeable observer of American culture, counted all of them on his list of "12 Cartoons No One Will Ever Have Nostalgia for," with Potato Head Kids placing second only to Kissyfur. Wrote Bricken: "The '80s were the heyday of children's animation, when weekday afternoons and Saturday mornings were packed full of cartoons. Some were great; some were just okay, and some were unbearably wretched. Here are a dozen '80s cartoons that don't deserve to be remembered at all, let alone fondly." http://io9.gizmodo.com/12-cartoons-from-the-1980s-no-one-will-ever-have-nosta-1657410102

History of the Great American Smokeout: www.cancer.org/healthy/stay-away-from-tobacco/great-american-smokeout/history-of-the-great-american-smokeout.html

Grenada relief mission: "Grenada toy-lift scheduled," by Peter Lord, *Providence Journal*, December 17, 1983, page A-04; "A reporter's notebook: Delivering toys to Grenada," by M. Charles Bakst, *Providence Journal*, December 25, 1983, page B-01.

First Surgeon General's Report on Smoking and Health: https://profiles.nlm.nih.gov/NN/B/B/M/Q/

Koop accepts Mr. Potato Head's surrender: "Hasbro's spud will kick the habit," by Neil Downing, *Providence Journal*, November 14, 1987, page A-15; www.upi.com/Archives/1987/11/19/Great-American-Smokeout-led-by-Mr-Potato-Head/7312564296400/

Arnold Schwarzenegger and the President's Council: www.thefreelibrary.com/MR.+POTATO+HEAD+TERMINATES+COUCH+POTATO+STATUS,+JOINS+WITH+THE...-a011963430 – 3/20/92

President Bush's remarks: www.presidency.ucsb.edu/ws/?pid=20905

Charness's comments: "A-peeling Mr. Potato Head turns 35: More than 50 million of the fabled Hasbro toy sold since 1952," *Providence Journal*, May 2, 1987, page A-02.

Hasbro stock historically: http://investor.hasbro.com/stocklookup.cfm

Providence Journal story on Stephen Hassenfeld's passing: "Legacy Hassenfeld style: 'Quiet passion,' consensus raised Hasbro to No. 1," by Neil Downing, July 2, 1989, page F-01.

Hassenfeld at 1993 Toy Fair: "Hasbro hits another 'home run' Revenue and net soared in '92, setting records," by Jeffrey L. Hiday, *Providence Journal*, February 9, 1993, page D-01.

Record year of 1993: "Hasbro profits and sales broke records in 1993: Foreign sales were strong, offsetting an unfavorable rate exchange," by Paul Davis, *Providence Journal*, February 11, 1994. Page B-01.

Number 169 on Fortune 500: http://archive.fortune.com/magazines/fortune/fortune500_archive/letters/H.html

A more detailed full story of Alan's stewardship of Hasbro during the 1989-to-1997 is told in *Toy Wars*.

CHAPTER FIVE: GOOD HEALTH, BAD GOVERNMENT

Stephen D. Hassenfeld Children's Center for Cancer and Blood Disorders: https://med.nyu.edu/hassenfeld/

Dr. William Oh: www2.aap.org/sections/perinatal/pdf/williamoh.html

Hasbro Children's Hospital groundbreaking: "The hospital that toys will build: Work begins on children's unit given by Hasbro," by C. Eugene Emery Jr., *Providence Journal*, September 20, 1991, page A-01.

Children's Hospital fundraising: "Children's wing tour underscores need for a new facility," by Felice J. Freyer, *Providence Journal*, October 28, 1992, page A-01; "Hasbro Hospital meets goal, sets a new one: An additional $3 million is targeted to be used as a pediatric outpatient clinic," by Felice J. Freyer, *Providence Journal,* May 28, 1993, page B-05.

"The Prince of Providence: The Rise and Fall of Buddy Cianci, America's Most Notorious Mayor," by Mike Stanton, Random House, 2004.

Ceramic tiles: "Work of small hands gives it a heart: The hospital's Circle of Clay eventually will have 10,000 tiles made by students in every community in Rhode Island. Most of the tiles project happiness, a few sadness and death," by S. Robert Chiappinelli, *Providence Journal*, January 23, 1994, page B-01.

More giving: "The new Hasbro Children's Hospital: 'People often gave more than we asked.' From small change to millions, fund raising was a community affair," by Karen Lee Ziner, *Providence Journal*, January 20, 1994, page A-08.

*****

Opening day at Hasbro Children's: www.youtube.com/watch?v =yi65s QMuEBU; "Opening Day at Children's Hospital: 'Now it's no longer just a building, it's a hospital," declares hospital president Bill Kreykes after yesterday's difficult but successful transfer of patients," by Felice J. Freyer, *Providence Journal,* February 13, 1994, page C-01.

*****

Secrets & Scandals: Reforming Rhode Island 1986-2006, by H. Philip West Jr., Rhode Island Publications Society, 2004, was a superb reference in writing about ethics reform.

State House history: http://sos.ri.gov/documents/publicinfo/tours/Activi-tyBook.pdf

*****

More on Cianci, and corruption:

In 2001, a federal grand jury indicted Cianci on extortion, conspiracy, racketeering, witness tampering and mail fraud charges related to City Hall bribery. During his 2002 trial, he was convicted of racketeering conspiracy and sentenced to 64 months in prison and fined $100,000. Once again, he resigned.

House Speaker Joseph DeAngelis agreed with Sundlun on the need to clean house. "I think it's important for him and I think it's important for this Assembly to set the tone on the first day, right in the beginning, that the most important thing we have to deal with is the public confidence," the speaker said. "Certainly I agree that it has, to a certain extent, been shaken and it is one of our obligations to regain that."

In 1993, after emerging from hiding, Mollicone was convicted of conspiracy, violation of banking laws and embezzlement, and was sentenced to 40 years in prison, fined $420,000 and ordered to pay $12 million in restitution. "Embezzler Mollicone to leave prison today," by Tom Mooney, *Providence Journal,* July 24, 2002, page A-01.

"There are not an inordinate number of crooked lawyers and judges in this state," Carol Zangari, head of the state Supreme Court's disciplinary board, said on TV. She did not speak tongue-in-cheek, although many viewers deemed 1991 a poor year to defend the judicial system.

"Don't try me in the media," Sarault said after he was arrested. "Please give me my day in court. I have entered a plea of not guilty to the allegations, and I persist in that plea." He did not persist for long.

*****

Verrecchia's warning: "Hasbro official sounded warning at '91 conference," *Providence Journal,* November 9, 1994, page B-01.

Voters approve four-year terms: "Voters give in, top officers to win 4-year terms in '94," by Brian C. Jones, *Providence Journal,* November 4, 1992, page A-01.

CHAPTER SIX: A NATURAL PROGRESSION

The Lost World tie-ins: http://adage.com/article/news/lost-world-jurassic-park-jurassic-sequel-set-promo-monster-lost-world-gains-250-mil-support-including-bk-jvc/69150/; http://articles.latimes.com/1997-02-11/business/fi-27406_1_universal-lost-world

Hassenfeld attends premier of *The Lost World*: "On the verge of summer Jurassic frenzy could be Hasbro gold mine," by G. Wayne Miller, *Providence Journal,* May 24, 1997, page A-01.

*****

Spielberg films *Amistad*: "Spielberg's real magic is off-screen: Movie stars are everywhere, but the one the fans wait around to see on blustery days in Newport is Amistad director Steven Spielberg," by G. Wayne Miller, *Providence Journal,* March 18, 1997, page B-01.

Spielberg's Ukraine roots: http://oralhistory.rutgers.edu/interviewees/30-interview-html-text/146-spielberg-arnold

Spielberg's only media interview while filming *Amistad* in Rhode Island: "Spielberg thanks Rhode Islanders for a great shoot," by G. Wayne Miller, *Providence Journal,* April 3, 1997, page A-01. "The people in all of Rhode Island have been fantastic," Spielberg also said. "We've had a great experience… It's been pretty amazing. We don't get this kind of hospitality everywhere we go." He expressed his gratitude to the thousands of fans who braved cold, snow, rain and wind for a glimpse of him and his cast and production team. "I would have invited them all inside to keep warm if we didn't have a crew of 100 already there," he said. On breaks, Spielberg had signed autographs, shaken hands and exchanged small talk.

Jurassic Park at 1993 Toy Fair: Story by Jeffrey L. Hiday, *Providence Journal,* February 9, 1993, page D-01.

O'Neill on Barney and *Jurassic Park: Providence Journal,* July 16, 1993, page B-01.

Krutick on a challenging climate: Story by Paul Davis, *Providence Journal,* February 11, 1994, page B-01.

Katzenberg, Hassenfeld and Charness speak with *The Providence Journal*: Story by Paul Davis and Jeffrey L. Hiday, *Providence Journal,* August 17, 1995, page A-01.

Goldner pitches *Transformers*: "The Business: Brian Goldner," *Hollywood Reporter,* June 14, 2017.

Special Rhode Island premier: "Movie Premiere to Help Change Kids' Lives: Hasbro to donate 100 percent of proceeds to four local charities," *Business Wire*, May 1, 2007.

Premier gala: "Premier gala at Providence Place: The buzz from Transformers," by Faye B. Zuckerman, *Providence Journal*, June 29, 2007, page B-01.

*****

New York Times on Japanese Pokémon cartoon: "TV Cartoon's Flashes Send 700 Japanese Into Seizures," by Sheryl WuDunn, www.nytimes.com/1997/12/18/world/tv-cartoon-s-flashes-send-700-japanese-into-seizures.html.

The *Times* story recounted what was described as a "vaccine bomb" intended to destroy a computer virus exploded on screen in a burst of bright red at about 20 minutes into the 6:30 p.m. broadcast. Red and blue lights flashed for a few seconds, and children suddenly fell ill. Some suffered seizures or convulsions and others vomited blood. Still more experienced headaches or said they felt carsick or confused. Many went to hospitals, where some, having difficulty breathing, were placed in intensive care. All recovered, but parents were alarmed, and medical professionals were puzzled by the reaction to a visual technique that was a common feature of Japanese cartoons, one that previously had caused no harm. Nintendo blamed Television Tokyo, which cancelled other broadcasts of the episode as police opened an investigation.

"'I was shocked to see my daughter lose consciousness," Yukiko Iwasaki, whose 8-year-old suffered a seizure, told *The Times*. "'She started to breathe only when I hit her on the back.'"

Said Saitama Medical School professor Toshio Yamauchi: "This may be the first case of mass suffering from photo stimulation. We would like to study this thoroughly."

In Pawtucket, Charness reassured consumers following the May announcement of Hasbro's acquisition of Wizards of the Coast, which brought Hasbro Pokémon rights, saying the situation was "totally resolved in Japan." The freak episode would not be broadcast in Hasbro markets, he said, "and the programming coming to North America will be carefully reviewed and edited to be sure there will be no adverse reaction from viewers."

*****

Barry Lynn comments on Teletubbies: www.au.org/media/press-releases/jerry -falwell-attacks-teletubbies

Falwell on *Today*: www.nytimes.com/1999/02/15/business/media-talk-falwell-takes-on-the-teletubbies.html

Shiffman on Furby: www.cbsnews.com/news/talking-toy-or-spy/

Columnist Andrew Marshall: http://www.independent.co.uk/news/furbies-banned-at-us-spy-base-1046935.html

Hasbro buys Galoob: http://www.sfgate.com/business/article/Hasbro-Adds-Galoob-to-Its-Toy-Chest-2988518.php

Hasbro closes Central Falls plant: "Hasbro closing its last R.I. plant: 'Tough decision' cuts 150 jobs in Central Falls," by Nora Lockwood Tooher, *Providence Journal*, February 4, 1998, page A-01.

Potato Head and League of Women Voters: http://library.lwv.org/content/head-polls

As Christmas 1996 approached, a theologian cited Mr. Potato Head in a *Providence Journal* op-ed column about a branch of Christianity, writing: "For the Christian liberal, the Holy Spirit is always the spitting image of the Zeitgeist. God is a kind of cosmic Mr. Potato Head: If you don't like his features, simply snap on others." The column: "Are we obscene or merely fatuous? By David Lewis Stokes Jr., *Providence Journal*, November 29, 1996, page B-06.

The *Toy Story* Burger King Mr. Potato Head French fry tie-in was not the first time Hasbro had partnered with the fast-food chain—Pot Head enjoyed a history with Burger King, and also McDonald's, Hardee's and Wendy's—but there had never been a campaign of this magnitude. Burger King was investing $70 million in ads, in-store promotions including life-size Pot Head standees, and other means in an attempt to persuade consumers that its new formulation of French fries, with "the taste that beat McDonald's," was superior. The chain was surging in popularity, its market share having increased a percentage point, to 19.2 percent, while McDonald's had lost 0.4 percent, dropping to 41.9 percent. Bring on the fries—and Burger King did, magnanimously, with a coast-to-coast "Free Friday" giveaway of small orders of the reformulated taters on January 2, 1998.

Details on the Burger King French fry campaign: "Mr. Potato Head Joins as Ally of Burger King: After Big Mac attack, McDonald's will face an onslaught on its French fries," *Los Angeles Times*, December 10, 1997, http://articles.latimes.com/1997/ dec/10/ business/fi-62456; "Burger King Campaign Is Promoting New Fries," by Constance L. Hays, *New York Times*, December 11, 1997, www.ny-times.com/1997/12/11/business/burger-king-campaign-is-promoting-new-fries.html

Hassenfeld and Pot Head's ego: "Girl trouble: Hasbro says these could be big," *Providence Journal*, February 15, 1998, page F-02.

Chicago Cows on Parade: www.chicagotraveler.com/cows_on_parade.htm

Marlene Parrish visits Rhode Island: "Rhode Island harvests appeal of Mr. Potato Head," by Parrish, *Pittsburgh Post-Gazette,* April 20, 2000.

*****

In Potato Head's home state, the "Birthplace of Fun" campaign elicited similar zaniness. For humorist Gerry Goldstein, it was an unequalled opportunity to showcase "Peregrine 'Perky' Spudd," the fictitious character in his long-running column about Americana (southern Rhode Islanders, more specifically) that drew favorable comparisons to Garrison Keillor.

"Perky, a retired potato farmer [has] just visited a new resident of our area, 'Salty' Spud," Goldstein wrote. "Salty Spud is one of our South County Mr. Potato Head statues. He's among dozens that are popping up all over Rhode Island this year in a state-sponsored tourist promotion. For my money, Mr. Potato Head is dynamite as a promoter of our shores but Perky hit me with distressing news: vicious rumors abounded that Mr. Potato Head no longer has anything to do with actual potatoes..." Now, Perky disclosed, they were all-plastic.

From: "Tater tales: From all-purpose tuber toy to all-state icon," by Gerry Goldstein, *Providence Journal*, May 15, 2000, page C-01.

*****

Cianci's marinara sauce: "As fundraiser, sauce lacking," by Alisha A. Pina, *Providence Journal*, August 19, 2014, page Main 07.

*****

Cianci brings attention to graffiti: "Cianci spearheads anti-graffiti program: Saying graffiti is a crime, not art, the mayor kicks off a campaign to rid the city of this form of vandalism," by Ken Mingis, *Providence Journal,* October 15, 1993, page B-01.

Cianci seemed obsessed with graffiti. Two years after the 1993 event, he was back on the frontlines of the war against tagging. Declaring that "I feel like Elliot Ness," Cianci on June 20, 1995, headed a late-night police raid on an apartment that resulted in the arrest of a 22-year-old man he called "the Al Capone of graffiti." Having violated terms of probation from a previous graffiti conviction, the man was immediately sentenced to three months in prison and ordered to serve 1,000 hours of community service on his release.

Cianci professed reluctance on personally leading the raid.

"I don't want to be a part of this," he said, "but I insist on being a part of it, because everywhere I go—community meetings—what I hear over and over is people asking me when I'm going to do something about graffiti. I have received well over 100 complaints."

It was a tacit admission that his much-vaunted "Graffiti-busters" had been a bust.

Nonetheless, Cianci was right: graffiti plagued the city, and the young man and an accomplice arrested during the raid were indeed in the Capone tagger league. Police seized from their apartment dozens of cans of spray paint, an air-compressor driven spray-painting machine, hundreds of photographs of graffiti, a scrapbook of the men's own work, and graffiti magazines.

"There's a whole subculture," Detective Lt. John Reis, who had coordinated a three-month investigation by four officers, told the press. "They even have their own art magazines."

The chief culprit, the detective said, had "put his 'tag' all over the city. He even climbed to the top of the Point Street bridge to put it up on the side there so people could see it from Route 195."

"Cianci rides graffiti posse," by Lee Dykas, *Providence Journal,* June 22, 1995, page C-01.

*****

"All eyes peeled for stolen spud sculpture - Mr. Hot Potato," by Marion Davis, *Providence Journal*, May 16, 2000, page B-01.

The story went on to related how Potato Head was undamaged in the Brown University caper and Carmen Sandiego plastered the statue with fake news stories and headlines.

Some were simply silly: "If you saw this potato eating alone, would you ask it to join you?" and "He could be your accountant."

But one protested Brown's refusal at that time to implement financial needs-blind admissions policies. Another seemed to indicate ignorance of the "Birthplace of Fun" campaign: "Brown students, public question the 'Disney-fication' of State. People demand to know why they are suddenly represented by a tuber."

Nonetheless, Carmen Sandiego showed contrition, writing: "Those students responsible for the theft of the Projo Mr. Potato Head earlier this morning are 'sorry,' sources said while they were writing this. 'We felt serious action had to be taken if we were to be heard,' typed one of the would-be criminals, who, as of yet, has not been caught."

The students never were.

*****

Tourism statistics: "Tourism's mighty power in R.I.," by Bruce Sundlun, commentary, *Providence Journal*, August 19, 2001, page B-07,

Assistant public defender case: "Lawyer admits larceny try on license plates: Miss Munson, who is a public defender, sought to have them made at the ACI," by Karen Ellsworth, *Providence Journal*, February 27, 1982, page A-05.

*****

Regarding license plate 1, Cianci explained that he changed a tradition dating to the 1950s "because Providence is the Number 1 city in the state," adding that he was also "tired of getting lost in the crowd."

Which, he claimed, he was.

"When these vanity plates came out, 10000 was a good number," the mayor said. "When I first became mayor, everyone knew what it was. It was a great tradition. (Now) every time I'm driving around I see 6000, 5000, 8000. I saw IOOOO, but it looks like 10000. I've seen 15000. I saw 9000. I don't want to play thousands of games; I want to send a message."

The city '1' plate, as it happened, was already registered to a Department of Public Works Jeep. When it came up for renewal, Cianci wanted it for his own.

"I could have taken City 2 or City 3 but that wouldn't have been appropriate," he said.

From: "Cianci's new license plate: 1-upmanship? The mayor's Lincoln has shed 10000 for a newly installed city plate that looks suspiciously like the plate the governor has on his Lincoln," by Ken Mingis, *Providence Journal*, May 31, 1996, page D-01.

*****

Hassenfeld's honorary degree from Roger Williams University: "Graduates are urged to serve: Brown University President Vartan Gregorian, the principal speaker, said service to neighborhood and nation is a duty, not solely the product of altruism," by Christopher Beall, *Providence Journal*, May 23, 1993, page C-05.

Hassenfeld's honorary degree ceremony at Fashion Institute of Technology: www.youtube.com/watch?v=tVbD99jjT8Q

House committee summary: www.congress.gov/congressional-report/105th-congress/house-report/829/1

Hassenfeld's personal moratorium on campaign contributions: "Hassenfeld swears off campaign donations," by Brian C. Jones, *Providence Journal*, April 23, 1997, page A-01.

Journal editorial on Hassenfeld's pledge: "Hooray for Hassenfeld," April 30, 1997, page B-06.

Chapter Seven: Corrective Measures

"Alan Hassenfeld: Cheers on Wall Street, mixed reviews in Rhode Island," by Nora Lockwood Tooher, *Providence Journal*, May 16, 1999.

Selya letter: "Alan Hassenfeld's contributions," *Providence Journal*, June 11, 1999.

Wizards of the Coast acquisition: "Hasbro collects the Pokemon set: The toymaker is spending $325 million for the maker of card games," by Nora Lockwood Tooher, *Providence Journal*, September 10, 1999, page F-01.

"Fiasco" headlined story: www.telegraph.co.uk/finance/4467013/Mattel-sale-ends-3.6bn-fiasco.html

Times story on Barad's departure: www.nytimes.com/2000/02/04/busi-ness/chief-of-mattel-steps-down-after-reporting-loss-in-1999.html

Hassenfeld asks Verrecchia to run Hasbro: "A life of Twister & turns: Over 43 years, Alfred Verrecchia rose to the top at Hasbro, and rebuilt the company along the way," by G. Wayne Miller, *Providence Journal*, May 25, 2008, page F-01.

Disney names Hasbro official toymaker: "Disney Finalizes Licensing Deals With Toy Makers Hasbro, Mattel," by Lisa Bannon, *Wall Street Journal,* September 21, 2000, www.wsj.com/articles/SB96949488491447621

Hasbro cuts 500 jobs: "Playing for keeps: Hasbro to cut 500 jobs," by Nora Lockwod Tooher, *Providence Journal*, October 13, 2000.

Layoffs reach 750: "Toy maker cuts jobs after first quarterly loss in decade," by Nora Lockwod Tooher, *Providence Journal*, February 9, 2001, page G-01.

Verrecchia is dead honest: "A life of Twister & turns: Over 43 years, Alfred Verrecchia rose to the top at Hasbro, and rebuilt the company along the way," by G. Wayne Miller, *Providence Journal*, May 25, 2008, page F-01.

Times on Pokémon: "Hasbro Has Loss as Pokémon Wanes," by Julian E. Barnes, *New York Times*, April 24, 2001, www.nytimes.com/2001/04/24/busi-ness/hasbro-has-loss-as-Pokémon-wanes.html

Brand-new game for Hasbro: "Coming of age: It's a brand new game for Hasbro, which has transformed itself in the last year," by Lisa Biank Fasig, *Providence Journal*, February 17, 2002, page K-01.

Hassenfeld says business is on track: "It's all in the games: Hasbro swallows $28.6-million hit on video games," by Lisa Biank Fasig, *Providence Journal*, July 23, 2002, page E-01.

THIN-TRONIX: www.toymania.com/toyshows/tf2003/full/hasbro_thin.shtml

Hasbro's 2004 annual meeting: "Hasbro annual meeting an exercise in brevity," by Paul Grimaldi, *Providence Journal*, May 21, 2004, page E-01.

Trump game: "Trump promised millions to charity. We found less than $10,000 over 7 ears," by David A. Fahrenthold, *Washington Post*, June 28, 2016.

First-quarter 2005 loss: "Hoping for sales force: Hasbro posts a loss for the first quarter," by Paul Grimaldi, *Providence Journal*, May 20, 2005.

Hassenfeld becomes non-employee chairman: "Hassenfeld, stepping into global advocacy role, will keep hand in Hasbro," by Paul Grimaldi, *Providence Journal*, August 31, 2005, page E-01.

CHAPTER EIGHT: 'A DIFFERENCE IN THE LIVES OF THOSE WE CARE ABOUT MOST'

The Business of Changing the World: Twenty Great Leaders on Strategic Corporate Philanthropy, by Marc Benioff and Carlye Adler, 2006.

Some information about the Hassenfeld Family Foundation is at www.grantmakers.io/profiles/v0/056015373-hassenfeld-foundation/

Brandeis business program: www.brandeis.edu/global/news/archive/innovation-center.html

Record Rhode Island Foundation grants: "Foundation gave out record $45M in '16 | Nonprofit set to honor contributors at annual meeting," by G. Wayne Miller, *Providence Journal*, May 24, 2017, page 4, section A.

Women's health centers in Afghanistan and Darfur: www.un.org/en/ecosoc/phlntrpy/docs/biographies_dialogue%20two_women's%20econ%20empowerment.pdf

Announcement of new Hassenfeld Children's Hospital in New York: http://nyulangone.org/locations/hassenfeld-childrens-hospital-of-new-york

Mr. Potato Head Unplugged, by Jim Davis and Brett Koth, Andrews McNeel, 2002.

ICTI CARE: http://www.icti-care.org/e/default.asp

Macy's Day Parade 2008: http://content.time.com/time/nation/article/0,8599, 1862565,00.html

Bridgestone commercial: www.youtube.com/watch?v=FTXCR5alGc4

"Promoting cannibalism": https://www.youtube.com/watch?v=wh6_vCchfnk

Illuminati: www.youtube.com/watch?v=zDOV1sTloyk

One person connected Mr. and Mrs. Potato Head to global conspiracy, writing: "I think the Illuminati might be using this commercial to sub consciously promote cannibalism. With what they have planned with 'agenda 21' it really makes you wonder."

Agenda 21 is a voluntary United Nations program aimed at promoting sustainable development and protection of the environment. But an alternative interpretation could be found, however, at the Dutch site Volkwordtwakker.nl, or People Wake Up (Truth Newspaper), which described Agenda 21 as: "Essentially designed to wipe out the human race, to the benefit of a small group known as the Illuminati, aka globalization, Rothschild Khazarian Mafia, summarized the Archon bloodline families, in our society carry the forefront as the 'financial elite'... The ultimate goal of the Illuminati is to own the planet for themselves, and to be operated by up to 500 million people may live as their serfs..." Everyone else? "The rest will be cut from the current population," Truth Newspaper predicted. The public-relations expert and former journalist Marc Jampole was more reasoned in his criticism of the Lays spot, but he, too discerned a nefarious message. "Eating another being of your own species is generally considered to be an abomination," he wrote on his blog. "Although the Potato Heads are not humans, they are stand-ins for humans with human emotions and aspirations, just like the various mice, ducks, rabbits, dogs, foxes, lions and other animals we have anthropomorphized since the beginning of recorded history. From Aesop and Wu Cheng'en to Orwell and Disney, authors have frequently used animals as stand-ins for humans in fairy tales, satires and children's literature. So when Mrs. Potato Head eats a potato, it's an overt representation of cannibalism—humans eating other humans." www.jampole.com/blog/a-tv-commercial-subtly-suggests-cannibalism-another-makes-fun-of-those-with-disabilities/

Inevitably, given the typical viewer response—*it's a good-humored spoof, for heaven's sake*—there was blowback to the backlash. "The entire purpose of this commercial is that the chips are so good even 'Potatoes,' themselves would eat them... please stop blowing things out of proportion. It's a funny commercial, so open YOUR mind and appreciate humour," wrote one commenter, www.youtube.com/watch?v=wh6_vCchfnk 153K. Wrote another: "I want chips now...☺☺☺"www.youtube.com/watch?v =WaUpjlSVA5Y 1.7K

Rickles' voice in *Toy Story 4:* "Here's how Toy Story 4 will honor the late Don Rickles as Mr. Potato Head," by Marc Snetiker, *Entertainment Weekly,* March 28, 2019.

Rickles and his grandchildren: www.maxim.com/entertainment/interview-icon-don-rickles

The BBC's Jon Kelly column: www.bbc.com/news/magazine-17871107

*****

Martinez video: www.youtube.com/watch?v=wkri1NUq9ro.
Full lyrics:

If you weren't born with it
You can buy a couple ornaments
Just be sure to read the warning, kids
'Cause pretty soon you'll be bored of it, ha-ha
Sexual, hey girl if you wanna feel sexual
You can always call up a professional
They stick pins in you like a vegetable

Kids forever, kids forever
Baby soft skin turns into leather
Don't be dramatic, it's only some plastic
No one will love you if you're unattractive

Oh, Mrs. Potato Head, tell me, is it true that pain is beauty?
Does a new face come with a warranty?
Will a pretty face make it better?
Oh, Mr. Potato Head, tell me
How did you afford her surgery?
Do you swear you'll stay forever?
Even if her face don't stay together
Even if her face don't stay together

If you want a little more confidence
Potatoes turn to French fries, yeah it's common sense
All you need's a couple more condiments
And a hundred thousand dollars for some compliments
It's such a waste
When little girls grow into their mother's face
But little girls are learning how to cut and paste
And pucker up their lips until they suffocate

Kids forever, kids forever
Baby soft skin turns into leather
Don't be dramatic, it's only some plastic

No one will love you if you're unattractive

Oh, Mrs. Potato Head, tell me, is it true that pain is beauty?
Does a new face come with a warranty?
Will a pretty face make it better?
Oh, Mr. Potato Head, tell me
How did you afford her surgery?
Do you swear you'll stay forever?
Even if her face don't stay together
Stay forever, stay forever
Even if her face don't stay together
Stay forever, stay forever
Even if her face don't stay together

Oh, Mrs. Potato Head, tell me, is it true that pain is beauty?
Does a new face come with a warranty?
Will a pretty face make it better?
Oh, Mr. Potato Head, tell me
How did you afford her surgery?
Do you swear you'll stay forever?

Even if her face don't stay together
Stay forever, stay forever
Even if her face don't stay together
Stay forever, stay forever
Even if her face don't stay together
Stay forever, stay forever
Even if her face don't stay together
Stay forever, stay forever
Even if her face don't stay together

The video resonated with viewers, prompting more than 113,341 comments to the official version Martiznez posted on her YouTube channel until comments were disabled.

"The woman in this video was beautiful inside and out," wrote one. "The man was gross inside and out. DON'T LET ANYONE TELL YOU WHAT TO DO WITH YOURSELF!! YOU'RE BEAUTIFUL INSIDE AND OUT!! Love yourself."

"This song has the perfect message for both boys and girls," one wrote. "What's wrong with being natural... embrace yourselves and if no one doesn't like you for you well that's them... don't let anyone bring you down or tell you that your ugly or fat."

Wrote a third: "I almost cry every time I hear this song. Melanie makes me feel better about myself and everyone that doesn't think he or she is pretty or handsome you are the way god made you and you are beautiful on the inside. just have a good personality and help other people with hard times and then you can feel better about yourself. you are all BEAUTIFUL!"

"Someone should show this to the human Barbie," wrote a fourth.

*****

Journal profile of Goldner: "A year after becoming non-employee chair, Goldner moves close in succession," by Paul Grimaldi, *Providence Journal*, February 19, 2006, page F-01.

Goldner becomes CEO: "Leadership change: Goldner replaces Verrecchia as CEO of Hasbro," by Paul Grimaldi, *Providence Journal*, May 23, 2008, page F-01.

Hassenfeld Boundless Playground: "Thanks to Hassenfeld, playground has boundless appeal for children," by Kate Bramson, *Providence Journal*, October 28, 2008, page B-01.

Hassenfeld's mother's funeral: "Sylvia Hassenfeld remembered as 'remarkable,' " by G. Wayne Miller, *Providence Journal*, August 20, 2014, Page Main 03.

Eulogy for Sylvia Hassenfeld: August 19, 2014, Providence, Rhode Island by Jehuda Reinharz.

Hall of Fame inductees: http://bit.ly/2EXvUIX

Two months after the Toy Halls of Fame festivities, another honor came Hassenfeld's way from Flag for Hope, the national organization that seeks dignity and respect for all Americans, and declares that "every American has a responsibility to make a positive impact in his or her community." Flags for Hope had honored or been supported by military leaders, retired Supreme Court Justice Sandra Day O'Connor, Muhammad Ali, John McCain, Colin Powell, Tom Selleck, Billie Jean King, Beach Boy Mike Love, basketball player Bill Walton, George Foreman and many others in its mission of fostering peace and understanding, "with no personal agendas, no politics—just a passion for our country and our flag."

Like the ones before, Hassenfeld had not sought this honor.

"An anonymous friend pulled us aside because they knew Alan would not brag about his charitable work," wrote Flag for Hope. "His friend wanted us to fully understand the depths of Alan's efforts… Most people will never know the scope of Alan's charitable work because so much of it is done quietly. We encourage our readers to Google 'Alan Hassenfeld' and understand the depth of his philanthropy. Alan has quietly devoted his life to making a difference in the world and we welcome him to our family."

CHAPTER NINE: RESPONSIBILITY

Hassenfeld's op-ed essay on eve of 2016 election: "Vote to improve R.I. ethics," *Providence Journal*, October 30, 2016, page 19.

"Ex-RI House Speaker Fox gets 3 years in prison," by Katie Mulvaney, *Providence Journal,* June 11, 2015.

"Former R.I. Rep. Gallison gets 51 months for stealing from dead man, disabled woman and nonprofit agency," by Tom Mooney, *Providence Journal,* June 16, 2017.

Hassenfeld's 2013 impassioned column on gun violence: *Providence Journal*, January 8, 2013, Page COMM 01.

DeSimone, Malik lose: "Truck-toll backlash ramps up in House races," by Patrick Anderson, *Providence Journal*, September 12, 2016, page 2, Section A; "DeSimone to wage write-in candidacy," by Karen Lee Ziner, *Providence Journal*, October 13, 2016, page 1, Section A.

Rhode Island Coalition Against Gun Violence vigil: "A call for 'moral outrage': Marking the Newtown massacre," by Donita Naylor, *Providence Journal,* December 16, 2016, page 4, Section A.

Protect Rhode Island Families Act: http://webserver.rilin.state.ri.us/ Bill Text /BillText17/HouseText17/H5510Baa.pdf

NRA Take Action release: June 28, 2017: www.nraila.org/articles/20170628/rhode-island-immediate-action-required-on-gun-control-bill

General Assembly approves legislation: "Domestic-abusers lose gun rights, private-sector workers get paid sick leave, it's easier for firefighters to get disability pensions," by Jacqueline Tempera, Katherine Gregg and Patrick Anderson, *Providence Journal*, September 19, 2017.

Rhode Island Senate 2012 survey: www.publicpolicypolling.com/pdf/2011 /PPP_Release_RI_0223424.pdf

Hassenfeld considers Senate run: "Hassenfeld says he's mulling run for Whitehouse's Senate seat," by Philip Marcelo, *Providence Journal*, February 24, 2011.

Hassenfeld's op-ed lambasting Washington: "Stop fiddling, you pols, and return to Washington now," by Alan G. Hassenfeld, *Providence Journal*, August 22, 2011, page B7.

Hassenfeld on the stand in trial of Doyle: www.ricentral.com/narragansett_times/news/local_news/former-ceo-of-hasbro-testifies-in-doyle-case/article_d6d55dd4-872f-11e6-9cd0-af4da2953596.html

The 2015 annual meeting: www.providencejournal.com/article/20150520/NEWS/150529837

Verrecchia, Goldner speak at 2015 annual meeting: "Game changing: Longtime executive Verrecchia retires as chairman, and CEO outlines future strategy," by G. Wayne Miller, *Providence Journal*, May 22, 2015

Names for babies, 2000 to 2009: www.ssa.gov/oact/babynames/dec-ades/names2000s.html

Stockton comments on *Frozen*: www.usatoday.com/story/money/mar-kets/2014/07/17/mattel-second-quarter-earnings-barbie/12773037/

Stockton fired: "Mattel Says Ex-CEO Stockton Was Fired: Toy maker's news release in January said he had resigned,," by Lisa Beilfuss, *Wall Street Journal,* April 9, 2015.

*****

Motley Fool: www.fool.com/investing/2017/07/31/mattel-struggles-as-bar-bie-gets-dumped.aspx

The publication added: "Adding insult to injury, the company also announced that Chief Financial Officer Kevin Farr will be leaving after 25 years with the company and 17 years in his current role. The market dislikes uncertainty, and having the CFO depart while trying to mount a full-scale turnaround didn't do the company any favors and probably contributed to the stock's continuing decline. In the wake of several years of disappointing results, Mattel laid out a plan last month to return the company to positive results. Mattel has already introduced new diversity-embracing versions of its iconic Barbie and Ken dolls and has plans to incorporate connected toys, online content, live events, and digital games into its offerings. Investors will have to wait a bit longer to see if that plan is ultimately successful."

*****

Zacks: August 16, 2017, by Neena Mishra, Zacks.com; www.nasdaq.com/ar-ticle/bear-of-the-day-mattel-mat-cm832586. The article noted the El Segundo, Califor-nia-headquartered firm's position as one of the world's three largest toy manufacturers (with Hasbro and LEGO), listed its leading brands, and some workforce and market statistics: some 30,000 employees in more than three dozen countries with products sales in more than 150 nations.

Developmental Psychology: willettsurvey.org/TMSTN/Gender/DoesBarbie-MakeGirlsWantToBeThin.pdf

*****

The Twitter bashing of Man Bun Ken was harsh, with additional comments including:

"What? Ken has a #manbun? That's not diverse, it's perverse. @Mattel @Bar-bie"

And: "Manbun == smooth plastic groin." It was a reference not only to Ken but to her on-and-off boyfriend, who both had nothing there. Both also lacked nipples, it is worth mentioning, although that, too, was standard in the doll-manufacturing industry.

And:

"Me to 9-yr-old son: Look at Ken

"9-yr-old son: Who's Ken?

"Me: Barbie's boyfriend.

"9-yr-old son: Who's Barbie?

"Me: 👏👏👏👏"

*****

The corporate culture inside Mattel and the company's fierce protection of its brands is told in *You Don't Own Me: How Mattel v. MGA Entertainment Exposed Barbie's Dark Side*, by Orly Lobel, Norton, 2018.

Bloomberg News quote on Georgiadis' departure: "Mattel Loses Another CEO But Shouldn't Lose Her Vision: Margo Georgiadis didn't have time to see her turnaround plans bear fruit," by Sarah Halzack, April 20, 2018, www.bloomberg.com/opinion/articles/2018-04-20/mattel-loses-ceo-margo-georgiadis-but-should-keep-her-plan

*****

Corporate Responsibility, Ethisphere, etc.: http://corporate.hasbro.com/en-us/community-relations/our-philanthropy; www.thecro.com/100-best/cr-magazine-reveals-17th-annual-100-best-corporate-citizens-list/#sthash.C0NXvkrI.dpuf

www.thecro.com/100-best/cr-magazine-reveals-17th-annual-100-best-corporate-citizens-list/#sthash.C0NXvkrI.dpuf; www.3blassociation.com/insights/2018-100-best-corporate-citizens; www.3blassociation.com/files/yMblCg/100BestCorporateCitizens_2019.pdf

Heart disease incidence: www.cdc.gov/heartdisease/facts.htm

Verrecchia related the story of his heart attack and stroke on August 31, 2017, over lunch with this writer at Massimo restaurant, Providence.

CHAPTER TEN: FEARLESS AND KIND

Early 2016 interview: With editor Mark S. Murphy, January 12, 2016, *Providence Business News*.

Hassenfeld's wealth: "Hasbro's Former CEO Just Became a Billionaire," by Tom Metcalf, *Bloomberg*, May 25, 2017.

Ilene Prusher story: www.haaretz.com/blogs/jerusalem-vivendi/the-color-of-water-a-fountain-of-hope-in-the-heart-of-teddy-s-jerusalem.premium-1.519066

Mechai Viravaidya: http://site.pda.or.th/

Viravaidya TEDxChange talk: www.ted.com/talks/mechai_viravaidya_how_mr_condom_made_thailand_a_better_place/transcript

Global Day of Joy: "Day of giving for Hasbro workers: One of the projects was refurbishing a community center at a middle school in Providence," by G. Wayne Miller, *Providence Journal*, December 16, 2016, page 3; http://newsroom.hasbro.com/mediakit/releasedetail.cfm?releaseid=1004363;Hasbro video, www.youtube.com/watch?v=P8YuZcv4Rt4

Trump insults: www.politico.com/magazine/story/2016/11/the-155-craziest-things-trump-said-this-cycle-214420

Points of Light: www.pointsoflight.org/blog/2016/09/29/building-culture-compassion-rules-kindness-give-kids-opportunity-show-they-care

Morton's post: "Building a Culture of Compassion, 'Rules of Kindness' Give Kids the Opportunity to Show They Care," September 29, 2016, www.pointsoflight.org/blog/building-culture-compassion-rules-kindness-give-kids-opportunity-show-they-care/

TODAY post: "7 Ways to Help Kids Stay Cool in a Heated Political Climate," by Amy McCready, June 14, 2016, https://community.today.com/parentingteam/post/7-ways-to-help-kids-stay-cool-in-a-heated-political-climate

Rules of Kindness: http://rulesofkindness.generationon.org/storywall

No Bully: http://newsroom.hasbro.com/mediakit/releasedetail.cfm?releaseid=929490; "Hasbro to sponsor anti-bullying effort in Pawtucket schools," by Patrick Anderson, *Providence Journal*, August 31, 2015.

Hasbro philanthropy and social responsibility: http://investor.hasbro.com/releasedetail.cfm?releaseid=959148;http://www.businesswire.com/news/home/20161027005932/en/

Hollywood Reporter interview: www.hollywoodreporter.com/news/hasbro-ceo-transformers-future-marketing-my-little-pony-boys-1012852

Merger rumors: https://seekingalpha.com/article/4044771-hasbro-mattel-merger-speculation-will-barbie-say-yes-g-joe; https://investorplace.com/2017/02/mattel-inc-mat-hasbro-inc-has/#.WcDzH8h95PY;https://themalaysianreserve.com /2017/04/03/warning-hasbro-mattel-merger-may-be-choking-hazard-for-disney/;www.latimes.com/business/la-fi-mattel-hasbro-20160205-story.html;www.thestreet.com/story/13991112/1/could-hasbro-s-blowout-earnings-reignite-mattel-merger-talks.html; https://seekingalpha.com/article/4085447-mattel-hasbro-merger-getting-improbable

Horasis panel with Hassenfeld: www.horasis.org/Horasis_Global_Meeting_2017-programme.pdf

Reuters story: http://www.reuters.com/article/us-hasbro-trump/u-s-companies-no-longer-know-rules-of-game-under-trump-hasbro-director-says-idUSKBN18P1MQ

Chewbacca Mom: "Chewbacca Mom's fame simply out of this world," by Mark Patinkin, *Providence Journal*, September 10, 2017, page 4, section A.

Verrecchias, Frascotti and Potato Head: "Mr. Potato Head refuses to be overshadowed: Among mega-brands at Hasbro convention, toy still holds hallowed place," by G. Wayne Miller, *Providence Journal*, September 10, 2017, page 4.

Hassenfeld on Don Levine: "Donald Levine, toy exec who developed G.I. Joe, dies at 86." *Associated Press* in *Washington Post,* May 25, 2014.

Toys 'R' Us: "Toys 'R' Us Files for Bankruptcy, Crippled by Competition and Debt," by Michael Corkery, *New York Times*, September 19, 2017.

Third-quarter results: "Hasbro Reports Revenue, Net Earnings and Earnings Per Share Growth for Third Quarter 2017," Hasbro release, October 23, 2017, http://investor.hasbro.com/releasedetail.cfm?releaseid=1044842

New Paramount deal: "Hasbro, Paramount extend partnership: 5-year deal continues relationship that brought Transformers, G.I. Joe to screen," by G. Wayne Miller, *Providence Journal*, November 4, 2017, page 5, section A

Hasbro takeover attempt? "Hasbro Sets Its Sights on Mattel: Potential deal would unite two biggest U.S. toy makers," by Dana Mattioli and Paul Ziobro, *Wall Street Journal*, November 10, 2017.

Community College of Rhode Island gift: "Hassenfeld Foundation gives CCRI $650,000," by G. Wayne Miller, *Providence Journal*, September 28, 2017, page 4, section A.

A week after the relief mission to Puerto Rico, Hassenfeld underwrote a second flight: "Hassenfeld foundation joins the relief effort," by G. Wayne Miller, *Providence Journal*, October 6, 2017, page 8, section A. A video of the relief effort: https://vimeo.com/242818546

*****

Hassenfeld's love of tennis and philanthropy crossed in 2017, when he paid for surgery and post-operative rehabilitation to heal tennis prodigy Tornado Alicia Black, whose career was sidelined at the age of 17 by an injury to her hip that she could not afford to fix. Hassenfeld stepped in after reading about her in September 2017.

The story was related in "Strangers Help a Former Prodigy Embark on a Comeback at 19," by David Waldstein, *New York Times,* Sports Section front page, October 23, 2017.

"If she succeeds in her comeback, Black said," Waldstein wrote, "she wants to open her own charity and address issues that have affected her life, like childhood homelessness. Black has said that she lived in homeless shelters with her family when she was young and that she also lived out of the family car for weeks at a time when she was 12.

"'No child should ever have to go through that,' she said. 'I hope I can be in a position to help.'

"Because her family used food stamps, childhood hunger is another issue dear to her, she said, as is the high cost of medical care.

" 'Someday I'd like to be able to help a kid get an operation they can't afford,' she said. "I think that would be a good way to pay everyone back for all their generosity to me.'

"Black said she was also interested in helping children get proper dental care. For the past several months, she said, she was embarrassed because she had the remnants of braces on her teeth. The wires were taken out, but she ran out of money before the attachments could be removed."

CHAPTER ELEVEN: REACH FOR THE STARS

Hasbro 2017 results: "Hasbro's mixed results: Despite lackluster 4th quarter, R.I. toymaker reports record 2017 revenues," by G. Wayne Miller, *The Providence Journal*, February 8, 2018. Also: https://investor.hasbro.com/news-releases/news-release-details/hasbro-reports-full-year-and-fourth-quarter-2017-financial

Toys 'R 'Us September 2017 bankruptcy filing: "Toys 'R' Us to Close 20% of Its U.S. Stores: About 4,500 U.S. workers will be affected; retailer filed for bankruptcy protection last year," by Paul Ziobro, *Wall Street Journal*, January 24, 2018.

Hasbro 2017 results conference call: https://seekingalpha.com/article/4144262-hasbros-ceo-brian-goldner-q4-2017-results-earnings-call-transcript?part=single

Mattel's 2017 results: https://www.prnewswire.com/news-releases/mattel-reports-full-year-and-fourth-quarter-2017-financial-results1-300592240.html

Toys 'R' Us to close all U.S. stores: "Toys 'R' Us Tells Workers It Will Likely Close All U.S. Stores: Failure of big-box chain would put up to 33,000 Americans out of work," by Paul Ziobro and Lillian Rizzo, *Wall Street Journal*, March 14, 2018.

Lazarus dies: "Charles P. Lazarus, Toys 'R' Us Founder, Dies at 94," by Michael Corkery, *New York Times*, March 22, 2018.

Georgiadis to leave Mattel: "Mattel CEO Margo Georgiadis is leaving the struggling toy maker after 14 months," by James F. Peltz, *Los Angeles Times,* April 19, 2018

Calderon describes her ICE imprisonment: "Guatemalan native speaks of weeks in ICE detention: Civil libertarians say case is emblematic of broken immigration system," by Tom Mooney, *Providence Journal,* February 15, 2018.

Hassenfeld learns of Calderon's imprisonment: "Supporters call for humanitarian release of R.I. woman held by ICE," by G. Wayne Miller, *The Providence Journal,* January 30, 2018. Hassenfeld learned during a previously scheduled lunch with me, and offered his help by phone during that lunch.

Stephen Brown on the case: "Guatemalan native speaks of weeks in ICE detention: Civil libertarians say case is emblematic of broken immigration system," by Tom Mooney, *The Providence Journal*, February 15, 2018.

Lilian is released: "ICE releases Guatemalan native, returns her family to Providence," by Katie Mulvaney, *Providence Journal,* February 13, 2018.

Carol Rose comments: "Lawsuit challenges Trump immigration practices after Providence mother's detention," by Tom Mooney, *Providence Journal,* April 11, 2018.

Details of ICE plotting to snatch immigrants: "Immigration officials conspired to arrest undocumented residents, says the ACLU," by Tom Mooney, *Providence Journal,* August 14, 2018.

Hasbro 1Q 2018 results: "With lights from Toys 'R' Us dimmed, sales plunge at Hasbro," Associated Press, April 23, 2018, as published in *Providence Journal.*

Mattel 1Q 2018 results: https://www.prnewswire.com/news-releases/mattel-reports-first-quarter-2018-financial-results-300637497.html

Power Rangers deal: "Hasbro picks up Power Rangers, other Saban entertainment assets for $522 million," by Ricardo Lopez, *Variety,* May 1, 2018.

Corporate honors: https://investor.hasbro.com/news-releases/news-release-details/hasbro-ranks-no-5-100-best-corporate-citizens-list. Also, www.businesswire. com/news/home/20180417006528/en/Hasbro-Named-America%E2%80%99s-Reputable-Companies

The Verrecchia Clinic for Children with Autism and Developmental Disabilities: https://www.bradleyhospital.org/philanthropy-news

Hassenfeld concerned Providence will declare bankruptcy: "Alan Hassenfeld on the state of politics and philanthropy in R.I.," by Mark S. Murphy, *Providence Business News*, January 12, 2016.

Line-item veto: "Our Turn: Alan Hassenfeld and Robert Manning, Put line-item veto on the ballot," by Alan Hassenfeld and Robert Manning, *Providence Journal,* May 25, 2018.

Flanders launches Senate bid: https://www.wpri.com/news/eyewitness-news-investigates/gops-robert-flanders-kicks-off-bid-to-unseat-us-sen-sheldon-whitehouse_20180327074902902/1082416389

Corazones Guerreros album: https://www.prnewswire.com/news-releases/ natalia -denegri-to-release-the-album-corazones-guerreros-as-producer-300625466.html

"The Truth" trailer: www.youtube.com/watch?v=TeKC24uAHP0&feature =youtu.be

Paige Alston story: "Four-year-old 'miracle child' honored at Hasbro Children's Hospital," by G. Wayne Miller, *Providence Journal*, March 30, 2018.

Hasbro 2Q 2018 results: https://investor.hasbro.com/news-releases/news-release-details/hasbro-reports-second-quarter-2018-financial-results

Mattel 2Q 2018 results: https://news.mattel.com/news/mattel-reports-second-quarter-2018-financial-results

CNBC approves of Mattel 3Q 2018 results: https://www.cnbc.com/2018/10/25/mattel-earnings-q3-2018.html

Motley Fool: "Mattel Posts a Surprise Profit as Cost-Cutting Takes Hold: After eight successive quarters of declines, the iconic toy maker is finally growing again," by Danny Vena, October 26, 2018. www.fool.com/investing/2018/10/26/mattel-posts-a-surprise-profit-as-cost-cutting-tak.aspx

Transformers' series box office: www.boxofficemojo.com/franchises/chart/?id=transformers.htm

Transformers 7 canceled: www.imdb.com/title/tt5090564/trivia?ref_=tt_trv_trv

Collider: "Paramount Officially Pulls the Next '*Transformers*' Sequel from Their Release Date Schedule," by Haleigh Foutch, May 23, 2018, http://collider.com/transformers-7-cancelled/#images

Hasbro's perspective on *Bumblebee*: correspondence with the author.

Layoffs and Pomerantz: "Hasbro: 'Difficult' changes in progress; won't confirm layoffs," by Tom Mooney, *Providence Journal*, October 18, 2018.

https://www.marketscreener.com/HASBRO-12874/news/Pomerantz-Law-Firm-Investigates-Claims-On-Behalf-of-Investors-of-Hasbro-Inc-HAS-27434420/

Hasbro 3Q results: "Hasbro, trying to find footing, posts weak 3Q," by Michelle Chapman, Associated Press, as published in *Providence Journal*, October 23, 2018.

Conference call: https://seekingalpha.com/article/4213243-hasbro-inc-ceo-brian-goldner-q3-2018-results-earnings-call-transcript?part=single

Associated Press story on Massachusetts officials interested in having Hasbro relocate: https://www.apnews.com/2a549b6311814cab8c68d5acfaf8123e

Pawtucket panic: "Mayor issues 'urgent' call to keep Hasbro in city: Company acknowledges it's 'evaluating several options' for its headquarters," by Tom Mooney, *Providence Journal*, November 8, 2018.

Mattiello and Raimondo want to keep Hasbro in Rhode Island: "Raimondo, Mattiello focus on keeping Hasbro in R.I.: 'I need to stay in front of them to make sure they won't leave,' governor says," by Amanda Milkovits, *Providence Journal*, November 10, 2018.

Gone from the U.S., Toys 'R' Us continued operations in Japan and China. "In Asia, Kids Can Still Drag Their Parents to Toys 'R' Us: Bankrupt in the U.S., the toy chain has 450 stores in Asia; company finds smaller is better," by Ese Erheriene, *Wall Street Journal*, November 25, 2018.

CHAPTER TWELVE: SANTA'S ELVES

The annual Christmas visit scene with Hassenfeld and Verrecchia occurred on December 19, 2016; while the details differ, the essentials of the visit remain the same year-to-year.

Jeanne Hebert wrote about Hassenfeld, enthusiastically, after this author asked if she were willing to contribute.

ACKNOWLEDGMENTS

To a great extent, the writer's life is a solitary existence (I am writing this at 4:45 a.m., I rest my case).

I have often said one does not have the choice to write, and having loved writing since early grammar school, this remains my truth. And yet, with few exceptions, only rarely does a writer ever really write alone. In the case of a non-fiction book such as *Kid Number One* involving so many interviews and interactions over such a long period of time, it is impossible.

So let me first thank my wife, Yolanda, for her patience and wise counsel during the writing of *Kid Number One*—and with all the other books and movies and writing and TV and more since when we met many years ago, on my luckiest day ever. Love you, Hon.

Deepest thanks to Alan Hassenfeld. A modest man of mighty means, he has devoted his life to the common good and so many people in the U.S. and around the globe owe him a huge debt of gratitude. Thanks to Alan's wife, Vivien. And thanks to his sister, Ellen Block; and Lori Holland, personal assistant and secretary at the Hassenfeld Family Foundation; and Alison Biondi, executive assistant.

Al Verrecchia, another man of means who gives back, is owed big thanks for sharing his time, memories and observations—which, like Alan, he has done for more than a quarter of a century, back to when I carried a Hasbro ID and freely roamed Hasbro headquarters while writing *Toy Wars*. Thanks also to Al's wife, Gerrie, and their children, Melisa Verrecchia, Michael Verrecchia, Lisa Verrecchia Montes, and Michele Verrecchia Levy; and their grandson, Austin Verrecchia.

I owe much to Barbara and Brian Goldner and I salute them what they have done to advance the common good. In its corporate and social-responsibility commitments, Hasbro serves as a model, proving you can both make money and do good. Henry and Hillel Hassenfeld are smiling somewhere.

Thanks also at Hasbro, past and present, to Duncan J. Billing, Karen Davis, Jen DeAngelis, Derryl DePriest, Julie Collins Duffy, John Frascotti, Katy Hendrickson, Dolph Johnson, Mary O'Connor, Jane Ritson-Parsons, Deb Thomas, and Paula Jean Walsh. Thanks to former Hasbro employees Wayne Charness, Kirk Bozigian, and David Hargreaves.

Appreciation to Rabbi Les Gutterman, longtime Hassenfeld family friend and spiritual force, a most wonderful man; to another wonderful person, Neil Steinberg, president of the Rhode Island Foundation, a major Rhode Island philanthropy; to Phil

West, ethics-reform leader and author; and to Garry Sasse, founding director of the Hassenfeld Institute for Public Leadership at Bryant University. Also, Natalia Denegri, Miami-based actress, producer, humanitarian and partner with Alan Hassenfeld and Ellie Block in Hurricane Maria relief efforts to the devastated island of Puerto Rico.

G.I. Joe collector, author and guru Dan Klingensmith Jr. helped me research the action figure's long history. Thanks to Shane Rhinewald of The Strong National Museum of Play, and Anna Yudina of The Toy Association

For background on Judaism in Rhode Island and earlier generations of Hassenfelds, thanks to Joshua Jasper and Kate-Lynne Laroche at the Rhode Island Jewish Historical Association; Aaron Ginsburg, Hassenfeld family genealogist; Harold Silverman, president, Congregation Sons of Jacob, Providence; the Newport Historical Society; Cheryl Fishbein; and Beth S. Veltri, executive director of Lincoln Park Cemetery.

In *Toy Wars*, I established the founding of Hasbro—nee, Hassenfeld Bros.—which I described as "by 1920," based on my research with Providence City Directories and other sources. I redoubled my efforts in *Kid Number One*, unearthing additional records that confirm an earlier origin (1917, to be exact) and provide more details of the Hassenfelds' earliest days in Rhode Island. In this effort, I was assisted by Nicole Lagace, Communications Director for Rhode Island Secretary of State Nellie M. Gorbea; Kenneth S. Carlson, Reference Archivist for the Rhode Island Department of State; Caleb T. Horton, an archivist with the City of Providence, Division of Archives and History; the office of Tax Assessor, the city of Providence; and the reference librarians at the West Warwick Public Library. They all have my gratitude.

At Hasbro Children's Hospital, my thanks to Dr. Phyllis Dennery, Pediatrician-in-Chief. At Lifespan, thanks to Jane Bruno, Elena M. Falcone-Relvas, Stacey B. Mihaly, Bill Murphy and David Levesque (now working for state of Rhode Island). I admire and thank Jeanne and Michael Hebert and their son, Ryan, for all they do.

Thanks to Lilian Calderon-Gordillo, Luis Gordillo and Gabriela Domenzain for providing background for passages in Chapter Eleven.

I extend again my appreciation to the late Sylvia Hassenfeld, who helped me with *Toy Wars*; my interview with her, now archived with other *Toy Wars* material at the University of Rhode Island's Robert L. Carothers Library & Learning Commons' Special Collections, was invaluable. So, too, was material from my years of writing about the late Bruce Sundlun, which I also donated to URI.

Gratitude to Dawn and Steven Porter of Stillwater River Publications for bringing *Kid Number One* to press. Thanks, too, to copy editor Ann C. Davis; Dawn Porter, who designed the cover and pages; and idexer Michelle Guiliano of Line by Line Indexing. Thanks to John Palumbo and Paul O'Hare at *Rhode Island Monthly*.

As always, special gratitude to my longtime screen agent and friend, Michael Prevett, of Circle of Confusion, the Los Angeles/New York talent agency and production studio; his ideas and inspiration over the years have enhanced my creativity. A shoutout to Michael, Ida Darvish, Josh Gad, Taylor Stuewe and Ryan Dixon for keeping the faith with *Toy Wars*. A shoutout, too, to Jim Ludes, my co-hosting and co-producing partner in our "Story in the Public Square" national PBS TV and SiriusXM Satellite radio show. Together, every week, we celebrate storytelling in all its many forms. Toys and entertainment properties, of course, tell many stories of culture and history, one of the reasons I have gone to lengths about many of them in this book.

I am lucky to have enjoyed the support over the years of colleagues past and present at *The Providence Journal*. Let me especially thank fellow staff writers Tom Mooney and Bill Reynolds; former publisher Janet Hasson; present publisher Peter Meyer; executive editor Alan Rosenberg; managing editor Mike McDermott; Kathy Hill, Whitman Littlefield, Michael Delaney, Kurt Mayer and former staffers Kate Bramson, Maria Caporizzo, Carol Kozma-Thomas; and former editor John Kostrzewa.

So there you have it, folks. It's almost 5 a.m. The birds are up. Time to write.

INDEX

The initials AGH, MLH, SDH, and SKH stand for Alan G. Hassenfeld, Merrill L. Hassenfeld, Stephen D. Hassenfeld, and Sylvia (Kay) Hassenfeld respectively.

ABOUT THE AUTHOR

This is G. Wayne Miller's 17th book. He is also a filmmaker, a podcaster, a *Providence Journal* staff writer, a visiting fellow at Salve Regina University's Pell Center for International Relations and Public Policy, and co-host and co-producer of the Telly Award-winning weekly national PBS TV and SiriusXM Satellite Radio show "Story in the Public Square." His books have won wide critical acclaim and been translated into several languages. Visit him at gwaynemiller.com and follow him on Twitter: @gwaynemiller

CPSIA information can be obtained
at www.ICGtesting.com
Printed in the USA
BVHW040824061119
562650BV00007B/11/P